TRANSFORMING
THE ORGANIZATION

TRANSFORMING THE ORGANIZATION

Francis J. Gouillart

James N. Kelly

McGraw-Hill, Inc.

New York   San Francisco   Washington, D.C.   Auckland   Bogotá
Caracas   Lisbon   London   Madrid   Mexico City   Milan
Montreal   New Delhi   San Juan   Singapore
Sydney   Tokyo   Toronto

Library of Congress Cataloging-in-Publication Data

Gouillart, Francis J.
   Transforming the organization / Francis J. Gouillart and James N.
Kelly
     p.   cm.
   Includes index.
   ISBN 0-07-034067-6 (cloth)
   1. Organizational change.   I. Kelly, James N. (James Newell).
II. Title.
HD58.8.G68   1995
658.4'063—dc20

                      95-5486
                      CIP

   4 5 6 7 8 9 0 DOC/DOC 9 0 0 9 8 7 6 5

ISBN 0-07-034067-6

*The sponsoring editor for this book was David Conti, the editing supervisor was Fred
Dahl, and the production supervisor was Pamela A. Pelton. It was set in New Caledonia
by Inkwell Publishing Services.*

Printed and bound by R. R. Donnelley & Sons Company.

McGraw-Hill books are available at special quantity discounts to use as premiums and sales
promotions, or for use in corporate training programs. For more information, please write
to the Director of Special Sales, McGraw-Hill, Inc., 11 West 19th Street, New York, NY
10011. Or contact your local bookstore.

To David Teiger,
the spirit of Gemini

CONTENTS

PART FOUR: RENEWAL

ACKNOWLEDGMENTS

Acknowledging all the influences that have gone into the writing of *Transforming the Organization* is a perilous task, for there have been many. To a large degree, the book is an assembly of many creative thoughts and approaches developed by others than ourselves. We have modestly attempted to place others' ideas on a common framework, and have used those ideas as the foundation for our own view of transformation.

C.K. Prahalad, from the University of Michigan, and Gary Hamel, from the London Business School, probably have influenced the writing of this book more than anyone else. The model which constitutes the base structure of our text was developed largely in partnership with them. In addition, both have been relentless apostles of growth and revitalization, at a time when the emphasis on restructuring appeared to be almost obsessive. The family of concepts they have developed, ranging from strategic intent, to core competences, to stretch and leverage (Chaps. 2 and 8), have been in our thoughts from the outset. The term *reframing*, object of Part One of this book, is borrowed from C.K.'s teaching. C.K.'s wonderful sense of large-scale mobilization, and his skill in leading executive workshops (both topics are featured in Chap. 1), remain for us the model we both aspire to.

We also owe an immense debt of gratitude to the Renaissance Strategy Group of Lincoln, Massachusetts, and to its three partners: David Norton, David Lubin, and Harry Lasker. David Norton is one of the two authors (Robert Kaplan is the other) of what has become a cornerstone of our transformation approach: the Balanced Scorecard (Chap. 3). Far beyond the Scorecard, David helped us develop the analytical underpinning of our bold biological metaphor, extending it beyond strategy and measures to include the world of technology and learning. David Lubin and Harry Lasker, his two associates, took it from there, showing us how learning loops can be identified from the Balanced Scorecard (Chap. 6), and how learning systems can be built to support those learning loops (Chaps. 9 and 12). Out of our joint work has emerged a new approach to reengineering—what we have termed *bioreengineering*—plus an entirely new view of individual renewal.

Michael J. Lanning and Lynn W. Phillips also have had a profound influence on our work through their pioneering thinking in the area of market focus. Both are principals with Lanning, Phillips and Associates. Phillips also teaches at the University of California, Berkeley, Haas School of Business. In the mid-eighties, Lanning and Phillips coined the Value Proposition and Value Delivery System concepts, then codeveloped these into their theory and graduate course "Building Market-Focused Organizations." We have learned much by practicing market-focused workshops under their passionate tutelage, and have made market focus an indispensable component of transformation (Chap. 7).

Professor Venkatraman of Boston University has long been an inspiration to us in our technology strategy work. Chapter 9, focused on information technology, is built entirely on a framework he developed a few years ago, entitled The Five Phases of IT-driven Transformation. We have watched Venkat electrify many large groups of senior executives with his technology insights, and we consider ourselves his modest students.

Robert Kaplan, professor at the Harvard Business School, has made two fundamental contributions to this book. First, he coauthored (with David Norton) the two seminal *Harvard Business Review* articles on the Balanced Scorecard. Second, he is probably the leading name associated with the activity-based costing technique, another cornerstone of transformation's economic modeling component (Chap. 4). We have worked with Bob for several years now, and we keep being struck by his insights and his indefatigable desire to keep on learning.

We also would like to acknowledge the help provided by Jean-Paul Figer from Cap Gemini Sogeti, our sister company, for sharing IT stories with us, and for helping us with many technology issues (Chap. 9). We also would like to extend our thanks to Jordan Lewis, for showing us how alliances should be used (Chap. 8), and to Philippe Haspeslagh of INSEAD and David Jemison of the University of Texas at Austin, for showing us how acquisitions should be managed (also Chap. 9). Special thanks also go to Thomas B. Wilson for his help on the rewards section (Chap. 10), and to Tom Wilson, from Sears, for sharing the Sears story. We also would like to thank the *Harvard Business Review* for allowing us to reproduce portions of its January/February 1994 article by Francis Gouillart and Fred Sturdivant entitled, "Spend a Day in the Life of Your Customer."

Our heart also goes out to the many firms who allowed us to use their stories. Whenever they have permitted us to do so, we have mentioned the individuals involved. In many cases, a client has been too modest to associate his or her name with the story of the transformation of a firm. We hope that both those who let themselves be dragged into the light and those who preferred to remain in the shadows will feel that this book is theirs.

Among such firms, we owe CIGNA Property and Casualty a mammoth debt of gratitude. Gerry Isom, its president, allowed us to feature him and his company's transformation throughout the entire book, making it possible for others to feel what he felt and learn from his experience. To say that we have learned from him would be an understatement. He agreed to let us start chronicling his work long before the outcome of the transformation effort at CIGNA P&C was known, with a quiet confidence that good work should pay dividends. We also owe a mammoth debt to Tom Valerio at CIGNA, through whom we built our CIGNA relationship, and upon whose help we constantly relied. Although many uncertainties remain today as to the outcome of CIGNA P&C's transformation, there has been tremendous progress already, and we hope he has gained a great sense of accomplishment from the experience. We also would like to extend our thanks to Ward Jungers and John Downham from CIGNA P&C, for letting us share their personal stories.

We are indebted to Gemini Consulting, our employer, for encouraging us to plan and write this book in the first place. Dan Valentino, Gemini's CEO, deserves special mention, for it was he who made it possible for us to free ourselves from our occasionally formidable client and managerial commitments. Gemini's wealth of experience in transforming corporations provided the raw material without which this book could never have been born.

Among the many Gemini consultants who helped us to build key stories, we would like to salute Peter Migliorato, John Garabedian, and the entire CIGNA team; Kee-Hian Tan (the anonymous Woodbridge Papers); Catherine Forster and Ellen Hart (mobilization); Nnaoke Ufere and Tonya Brenneman (Du Pont); Alan Meekings (Chap. 3, Rolls-Royce and Network South East); Mark Schennum (Rolls-Royce); Bill Beizer (activity-based costing and HEB); Nimi Natan (service-level assessment at CIGNA); Kees Been and Harry Gumble (Monsanto); Hank Pereth (Du Pont, Circleville); Duane Dickson (Union Carbide); Bob Fritz, Scott Frederick, and Carl Smith (telephone service activation); Gail Breslow (Air Products and Chemicals); Howard Radley (AIB); Bob Frisch (Sears); Ron Konezny and Bill Wallace (Concert); Victor Nau and Franklin Gold (Zeneca); Klaus Baumann and Konrad Reiss (SPAR, Tchibo); and Jean Hoepffner (France-Telecom). A special note of thanks also goes out to Jay Doherty for coming up with the "Vitruvian Man" representation of the 12 biocorporate systems.

We would like to thank the writing and support team, without whom this book would not have been produced. Our Information Services team provided focused, timely research support. Riccardo Lloyd d'Orsainville and Jaspa de Pastor put up with our unreasonable expectations with great patience. Tom Lloyd and Terry Brown provided invaluable research, writing, and editing input. Together, they helped us to make sense of the many first drafts and to bring the book to its final form. Peter Bielby kept the whole process on-track. McGraw-Hill has been a wonderful partner for both of us. Philip Ruppel in the early stages, and David Conti throughout the process, provided both the coaching and the firmness needed to bring this book to life.

Finally, we offer our most profound gratitude to our wives, Laura Gouillart and Francesca Kelly, who not only put up with impossible hours and schedules, but provided significant insights of their own.

FRANCIS J. GOUILLART   JAMES N. KELLY
Cambridge, Massachusetts   *London, England*

A FRAMEWORK FOR TRANSFORMATION

There's a certain feeling of presumptuousness that one must overcome before writing a book about business management. Looking at the already encumbered business sections of the world's bookstores, we were forced to ask, "Do we really have something unique and valuable to offer?" After careful analysis of the many fine books out there, we believe that we do, and from several standpoints.

Most business books are long on conceptual models but short on real-life cases. After many years of living within the transformation drama of major global corporations, we thought it was time to share what we have learned. Consequently this book is, above all, a firsthand account of the transformation of many large corporations as seen through the eyes of two insiders.

In addition, nearly all business books deal with isolated problems within the corporation. Many are exquisite treatises on individual organs of the company and the associated ailments that grieve them. Others are self-proclaimed "manifestos," implying that the prescription offered, no matter how one-dimensional or localized, can cure all of a company's ills. In reality, very few of them offer an approach of sufficient scope to impact the corporation as a whole.

We believe, however, that corporations are inherently *whole*; that no individual therapy should be administered without considering the consequences upon the entire corporate body. We also believe that there are no miracle drugs, that no single therapy is ever enough to induce complete health. That is why this book is about the entire business, not any one part, and that is why the approach it proposes is holistic.

This book is wider in breadth and broader in scope than most other business management books. It will carry you from "hard" disciplines, such

1

as customer studies and cost analysis, to "soft" disciplines such as team building and individual renewal. It will propel you from the hardship and pain of restructurings to the invigoration and elation of business growth and organizational renewal. It will link the technical to the emotional, weaving technology to human feeling with a common thread. It will place you in the higher echelons of management, then let you experience the anxieties of the rank and file. Hopefully, it will let you *feel* what transformation is about in all its dimensions, to help prepare you for the day when *your* company begins to transform itself, if it hasn't begun already.

We intentionally emphasize the perspective of senior managers, often that of CEOs, for their viewpoint is, by definition, the broadest. Their responsibility is for the well-being of the whole corporation, which is what this book is about.

At minimum, this book is a synthesis of everything we know about how corporations manage themselves. It is an attempt to integrate a broad spectrum of traditionally disjointed disciplines such as strategy, reengineering, information technology, and behavioral sciences. We have learned from many masters, and hope that the many acknowledgments in the book pay just homage to their enormous contributions. We have modestly attempted to synthesize what we have learned from them, and to integrate their views into our own framework.

Our hope, however, is that this book is much more than a collection of best practices in management. Our intent is for it to successfully introduce a new theory of business: *Business Transformation*.

The underlying premise of business transformation is that the complexity of a modern corporation defies mechanistic description, that a corporation is tantamount to a living organism—the *biological corporation*. We think of companies as living, volitional beings—like people—complete with body, mind, and spirit. Companies are born, they grow, they get sick, they recover, they mature, and they grow old. Companies think, they choose, they learn, they work, and they feel. Every company is unique, its personality developed through a combination of choice and environmental influences. Some are smarter than others, some stronger and faster, some healthier, some more moral. Many are honest and well intended. Some are charlatans: morality is no object. Some have a strong identity built upon clearly defined values. Others suffer an "identity crisis," their values missing or ill-defined. And like people, companies are mortal—they can die. Unlike our own demise, however, theirs is not inevitable.

For the biological corporation, we believe the secret of eternal life resides in its ability to orchestrate the simultaneous transformation of all its systems in a unified pursuit of common goals. Considered in isolation, technology may pull a company in one direction, its work architecture in another, and its reward system in still another. The challenge is to consider and work within all systems simultaneously, keeping them aligned during the transformation. This book presents perhaps the first picture of how these systems—the 12 *biocorporate systems* we propose—are actually interconnected in successful companies, and how misaligned systems can be brought into solidarity.

Genetics teaches us that the genetic imprint, or *genome*, which makes every person unique is carried within each of a person's 23 chromosomes—the big is in the small, and the small in the big. In a like way, the 12 biocorporate systems must proceed from the same "genetic imprint," so that each system represents a continuous expression of all the others. Business transformation proposes such a genetic model of the corporation.

Leaders are responsible for creating and maintaining the genetic imprint that makes a corporation unique and keeps it competitive. Once just decision makers and gatekeepers of information, leaders now assume a completely different role: genetic architects of the biological corporation. This new role, when properly understood, allows them to inspire the development of all biocorporate systems, without having to manage the details of any single one.

Weaned on a mechanistic view of business, most modern leaders are not yet fully prepared for the magnitude of the challenge facing them. Few of them have studied such things as process design, shareholder value theory, and IT strategy; and fewer still are comfortable, let alone intimate with, the latest concepts of team building and individual renewal. Only a handful have tried to mix all these together to meet the challenge of large-scale transformation.

We hope this book will help them to do so.

FROM MACHINE TO LIFE:
A NEW PHILOSOPHY OF BUSINESS

The need for Business Transformation represents a fundamental shift in the relationship of the corporation to individuals and to society as a whole. Simply put, corporations need to reconnect with the people that comprise them.

Born in the Industrial Age, our model of business has been a mechanistic one. Corporations have been economic agents in an efficient market system, parts of an ever expanding, ever more complex machine. Caught now in the Communications Age, we have stretched the models of the Industrial Age to the limits of implosion. It is time to replace our mechanistic view of business with a more organic one, and to endow the recently discovered biological nature of our corporations with a new spirituality that recognizes the sanctity of individual human life and has compassion for individuals.

We have moved beyond the Industrial Age, but our business model is still rooted there. Some say that the ability to manage the flow of information represents the basis for the new business model of the Communications Age. We submit, however, that more is involved than that. The communications revolution is merely the facilitator of a more fundamental social and business influence: an unstoppable trend toward *increased connectivity*. As more and more parts of the machine have learned to talk to each other, connectivity has become the dominant feature of modern business. As the trend continues, the role of corporations within society must change.

The entire history of civilization, and therefore of business, is one of increased connectivity. Verbal and written communication represented the level of connectivity needed to form the earliest civilizations. Gutenberg's printing press raised connectivity to a new level, spreading knowledge that would eventually undermine the simple tyrannies of church and monarch. The rights of church and monarch were displaced by the rights of individuals, giving birth to the democratic movement and culminating in the great revolutions of the eighteenth century.

The age ushered in by the Industrial Revolution and lasting until our own time was largely driven by technology, but its most important manifestations were social. It freed us from drudgery and physical isolation, and led to urbanization. The rhythm of life changed profoundly, and because the spirit of the Industrial Age was mechanical, the qualities of the social institutions it created (bureaucracy, hierarchy, command-and-control systems, and specialization) were machine-like as well. The line worker became a cog in a wheel, with no sense of personal connection to the company and often with no sense of communion with the environment.

And so the Communications Age is upon us, replacing the Industrial Age. As was true of earlier social transformations, this one is increasing the level of social complexity and leading to profound changes in society, to which the company—the dominant institutional creature of the Industrial Age—must adapt.

Viewed from the perspective of the individual, speech, writing, printing, telephones, radios, and televisions all represented technological advances that increased the size and scope of our connectivity networks. Now we can fax, videoconference, and computer-network with all parts of the world, on demand. Our networks are growing inexorably in both size and complexity, and that growth probably will continue

What is true at the individual level is also true for corporations. Companies are forming alliances and partnerships with their suppliers and customers, becoming parts of networks, even networks of networks. The physical and financial boundaries between companies are blurring, and the trend probably will continue.

But while the individual networks expand, and while *business* networks become *knowledge* networks, there is a human element that warrants careful attention and nurturing. Connectivity can be a double-edged sword, triggering either greater individual isolation or a greater sense of community, depending on the role companies choose for themselves in the future.

On the pessimistic side, increased connectivity of the electronic variety may cause a loss of genuine human contact. We will continue to lose our ability to feel and touch each other. Encounters become simulations, contrived by electronics. We don't touch, smell, or feel emotional about the things and people we interact with, because they are not *there*. A credit card doesn't have the feel of a gold coin; talking to your boss on the phone isn't the same as playing golf with him on weekends; and electronically swapping production schedules with a supplier isn't the same as doing it over a beer in the pub. We used to have *physical* experiences when on the job. We have fewer and fewer of them now, and we miss them.

The economic logic of business has taken over. Old social contracts have expired, and they are being replaced by more Darwinian models of individual survival. The rural textile plant in the southern United States now competes with Taiwan. The wider the network becomes, the greater the need for a new compassion, because there are human voices to be heard, crying out in the emotional silence.

Another more optimistic scenario is possible, the one we encourage in this book. Corporations *can* provide the new caring that so many seek. This will not happen in the paternalistic fashion of the previous generation, and we are not likely to see a return to guaranteed employment. But it *will* happen in different forms.

Successful corporations will develop a new role built around the invention of a new social contract. We believe we will see corporations taking responsibility for the renewal of individuals, helping them to acquire new skills. We will see corporations redefine the boundary of their responsibility, accepting accountability for the way they use resources and contribute to the environment. Corporations probably will play a major role in the renewal of education in many countries, and become involved in the solution of major societal ailments. Most importantly, they will build a new pride in the people who are part of them.

This book is a first attempt to define this new *spirituality of business.*

BUSINESS TRANSFORMATION

Our work with some of the world's largest corporations has convinced us that *Business Transformation is now the central management challenge and the primary, if not the sole, task of business leaders.*

The program of Business Transformation presented in the pages that follow is not a theoretical model based on a few new insights and hypotheses about how firms change. It is a tried-and-tested system, a proven and powerful agent of corporate evolution in industries ranging from chemicals, electronics, pharmaceuticals, and auto-making, to telecommunications, aerospace, railways, and financial services.

It is a living methodology. Each day we learn more and more about business transformation—about what works, and what leads to dead-ends; about how strategies and visions can be translated into action programs at every level of an organization; and about the role of business leadership in the alchemy of transformation.

The biological model of Business Transformation that we shall be exploring in this book consists of four broad categories of therapy, what we call The Four R's of Transformation (see Fig. I.1):

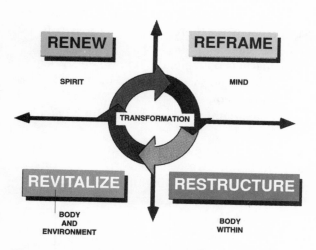

Figure I.1. *The Four R's of Transformation.*

Reframing

Restructuring

Revitalization

Renewal

We define Business Transformation as *the orchestrated redesign of the genetic architecture of the corporation, achieved by working simultaneously—although at different speeds—along the four dimensions of Reframing, Restructuring, Revitalization and Renewal.*

The four R's are to the biological corporation what the "three R's" of Reading, wRiting and aRithmetic are to schoolchildren: the life skills it needs if it is to survive and thrive.

Reframing is the shifting of the company's conception of what it is and what it can achieve. It addresses the corporate *mind*. Corporations often get stuck in a certain way of thinking, and lose the ability to develop fresh mental models of what they are and what they could become. Reframing opens the corporate mind and infuses it with new visions and a new resolve.

Restructuring is a girding of the corporate loins, getting it to achieve a competitive level of performance. It deals with the *body* of the corporation, and competitiveness—the need to be lean and fit—is the primary consideration. Restructuring is the domain where payoffs are fastest and cultural difficulties are greatest, often making layoffs and the anxieties associated with them an unavoidable side effect. The payoffs, however, if invested in revitalization and renewal, can be used to heal the wounds, if not lessen their severity. Many companies stop at restructuring, cajoled into contentment by their "quick wins." But they won't gain true health unless they use those wins to fuel longer-term transformation programs.

Revitalization is about igniting growth by *linking the corporate body to the environment*. Everybody wants to grow, but the sources of growth often are elusive, making the process of achieving growth more challenging and protracted than restructuring. Of all the four R's, revitalization is the single greatest factor that clearly distinguishes transformation from mere downsizing.

Renewal deals with the people side of the transformation, and with the *spirit* of the company. It is about investing individuals with new skills and new purposes, thus allowing the company to regenerate itself. It involves creating a new kind of metabolism, the rapid dissemination of knowledge inside the firm, and it involves the cultivation of a reflex of adaptation to environmental changes. Renewal is the most subtle and difficult, the least explored, and potentially the most powerful of transformation's dimensions.

Companies are living organisms. Like people they need holistic medicine, not organ-by-organ treatments. In this book we hope to show, as we have already shown in our work, that the four-R model represents a uniquely powerful way to tap a company's hidden reserves of energy, and transform it into something far better than it had ever dreamed of being.

FROM CHROMOSOMES TO BIOCORPORATE SYSTEMS

The essential physical, mental, and perhaps even the spiritual quality of each human being can be traced back to a unique human genome and its 23 sets of chromosomes. The structure of this book is based on our proposal that 12 "chromosomes" comprise the biocorporate genome, three for each of the four R's. Each chromosome spawns a *biocorporate system*, and one chapter is devoted to each of them.

Together, these 12 corporate chromosomes represent the integrated "software" that governs biocorporate life. Each chromosome and its corresponding system can be considered independently, but no one acts independently of the others. For example, the mobilization chromosome (Chap. 1) is most vigorous when the vision (Chap. 2) and market focus (Chap. 7) chromosomes vigorously exchange their genetic code. Similarly, organizational development (Chap. 12) must reflect the firm's vision (Chap. 2), its system of goals and measures (Chap. 3), and its work architecture (Chap. 6).

In other words, *each cell within the biological corporation carries the imprint, or genome, of all 12 corporate chromosomes.* It is therefore important to bear in mind that, although each chapter of this book is dedicated to only one chromosome, it is really the same story told again, but from the standpoint of a different protagonist.

The role of the CEO and the leadership team is to act as *the genetic architects of the corporation.* As such, they are not concerned with the minutiae of corporate life, but with splicing the right genes, of the right chromosomes, at the right time, and in the right place to enable the 12 biocorporate systems to interact with each other in the best possible way. In other words, it is leaderships' job to create the unique genetic architecture that comprises the biocorporate genome, not to construct and control every cell within the corporate body.

It is tempting for leaders to get involved with the details, but the details can obscure the view of the business or corporation as a whole. For example, CEOs should design the mobilization process, but not the composition of individual teams; they should create a vision, but let each line of business develop a strategy consistent with the vision; they should articulate an operations strategy, but leave it to others to decide whether to shut down a particular plant; and they should encourage business units to share knowledge among themselves, but not supervise individual, cross-business initiatives.

As genetic architect, the leader's job is essentially that of programming the "code" of the corporation. Viewed from this perspective, each chromosome and its corresponding biocorporate system may be translated to a high-level leadership task (see Fig. I.2, and the following section).

THE THREE REFRAMING CHROMOSOMES

1. *Achieve mobilization.* Mobilization is the process of mustering the mental energy needed to feed the transformation process. It involves

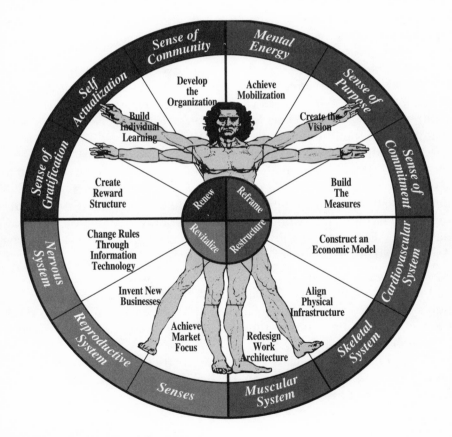

Figure I.2. *Transforming the Organization.*

expanding the realm of motivation and commitment from the level of the individual to the team, and finally to the entire organization. In human terms, it musters and liberates the *mental energy* needed to feed the transformation process.

When Don Petersen unleashed Employee Involvement at Ford, when Jack Welch created the Work-Out process at General Electric, they were mobilizing their companies for major change.

In our discussion of mobilization, we witness Jan Timmer energizing his entire firm at Philips by holding, for example, a huge, global videoconference as a symbol of the new way to compete. We also follow the impact of his "top-down" approach, all the way to a cafeteria meeting inside the large electronics conglomerate.

2. *Create the vision.*   Mobilization creates potential in an organization; it prepares it to create a better future. Vision provides a shared mental framework that gives form to that future. It must be challenging, representing a significant *stretch* from current reality, becoming the firm's new raison d'être, its most passionate aspiration. In human terms, it creates a sense of purpose.

Bill Gates' vision of the computer business—in essence, that software, not hardware, is the name of the game—is one example of a powerful vision. Another is Ted Turner's vision of a global news network, which he realized with CNN; another, Sam Walton's vision of discount retailing, manifested in the resounding success of Wal-Mart.

In our discussion of creating the vision, we follow Jerry Blumberg's efforts at DuPont Nylon, and his creation of a completely new approach to a staid chemical business. We discover how John Neill's vision of shared-destiny relationships with suppliers and customers helped to turn Unipart's third-rate factories into world-class players. And we witness the determination of CEO John Hall in his fight for the independence of his firm, Ashland Oil, in the middle of a takeover attempt.

3. *Build a measurement system.*   Once the company has been mobilized, and armed with an inspiring vision, leadership must translate the vision into a set of measures and targets, and define the actions needed to reach the targets. In human terms, the measurement system creates a *sense of commitment.*

Motorola used the quality process and metrics to drive its transformation; Xerox used a combination of benchmarks, particularly vis-à-vis Japanese competitors, and a quality process to regain its competitiveness; Taco Bell's transformation was driven by customer service measurements.

In our discussion of measurement systems, we see how Rolls-Royce, in deep financial straits, used a cascading system of performance measures in its comeback; how the measurement system helped to transform a culture that had been steeped in tradition; and how the people of the company brought it back to life. We learn how Network South East, part of British Rail, used a cascading set of key performance indicators to turn a lackluster railway into a customer-focused supplier of travel services.

THE THREE RESTRUCTURING CHROMOSOMES

4. *Construct an economic model.* Constructing an economic model involves the systematic, top-down disaggregation of a corporation in financial terms, from shareholder value considerations to activity-based costing and service-level assessment. It gives the company a detailed view of where and how value is created (or destroyed) in the firm. The economic model is to the corporate body what the cardiovascular system is to the human body. Just as the cardiovascular system supplies oxygen and other vital nutrients wherever they are needed throughout the body, so the economic model transports resources to where they are most needed inside the corporation.

AT&T, Hanson, and Coca-Cola are examples of successful companies that are strongly driven by shareholder value considerations.

In discussing the construction of the economic model, we see how Sears proved that it understood its economics better than the financial market did, revealing the hidden value of the strategy it launched 12 years earlier. We see how how Monsanto Plastics used economic analysis to reconfigure its product line.

5. *Align the physical infrastructure.* The redesign of a corporation's physical infrastructure is one of the most visible and telling measures of the overall health and strategic direction of a company. It is the corporate equivalent of the skeletal system, the network of facilities and other assets—plants, warehouses, trucks, barges, machines, etc.—upon which work processes, the muscles of the business, depend. Like bones, the physical assets of a company are relatively fixed and rigid, resisting movement beyond their design. Some are like the spine—when they fall out of alignment, they pinch vital nerves, causing pain and partial paralysis. Others may fracture under stress, immobilizing whole sections of the corporate body and requiring mechanical realignment to allow the healing process to occur.

Johnson Controls and Hewlett-Packard, for example, continuously reconfigure their physical facilities according to their "focused factories" strategy.

In discussing physical infrastructure, we show how Ken Iverson shaped the operations of Nucor. We see how Praxair changed the rules of the industrial gas industry by providing on-site gas production facilities to customers. We discover how the Circleville plant of the DuPont corporation took its destiny into its own hands.

6. *Redesign the work architecture.* In the corporation, work gets done through a complex network of processes, the *work architecture.* Work processes are the vehicle of business life, the biocorporate equivalent of muscles. Like muscles, they can be considered in isolation, but are in fact so interconnected that a change in one may affect them all. Also like muscles, they must continuously adapt to the demands placed on them or fall into atrophy from lack of stimulation. If properly configured and aligned, and if properly orchestrated by an integrated set of goals and measures, they produce a symphony of value creation so fluid that process boundaries seem to disappear.

The first two genes of redesigning the work architecture involve principles of classic reengineering. The third gene brings reengineering into the realm of *bioreengineering.*

The dramatic reductions Hallmark Cards achieved in its design and printing cycle time demonstrated the power of reengineering. The success of Detroit's Big Three auto makers in shrinking new model development time enabled them to catch up with their Japanese competitors.

As we discuss the redesigning of the work architecture, we follow how phone companies struggle to avoid having "leaky pipes" when customers call for service. We also visit Union Carbide, and analyze how the company raised itself from its status of wounded animal after a ferocious takeover attempt, to become one of the best performers on Wall Street.

The Three Revitalization Systems

7. *Achieve market focus.* Revitalization implies growth, and focusing on customers is a good place to start, for providing the benefits customers seek—often new, as yet undiscovered benefits—is what leads to business growth. Market focus is to the corporation what the *senses* are to the human body, connecting the corporate mind and body to its environment.

Rubbermaid has shown how identifying customer needs and quickly designing products around those needs can revitalize a company even in an industry as prosaic as rubber goods. Johnson and Johnson is another company that has sustained its customer-driven creativity over the years.

In discussing market focus, we describe how Air Products found a new business by listening to hospital orderlies. We observe how a small retailer, Idylwilde Farms in Acton, Massachusetts created an inspiring offering for its customers. And we witness how two chemical service companies, Nalco and Betz, have turned other companies' problems into their own opportunities.

8. *Invent new businesses.*   Growth also comes by starting new businesses from scratch. This requires the cross-fertilization of capabilities that are often scattered throughout a firm's business portfolio, and the creative assembling of them to develop new offerings. In many cases the capabilities of other firms are required, spawning alliances, partnerships, mergers, or acquisitions. Inventing new businesses brings new life to the corporation; it is the corporate equivalent of the human *reproductive system.*

Canon leveraged its optical and small-motor knowhow into a strong global position in copiers; NEC was one of the first companies to exploit the convergence of computing and telecommunications.

As we explore the inventing of new businesses, we see how the entire DuPont empire is built on a few, hard-to-manipulate catalysts.We see how Sears used its customer knowledge as a launchpad for its Discover credit card and, more broadly, for its "socks and stocks" strategy. We see how BT (British Telecom) and MCI wed their competences and gave birth to a new enterprise. And we observe the courageous formation of First Trust Bank, as a result of the merger of two separate institutions against a backdrop of Nationalist vs. Unionist conflict in Ulster.

9. *Change the rules through information technology.*   Technology can often provide the basis of new ways to compete. Information technology, in particular, can redefine the rules of the game in an industry. Technology is the equivalent of the *nervous system* in the human body, connecting all parts of the body and allowing it to experience sensations produced by the environment.

Federal Express's ability to track packages was a powerful service differentiater in the courier business. Progressive Insurance's ability to settle claims on-line with centrally connected, hand-held devices rewrote the competitive rules in the insurance industry.

In seeing how technology can change the rules, we observe how Citibank allowed its brokers to apply "on-line" for mortgages. We see how ERAM, a French discount shoe manufacturer, connected its supplier network through technology. We see how G7, the Paris-based taxi company, is revolutionizing service in a traditionally low-tech industry. We discover how Zeneca is using information systems to help reinvent its industry.

THE THREE RENEWAL SYSTEMS

10. *Create a reward structure.*   Rewards aren't the only motivators of people, but they are very powerful ones. When they are misaligned with corporate objectives, they can be equally powerful demotivators. The compensation system should reward risk-takers, and encourage people to link their own futures to the transformation of the company. The reward structure builds a *sense of gratification* among individuals in the corporation.

Goldman Sachs, in the investment banking field, Coca-Cola in soft drinks, and Heinz in the food business, are examples of companies in which rewards are strongly linked to performance.

In discussing rewards systems, we show the basis of rewards in the Balanced Scorecard, and how to link rewards systems to organizational performance. We watch how Lloyds Bank's shareholder value-based bonus system helped to transform the company. We witness how Tchibo, the coffee manufacturer, employed a performance-linked reward system to good effect. We return to Unipart, seeing how it extends its reward system beyond corporate boundaries.

11. *Build individual learning.*   There can be no corporate transformation without the transformation of a large number of individuals. Companies must commit themselves to the development of their people by encouraging the acquisition of skills and by cultivating mutual learning. Individual learning promotes *self-actualization* in the individuals who make up the company.

Federal Express has always understood the link between customer loyalty and the service-orientation of its drivers, and invests heavily in increasing employee skills with sophisticated electronic learning systems.

In discussing individual learning, we observe how Unipart invests in the development of skills for their employees. We see how France-Telecom handles the problem of reskilling displaced employees.

12. *Develop the organization.*   Companies need to organize themselves for learning, so that they can adapt, constantly, to their changing environments. Developing the organization fosters a *sense of community* among individuals.

Dow Chemicals was one of the first companies to adopt the controversial matrix structure, but has now abandoned it in favor of a spider's-web arrangement, in which multifunctional teams periodically coalesce around customer applications, quite independently of formal, reporting relationships. Asea Brown Boveri's CEO, Percy Barnevik, uses organization design to combat bureaucracy and force ABB's business units to remain small.

In discussing the development of the organization, we observe how SPAR, the German retailer, went from being a sleepy company to becoming an aggressive competitor by leveraging the power of its network of stores. We see how Swedish Post transformed itself from a bloated bureaucracy with no pride to become an entrepreneurial network of some 1500 individ-

---

ual businesses. We see how John Brown, a key component of Trafalgar House's engineering division, linked its 160 offices around the world through technology, creating a "global office with electronic corridors."

CORPORATE EVOLUTION

The 12 biocorporate systems don't exist in isolation. They are perpetually being challenged to adapt to changes in their environment (such as the arrival of new competitors and technologies), shifts in the attitudes of customers and regulators, and signs of the impending extinction of their industries. Gestetner almost expired when xerography destroyed the duplicator market it had invented. Wang was rocked to its foundations when the word-processing hardware market it had dominated was colonized by general-purpose PCs. The mechanical "one-armed bandit" was rendered obsolete by microprocessors and video games.

An ability to sense environmental change, and whether it carries threats or opportunities, is essential for survival, because the biological corporation is always evolving. Rewards systems are changing, work architectures are being redefined, visions are being refreshed. We once assumed that corporate evolution consists of long periods of stasis, punctuated by periodic adaptations, but the pace of change is too fast for that now. Now, the company needs to adapt every day.

In the natural world, evolution is driven by chance mutations and natural selection. Very occasionally, the DNA replication system makes a minor mistake. Almost invariably, these errors are harmful, killing the mutant life-form before it can breed. An infinitesimally small proportion of errors are advantageous, and the mistake is passed on. Malaria kills over a million people each year. Hemoglobin S is a mutant hemoglobin gene, which happened to protect its carrier against malaria. A tiny copying error, the odds against which were astronomical, has lifted the threat of a deadly disease from millions of people.

A company need not wait to get lucky. Armed with a map of its genome, its leaders can splice a few processes and change its systems to adapt to environmental change. This book represents a modest first step in that direction.

INTRODUCING GERRY AND KARL

Business Transformation penetrates deeper and broader than conventional change programs, generating therapy for the whole company. It works only if everyone, from the CEO to the truck driver and order-entry clerk, is persuaded to become involved and committed. It is neither a "top-down" nor a "bottom-up" process; it is both, simultaneously. To illustrate the point, we devote part of each chapter to the personal experiences of two transformation protagonists.

From the top-down perspective, Gerry Isom, the real-life president of CIGNA Property & Casualty, guides us through the transformation experience from the point of view of the leader. We wish to express our deep gratitude for his willingness to share his experience of what has been, thus far, a successful business transformation.

From the bottom-up perspective our guide is Karl, a fictional grade-12 scheduler at a paper company we shall call Woodbridge Papers. Woodbridge Papers is a fictitious company, but the story of its transformation, as seen through Karl's eyes, is based on a real-life case.

Will Gerry Isom Make It at CIGNA Property and Casualty?

When Gerry Isom left Transamerica to become President of the three-billion-dollar CIGNA Property & Casualty (P&C) in March 1993, his mission was simple: stem the losses, and turn the company around.

CIGNA P&C was in deep trouble. A series of major catastrophes—the San Francisco earthquake, hurricanes Andrew and Hugo, riots in Los Angeles, and floods in the Midwest—had combined with an intrinsic lack of competitiveness and an outbreak of unforeseen compensation claims (largely stemming from new government environmental rulings), to create a crisis that some believed was terminal.

On his arrival, Isom found a culture in tatters. Morale was almost nonexistent, agents were leaving what they saw as a sinking ship in droves, and the firm was losing underwriting talent at an alarming rate. The departments had isolated themselves from each other; there was precious little team spirit left, even at the top; and relationships between the P&C division and its parent group were strained, to say the least.

Isom was keenly aware of the fact that his "outsider" status had created fears that he would "slash and burn." *Reframing,* therefore, was his first priority. He would have to quickly shape and communicate a new vision, and build personal credibility in the process.

At the same time he knew there was no choice: Some of the harshest aspects of *restructuring* could not be avoided. There would be major layoffs, particularly at the Philadelphia headquarters. He would have to get out of some businesses and prune the company's surplus facilities, including at least one of its four U.S. marketing centers.

Isom believed that the solution to the problem was *revitalization*: getting the firm to grow again. Restructuring was necessary, but not sufficient; he would have to focus the firm on its future. He had learned from experience that employees would find it difficult to envision a thriving firm in the midst of a layoff program, but he would talk about investment and expansion and hope for the best.

He also was convinced that, ultimately, the *renewal* of CIGNA P&C's people would be key to long-term success. He planned to replace a few people at the top, but the rest would have to renounce the past and concentrate on making CIGNA the best property and casualty firm in the business. This could be achieved, Isom believed, only by enriching the skills of everyone in firm, with the claims agents and underwriters as a top priority. New partnerships would have to be forged with independent agents, and eventually everyone would have to realize that the business was about inventing new markets and businesses more quickly than competitors, about rewriting the rules of the whole industry.

The tale of CIGNA P&C's transformation, which we tell in the following chapters, is unfinished. Since Isom's arrival, CIGNA has raised itself from the status of floundering firm to that of average competitor. There are clear signs of improvement, but the really tough work still lies ahead.

The Transformation of Karl, the Grade-12 Scheduler at Woodbridge Papers

Woodbridge Papers is part of the packaging industry, with six plants located and managed regionally in North America. Its main customers are printers, who supply companies like Campbell Soup with the wrappers that adorn their cans and packages. Karl, a smart but cynical scheduler bent on "serving his time" until retirement, is a most unlikely hero of a business transformation program.

Although Woodbridge is the market leader, it has been losing market share to one of its competitors, Mountain View Papers, which offers printers a much faster delivery time.

Karl's schedule accounts for a significant part of the order-to-delivery time. He's the guy you call if you really want to know what's happening to your order. He hides in a corner of the plant, well away from prying eyes of executives and busybody consultants.

"*Mobilization,* that's a good one," he mutters, as he reads the latest pronouncements from on high. He'll be darned if he'll sign up for any of the new "task forces" being formed in his plant. He dismisses the whole exercise as "kids' stuff."

There have been a lot of memos and briefings about a new "vision," and a new emphasis on service and lead time. Karl yawns in the back row of a plant staff meeting, watching "the vision video" issued by corporate communications. It goes in one ear and out the other. It is not that he's stupid; it's just that he finds it hard to translate all the high-sounding words into something he can sink his teeth into.

He's a scheduler. His job is to make production commitments, and meet them. That's what he gets paid for, and that's what his occasional bonus is based on. He's good at his job, and he knows that one sure way to mess up is to promise quick delivery when you're not sure you can do it. The plan to shrink the order-to-delivery time looks to him like trouble, so why would he endorse it? Nobody's *measuring* him on it!

Karl *would* truly love to know what it really costs each time he switches from one batch of paper to another. He would like to understand the basic *economics* of his job. But that information doesn't exist. Some young staffers from HQ came to do something called "activity-based costing." They said it was just what he wanted, but he heard nothing more.

Karl also has strong views about what can and can't be done. He has views about *physical infrastructure,* for example. He has never been able to convince the powers-that-be to cut to length and width right in the plant. Instead, they ship semifinished products to a Chicago warehouse 100 miles away, where his plant's products are cut to width and length along with those of two other plants. Rolls get lost, people forget to send the specifications, trucks skid off icy midwestern roads. In other words, they spend a lot of time tracking rolls through the inventory system and the transportation log. That's another cost he'd like to see in black-and-white.

"It's a waste!" Karl has insisted time and again. "Let me cut my paper at the end of the line, and I guarantee things will go better." But that's up to manufacturing's big boss at HQ, and he doesn't even know they have to cut to length and width! "What's the use?" Karl grumbles. "I've been saying it for years, and nobody listens."

Despite his ornery reputation, Karl is asked to get involved in the *work redesign* effort—Woodbridge's version of the new reengineering craze. His colleagues are telling him to get along better with customer service and transportation, because they're all part of the "order fulfillment process."

Yesterday, they even had customers in the plant. They call it a *market focus* initiative. It was interesting to meet people who buy the stuff. They explained what they do with the paper, and what can go wrong when they print on it; "machinability" problems, they call them.

The marketing department and the customers who dance to the rhythm Karl sets see scheduling as a black art, and Karl as the local witch doctor. There are occasional outbursts from HQ about how long it takes to make the stuff, but Karl sets them straight with a few choice epithets about the facts of scheduling life in the paper business. He lets them screw up his schedule when they shout really loud, or when the CEO gets involved.

But he *will* feel a little guiltier, now that he's met them.

Another headache for Karl are those trial runs they do when they're *inventing* new kinds of paper. They are tiny little runs, and they mess up the schedule like you wouldn't believe. And the engineers are all over the machine for hours, taking samples, checking gauges, and analyzing effluent. "Give me my machine back!" Karl screams silently. "I've got a job to do."

And the new SAP information system...? "An apt acronym," says Karl. It was a piece of *information technology* that would give them everything they needed, including consolidated forecasts for all divisions to help with scheduling. But Karl knows about "garbage in, garbage out." The program produces dog food in an elegant wrapper. Machine-time standards, by paper grade, haven't been updated in five years, and they're so hopelessly inaccurate that capacity projections can be wrong by as much as 50 percent. Karl knows he is better off using his experience.

It would be helpful to embed Karl's experience and scheduling methods in the program and make his numbers available to the capacity planners in transportation and materials sourcing; but nobody has taken the trouble to understand what he has to offer. The SAP implementation team visited him once, but they were too busy selling him on the package to listen to what he had to say.

Karl knows which side his bread is buttered on. He reports to the plant manager, and he knows how his boss is *rewarded*—by cost per ton and throughput (how many pounds of product he gets out of the door each month). "Don't bother me with lead time," Karl says, "I'm helping my boss to maximize machine utilization, and that's that."

Still, Karl would love to learn new skills and participate in his own *renewal*. He went to classes on accounting for non-accountants at the local college. He learned a lot, but he'll never do anything with it. He also attended classes on SAP. That was more relevant, because they were installing SAP in his plant, but he got lost in the technical part. Besides, he won't use the program if he can help it.

On *organizational* issues Karl has strong opinions, as he does on most things. For years, Woodbridge has been blowing hot and cold on the idea of centralizing the scheduling of its six plants. Each plant has its own Karl, and he knows them all. They're a brotherhood; they meet once a year, talk on the phone a few times a month, and share a deep dislike for a head-quarters fellow called "central scheduling manager."

Unlike the Karls of this world, central scheduling managers change all the time, and each one wants to do things differently. Karl knows the arguments for centralization: it would allow Woodbridge to optimize across plants; it would permit one plant to pick up the slack, if another was down or too busy; and the plants could operate as a network rather than as stand-alone units.

Karl's response is that they've tried it and it doesn't work, because when push comes to shove you want quick decisions, and having a guy on-point in each plant is the only way to get them.

Thus Karl secures his bunker. And if they want to smoke him out of his foxhole, he'll give them a good fight.

REFRAMING

In the movie *Moscow on the Hudson*, there is a scene in which the protagonist, played by Robin Williams, has a mild nervous breakdown in a grocery store. A recent immigrant from the Soviet Union, he is walking down an aisle stocked with coffee, soap, toilet paper, canned foods, etc.— all products considered luxuries in his former home. Not only are they available, there are multiple brands of each. The sheer number of choices overwhelms him, and he breaks down, weeping in the aisle. Later, he explains to a friend that in Moscow, where they had nothing, they had learned to "love their misery." By a terrible irony, giving up the misery felt like losing a love.

Transformation is a lot like that at first. It's the time when corporations leave the secure walls of the castle and step into unexplored territory. Though the dynamics of success may eventually lead to elation, it's not much fun in the initial stages. There are walls of reluctance and denial to break through; old values to discard, and new ones to assimilate. And that's usually painful, because the ramparts are thick, and they are made of human emotions and prejudices.

Reframing is about breaking through those walls and becoming mentally prepared to move beyond them. It deals with the mind, with fundamentally changing the source of a firm's motivation, the standard for its judgments, and the values that underlie its sense of emotional well-being. It's about convincing hundreds or thousands of people to adopt a new mental framework, when their loyalty tends to rest with the status quo. It's about creating confidence in the outcome of a massive transformation, when that outcome is by definition uncertain.

It is not a simple task. Few of us are natural explorers. Fewer still are willing to gamble the present against the hope of a better future. Contentment lies within existing prerogatives, customers, budgets, and areas of responsibility; enough so to make us fiercely protective of our existing positions. The "now" is familiar, the pace is controllable, and people can define themselves in relation to that pace. Things are just fine the way they are.

Family compounds this resistance, making conservatives out of almost all of us. We think of our spouses, our kids, their financial future, and our need for their respect and approbation. Why risk coming home one evening and having to explain that you're not the divisional manager anymore, that instead you've been asked to spearhead the relocation of a key facility to Georgia or to drive the redesign of the order fulfillment process? Even if it marked a genuine advancement, would they understand?

And what if you lose in a reshuffling, end up demoted or even redundant? And what if you *don't*? Transformation is hard work—long hours, more travel, weekends away from home, new responsibilities, new bosses, new enemies. Why support something you have every reason to fear?

On top of that, transformation invariably involves someone else telling you that you need to change. That means what you have been doing is wrong, inadequate in some way. Whether insiders or external change agents, why trust people who live off your pain, whose job is to define your failure? "Who do these guys think they are?" you mutter to yourself. "And why start with me? Surely there are better targets, sicker parts of the company!"

Rationalization is a powerful force. It's relatively easy to pile argument upon argument against change. One way or the other, however, those arguments will reveal themselves not as true reasons to stay the current course, but rather as means to evade judgment about the way things are, versus the way things might and ought to be. And while it's possible to evade judgment indefinitely, it is not possible to avoid the consequences of the evasion. Like humans, corporations must choose to master their own fate, or doom themselves to be mastered by it.

In that sense, reframing is an act of claiming corporate self-responsibility, the prelude to releasing the potential for change lying dormant in the vast majority of large organizations. It is the self-imposed task of breaking apart the organization's "conventional wisdom" (its existing mode of thinking, mindset, or paradigms), abstracting the useful elements, bringing in new materials as required, and constructing a new mental framework for the firm.

Reframing is governed by three chromosomes and their corresponding biocorporate systems, which are the subjects of the three chapters in Part

One. The first, described in Chap. 1, deals with achieving the large-scale mobilization required to transform an entire organization. Mobilization involves mustering the mental energy required to motivate the organization's people throughout the transformation process. It is in this stage of reframing that people—both the leaders at the top, and the workers on the shop floor—overcome the resistance and denial associated with change. It is here that they begin to believe in the promise of a brighter future, whatever that future might be.

The second reframing chromosome, described in Chap. 2, deals with creating the vision, arming the organization with a sense of purpose that will sustain its newly found motivation over time. The vision gives a more tangible form to the promise of a brighter future. It becomes something people can get a sense of, something they believe is attainable, and something that they can see coming closer as they continue to change over time.

The third reframing chromosome, described in Chap. 3, deals with establishing the measurement system. It is hard to motivate individuals to change their behaviors, until they can see with their own eyes the impact of their new behaviors. Measures allow our minds to test the hypotheses we formulate about which causes produce which effects, and to verify on a rational level that we are on our way to higher plateaus of performance.

The order of the chapters implies a sequence of activities. This is made necessary by the construction of a book, but it does not represent an actual chronology of transformation. Transformation needs to occur simultaneously, although at different speeds, along multiple dimensions. In the end, even the order in which we introduce the three systems of reframing may seem odd. In particular, it might seem more logical to start with a vision and build a mobilization process around it. But a vision can only take seed in fertile ground. Mobilization provides a critical preparatory period that loosens and enriches the company's "psychological ground," creating an environment in which the new vision can flourish.

The complex sequence of activities involved in reframing is far from fixed, many possible combinations of events will make all three components finally come together. Like people, different companies choose different pathways of change, even when they are heading for the same destination. No one pathway is necessarily better than another—all are strewn with roadblocks, and errors are inevitable along the way. In that sense, the order ultimately doesn't matter. And besides, it is on the uncharted course that new discovery is most likely to occur.

ACHIEVING MOBILIZATION

Transformation is conceived in the individual human mind, but it is born in the mind of the corporation as a whole. It is the result of a choice, an act of will, made first by one, then by a few, then by many, and finally by the critical mass needed to make radical change happen. Unlike mere *change*, which can occur by default, *transformation* is the result of an enduring, organizationwide motivation and commitment to achieve a common set of goals. *Mobilization* is the means of creating that shared motivation and commitment.

The mobilization chromosome governs the process of mustering the mental energy needed to feed the transformation process. It involves expanding the realm of motivation and commitment from the level of the individual to the team, and finally to the entire organization. Creating the mobilization system involves working from the leadership level down, and from the grass roots level up. There are four genes in the mobilization chromosome, requiring the following four primary tasks for the genetic architects of the corporation:

1. *Developing leaders.* Those who lead the transformation process largely determine its course. Therefore, the CEO's choice of leaders and of methods for developing future leaders sets the tone and direction of the company's future. The CEO acts as a role model, and induces the senior leadership team to do the same. Senior leadership, in turn, encourages key qualities of transformational leadership at lower levels of management, and so forth, creating a top-down, cascading migration of responsibility, motivation, and commitment, down and throughout the organization. Few people are born to lead this kind of effort; most grow into their role, and there are techniques that can help develop the needed leadership skills. CEOs, for example, often find a personal coach and confidant helpful. On a group level, senior executives often find it necessary to plunge into a *Valley of Death* meeting to get the transformation process underway.

An intensive executive meeting held away from corporate facilities—an offsite—is a highly effective means of focusing senior managers' attention on transformation. Offsites also provide an ideal forum for naming transformation leaders, who together will drive the transformation process as *the executive steering committee, or executive team*. The steering team usually consists of the CEO and a handful of direct reports, four to eight people in all. Its role is to direct the overall transformation effort, remove obstacles to that effort along the way, and personify the energy, motivation, and commitment needed at all levels of the organization. Each member of the group assumes personal responsibility for some aspect of the transformation program, and for delivering the results associated with it.

2. *Creating wide-band, interactive communication.* Once the leadership has been enlisted, the change effort is taken to the people. This stage of mobilization involves creating a wide-band communication process, involving the whole company in the effort. From the top, using vehicles such as *town meetings,* the CEO takes a highly visible role, making it clear that he or she is personally driving the effort. The emphasis here is on width rather than depth. Interaction is the key.

At lower levels of the organization, people actively involved in transformation projects play a key communications role. They are most effective when temporarily (meaning several months to a year, or more) relieved of their former duties to become *full-time change agents.* Generally these are high performers, people who are well respected and to whom people listen. Precisely because they are high performers, there is often resistance to extracting them from their jobs. In such cases the CEO can make great, symbolic strides by intervening and persuading their bosses to release them. When 30, 100, 300, or even more of the most talented people in the firm are dedicated to the transformation effort, people at all levels of the organization start to take notice.

3. *Encouraging the formation of "natural work teams."* The bottom-up component of mobilization takes hold through the work of a relatively large number of small groups, or *natural work teams,* who focus on solving specific problems. These teams have dynamics of their own, and require careful management. A full-time change agent is part of each team, ensuring lateral and vertical coordination between teams and, thus, integration of the team's work into the overall transformation effort.

The composition of the team is critical, requiring cross-functional representation to foster fresh insights born of a comprehensive view of the business. Only such diversely populated teams have the detailed *granular* knowledge of what needs to be done, and it is up to them to define action steps that yield measurable benefits. The action steps often are carried out by *subteams,* spawned by the natural work team and held in orbit by its focus.

Because natural work teams operate in the realm of specifics, the role of the executive leadership team is primarily that of facilitator, communicating faith in the team process, insisting on measurable benefits, and leading celebrations of early success.

4. *Preparing individuals for the cycle of change.* Since transformation is conceived in the mind of the individual, the lens of the corporation must ultimately focus on the individual employee, helping him or her to accept and adjust to the many changes under way. Individuals must undergo an *emotional cycle of change* before organizational change can occur. In other words, a critical mass of people must experience *personal transformation* if corporate transformation is to succeed. *Coaching and feedback* can help people in their quest for personal transformation.

In helping the individuals of a company through a cycle of change, the leadership team's role is to become an open book, a living demonstration of completing the cycle. This may involve an unfamiliar sharing of more wants and needs, disappointments and victories, as well as an open display of giving up one's personal "comfort zones."

When mobilization efforts fail, it is usually because leaders fail to engage all four genes in the process. Many companies rely almost solely on the "top-down" component, putting their trust in executive workshops and team building. Such efforts fail due to lack of interest at the bottom. Others focus just on mustering the troops from the bottom-up, sending task force upon task force to tackle "total quality" or to reengineer processes independently of each other. Typically these efforts produce mixed and conflicting results, or generate impossibly ambitious recommendations that, lacking guidance and obstacle-removing support from the top, never get off the ground.

The key to successful mobilization is to create a groundswell, which is guided by middle managers, who are directed and coached by senior managers, who are led by the CEO. It is neither a top-down nor a bottom-up process, but both simultaneously, working for and with the middle. The result is a controlled but inexorable stampede of motivation, commitment, and action, with the CEO riding at the head of the herd.

DEVELOPING LEADERS

Connoisseurs of the business cliché are well acquainted with the ritual obeisance in the chairman's statement to shareholders: "To the employees and staff, our most precious assets, without whom none of this would have been possible." There is a certain blandness in these statements, as if the writer were aware that people somehow play a key role in business success, but just can't find the right words to say it.

CEOs can't afford such lack of clarity, for there can be no business transformation without the transformations of the working lives of "the employees and staff." While it may seem obvious to some, the idea is troubling to many executives. It is difficult to grant the emotions of the group precedence over an elegant business solution. If the analysis is right, they may think, then people will see the value in the approach, and the change will surely occur. The analytical will prevail over the emotional.

This curious tendency to see business as an island of reason in a turbulent, emotional sea is said to be linked to the dominance of the analytical, left side of the brain. Left-brained thinkers tend to assume that the entire world is left-brained, that reason and the products of clear thought need no advocates but themselves. The grim reality may reside closer to a view that there is a strong right-brained, if not hairbrained, contingent out there, and it is upon their contribution that success depends. For the CEO, accepting this reality is prerequisite to beginning the mobilization journey.

The Eagle Has Landed

March 1993 marked the arrival of Gerry Isom as the new president of CIGNA Property and Casualty. After becoming acquainted with his new Philadelphia surroundings, he immediately undertook a two-week field trip, leaving many in Philadelphia to wonder whether their new leader had had a sudden change of heart.

"I wanted to see things with my own eyes," Isom remembers. "This first impression turned out to be determinant for me. It helped things gel in my mind very quickly."

His most immediate preoccupation was with the development of a leadership team. He remembers the good part, and also the painful part. On the positive side of the ledger, he encountered motivated, eager collaborators who had simply, as he puts it, "been starved for leadership."

"I had several two-hour meetings with members of the previous leadership team," he recalls. "You can usually tell who's going to make it, and who isn't. Many were wonderful, raring to go, welcoming the anticipated change. Many knew exactly what needed to be done."

There was also great pain, though. During his first stop, Tampa Bay, Isom began to notice underwriting and pricing practices that struck him as ineffective and, in some cases, downright odd. He questioned one of the executives who had been traveling with him about whether what he had just observed matched what they actually did.

"This is how we do it," the executive confirmed, somewhat anxiously.

Isom pointed to the flaws of the approach, relying on his own underwriting background. He spent time detailing how he thought it ought to be done, patiently coaching the executive about where to go.

During their next stop, Sacramento, the same discussion took place. Upon discovering that the office was using the same flawed approach, Isom once again detailed for his colleague where he wanted to take underwriting. He could tell that the new approach was too much for his colleague, that the train was moving too fast. The executive also knew he'd reached the end of the road. He looked straight at Isom and said, "I'm not going to make it am I?" He looked almost relieved when Isom gently agreed. The executive submitted his resignation shortly thereafter.

Gerry Isom is a compassionate man. He remembers this moment with emotion, the inexorable conclusion of a several-week attempt on his part to help his colleague find a place in the new world. "In the end," he says, "the organization had done this man a terrible disservice by pushing him into responsibilities he had not been prepared for. In those situations, I always find it better to face up to the issue quickly, rather than let it drag."

Shortly thereafter, Isom focused on redefining the relationship of the Property & Casualty Division with the parent corporation.

"While everybody's intentions were pure," Isom comments, "a strange dynamic had developed between the division and corporate. In particular, the mission of P&C's financial staff had evolved into an ambiguous one. On one end, they were tasked with supplying P&C's management with the necessary financial information, which is what you'd expect. On the other, they'd developed the habit of filtering the information they distributed inside, and leaking selected other information to corporate, unbeknownst to the P&C management team."

Isom confronted the issue head-on. The corporate management of CIGNA was as surprised as Isom had been. With the endorsement, Isom installed a new financial team. A foundation of trust was beginning to be built.

In May 1993, Isom reorganized P&C, creating three divisions where previously there had been two.

"I needed to bring things in focus," he says. "The picture was blurry."

From Transamerica, his former company, Isom brought two of his senior managers, Dick Wratten and Bill Palgutt, both with strong underwriting backgrounds, to lead two of the three newly formed divisions. Interestingly enough, Wratten and Palgutt are quite different from Isom. Wratten is an intuitive, street-smart executive who can look you in the eye and instantaneously assess the risk you represent. Palgutt is deeply analytical, continuously pursuing new creative thoughts and testing them on you. Many have characterized Isom as a blend of the two, with the pragmatism of Wratten and the conceptual depth of Palgutt.

Meanwhile, Isom was working hard at building a new partnership alliance with some of the executives from the previous management team.

"This was key," Isom points out, "for you can't simply build a team with outside recruits. This is where Jim Engel, the head of claims, Dennis Kane, the head of the third business unit, and Rich Franklin, the chief underwriter for Wratten, came in. Two hours with Engel, and I knew we had a partnership. I met Kane at the Dallas airport, and I immediately knew he was running a good operation. As for Franklin, I could see him get excited on our field trip whenever I explained what I wanted underwriting to become. I knew he'd be a tremendous asset."

Isom's team was now close to complete. From July to September 1993, he focused on changing the approach to segmentation and pricing, while implementing some dramatic restructuring measures (more on this later). By October 1993, Phase 1 of the transformation was over. So far, the effort had concentrated on building the leadership team and stopping the bleeding. Isom was ready to move to the next stage: a larger-scale mobilization.

FINDING A PERSONAL CEO COACH

In their role as leader, CEOs are often lonely people. They may be awakened or enlightened by an article, a subordinate, or the advice of friends, but it rarely goes further. They feel obliged to keep their emotions under tight rein—always cool during crises, always maintaining that facade of optimism. Though perhaps naturally gregarious, they rarely have an opportunity to talk in confidence to anyone about their own problems. Close colleagues can't play the honest broker, because they have their own agendas or are themselves part of the problem. Neither do life-partners typically fill the bill, because their emotional involvement tends to overshadow their perception of the situation, producing cognitive distortions.

Many CEOs find solace not with a "right-hand man," but with a father-confessor of sorts, an experienced "coach" with whom to address an agenda uncluttered by taboos or "no-go" areas. The coach may be a peer from an unrelated business, a professional consultant, a university professor, or the chairman of the firm. It is an intimate relationship, to be handled with care by both parties. In some cases the coach may attain "guru" status, acquiring power proportionate to the CEO's own, opening doors to Machiavellian influence.

On the positive side, this personal coach may provide that extra bit of courage needed to step out into the unknown realm of transformation. After all, the stakes are high for both the CEO's career and the company's future. And CEOs, like most people, tend to prefer the safe, the normal, the status quo. Perhaps that is why they usually embark on transformation programs either at the beginning or near the end of their terms. At the beginning, they have a fresh view of what can be done. Near the end of their tenure, they begin to think in terms of their legacy and of their place in corporate history.

In either case, they are motivated by a desire to make a mark, to change things for the better. Unfortunately, such is not the motivation of most business leaders. Most leaders are motivated not so much by a desire for positive change as by a desire to avoid pain—the disapproval of the board, angry shareholders, a disgruntled leadership team. For this kind of leader a jolt is often required, one which demonstrates that *not* changing will be more painful than changing.

INTO THE VALLEY OF DEATH

One effective "mobilizer" of management teams is a two- or three-day executive workshop, typically held off-site, which we call the "Valley of Death" experience.

Its purpose is brutal: to make the executives feel so much pain that they emerge convinced that *anything* is better than the status quo. How far down into the valley the participants are led depends on how bad things are. In the most serious cases, nothing about the workshop is polite or comfortable, because it's in the very depths of the valley that self-discovery generally occurs.

A typical workshop begins quietly, but builds in pitch. During the first day the CEO invites someone, often an outsider, to present interesting cases or frameworks to illustrate how great companies succeed and where growth comes from. The aim is to engage the rational, left side of the brain of the participating executives.

The second day is when everyone's life is turned upside down. Suddenly the CEO is on the attack, challenging the company's major management processes, analyzing the history of the firm, questioning the management culture, and berating financial performance. The company is in dry dock, all the barnacles are revealed. The CEO is brutally accurate, matching indictments to the appropriate defendant, himself included. The accusations are relevant, and hit home. Everyone becomes profoundly uncomfortable. The corporate mind has been accused, tried, and convicted. Its head bloodied and bowed, it stands, awaiting sentence.

On the third day comes the reprieve. With the grim reality fresh in their minds, the participants start to work on solutions, plans they will take back with them and act upon. It is time to start generating immediate results.

The degree of brutality in the process depends on how deep the company's problems are and how firmly entrenched its state of denial is. Sometimes, exigency calls for a plunge into the valley on day one. In one such case, the workshop began with a slide of the cover of a well-known business magazine. It was dated one year hence, and the cover story was the collapse of their company.

On another occasion, one executive became obstinate right at the beginning, and refused to participate. As far as he could see, the workshop was a ridiculous child's game. The CEO fired him on the spot, clearly indicating that participation was nonnegotiable. Sometimes actions like these are necessary to prevent workshops from degenerating into bitter mud-slinging matches between people with irreconcilable positions.

An approach used successfully by some CEOs is to invite an outsider to play the role of a corporate raider. The raider stands before them and makes a detailed, formal presentation of how he plans to "take them out" with a hostile takeover bid. The ammunition is standard shareholder value analysis, but the delivery is pure theatrics. Jerry Blumberg, the president of the Nylon Division of DuPont, calls his character "Louis the Liquidator," and has conjured him up on several occasions. We shall return to Jerry Blumberg and to the vision he created for DuPont Nylon in the next chapter.

It's extraordinary, but otherwise sober executives can become incandescent during sessions of what some would consider hokey role-playing. When Louis the Liquidator attacks, executives get mad—they challenge the data and fight back. They start talking poison pills and staggered boards to keep the predator at bay. They want this guy to go away tarred and feathered, and sometimes they feel the need to do the job themselves. On several occasions, Louis the Liquidator has left town under heavy protection.

Another approach is aimed directly at the CEO. It goes like this: "It's a hundred years later, and you've been in your grave for years, Mr. CEO. So let's talk about the legacy you left. What? You've never heard of Martin Van Buren, or James Monroe? They were American *presidents,* but almost no one remembers anything about them. Now, why should anyone care that you created the best customer service in the cosmetics industry?"

In a derivative approach, executives are asked to guess what their mothers think of the company and their role in it. (This exercise must lead to some intriguing phone calls after business hours!) This takes the concept of *legacy* out of the business context and into the realm of the common man. Mothers rarely have a deep understanding of the firms their offspring run. They know the company name and they know that the job pays well, but that's about as far as it goes for most of them. It makes some people uncomfortable when they realize that what they do doesn't really matter all that much to the world at large, much less to their mothers. Others become annoyed with themselves, realizing that if the right solution really is as simple as they have been saying it is, then they should be able to explain it to their mother.

Another line of questioning that sometimes hits home goes like this: "Tell me what you thought of the company when you joined it at age 25. Now tell me what you think of it now." They reminisce about how, at 25, they thought the firm was flexible, dynamic, and bursting with opportunity. Then they flash to the present and speak of rigid bureaucracy, of how impossible it is to get anything done.

A variation on the same theme is to ask executives: "What would you say to your son or daughter if one of them wanted to apply for a job with your company?" Some of them, after really searching their souls, respond with something like: "I would advise them against it; we aren't going anywhere, so there's no point."

The Valley of Death experience is a way of helping a company's leadership team face the realities of the present. It makes the pain of maintaining the status quo concrete, real, visceral. Sometimes it's enough to galvanize leaders into action.

CREATING WIDE-BAND, INTERACTIVE COMMUNICATION

Mobilization of a small group of executives on mahogany row is a propitious start, but only a start. *Everyone* needs to be mobilized, so how can the leaders of large companies reach out to the several thousand people who comprise the corporation?

Philips, the Dutch electronics giant, has mastered the art of wide-band, two-way communication under the leadership of its CEO, Jan Timmer.

The company's top 150 executives had been converted. They were aligned with the basic purpose and intent of the transformation: the revitalization and renewal of a company on the brink of death. The 150 new zealots went out into the company, holding extensive discussions with a thousand of the next most senior managers. The message was then cascaded down to the third and fourth levels, always with interactive discussions.

As a culmination of the effort, and to celebrate its 100th birthday, Philips organized a two-way dialogue with all its employees: an electronic town meeting of gigantic proportions. As a birthday present, the telephone company granted Philips free time for a simultaneous, worldwide video link. Tens of thousands flocked to convention halls and stadiums to participate in the proceedings.

The event was produced with the professionalism of a network TV show, and had an extraordinary mobilizing effect.

Although the number of participants was huge, people realized that the company's very survival required a complete change in the way Philips and its people worked. People in the components division began to see what the television division wanted to do, and how they could help. Assembly people began to see how they could contribute to projects such as the race to produce a commercially viable version of high-definition television (HDTV). On their own, people in all divisions recognized that projects of that type would need the cross-fertilization of various divisional capabilities.

People became visibly moved by the need to preserve the Philips heritage, and the event ended with the promise of creative breakthrough in the air. The event triggered multiple local problem-solving sessions in the various countries, plants, and distribution centers. Ultimately, the leadership and work force of each unit committed to the new vision of Philips, and followed through with action. Later, Philips extended its mobilization to suppliers and partners, who account for a significant part of the value-added in its products.

Successful mobilization events guide employees through the same reframing cycles already experienced by leadership. They break existing frames and create new ones, in the process taking employees through the rational, emotional, and political conversions experienced at the leadership level. Like their leaders they may feel demoralized and angry at first, but eventually the first few steps become clear, as they begin to sense that transformation is within their grasp.

When Cafeterias Become Strategic

To get a feel for large-scale mobilization, we will "listen in" on one of the early Philips town meetings. At the time, the firm was in dire straits. In a ferociously competitive environment and badly strapped for cash, it had already sold some businesses and was in the midst of laying off employees. The air was thick with distrust and despair. Everyone was on-edge.

One evening, about 100 people were invited to the canteen in one of the company's plants. The manager of the division, the plant manager, and a facilitator presided. They explained that top management had initiated an action program to cut costs. But that top-down change was not enough, they said. Everyone had to be involved, hence these town meetings. Be frank, they urged. No subject was taboo. All questions would be answered.

The division head started the proceedings with a brief address.

"A town meeting is a very old idea," he said. "When there was a crisis in the village, the people came together and talked about it. I was told you do not fully understand what's going on at Philips. I will try to explain. We're like a married couple who have overextended ourselves financially. We already have a mortgage, and have been forced to borrow more just to make ends meet. Now our income won't cover our monthly payments. We're hurting, both financially and emotionally."

That was it. He sat down and invited questions.

"Would the company ever consider shutting down our plant and sourcing our product from somewhere else, maybe the Far East?" someone asked.

A moment passed. "No, I don't think so," said the plant manager. "Philips can't be solely dependent on the Far East. As I say, I don't think so, but there may be more nuances that change that view in the future."

"Don't you mean that the Far East doesn't yet have the required capacity?" chimed in a more cynical member of the audience. "That will change in a few years. What will happen to us then?"

"I can't address that," replied the plant manager, stifling his anger at the insinuation of dishonesty. Fortunately, a more sanguine participant stepped in with a positive slant on the same issue.

"We all know that customer [X] has quality problems with us. Even so, we still supply them with 50 percent of their needs. What would happen if we could consistently deliver quality?"

As that thought sunk in, an apparently trivial question came from the back of the room: "Can we have warm food in the canteen again, and clean tables?"

The plant manager buried his face in his hands. The firm was struggling for its very survival, and here they were discussing warm meals in the cafeteria—and in front of the division president! He wanted the earth to open up and swallow him, but he had promised to respond. That was the rule.

"It was so darn expensive," he said. "Someone, how much were the yearly costs of the canteen?"

"It cost us $100,000 per year," a line manager offered.

"It was a very difficult decision to make," the plant manager said, "but we decided that we couldn't afford it. We had more urgent use for that money."

"That's no way to treat us," someone else protested. "You want us to be a team, and then you make unilateral decisions that affect our daily lives. We liked the stupid cafeteria!" The atmosphere had become heated. It was clear there was more at stake here than met the eye; the entire room had become involved.

"Why not make it so we pay more per meal? We'll absorb some of the cost." someone shouted.

"Yes, we thought of that," the plant manager replied, "but the fixed costs will stay. In three or four months, you'll find that a sandwich from home is much cheaper. Sales will go down, and the fixed costs will stay."

Unable to get them off the subject of the canteen, he was at first flustered. But later, during the 15-minute coffee break, he reconsidered. When he took the podium again, he opened with, "I want to come back to that canteen issue again. During the restructuring, we underestimated the value of the cafeteria to you, and we might not have explored all possible alternatives. If you can come up with a way to keep it open that is affordable, we'll do it. Cornelius [one of the more vocal employees] will chair a small team of four to five people. In two weeks, they'll issue a report and recommendation, if there is one. At that point, we'll let everyone know what's going to happen."

The simple promise of resolution for an otherwise minor issue marked the emergence of a new attitude. Before the night was over, they had reviewed the role of trial runs versus volume production. They had discussed the need for, and how to cover the costs of, more training to develop the skills needed for the move to more complex products and production systems. They had discussed the desirability of focusing the marketing effort on four primary customers.

The division president and the plant manager had forged a new partnership, born of their shared trials in a rough canteen. Stronger bonds had been created among the employees. They were still fragile, but they held promise.

A Brown Paper Fair at CIGNA P&C

It's October 1993, and Gerry Isom has been at work for six months. His leadership team is largely in place. It's time to "crank up the machine a notch," as Isom puts it, and to tackle the broader issue of mobilizing the entire organization. His first salvo includes a barrage of newsletters, speeches, videos, and work sessions. But it never seems like enough. The typhoon Isom conjured up at the Philadelphia headquarters is causing scarcely a ripple on the still waters of the distant claims and marketing offices.

He decides to experiment with a more radical approach. He will invite mass participation in the redesign of all major processes in the firm, using a technique called the "brown paper" that he has recently been introduced to. It isn't rocket science; simply a large process flow diagram constructed on butcher paper by a multidisciplinary team of people involved in the process.

Today, Isom is to see how it has gone. He has invited all the teams to come and display their brown papers in the main cafeteria, and to share their discoveries with the other employees.

"Move it over to the right a bit!" a claims adjuster yells to the group, as they fumble the 20-foot piece of butcher paper along the cafeteria wall. Bedecked with colored Post-its™, boxes, and lines, it reminds Isom of a Chinese dragon.

"So, this is one of the claims processes?" Isom asks of the claims adjuster.

Looking tired, he nods. "Yep, we spent most of the night finishing it up. This one is the claims process in the worker's compensation department." The energy in the man's voice belies the bags under his eyes.

"Run through it for me, will you?" Isom asks.

"These are the steps we follow," the claims adjuster complies, eager for a chance to shine in front of the big boss. "Those red flags show what's wrong with the process. See this one? It often takes up to three months before we're notified of a claim. By then the policyholder has already gathered all the lawyers and the doctors he can find, and you lose all chances to get a reasonable settlement by paying promptly. By then you're in heavy-duty litigation, and everybody loses. Except for the lawyers, of course," he adds with a grin.

Around the room, there must be 30 other papers hanging on the walls. It looks like the work of Christo, the artist whose sculptures involve wrapping up famous monuments, such as the Pont-Neuf in Paris and the Golden Gate Bridge in San Francisco. In this case the monument is the third floor of the main building of CIGNA Insurance at 2 Liberty Place, Philadelphia.

Despite the claims adjuster's enthusiasm, Isom is becoming a little nervous. Not many people seem to be turning out for the show. Although everyone in the home office has been invited to attend, it's very close to the 10 A.M. start time. What if no one shows up?

At 10:15, three systems people arrive. They huddle together for comfort, apparently intimidated by the transformation of their canteen. They move furtively from wall to wall, their eyes saying, "Don't bother me, I'm just browsing." Some 15 minutes later, one of them, a middle-aged man, breaks the silence while standing in front of the brown paper depicting the new product development process, the part that shows the history of an unsuccessful attempt to develop a new insurance product for golf courses.

"Hey, I remember this," he says to the woman stationed next to it, "but it isn't quite right. You see here," he says, pointing to the claims handling area, "we didn't classify the claims we received. That's where the real learning would have been. Lots of things can go wrong on a golf course—getting hit by a golf ball, twisting an ankle in the trap, lightning strikes, accidentally planting a club in someone's face. Heck, I remember one case where the pro ran off with the cash box. He had a gambling debt, or a mistress, or something...."

Isom overhears. That systems guy seems to be a walking encyclopedia on golf course insurance. The brown paper is stirring up old emotions, memories of an unsuccessful entrepreneurial effort. Isom wonders how that knowledge can be put to use.

As if hearing the silent question, the systems guy continues. "If we could have just put that knowledge onto a desktop computer at the moment the claim was made, linked it to underwriting, and built a golf claims library, we could have become the world's experts on golf course insurance. If we'd done that, we would have had a jewel of a product. We'd own the golf business by now."

The woman hands him a yellow Post-it™, inviting him to make a note of his remarks, stick it on the appropriate spot, and write his name and extension number on the brown paper.

Isom can't believe it. This fellow has just elucidated a perfect example of implementing a specialist strategy, what Isom had formulated as the future orientation for CIGNA P&C!

By 10:30, the room is filling up. Debates have started in front of just about every brown paper. Isom feels better. He circulates quietly, stopping occasionally to answer questions or listen to suggestions, but careful not to pass judgments at this stage.

By 11:30, the room is packed. Suddenly, the crowd parts and the room falls silent. Heads turn to the door and Bill Taylor, Chairman of the CIGNA parent company, strolls in and starts shaking hands and asking questions.

Soon both Isom and Taylor are totally surrounded, as people point out the financial implications of the ideas on the various brown papers. They could save $1 or $2 million in interest by collecting money through a lock box rather than waiting for checks to clear; save $3 or $4 million by filing claims with reinsurers more quickly; $6 or $7 million simply by making sure the phone gets answered when agents call for quotes. All simple, obvious stuff, but the combined streams of savings add up to close to $100 million.

The change agents call it "the business case." They seem to have a name for everything, particularly the obvious.

A hundred million dollars won't be enough to bring the company back to health, but it's a start. More importantly, several employees have ideas about how they can add money to the bottom line. They are excited, literally elbowing their way around to show their boss what they can do differently. It's a new feeling, for both the President of P&C and the CEO. For the first time, they are certain that transformation has begun.

ENCOURAGING THE FORMATION OF NATURAL WORK TEAMS

Individuals can accomplish only so much on their own. A Lone Ranger is rarely an adept transformation agent; it's hard to stay motivated on one's own. People derive energy from each other, and that is why teams are so important.

Transformation efforts typically spawn numerous *natural work teams*, each addressing a part of the change program. A large transformation effort can run 20 or 30 main teams at any one time, and each main team often begets a brood of "sub-teams." For example, an order-to-delivery team may commission *(charter)* several sub-teams to investigate specific parts of a main process such as order entry, scheduling, manufacturing, transportation, or invoicing.

The key to the success of natural work teams lies less in the workings of each individual team than in the coordination and integration *across* teams. When well chartered and resourced, natural work teams usually succeed. If charters are vague, if they overlap with those of other teams, or if there is an insufficient commitment of resources, teams become millstones around the corporate neck.

Fostering Courage through a Team

A man we will call Merv Previn is the head of the actuarial department for a large insurance company, and one of the 12 members of the Life Insurance Division's Executive Committee. He has also just become a reluctant "sponsor" of the reengineering team for the whole financial area at headquarters. He knows what that means—cutting costs—and isn't exactly enthusiastic about the prospects.

A bald, bespectacled, mild-mannered man, he tends to avoid confrontation. In management meetings he participates discreetly in noncontroversial areas, sticking to the facts and refraining from offering anything that could possibly be construed as a statement of opinion.

Analysis is his life, cultivated through his Wharton student days and mastered in his 20 years in the actuarial business. Through his thick glasses, he may fail to recognize a colleague in the elevator, but somehow he can always pick the relevant number on complicated spreadsheets, even from across a room.

To the people under him he is warm, almost paternal. He spends long hours with the younger actuaries, occasionally staying late for actuarial jam sessions. It is then that his wry sense of humor, normally concealed, shines. But few outside of his actuarial department see this warmer side, so he comes across as a left-brained, numbers man. The perception saddens him, but he never seeks to change it. Actuaries, he thinks, can't afford to be considered emotional.

When a major transformation effort begins at the Life Division, Merv becomes uncomfortable. Things are moving too fast. There's barely time to run the numbers. The impetuousity of the change agents, their appetite for immediate results, puts more and more pressure on the department. He tries hard to get involved, but there is a distant quality to his analyses. He presents them as "exercises," and skillfully avoids having to assign real cost targets to individual departments, safely hiding behind aggregated numbers and "full-time equivalents."

As the effort proceeds, the pressure from the top increases. The president begins to tell his direct reports to "suggest" achievable cost-cutting and head-count reduction targets. He wants action. The tension rises with each consecutive meeting. Some of Merv's colleagues are suggesting downsizing strategies such as "shooting every fifth actuary."

A fellow we will call Paul Jones, a young accountant who carries a tremendous allegiance to Merv, has become a member of the team responsible for reengineering the financial area. His involvement has made him the unquestioned expert on all matters pertaining to the "business case" and financial goal-setting. What he has learned on the team makes the conclusion inescapable: Merv is dithering. But unlike others on the change team who are simply critical of Merv, he spends a lot of time putting himself in Merv's boots, knowing the gut-wrenching dilemma he's wrestling with. He takes it upon himself to talk to Merv privately.

He starts with one-on-one meetings, which are tense for both of them. Jones feels like a son offering unsolicited advice to his father. Merv wonders if his young disciple has defected to the enemy. It's tense at first, but over time, Merv realizes that Paul really wants to help him.

"Merv, you've got to let go," Jones tells him. "Let go of the darn analytics and the rational stuff. Step in front. Mobilize your troops. Reach for the stars, and the impossible will become reality."

Sometimes Jones scares himself with this evangelical tone. What is this language coming from his mouth? Perhaps it's time to bring in an exorcist. But no, he is right. There's a job to be done, and hard decisions often refuse to yield to analytical rigor.

It doesn't seem, however, that Merv will budge. He remains steadfast, saying, "I simply don't see how one can cut costs in these proportions. It just isn't possible."

But shortly after Christmas, Merv calls a team meeting. "I've come to clear the air," he begins awkwardly. "I know that most of you think I have been reluctant to lead the way in this downsizing thing." They watch him suspiciously, expecting another diatribe on why it can't work. "I have decided—." He stops in mid-sentence, the pain of the decision apparently overtaking him.

"What do you think of me?" He almost blurts it out. "Have I been wrong, acted wrong? Do you believe I'm not stepping up to my responsibilities?"

It's a strange act of courage for this introverted man. It's almost impossible to imagine Merv Previn asking such a question of a close friend, let alone of a group of mostly lower-level employees at the company. Paul Jones is stunned. Everyone senses that something important is happening.

He wants feedback, and he gets it—delivered in hushed, supportive tones. The team, which was ready to attack him, has become a support group, helping a man with a difficult problem to gather the mental strength to face the inevitable. Some of the voices become thick with emotion. People are gulping too often, and too slowly.

Merv listens, his resolve building. Finally, he goes on. "I've been talking with my direct reports," he says "and they agree ..." The team recognizes the hand of Paul Jones. He has been working at all levels in the actuarial department, getting Merv's managers to put pressure on him from their end as well. They know that Merv's protective instinct toward them, though well intended and appreciated, is ill-founded. They don't want protection anymore. They want to get on with it, and stop living in the past.

"We are willing to commit to a 30 percent cut in our total costs," he says, staring at the floor. This is a huge number, far greater than they had hoped. In what must be the hardest moment of his professional life, Merv Previn has committed a prodigious act of leadership. To his own surprise, and among his newly made friends, he starts to feel good about it almost immediately. He knows he's doing the right thing. He gets up, smiles as he shakes hands with each member of the group, and leaves the room.

PREPARING INDIVIDUALS FOR THE CYCLE OF CHANGE

We have heard the messages from our leaders: exhortations for change, visions of glorious tomorrows with singing and dancing from headquarters to the shop floor. At long last, the generals have taken command. Now let the troops follow them to victory!

Unfortunately, it just isn't that easy. Generals do not victories make; captains, sergeants, and foot soldiers do. It is they who are out there in the trenches when the leaders take command. Often they are ill-equipped, and they're not budging an inch. They see blood, guts, and paychecks, not glorious tomorrows. They've seen too many officers come and go, too many battles fought and lost, to willingly storm the barricades and start transforming the company.

But the transformation can't start until *they* are transformed. *One at a time*, their hearts and minds must be filled with the motivation and commitment, until a critical mass has been reached. Then change can begin.

Karl's Personal Transformation Begins

Karl, our grade-12 scheduler at Woodbridge Papers, doesn't give a hoot about "transformation." He has seen it all before, and learned to duck. "This too shall pass," is his motto.

But very recently, one of his friends, the plant's support services superintendent, cornered him in the canteen and convinced him that this time it was going to be different. They talked until everybody had gone back to work, scratching little drawings on napkins. Karl's friend was a full-time change agent on the transformation project, and he'd already gotten quite an education. Responsible for presenting stuff to the "big boss" every two or three weeks, he was charged up about what was happening.

The plant superintendent has some ideas about what the plant could become, and he's canvassing for support. He tells Karl that the plant needs to be more flexible, particularly in scheduling, and that he needs Karl's help.

The superintendent is someone Karl can trust. He *likes* him, for heaven's sake, even with his weird ideas, and he wants to make him happy. Although younger than Karl, he's been around for a while and knows the business. So Karl listens—with deep reservations and occasional outbursts of defensiveness—but he *listens*. Then suddenly, he finds himself *involved*. He's no longer ducking some cold, mechanical corporate program; it's a pair of pals chewing the fat and figuring out how to do things better, and somehow it's all part of this thing called *transformation*. Karl feels his precious cynicism starting to desert him.

The plant superintendent meets with Karl periodically, building an even deeper level of trust. The superintendent suggests that maybe Karl should develop a better relationship with transportation. Maybe sending them a memo every two weeks that catalogues their incompetencies isn't the best way to cut that order-to-delivery cycle time. The transportation folks account for a third of the cycle time, he points out. Like it or not, Karl is joined to them at the hip, so they may as well behave like Siamese twins. Karl raises his hands above his head in mock surrender.

For Karl, it's like having a personal trainer, someone to seek out for advice, and he takes the advice. Soon, gaining a progressively broader view, Karl starts trying to develop a real partnership with transportation. Lead time becomes a priority for him, and he starts sharing his view with schedulers in other plants, developing a better rapport with them in the process. The embryo of a network of corporate schedulers is beginning to take form. Karl, assuming a leadership role, starts to become a critical node in that network.

Unbeknownst to Karl, Woodbridge's CEO has taken notice. He is watching the birth of a *leader,* perhaps a corporation's most valuable asset. He needs such leaders, people willing to drive the transformation effort in their areas. Karl has become a small fire, slowly building on a barren and frigid landscape. More like him, if carefully fanned and fueled with care and patience, could envelop the whole company in a purifying conflagration that would fuel the engine of a corporatewide transformation.

The Individual Cycle of Change

Now that he has "signed up," Karl is in for quite a rodeo ride, though he doesn't know it yet.

Many have noted the parallels between the emotional cycles people go through when struggling with change, and those people experience when facing sickness or death. And just as counseling is recommended to someone fighting a grave or terminal illness, so it is helpful to those confronting transformation.

The Kübler-Ross studies of people coming to terms with death revealed a standard emotional pattern, starting with denial and moving through anger, bargaining, depression, and, finally, to acceptance.

Karl acts true to type. "No, nothing's broken," he tells the change agents at first. "Go talk to transportation—that's where your problem is. They're so incompetent!" *(Denial)*

Then Karl gets angry with many people, but mostly with those change agents. "Why are you bugging me?" he snarls. "What have I ever done to you?" *(Anger)*

A little while later he calms down, because he knows it's no use. Still, he wants to negotiate the diagnosis. "Things aren't so bad when you really look closely at it," he whines, pulling out a sheaf of handwritten memos and notes. "I've done a bunch of interesting things over the years. Take a look—what do you think?" *(Bargaining)*

Next he becomes maudlin; no more feisty denials and no more negotiation; just a feeling that the sky's falling in on him. "I never thought it would come to this," he whispers, close to tears. *(Depression)*

Finally he resigns himself to the inevitable. "I'll do what I have got to do," he says with resolve. *(Acceptance)*

Karl needs help at every stage of the cycle because: First, he is in pain through most of it, and won't change until the pain has been relieved; and second, he could get stuck in any of the stages, and every time you lose a key person like Karl the transformation momentum drops. In other words, companies can't afford to lose too many Karls along the way.

It's the responsibility of CEOs to make sure they don't. Here CEOs almost play the role of missionaries, trying to release as many people as possible from the cycle of suffering. The more that get through, the greater the chance that transformation will occur.

Explaining this emotional cycle of change beforehand can be helpful. If people know what sort of roller-coaster they'll be on, they're more likely to hang tough.

Embedded in the emotional cycle of change is an uncomfortable truth; namely, that individuals, working in teams, can bring about radical change, but in producing that change they may feel that they are threatening their own futures and those of their friends.

The evidence suggests that this fear is unfounded, at least as far as a change agent's own career is concerned. In fact, those who embrace change and become its champions almost always survive it. The reason for this is simple: Transformation "talent" is extremely rare and valuable. Firing effective transformation leaders would be like firing your doctor for making you well. A commitment to change is far more likely to advance your career than to end it.

But the same is not the case for friends or colleagues. It is in the nature of transformation that change agents, including CEOs, will make decisions and dispositions that affect people close to them. In these circumstances, the way to be true to one's friends is to follow the example of Karl's friend and do all you can to persuade them to give their support to the transformation process. Those who won't be persuaded must accept the consequences of their apathy.

CREATING THE
VISION

O n the streets of Manhattan, people would call them crazy. But at the winter Olympics, it's common to see slalom racers sitting against trees, eyes closed, swaying and moving their hands like overdressed exotic dancers. They aren't insane; they're creating a mental image of the perfect run, and it is a proven means of enhancing performance. More than physical prowess, more than thinking about beating someone else, it's mental focus that makes the Olympian.

Companies, too, need mental focus, a sense of purpose. That is the function of the second corporate chromosome: *creating a vision.* Mobilization creates potential in an organization; it prepares it to create a better future. A vision provides a shared mental framework that gives form to that future. The visioning chromosome has three genes, requiring the following three primary tasks of the CEO:

1. *Developing a strategic intent.* A strategic intent is a picture of the company's ultimate purpose, the corporate equivalent of envisioning that perfect ski run. It is an aspiration representing the convergence of the analytical, emotional, and political elements of the corporate mind. Analytically, it is based on a dispassionate diagnosis of the company's competitive situation *vis à vis* its customers and cost structure. Emotionally and politically, it is the banner that captures the imagination of the entire firm, and around which people will rally.

Just as people are limited by their view of themselves, so are companies. Developing a strategic intent is the CEO's chance to *stretch* the company's view of itself, to extend the boundaries of the company's industry, to trash the orthodox rules of engagement. The world is full of opportunities for the strategically imaginative. As Ray Charles put it, "Any dream that's any good is a little bit crazy."

This is the heart of CEO territory, where individuals make their mark on the corporate annals. Collective processes rally people around a strategic intent, but the intent itself is the child of the leader's creativity, carefully nurtured and cultivated over time.

2. *Prioritizing expectations among constituencies.*   Driving a company toward its strategic intent involves balancing the expectations of the various constituencies that have claims or designs on the company's resources and wealth. In market-driven economies the shareholder is one of the premier constituencies, but customers, competitors, employees, regulators, suppliers, communities, pressure groups, and many other spheres of influence have a bearing on the daily decisions of the company's management.

The role of the leader is to navigate the corporate trawler through the shoals of value, in constantly changing waters where fishing rights are ill-defined. A clear articulation of what the company hopes to accomplish for each constituency—a combination of a statement like Johnson & Johnson's credo and the daily behavior of the CEO—help to communicate the firm's priorities.

3. *Establishing values.*   Behind every strategic intent, and guiding the balancing of constituencies, is an underlying set of values and beliefs. Explicitly or by default, values and beliefs guide the decisions of corporate life. It is the leader's task to ensure that they are aligned and consistent, rather than mixed and contradictory.

Values define the firm's *nonnegotiable behaviors,* as well as provide the guideposts for navigating through gray areas. They set forth the "do's" and the "don'ts," the "always, under any circumstances" and "the never, under any circumstances." They are the essence of the corporate culture.

Values keep a company together and give it resilience. They are expressions of its "personality," determining its attractiveness to employees, customers, and all others who have a say in whether the firm will prosper. Publishing values is a good idea, but *living* them day in and day out is what really counts in the end.

For the CEO, creating the vision is more art than science. The interplay of the three visioning genes is intricate, defying definition through analytical rigor. Except in rare cases, strategic intent is discovered gradually, after repeated experimentation, not through sudden insight. While the intent takes form, balancing constituencies can be like playing a game of chess in which the rules change with every move. Embedded in the corporate culture, many "values" may not be values at all, may instead be sapping corporate energy and impeding the change process. And changing embedded values is never easy.

Creating a vision is of critical strategic importance. Striving for strategic precision in the creative process, however, can be a fatal mistake. That precision comes later, with the definition of market focus (Chap. 7) or the inventing of new businesses (Chap. 8). Because it lies equally in the analytical and emotional realms, creating a vision belies detailed programming. Like wine, words can describe a vision in detail, but the real test is in the tasting.

DEVELOPING A STRATEGIC INTENT

A strategic *intent* is the core of a vision. It is, in essence, the firm's "ambition in life," a central motive designed not only to capture the imagination of the entire organization, but also to extend boundaries within the realm of the possible. *Stretch* is the sine qua non of strategic intent.

There are many classic examples of strategic intent: AT&T's aim for universal telephone service; Coca-Cola's drive to put its product "within arm's reach" of anyone in the world; Pepsi's commitment to "defeat Coke"; or Toyota's design to "beat Benz." Some intents may be financially oriented, such as the vow of Eastman Chemicals, formerly part of the Kodak empire, to grow from a $3 billion company to a $20 billion company by the year 2000. Other companies may choose a more subjective, customer orientation, such as British Airways' vow to become the world's favorite airline, made at a time when it was clearly one of the world's least favorite.

Whatever its focus, an effective strategic intent directs a company beyond the pale, forcing it to banish limits on what it thinks it can accomplish. It is ambitious enough to require strenuous and prolonged effort, but realistic enough to be a source of focus and motivation.

That's a lot to ask of a simple statement, and even more to ask of its author. In fact, the leader's task is not so much to articulate a strategic intent as it is to give it life. It's as if, as many sculptors believe, the vision is already there, buried within the company and its businesses, awaiting the hand of the leader to bring it out. It usually begins as a "dumb vision," a hypothesis in the CEO's mind, not as a lightning bolt of inspiration. Then, without fanfare, he or she launches experiments to test the intent, to see if it captures and motivates the hearts and minds of the people it touches. After repeated stops and starts, the intent seems to reveal itself. That is when people look at it and say, "Of course!" Then it can be presented to the company and the rest of the world as a fait accompli.

There is no standard pattern for developing a strategic intent, no 10-step process guaranteed to create one. There are, however, a few general guidelines:

Be bold. There's no getting away from it: Strategic intent requires guts and nerve. Alfred Hitchcock, when asked why the hero in one of his movies didn't call the police when he found something suspicious, said, "Because it's boring." Boring platitudes about shareholder value, customer service, quality, or environmental responsibility are not the stuff of compelling visions.

Too many CEOs are easy on themselves and their companies, dreaming merely of joining their industry's ruling class, of becoming one of its top three or four players. It rarely occurs to them to forget the competition; that being the industry leader is a means, not an end; or that they can achieve outright leadership through revolution. "Be in the top ten percent ... " just doesn't compare to "Put a Coke within arm's reach of every citizen in the world."

Be broad ... Does a commuter rail company want to provide superb train service to its customers? Absolutely. But stating so is far too limiting to be a strategic intent. A strategic intent might be: *to make rail-based commuting the preferred, land-based link between home, office, and airport in major metropolitan areas.* A strategic intent needs to encompass the business as a whole, and more—it should allow, even imply, extension into completely new businesses.

... but not too broad. It is possible to be too ambitious, however. One must wonder, for example, if Bell Atlantic and Southwestern Bell will ever excel as total communications and entertainment groups. Trends in technology clearly point to a convergence of the two markets, which invites strategic intents designed around that convergence. Does that imply, however, that building a single, monolithic business is the right way to go? If so, will telephone companies manage to successfully integrate with cable TV groups and movie studios? Visionary leadership means treading that fine line dividing boldness and breadth from posturing and hubris.

Look a long way ahead. A strategic intent brings the future to the present. The idea is to start 5 to 10 years from now, and work backward. If Eastman Chemicals is going to be a $20 billion company in the year 2000, what does it have to be in 1998, 1996, and so on? Starting from the future enables the CEO to make a radical departure from the present, which opens the door to immediate, radical change. The conventional approach, starting from the present, may move a company toward its intent, but usually too slowly. The tendency is to sketch out incremental moves that preserve too much and alter too little. The revolutionary excitement is lost.

Once adopted, the strategic intent becomes the rallying point for leadership. It is up to the leadership team to align themselves around the corporate ambition and become the role models of it. It is never easy. Sometimes it is impossible, given the existing leadership structure. At British Airways, for example, Sir Colin Marshall found it necessary to replace the vast majority of his leadership team. He brought in new people from within and outside the company. Many knew little about airlines but had the marketing skills and, more importantly, the conviction needed to drive British Airways toward its strategic intent. If senior people who lack faith in the vision are left in their positions, they will surely make infidels of others.

The Crown Jewels of DuPont

Nylon is one of the world's most important products, touching the lives of literally billions of people around the world. Invented in DuPont laboratories in the 1930s, it has revolutionized not only the appearance of women's legs, but the entire garment industry, the automotive tire industry, and countless other business segments. Since DuPont built its first Nylon manufacturing plant in Seaford, Delaware more than half a century ago, Nylon and its related products have become the crown jewels of DuPont's family of world-class businesses. Nylon alone accounts for over $4 billion of DuPont's projected 1994 sales of $37 billion and 19,000 of the giant's 114,000 employees around the world.

In 1992, however, Nylon was showing signs of becoming a "mature" business at DuPont. Sales were flat, profits were down, and the prospects for growth were not bright. Beyond the recession that was affecting European markets, a general lack of vitality engulfed this once proud business. While sales of Nylon surged globally, DuPont was losing competitive ground. Ed Woolard, Chairman of DuPont, was concerned enough about the problem that he put Jerry Blumberg, an experienced executive in the chemicals business, in charge of the entire Fibers Sector to get things back on track.

The fibers sector included Nylon, as well as Lycra®, Dacron®, and other business units. Blumberg's background includes a long stint in Tokyo as the head of DuPont's Asia-Pacific operations. In 1990, he returned to Wilmington headquarters as senior vice president in charge of Corporate Planning and Human Resources. It was during this time that he encouraged DuPont to take $1 billion of cost out of the company's overhead. His management style is marked by modesty, a bias for action, and focus on shareholder value.

When he took the reins of Fibers in 1992, Jerry's first move was to take stock of each business in his portfolio. It quickly became clear that Nylon was the one business most in need of attention. As he sized the businesses up, the people at Fibers were sizing him up. They viewed him as an outsider, especially in the Nylon business, because his experience at DuPont was predominantly in chemicals. The employees of Nylon, accustomed to being performance leaders in a leading company, were confused and frustrated that the business was falling below everyone's expectations. It was not an easy time for Woolard, Blumberg, or the employees of the Nylon business. The Nylon business needed a new vision, a new strategic intent.

Jerry knew that one component of that vision was growth. He had witnessed how downsizing had consumed many companies during the eighties and was determined that the fix for Nylon would not simply be a cost-cutting exercise. Therefore, his first step was to find out what to fix. He led an extensive analysis of the Nylon business, performed by a team consisting of individuals selected for their intelligence, experience, and objectivity, gathered from different geographical, functional, and business operating units across DuPont. The purpose of the analysis was to build a realistic assessment of the current and future requirements of a "healthy business" in which efficiency and growth were equal partners.

The team found that there were, indeed, significant competitive, operational, cultural, organizational, and strategic performance gaps that existed for both the current and future performance requirements for Nylon. The results of the analysis were not popular throughout Nylon; many felt the business was doing just fine. The resistance to accepting the reality of the situation was higher than anyone expected.

With the facts in hand, Blumberg developed a new strategic intent for the business. He believed that DuPont must have the world's best Nylon business by every standard of performance. This was not a motherhood statement to Jerry—he *meant* it—as evidenced by the fact that the vision has now been translated into an internally circulated document that blueprints Nylon's future.

Blumberg is passionate about growth, believing that the key driver of growth is linking the business to the customer. The Nylon business got sleepy, he believes, because it viewed itself as a manufacturer, when in fact it has a wealth of technologies that can help customers make more intelligent choices. He envisions, for example, customers designing their carpet on a computer screen, complete with color, thickness, and type of fiber they want. They would be counseled on-line, electronically, by specialists. The next day, they would get the carpet installed at their home or office with a 100 percent service guarantee attached, and a commitment to recycle the carpet at the end of its useful life.

He sees this type of business as an emerging business paradigm in which companies form strings of mutually beneficial alliances and partnerships. By contrast, he laments the cost-driven model used by so many businesses today. "For example, the distribution of carpets is a shame," he says. "The benefits story of Nylon-related products is never told in the stores. Three of every ten customers go into a carpet store wanting a Stainmaster® carpet—durable, stain resistant, and easy to maintain. But only one in ten comes out with the right fiber. Why? Because the existing supply chain tends to drive everything down to price, which is suicidal. Everybody loses. Customers don't get what they were looking for. The carpet manufacturer gets dragged into a no-margin business. And we, the fiber manufacturer, are forced to compete on price alone in a very capital intensive industry." Blumberg and DuPont are committed to changing this antiquated model, hoping to revitalize the entire supply chain such that more value is produced and received at every step of the way.

Blumberg also realizes the practical reality that a vision will not take hold unless the company becomes committed to real projects that move toward the vision. He immediately launched a major transformation effort to achieve the strategic intent, dubbing it the "Generation Program," consistent with the concepts of health, growth, and vitality. The label, however, was secondary to the approach he designed to the Nylon business in collaboration with Woolard and the leadership team. Recognizing that overcoming resistance to change was going to be a determining factor in the turnaround, Jerry decided that Generation was going to have to begin as a top-down program. The stakes were very high. Employees, security analysts, and the media were all watching intently. Would Blumberg and the Nylon leadership succeed?

To say that the Generation Program succeeded beyond anyone's expectations is an understatement. The success of the Nylon business Generation Program has changed DuPont forever. Many security analysts attribute the recent surge in DuPont stock price—close to 30 percent—to the turnaround of Fibers, particularly of Nylon. The Nylon business created cash flow in excess of $400 million in 1993 and another $120 million in the first nine months of 1994, enjoyed record profitability, and most importantly, created numerous growth opportunities that are beginning to revitalize DuPont's Nylon business. How did the Generation Program succeed so impressively?

To Blumberg, there are clear and unmistakable reasons for these record-breaking achievements. Most basic, he says, is that, "Ed Woolard supported us throughout the effort." Aligning Nylon's leadership team was a problem at first. Recalls Blumberg, "As we started Generation, some of the Nylon business managers had trouble facing our performance reality. My job at that point was to insist that they either support the program, or get out of the way. I also knew that this thing had to work fast. We simply didn't have time for some drawn out affair that would keep the organization in a state of turmoil. We had to produce credible results—and fast. At times, it seemed as if we were all in a fishbowl. But the good news is that the people in DuPont quickly understood that a healthy, growing company was a much better alternative than trying to hang on to the chronically flat-sales, bloated staffs, and ineffective organization that we had when we started Generation."

Blumberg says that getting all the employees to understand the need for the changes and win their support was a major challenge. To drive home the need for change, he and the Nylon leadership embarked on a "get healthy" program, which involved literally all of Nylon's 19,000 employees as part of the mobilization effort. In the early days of Generation, employees were asked to review the major initiatives underway in Nylon and determine whether they were consistent with the goals of Generation. As a result, 160 of the 800 initiatives underway were stopped. This immediately saved $14 million through cost avoidance. It was an auspicious start.

The early mobilization efforts focused on determining the level of services necessary to support a "healthy" Nylon business. As a result, they discovered they could dramatically reduce the amount of work required to support operations. Consequently, over 4000 people were laid off. "It was the most painful part of Generation," remembers Blumberg, "separating employees is not something that is taken lightly at DuPont."

All of the 26 major manufacturing sites were examined from two critical perspectives. The first was to determine if each site was operating according to best practice standards. Significant operational improvements were made after the cultural barriers surrounding each manufacturing site were set aside to allow outside scrutiny. Even more value was found when the total strategic performance of all of Nylon's manufacturing capacity was considered in the context of the global market. They discovered that significant idle capacity existed. As a result, several plants were downsized and one complete site was shut down.

Mobilization was not just a single act or event, but there was a critical period that Blumberg considers a "defining moment of truth" for Generation. In the summer of 1993, frustrated that the pace of change wasn't fast enough, the leadership launched what is now termed "the 90-day war" to push the organization to accept the new reality. The 90-day war set real, tangible goals and developed specific action plans, accountabilities, and progress reviews for all of the Nylon business units. It was the equivalent of a "full court press" in basketball. Looking back, Jerry credits this intervention with bringing the leadership of Nylon together, both in terms of their level of emotional commitment and their shared sense of purpose regarding what Generation meant to the Nylon business's future.

Growth and health are synonymous to Blumberg. A core tenet of his vision is to double the size of Nylon by the year 2000. While this represents only a 10 percent real growth rate over the next six years, it represents a fundamental and radical transformation of the Nylon business, which has had virtually zero growth over the last five years. Being able to grow and sustain growth is a competence that Blumberg and the leadership team are working hard to ingrain in the culture of a renewed Nylon business.

To jump-start the organization's interest in growth, Jerry and the leadership team organized a global "idea fair" to bring together hundreds of people from all parts of the Nylon organization and the broader DuPont organization. In a series of idea generation sessions focused on how to expand the Nylon business, a wide range of creativity was unleashed, which resulted in over 400 workable ideas. Of these, 10 projects were initially funded and launched by the Nylon leadership. The projects span a wide range of new opportunities, which have created substantial enthusiasm within Nylon. One of the most promising projects involves a pilot in the garment packaging business, which again illustrates DuPont's vision of generating greater value to be shared throughout the supply chain.

He explains that the garment industry, too, is trapped in the same cost game as carpets. A garment packager takes the specifications from a retailer, designs the garment without understanding the materials and the properties of the materials available, invites quotes from low labor-cost manufacturers in the Far East, and grants the work to one of them. Once produced, the garments are shipped by boat, taking weeks to reach retailers' floors. Everybody hopes they forecast demand accurately—a cinch in the fickle fashion industry—because when they don't, the retailer runs out of merchandise, and it takes weeks or even months to replenish the stock.

What about changing colors, modifying the properties of the fabric, or making tailor-made clothing affordable through technology? Forget it under the current model operating in the garment industry. DuPont hopes to brighten those prospects.

Achieving both efficiency and growth meant changing the organization structure, which Blumberg remembers as a major challenge. DuPont integrated all of the world-wide Nylon business organizations into one flat and highly focused organization. Prior to Generation, Nylon units existed as individual, semiautonomous "islands." Business units developed Nylon intermediate products, tires, carpets, textiles, and other products. Each operated its own assets and each developed organizations to address the various markets around the globe. This led to "stovepipes," which impaired collaboration. Overlaying these islands, autonomous functional groups such as R&D, human resources, and engineering made things even more complex.

Generation mobilized the employees of Nylon to create an integrated model of the business, which had never before existed. It encouraged the organization to think and act more broadly in pursuing customer-facing opportunities. Today, the Nylon leadership makes decisions regarding capital investments, asset management, growth, and operations from a "total Nylon" perspective. Market-facing teams are empowered to pursue growth opportunities aggressively and with maximum freedom to move across all of Nylon to serve customers. Nylon leadership is helping the organization develop the skills and competencies needed to become a growth-oriented business. The renewal of people is a major theme as Nylon strives to learn new ways of serving customers. Everyone now knows that even more skills are needed in order to realize the vision. As a result, there is one Nylon organization supporting many market facing teams, working and learning interactively instead of sending notes across "islands of Nylon."

Blumberg's vision for Nylon did not end with the "getting healthy" activities. He had launched an effort he called "blueprinting" early in the Generation program. The blueprinting process was Blumberg's way of taking his broad vision for Nylon's growth and health and having the organization's best minds think creatively about how to turn that vision into a reality. The resulting blueprint is a road map for all the employees to use in building the future DuPont Nylon business.

A cross-functional team of DuPont's best and brightest future leaders and the Nylon Leadership Team developed and documented an extensive design of the future state of the Nylon business. The result, after six months of rigorous design, is a hefty document called, *DuPont Nylon Blueprint for Health and Growth*, which contains the models, requirements, and plans for the future of the world's best Nylon business.

Blumberg believes that the blueprinting process has done more to give employees a sense of ownership in Nylon's future than anything he has seen in his career with DuPont. The leadership and the blueprinting teams worked together in an open, often tumultuous, process. All parts of the organization were able to participate. The final result is a plan that has already helped the new Nylon business achieve record levels of profit.

Is the job done? Blumberg laughs and says, "We all know we've just started. One of our beliefs is that we are all going to have to learn, again and again, how to meet the needs of customers throughout the world. We'll never get it completely right because everything is changing and always will be changing. I think we've learned that the need to change our business to meet customer requirements as an essential part of our health as a company. If there is a learning organization, Generation has mobilized us all for that purpose. We intend to follow the basic elements of Generation (facing reality; mobilizing for change; blueprinting the future; realizing our goals; learning effectively; and developing organizational speed) as a means of staying aligned with our customers. Now that we have committed to being a growth company, we'll continue to push the Generation growth process in everything we do from now on."

Gerry Isom Redefines the Future of CIGNA Property and Casualty

Between March 1993, the date of his arrival at P&C, and October 1993, when he launched his major mobilization effort, Gerry Isom was a busy man. We saw in Chap. 1 how he assembled his new leadership team during that period. He also used those early months to develop his vision of what CIGNA P&C ought to become. On July 31, 1993, he delivered a major address to CIGNA's senior officers, specifically tackling the difficult question: "Can CIGNA P&C dig itself out of the hole it's in?"

By then, Isom knew his audience well, and he built his speech accordingly. The address started with some analytical evidence delivered with surgical precision, and progressively rose to higher motivational planes, culminating in a gigantic crescendo. Isom showed that P&C could be turned around, because some competitors actually make money in the property and casualty business, and he committed to returning the firm to profitability, if everyone helped. The support was immediate and overwhelming.

Isom's vision involved a fundamental switch from being a "generalist" P&C firm to become a "specialist" firm. A generalist firm is essentially a claims and underwriting factory, providing products and services to agents. As Cincinnati Financials does so successfully, it builds relationships with agents and relies on them to sort out which risks to underwrite and which to pass on to competitors. A specialist firm, by contrast, selects specific types of risk it wants to underwrite. It focuses on specific businesses or customer segments—specific groups of end-users of insurance products—whose risks the insuring company uniquely understands, and they use that expertise to draw agents into a partnership to serve those end-user groups.

An insurance company with a unique understanding of wine-making, for example, will most likely have a lower loss record for related products than a company with little experience in the field. It can better project what may go wrong, such as the probability of losing a crop or the likelihood of a fermentation process going awry. Moreover, because it knows the business so well, it may counsel its customers on how to reduce risks. It might inspect a vineyard, for example, and provide the manager with information about a new pesticide or frost-control technique. At the winery, it might suggest things as simple as fire extinguishers where there are none, or more subtle things such as better lighting in a work area. With its unique knowledge base, a specialist firm understands its customer's risks more fully and can recommend more focused action to reduce them. Consequently, specialist firms are typically the lowest cost and the most sought-after providers in their segment.

"The P&C business is a squishy part of the insurance business," Isom states, "and not everybody understands that. Unlike life insurance, where you can predict everything statistically through mortality tables and other tools, the P&C business involves a personal evaluation of the risk you take by undertaking tiny segments of the market. That's why knowledgeable underwriters are so important."

Isom knew that the best performers in the P&C business, starting with AIG and Chubb, were specialists, and he wanted to quickly move CIGNA P&C in that direction. The problem was that, historically, they had followed what might be termed a hybrid strategy. They had ostensibly adopted a specialist strategy, but in practice they were pursuing so many segments with such a small resource commitment to each that they had de facto reverted to a generalist approach. Consequently, agents didn't understand what risk CIGNA P&C truly wanted to underwrite; they were confused about CIGNA's "appetite," as insurance people call it.

Agents not only were confused, many of them became alienated by what they perceived as CIGNA's arrogance. In implementing its segmentation scheme, CIGNA demonstrated an apparent intent to bypass the agents. "We don't really need you," the strategy seemed to say. "You are irrelevant, because we can go straight through you to the policyholder." This attitude, combined with a drop in service levels to agents, induced many good independent agents to quit using CIGNA P&C as one of their principal carriers. At the same time, the best agents inside the firm were defecting to other companies. This left CIGNA in double trouble. Independent agents no longer trusted them, and sought them out less often. Internally, they were left with a stable of relatively unskilled agents, who stayed on and were quietly passing on bad risks to the company.

"Agent relationships were even worse than I had thought," Isom later confessed. Understanding all of this, Isom wanted a whole-hearted commitment to a specialist strategy, including the development of a close partnership with independent agents and a reskilling and renewing of their own agents. To make the specialist concept real, he first established a preliminary, financially based strategic intent: to become one of the top quartile performers in the industry, as measured by combined ratio, a measure of overall profitability in the insurance business.

Critics will point out that this vision is neither particularly original—most insurance companies claim they want to be specialists rather than generalists—nor particularly compelling—being in the top 25 percent of an industry hardly appears to be a stretch goal. In CIGNA P&C's financial context at the time, however, these were large aspirations indeed, though modest in the context of the P&C business as a whole.

Modest though it was, Isom's vision began to lift the company out of its long-standing morass. For the first time in recent memory, hope timidly lifted its head at CIGNA P&C.

PRIORITIZING THE EXPECTATIONS OF VARIOUS CONSTITUENCIES

We have all read vision statements like: "We will be the premier supplier of products and services in all markets where we intend to compete; achieve excellence for the benefit of our shareholders, customers, employees, and our mothers; and otherwise make everyone rich, healthy, and metaphysically balanced, while remaining focused and having fun."

Okay, so it's a bit of a caricature, but most alleged visions statements have that sort of feel to them. They typically even follow a similar structure: First, a set of bold statements full of flowery adjectives like *premier, excellent,* and *world-class*; second, a vague reference to how the firm will compete, or "win"; third, a pledge to the *constituencies*—shareholders, customers, employees, and mom; fourth, a statement of grand, altruistic intent to make the world a better place, promptly corrected by a pledge to remain focused; and finally, often, a reference to *fun.*

A good way out of this trap of banalities is to map each of the firm's constituencies to an intent of how the firm will serve them. In most companies, dedicated functions serve individual constituencies, which is fine as far as it goes. But just as wars are too serious a matter to be entrusted solely to the military, so leaders cannot allow purchasing to be in sole control of supplier relationships or let marketing and sales unilaterally decide how customers should be treated. That is why it is important for leadership teams to retain ultimate control of constituency management. It is up to the leadership team to establish behavioral ground rules for dealing with constituencies, and to articulate the philosophy of relationships upon which those rules are based. The goal is to gear the entire organization, not just an isolated function, toward both managing and fulfilling the expectations of shareholders, customers, suppliers, and, of course, good old mom.

Unipart's Constituency-based Vision

The Unipart Group of Companies (Unipart) in Great Britain has gone so far as to explicitly define its vision in terms of its constituencies. The vision itself is simple, perhaps even simplistic at first glance, but it has played an integral role in providing the motivation, commitment, and sense of purpose the company needs to succeed.

The company was founded in 1987, the result of a buyout of the former British Leyland, consisting of a successful marketing division and a third-rate manufacturing operation. Under the leadership of John Neill, group chief executive, it has since become one of Europe's leading independent auto parts suppliers, with annual sales of $1.1 billion, 23 percent of which is exports.

Unipart consists of a number of businesses. Unipart DCM provides "demand chain management services" for a number of leading auto makers; Unipart International develops and markets an "all makes" range of parts to the automotive repair market under the Unipart brand; Unipart Industries (including Oxford Automotive Components, Premier Exhaust Systems, and Advanced Engineering Systems) makes original equipment for Honda, Land Rover, Rover, Saab, and Toyota. Unipart also owns UniqueAir, a cellular phone service supplier; UIT, an information technology company; and Complete Communications, a creative communications group.

Unipart's vision is summarized in a set of nine statements (see Fig. 2.1). Most companies stop at something similar to Unipart's Group Mission Statement (from which, Neill asserts, the other eight can be derived). Unipart, however, spells out its vision in greater detail, with explicit focus on key constituencies. The people of Unipart, and everyone who knows the group well, have become familiar with these and other "tools for thought" that play key roles in Neill's tireless evangelism.

1. Group Mission Statement

The Unipart Group of Companies aims to be an enduring upper-quartile-performing company, in which stakeholders are keen to participate, performing principally in the automotive-related market by:

Pursuing our values

Ensuring the continuing relevance and synergy of the divisions' missions

Creating an environment within which the divisions can and do pursue their mission

2. Group Philosophy

To understand the real and perceived needs of our customers better than anyone else, and to serve them better than anyone else.

3. Group Corporate Goal

To make the Unipart logo the mark of Outstanding Personal Customer Service.

4. Lifetime Customer Relationships

We will strive to build lifetime relationships with our customers, and we realize that to do so, we will need to harness the intellectual energies and creativity of all our stakeholders, based on long-term, shared-destiny relationships.

5. The Supplier Partnership

We see our suppliers as stakeholders, and are increasingly working in partnership with them, continuously striving to make our total enterprise activities, from raw material to the end-user, as lean and efficient as possible through a process of continuous mutual learning and up-skilling, underpinned with the confidence of a long-term relationship.

6. The People Commitment

We will strive to create a community of employee stakeholders who are committed to the company, the customer, quality, and continuous improvement.

Figure 2.1. *Unipart's nine-part dream.*

7. Interdependence with the Community

We realize that the vitality of the communities in which we trade and from which we recruit is crucial to our prosperity, and we will lead or participate in our community, sometimes in partnership with others, for our mutual long-term benefit.

8. Unipart's U's Vision

To build the world's best lean enterprise.

9. Unipart U's Mission

To train and inspire people to achieve world-class performance within Unipart and amongst its stakeholders.

Figure 2.1. *(Continued)*

Unipart's nine statements embody the spirit and vision that has given Unipart a sense of purpose, emphasizing its strong commitment to *shared-destiny relationships*; which means, building long-term partnerships with its constituencies. They are consistent; they are all deducible from the group mission statement; and they are linked to and supported by a rich and actively promoted philosophy. (For more on Unipart's constituency-based approach to business, see Chap. 10.)

Tilting Excessively to One Constituency

In the absence of constituency maps and philosophies such as Unipart's, companies tend to overemphasize a single constituency, often the shareholder. This emphasis may serve to get people focused and drive performance, but it usually leads to long-term problems.

RHM, the UK miller and baker, singlemindedly concentrated on shareholder value for 10 years to the detriment of employees, suppliers, and customers. It drove its return on investment up significantly, but when it could no longer sustain such high returns, it was taken over. RHM never got the vision message, especially with respect to managing its constituency relationships. It remained stubbornly wedded to the old command-and-control model and confined its change efforts to creating shareholder value. As a result, the company ran into a wall. Nobody got mobilized, and transformation didn't occur.

An exclusive emphasis on improving internal efficiency—often evident in an obsessive focus on quality and reengineering—can also cause problems. IBM has long had a process-dominated culture, and has been rumored to suffer from the disease of overly intense introspection. The case of the Wallace Corporation, which in the space of a few years went from being a Baldridge Award winner to being in Chapter 11 bankruptcy, illustrates the same point.

Some firms, in their single-minded state, start behaving like alcoholics, driven to destruction by their obsession. They close themselves to the world around them and get weaker. Even great companies such as Xerox and Motorola, in their drive toward quality, or DuPont, with its safety program, can sometimes become irrational in their enthusiasm, closing themselves to the critical influence of other constituencies. If internal health is all that matters to a firm, it runs a risk of dying completely healed.

Of Predators and Shareholder Value at Ashland Oil

While a bias toward one single constituency is clearly not a good idea, corporations need to be aware that companies and individuals obsessed with shareholder value make dangerous predators. Raiders and LBO specialists, in particular, make their career on the premise that they can take apart companies that cater to multiple constituencies.

CEOs definitely worry about shareholder value, checking their stock price several times a day. But if they focused *solely* on managing for shareholders, they would simply sell, not try to grow, the ailing business that is losing money; they would probably stop funding some of the more "blue sky" R&D programs; and they might worry less about firing 3000 people at corporate headquarters.

Like nature's predators, corporate raiders target the weak or the slow, so the name of the game is to be strong and fast—to make sure that all the value in the company is visible, reflected in the stock price.

In the mid-eighties, the Ashland Oil corporation was the object of a takeover bid by the Belzberg family of Canada. Ashland Oil was, and still is, a diversified conglomerate, primarily based in the Kentucky and Ohio regions, built around a petroleum refining business. At the time the company also owned Valvoline motor oil (one of the three leading brands in the U.S.), the successful SuperAmerica convenience store chain, one of the largest asphalt-paving businesses in America, a small oil and gas exploration and production arm, a specialty and commodity chemical business, the second largest chemical distribution business in the U.S., two coal companies, and, for good measure, an engineering business.

The Belzberg attack was traumatic, and it took the presence of mind of John Hall, Ashland's CEO, for Ashland Oil to survive relatively unharmed. The first round went to Ashland when the Kentucky legislature intervened and passed a law, effectively protecting Kentucky companies, and therefore Ashland, against unfriendly take-over bids.

Hall knew, however, that this was only a reprieve. Predators would eventually find a way to get around the legislative obstacles. The long-term problem remained, and he was at a disadvantage. Like most managers of his generation, Hall was unfamiliar with the raiders' tool of shareholder value creation. He was an engineer and a shrewd negotiator, who had developed an instinctive sense for business; without the knowledge of the raider games and their investment banking plays, he had been totally blindsided by the Belzberg attack. But he was willing to learn, so he immediately went to school on shareholder value.

After consulting Harvard professors and investment analysts, he concluded that the stock price was indeed too low, making Ashland vulnerable to a breakup bid. He knew he needed to act, and now he knew what to do. He initiated a stock buy-back program, funded by forming what at the time was the largest ESOP in history. He sold the engineering company, as well as part of the coal businesses in a public offering. He also worked with the Kentucky legislature to pass a law requiring Belzberg to own 80 percent of the stock before he could effect consolidation. By the standards of modern, value-based restructuring, these may seem small steps; but for a conservative, paternalistic company from Kentucky, it was a gutsy move. At corporate headquarters, it felt like the mother bird was pushing the chicks out of the nest before they could fly, and the chicks didn't like it.

The stock price immediately shot up, reflecting Ashland Oil's new focus on the shareholder. More importantly, every division of the firm and every department at corporate headquarters understood that, from here on, they would have to justify their existence. John Hall had sent a signal that shareholder value would be neglected no more. The paternalistic tradition of the firm was out. Everyone in the company would add value—or face the inevitable.

THE EMERGENCE OF ALTERNATIVE CONSTITUENCIES

Traditionally, firms have worried about their competitors, their suppliers, their customers, and their regulators, which is the list Michael Porter offered the world in the mid-eighties. There are other constituencies, however, and more and more businesses are building their vision around them as well. This is what is behind the emerging of the *stakeholder* model, which sees firms as integral parts of the social fabric.

Ben and Jerry's, the ice cream maker in Vermont, is one such business. It can be described as an ecologically and socially concerned, late incarnation of the hippie movement. It uses only natural products, for example, and until recently maintained a fairly egalitarian, seven-to-one ratio between what it paid its CEO and what it paid its lowest-echelon employee. The firm's need to attract a new CEO, however, forced Ben & Jerry's to abandon this principle.

Tom's of Maine, the toothpaste company, is another example. In a market dominated by multinationals like Procter & Gamble, Lever Brothers, and SmithKline Beecham, Tom's of Maine is competing by means of a vision based on a philosophy of health and ecology. Esprit, the clothing manufacturer, also is driven by social conscience as much as by shareholder value. And the U.K. retailer, Body Shop International, wears its conscience on its sleeve, much to the benefit of shareholders.

In all likelihood, corporations will take on a more dominant role in what has traditionally been the domain of government. As the disgruntlement with government excess and waste continues to mount, people will look to the more efficient private sector to lead the way in improving society as a whole. Inner city revitalization and education are two of the most likely candidates for increased business involvement (also see Chap. 12).

ESTABLISHING VALUES

Have you ever noticed how good companies almost always seem to have strong values? In many cases, a company's strength is not so much in its strategy or even in its products, but rather in the way it behaves.

Disney, for example, is a class act. Yes, you can point to all the great things the company has done—the theme parks, the movies, the animation—but what is really wonderful about Disney is the people and the sense of fun they communicate in their work. One of the authors was once at EuroDisney with his family (in spite of its financial woes, EuroDisney exhibits the same standards of service as the rest of the Disney empire). His wife and he were waiting in a cafeteria line trying to shuffle two trays of food, one baby carriage, and one baby, all while assisting their other child. Before they knew it, a young woman had appeared from behind the counter and was escorting both the baby and the baby carriage to a baby chair at one of the tables. It was such a simple act, and yet it made the whole trip worthwhile.

Where does that kind of voluntary, genuinely caring behavior come from? Clearly, it doesn't come from a policy directive telling employees to cheerfully escort parents to their tables with their food trays, their baby carriage, and their baby. Certainly, that person was not going to get a higher bonus because she helped. This is simply the way things get done at Disney. It is embedded in their *values*—in the people they hire and the way they train about service. Whether in France, Japan, or the United States, the distinctive, genetic marker of Disney's value for service is consistent and unmistakable.

Values make the corporate "person." They are acquired attributes, which combined with the genetically inherited traits of the biological corporation create a corporate "personality" that touches everyone inside and outside of the company. Just as parents exert the strongest influence on the development of values in children, so leaders exert the strongest influence in a corporation. It is their responsibility to splice the right values inside the company. They are an integral component of the cultural imprint that can make or break a company.

Unlike strategic intents and constituency maps, which may not be relevant to many in the company other than the top management team, values reach everywhere, touching people both within and outside the company. A company's values attract or repel customers and suppliers; they induce people to join the firm, or existing employees to quit; they predispose people in positions of power—regulators, planning officials, etc.—for or against the company; and they encourage or deter the formation of alliances and partnerships. In short, they represent the essence of a corporation's character and are a key determinant of its personality.

All companies have personalities. Citibank, for example, is known as an aggressive company with a strong belief in technology, making it attractive to fast-trackers, less so to security seekers. Merrill Lynch also is an aggressive firm, known for rewarding its high performers well, which makes attracting good talent relatively easy. In the generally slow-moving and conservative insurance industry, Prudential and AIG stand out as fast-moving innovators. New York Life, by contrast, has made a virtue out of its somnolence in the 1980s. Having emerged unscathed from the collapse of the junk-bond and real estate markets (because it did not participate), it is now perceived as a stable, reliable institution.

Most telephone companies are still dominated by the values of their formerly regulated environment, worrying about their network and their relations with the regulators. Only a few of them have successfully made the leap into the wilds of the unregulated side. Some of them are unwilling to change their values and personalities with the changing times. MCI, on the other hand, is starting to look more like an investment banker than a long-distance provider, making its Concert partnership with BT (formerly British Telecom), the long-regulated and staid British telecommunication conglomerate, a culturally interesting one.

A strategic intent provides the core image of a vision, an image of the future to strive for. Constituency management ensures that everyone joins the journey toward the vision. *Values* provide the bond to keep everyone together along the way.

Emerging Values at CIGNA P&C

Gerry Isom communicated his new vision for CIGNA P&C at the end of July 1993. Shortly thereafter, he put another stake in the ground.

As a seasoned veteran of the industry, he knew that the insurance field is dominated by analytical constructs and actuarial thinking. To transform CIGNA P&C, he knew he needed to cater to the analytical side of his firm and present a conceptually articulate picture of the vision. He had taken that step through an executive meeting, a letter to managers, and a communications campaign. As a "people person," however, Isom knew that the vision had to appeal to the hearts of CIGNA's people as well. This, he thought, required the development of values the whole firm could identify with.

He began a dialogue with his leadership team and, later, with the firm-at-large during multiple field visits. The values that emerged came from all over. Isom liked that. As far as values were concerned, he was a committed eclectic.

"Focus on making money" was the first one, a simple principle that the firm appeared to have forgotten. It made it okay to be entrepreneurial, as long as you knew what you were doing, and it also triggered discussions about *how* to make money in the insurance business.

"The culture is the hardest part," Isom states. "We used to have a process-based culture, not a profit culture, one where people prepared and sent reports without even thinking why they did it. We changed all of that."

In insurance, making money is a matter of playing the odds, always keeping them in your favor. It requires spreading risk across a large, cultivated population to create a statistically predictable distribution of claims. Some of CIGNA's managers had forgotten that simple principle. They would look at a customer file and notice that there hadn't been a significant number of claims in recent years. Fearing a loss of business, and forgetting that statistical profiles capture norms, not realities, they would lower the premium to help ensure the ongoing business. This would happen again and again until, ultimately, the probability profile would finally shift. Ultimately, the claims would come in, collapsing the profitability of the account.

"Work cooperatively across business units" was another value. It reinforced the specialist thinking by acknowledging the existence of discrete business units, while encouraging the sharing of resources and information across them. Underwriters felt good about it because it legitimized their special knowhow. It also signaled to claims and systems people that there would still be room for shared resources under the new regime. This value also applies to the new relationship Isom wants to establish with corporate, one of trust and empowerment rather than micromanagement and control.

"Both P&C and corporate had developed bad habits," he suggests. "We had forgotten to trust each other, and were playing games. Today, if I need anything, I call, and everybody's quite helpful. They do the same."

Another new value was "build service-based relationships with producers" (producers are the independent agents and brokers who act as intermediaries between policyholders and insurers). To an outsider this might seem self-evident, even trite, but CIGNA P&C had been neglecting its producers, and the value of that relationship needed explicit affirmation. It also raised interesting questions about what "service" means for a property and casualty company.

"Stress professional pride" was another, and a sorely needed one at that. Under barrage from the parent company, outside ratings agencies, and stock analysts, the division had become a group of the walking wounded. One of Isom's most gratifying moments came when that pride showed itself a few months later. The bottom line had already started to improve and a young underwriter said to a member of the President's Executive Council (PEC), "You see, we weren't losing money because we were stupid, we were just badly led!"

Another value, which Isom has never publicly articulated but which he exhibits every day, is a belief in technology. He believes insurance is an information game, making technology and how it is used of critical strategic importance. He displays a keen interest in all technologies that allow for the freer circulation of information across agents, underwriters, and claims; and he has displayed a willingness to invest significantly in that area.

He also strongly believes in empowerment. He will gladly communicate the general direction of the company from the top down, as he did with the articulation of the specialist strategy, but he is very reluctant to force decisions on anybody. He is, however, relentless in his expectations, and will come back at you in a variety of ways before he gives up.

"My job is simple," he states. "I fly at 40,000 feet and watch the jigsaw puzzle come together."

None of these values is particularly new or startling. In fact, they are predominantly common sense for a property and casualty company. Even so, they had been lost, forgotten, or stifled at CIGNA P&C, and Isom brought them back to the surface. Simple though they seem, they were designed to be specific enough to pinpoint the errors of the past, yet broad enough to engage his troops in fleshing them out in more detail.

The development of CIGNA P&C values continues. Every day, in some corner of the firm, there is a discussion of what each value means. Many observers have felt that these discussions are repetitive and shed little new light, but Isom knows that the process of developing those values and of keeping them in the forefront of the collective mind is as important as their content. And he never misses an opportunity to talk about the values to new recruits.

He is sometimes reproached for his missionary zeal. "You don't understand," he laughs. "This is what makes my job fun."

Karl and the Woodbridge Vision and Values

We left Karl being slowly awakened by his friend, the plant superintendent, to the need for a transformation. He had found himself excited and willing to get involved. Since then, things have become dangerously real. Karl is now spearheading a team in charge of redesigning the entire order-to-delivery system across all plants. That's a big deal for Karl, because he's only one of six plant schedulers, and the order-to-delivery process is a whole lot bigger than just scheduling. He now has temporary redesign jurisdiction over areas he knows next to nothing about, such as order entry and transportation.

Karl isn't sure why they picked him. One of the change agents said it was "because you're naturally uncooperative." One of his colleague told him that the actual words used were: "If you can get that grouch to play along, you've got it made." But Karl can't believe that's the real reason. He's intrigued and, let's face it, more than a little flattered.

"Where should I start?" Karl asks himself. He knows that so much is wrong in the order-to-delivery system that it is overwhelming. Perhaps "sorting through a trash pile" would be a more suitable charter for his team.

Inspiration suddenly strikes. "I'll start with the vision, of course. Vision is the source of everything." So he gets hold of a copy of the Woodbridge Papers mission statement and reads with bated breath:

> We will be the North American leader in producing and delivering printed packaging paper through unmatched service levels and through an advantaged cost position resulting from economies of scale.

Wow, that's a mouthful! Let's see, he thinks to himself, "service"—that has something to do with order-to-delivery. And "economies of scale"—that might imply something about centralizing the order-to-delivery process. But it's all too vague. Karl needs something he can sink his teeth into.

Reflecting upon it all, Karl decides that although the mission statement may not be very helpful, the values of the firm are changing all around him. The company is taking this "teamwork" thing seriously, and he'll have to make it work on this project. He has a series of conference calls arranged with the five schedulers from other plants, and it's up to them to come up with something. The Vice President of Manufacturing is their "sponsor," which seems to mean that he calls every two days and asks how much progress they've made.

They have a "facilitator" who helps him set up for his phone calls and team meetings. She annoys him at times with her insistence on "process." They knew how to do meetings before this young woman from headquarters showed up, so what's this fuss about agendas, time contracts, and all that mumbo-jumbo?

She even scolds him occasionally. It's done in good fun, but she scolds him nonetheless. Whenever he starts bad-mouthing the guys in the transportation department, for example, she frowns. He shrugs his shoulders in disgust, but he's been doing less bad-mouthing these days. And he's got to hand it to her, she does a lot of the leg work: arranging the meetings for him, writing up notes, and making sure that they all know what the meeting is about. Her obsession with process has created a discipline that gets them through their work.

One of the most remarkable things for Karl has been the discovery that talking with colleagues can actually be useful. During yesterday's conference call, the Canadian scheduler mentioned that he was running out of vermilion paper. They had just finished a vermilion run at Karl's plant and had paper left over, so Karl arranged for it to be shipped to Canada. And the fellow in Chicago told him that they obtained a significantly better yield by doing "hot-slitting" (cutting the paper off right next to the paper machine, before it cools off). Karl has decided to try it as soon as possible.

Also, it's fun to talk about his job with other folks who do the same thing. He has actually found himself looking forward to some of the meetings. He still grumbles about them, of course, but that's just because he has his "grouch" reputation to live up to. He's not quite ready to shed his old persona.

BUILDING THE MEASUREMENT SYSTEM

No one likes a hypocrite, or so the saying goes. A hypocrite professes to live by one set of standards, but acts upon another, often driven by an insidious hidden agenda. By contrast, most people admire the person of integrity. The person of integrity "walks the talk"; his or her actions are based on goals, which support higher level goals, which ultimately support a set of high-level values. The hypocrite seems to have no sense of commitment to his stated values. The person of integrity does. We come to know the difference by *measuring* the alignment of their actions, goals, and values.

A company, too, can be hypocritical. It may articulate an inspiring vision and set of values, but act on an entirely different set of standards. Unlike the human variety, however, corporate hypocrites are seldom conniving. Rather, they simply lack the integrated set of goals and measures— the measurement system—needed to translate vision and values into actions that will move the company in the right direction.

Ideally, both human and corporate life is a process of goal-directed action, and success is measured by the achievement of goals along the way. Just as human integrity depends on aligning actions to goals, so does corporate integrity. And just as the person of integrity demonstrates a sense of commitment by measuring himself against his stated goals, so does the biological corporation.

The biological corporation's sense of commitment to its vision and values is represented by its measurement system. Building the measurement system is the function of the third corporate chromosome. The measurements chromosome has four genes, implying four corresponding tasks for the genetic architects of the corporation:

1. *Developing top-level measures and targets.* A physical measurement system is built upon a set of standard units that represent common attributes of different physical things, such as meters for length, kilograms for mass, liters for volume, seconds for time, and others. In the same way, a corporate measurement system is built upon a set of standards representing common performance attributes from different business perspectives.

The Balanced Scorecard (BSC) is one way to build such a measurement system. It's a way to translate the vision of a company into a high-level set of goals and measures that act as the standard for all other measurements. It takes a high-level view of the company, asking: "What should the company look like from a customer perspective; a financial (shareholder) perspective; an internal operations perspective; and an innovation and learning perspective?" Within each of these domains, a set of strategic goals is established, with corresponding measurement targets attached. Ideally, if these strategic targets are reached, the vision of the firm is attained.

Because they are tied to a balanced set of perspectives, this set of "strategic vectors" provides leaders with the "instrument panel" they need to assess the impact of activities and initiatives throughout the organization. Ideally, even small localized initiatives, directed by their own goals and measures, can be linked through a chain of cause and effect to their impact on the targets and measures established at the top. Thus, the goals and measures leaders adopt at the outset create the motivating force and the integrating framework for the activities of the entire organization. The leader's role here is to develop the BSC or some equivalent of it, thus providing the basic template for the entire transformation effort.

2. *Building connectors across the top-level targets.* As millions of forgotten New Year's resolutions prove, goals and targets remain empty wishes until and unless action is taken upon them. In this step, leadership sets the stage for action by identifying the cause-effect relationships, or *connectors,* across the high-level targets. If the targets are correctly formulated, then there is an intrinsic flow within the BSC. Learning and innovation targets drive operational and process goals; achieving operational and process goals leads to positive customer indicators; and ultimately, high scores on customer goals translate into favorable financial results.

The logic that translates "back room" indicators into "front room" financial results is one of the keys to healthy corporate life. It provides the conceptual architecture needed to build a hierarchy of cause-effect pathways down and throughout the corporation, making it possible, for example, to trace the financial impact of reducing the order fulfillment time from 30 days to 3. By building logical connectors across top-level targets, the foundation is laid for deeper probes into the cause-effect relationships that drive corporate performance. As the cause-effect pathways start linking and intersecting with others, they begin to form a web of *metabolic pathways* across all 12 biocorporate systems, which allows leaders to model the impact of proposed initiatives or to track the progress of initiatives already underway, ultimately linking them to high-level targets of all four dimensions of the BSC.

Building this web of linkages typically proves to be an extremely valuable mobilization exercise for leadership. It gives each member of the leadership team an opportunity to describe his or her own mental model of how the business works, while learning from the views of colleagues. It establishes a common framework for thinking about and planning the complexities of the transformation process.

3. *Constructing a bottom-up business case for change.* While the leadership team develops the top end of the measurement system, it pays to have teams already at work in the field. Their focus is identifying opportunities to improve day-to-day operations and quantifying the potential benefits. Usually the leadership team provides broad operational targets, such as to find $300 million in cost reductions. Working with the field-based teams, their goal is to identify a set of opportunities that can yield immediate benefits. The sum of what they find constitutes the *business case for change.*

Developing the business case involves building a bottom-up set of measures and targets, but the focus is not necessarily on building a measurement system. The emphasis is on generating enthusiasm and on finding the resources to fuel the transformation effort, not on aligning the bottom-up measures with those at the top. That will come later.

The business case gets people excited. Typically, the people involved have seen many of the problems for years, but have never had the license to do anything about them. Now they not only recommend solutions, but they can also show the financial impact the solutions will have, making them confident that action will be taken. Moreover, when they are unleashed to improve processes that span different functions, they often unveil new, creative ways to do the work, generating even greater potential benefits than might have been anticipated. The leadership team's role at this stage is to demonstrate a bias toward action and to encourage the team to put points on the board quickly.

4. *Connecting bottom-up and top-down measures.* The last step in building a measurement system involves connecting top-down and bottom-up measures. If the measures and targets are to be relevant at all levels of the firm, they need to be unpacked into a set of *key performance indicators*, each tied to a specific process and clearly linked to the higher, strategic measures. This process is carried out through facilitated work sessions, in which employees creatively map the detailed connections between their opportunity-driven measures and the top-down measures developed in the Balanced Scorecard.

The mapping process consists of building causal connections from the lower level goals to high-level goals, and ultimately the measures of the BSC. What emerges is an integrated "tree," or hierarchy, of measurements, linking initiatives and actions at all levels of the organization to the BSC.

Leaders play the pivotal role at this stage, managing a periodic, structured review process in which the leaders of initiatives at all levels of the organization gather to assess progress and to ensure that all initiatives, through their goals and measures, are aligned.

DEVELOPING TOP-LEVEL MEASURES AND TARGETS

Faced with declining competitiveness, most corporations look for a way to improve through process redesign initiatives. They have a varied menu to choose from: process redesign; process reengineering; enhanced process redesign; process redesign with a breakthrough; and super-enhanced process reengineering with added vitamin C. Some of the variations on the reengineering theme are very effective, but all of them start from the assumption that we know what we want to redesign. None of them tells us which processes should be redesigned, or which to redesign first.

Much has been made in the reengineering literature, for example, of Ford's redesign of its accounts payable process in the early 1980s. But at a time when Ford was finding it difficult to make cars people wanted to buy, one must wonder why the accounts payable process was given a high priority.

The Balanced Scorecard gives leaders the compass they need to choose target initiatives, prioritize them, and track progress, with the assurance that process redesign initiatives under way will serve the long-range strategic objectives of the organization. It precludes launching major initiatives at random, minimizing the chance that people and resources will be wasted by working on the wrong problems, or by improving operations in an isolated process while the company's ability to compete continues to decline. Jumping head-first into a major process redesign is like a surgeon reaching for a scalpel before the patient's problem has even been diagnosed.

When Karl Gets Schizophrenic

Karl's getting somewhat overwhelmed. This is a big job, this redesign of the order-to-delivery process at Woodbridge, and he's not sure whether he's up to it.

In the last chapter, we found him struggling to draw inspiration from the corporate vision statement. There was little help in its broad-based bombast. Now, Karl is ready for a 180° turn. If the vision is of no help, he'll start at the other end, very pragmatically, with what hurts. He takes the doctor's approach, using the proverbial "what happens to be the trouble?" line. He begins to interview selected people he knows, asking them to focus on Woodbridge's challenges in the order-to-delivery area.

He learns that Woodbridge is indeed the number-one competitor in its market, with close to 50 percent market share. Many worry that it's losing its leadership position, however, a fact corroborated by a gradual erosion of market share over the last five years. Mountain View, the third largest competitor, seems to present the biggest threat. People are saying that Mountain View offers better service, particularly with respect to lead time. But most worrisome of all is that Woodbridge has been unable to hit its corporate target of 25 percent return on net assets (RONA) for the last five years, thereby preventing the executives from earning significant bonuses. Now, that's a *real* problem!

But what to do about it? Karl remembers an article about a monkey beating Wall Street pros by throwing darts to pick stocks. That's how he'll pick the issues he'll address. Somewhere in the center of the dart board are "service issues," whatever that means. Service seems to be the principal problem, particularly "lead time to delivery." This is the reputed deficiency area, and that's what he has inherited responsibility for.

But he needs more information. He learned that in college: When in doubt, after you've sorted through hundreds of pages of case material, say "I need more information," and the teacher will let you off the hook.

"How will I know what constitutes a good and a bad performance?" he wonders.

Karl decides to get some benchmarking done; he heard that's what Mountainview has done. Ah, the soft whizzing noise of competitive information! He calls five consulting firms, asking them whether they could come and benchmark the service area at Woodbridge, and gladly they all say, "You bet." They show him reams of tantalizing data they'd be willing to share for a fee. It's a festival of dark suits and color slides. L.L. Bean, Xerox, Honda, Mrs. Field's cookies, Disney, Taco Bell! An orgy of "best practices" in the service area. Two firms even offer him databases he can sort through right on Woodbridge's computer. For $30 thousand he can buy a copy of the order-to-delivery cycle of a leading manufacturer, complete with metrics and plant layout. For another $10 thousand, he could purchase the engineering plans of the F-16.

Karl now understands how the best companies in the world deal with service, but he needs to know about his own industry: packaging paper. In particular, he has to worry about Mountain View, the competitor who's gaining market share on them. He goes to the benchmarking well once again, this time focusing on his own industry.

What he gets is a blurry picture. On the one hand, Mountain View is clearly better on the order-to-delivery lead time. It takes them 10 days to make and deliver the paper, while Woodbridge takes 30. That appears to Karl to be a big deal. The advantage clearly also lies with Mountain View on responsiveness: Mountain View is described by customers as "flexible," "accommodating," and "pleasant," while Woodbridge is perceived as "arrogant" and "stiff."

On the other hand, Woodbridge has a broader product line than Mountain View by a large margin. Woodbridge has 440 items in its line, Mountain View only 125. Karl doesn't know whether that's good or bad, and his brow wrinkles in puzzlement.

Karl's just can't seem to figure out what drives Woodbridge's order-to-delivery process. The dilemma is particularly strong given the breadth of the product line. On the one hand, he assumes that the product line is too broad, and shows that many of the lead-time problems are there. Working late at night in his office at home, he writes on his flip chart:

> Our product line is too broad. It clogs our production and logistics system. It slows down our order-to-delivery cycle and increases our cost. It also hinders our responsiveness. Consequently, our competitors are able to cherry-pick our product line and take market share away from us. This is why we've been unable to hit our return on net assets target.

Well, that's not a bad scenario. It has some elegance to it. It has causality and drama built into it. The prescription is also pretty clear. Prune the product line! Let's wheel in Edward Scissorhands and start clipping trees.

Simplify, streamline! He goes to bed with visions of a French garden with neat alleys and small, carefully spaced bushes.

He wakes up in a sweat at four in the morning. What if the wide product line is in fact a good thing; what if customers like it, even depend upon it? Karl fumbles in the dark, rips off his flip-chart page from last night, and starts writing again:

> Our product line is broad, and we like it that way. It differentiates us from competitors. If we can find a way to deal with the complexity of our product line in our manufacturing and distribution operations, then we'll get our market share back and reach our financial targets.

Now, he thinks, that's not exactly a full scenario, but it seems like a heroic starting point. The conclusion is appealing, but the middle is speculative at best! Karl has no idea what it would take to align the operations to cut lead time and still have the world's most diverse product line. But it's an idea. This time he dreams of an Amazon forest with dense vegetation and giant trees.

Karl finds himself becoming schizophrenic. Confused, he feels he could take his entire company down two very different strategic paths: the first a cost-based, commodity-oriented one, the second a product-based, more differentiated one. He, just a scheduler in one of the six Woodbridge plants, finds himself holding the keys to the kingdom. And it isn't a very comfortable position to be in.

Building a Balanced Scorecard.   Though Karl may not know it, he is wrestling with one of the biggest challenges that CEOs face: figuring out which actions are possible, and anticipating what the results will be.

To become a true corporate doctor, Karl needs to learn two things. First, he must figure out what measures really matter and what a "normal" level for those measures would be. Doctors know that body temperature is important, and that it needs to be around 98.6° Farenheit; significantly above or below that, and the patient is in deep trouble. Similarly, blood pressure is a helpful predictor of health, and needs to remain below 100 millimeters of mercury for the systolic, 160 for the diastolic pressure.

Second, Karl must learn about cause-and-effect relationships in the corporate body. It's one thing to know that body temperature needs to be in the 98.6° range, another to know that the patient's temperature is 106° because she has malaria. Unless Karl understands the cause-and-effect relationship between malaria and body temperature, he can't be terribly effective as a doctor.

The Balanced Scorecard (BSC) is designed to provide the standards of a company's health and the means to trace performance problems to their cause. It was originally developed by Robert Kaplan and David Norton. Kaplan is a professor at Harvard Business School, and Norton heads the Renaissance Strategy Group in Lincoln, Massachusetts, a rapidly growing consulting firm.

The BSC provides a way to translate a vision or high-level strategy into goals and measures for four different constituencies (see Fig. 3.1). Although it assumes that the vision and strategy are in place, the discipline involved in developing the BSC often leads to a reevaluation of both. It consists of a set of logically linked pairs of goals and measures (*strategic vectors*, in BSC parlance) generated within each of four perspectives:

1. *The shareholder perspective,* stated as financial goals (return on equity, return on net assets, yield, etc.)

2. *The customer perspective,* stated as customer goals (market share, percent of repeat business, number of complaints or returns, etc.)

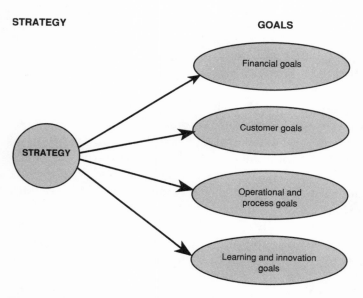

Figure 3.1. *The Balanced Scorecard.* (SOURCE: The Balanced Scorecard, *David Norton, Renaissance Strategy Group, Lincoln, MA, and Robert Kaplan, Harvard Business School.*)

3. *The internal organization perspective,* stated as operational or process goals (order fulfillment time, product development cycle time, costs per unit of production, etc.)

4. *The future capabilities perspective,* stated as learning and innovation goals (percent of jobs filled from within, number of people trained, period between job rotations, etc.)

In the context of the 12 biocorporate systems, the BSC turns the measurement system into the backbone of the transformation design and the instrument panel with which to guide it. When the corporation's measurement system is built around the BSC, leaders can build cause-effect pathways from top-level targets and measures, right down to the primary processes and systems that drive them. By tracing through these pathways, leaders can identify a series of improvement initiatives and prioritize them, not just logically, but also in terms of their impact on corporate performance.

BUILDING CONNECTORS ACROSS TOP-LEVEL TARGETS

The real value of the BSC lies less in the process of goal-setting than it does in providing a theory of cause and effect, one that links operations, culture, and customers to financial performance and, ultimately, to strategy. Most companies lack a theory of cause and effect, and the BSC provides them with a way to build one, with the top-level goals as a starting point. The company's leaders form hypotheses or "what if" experiments, much like those Karl developed about the product line at Woodbridge, and then define the path of cause and effect to test their validity. Once they have hit on a viable system of cause and effect, they can take action with reasonable certainty that the outcome will be desirable. Over time, by forming, testing, and validating a series of hypotheses, the cause-effect chains begin to form a map of metabolic pathways, and a model of the interplay of the 12 biocorporate systems begins to emerge in all its complexity.

There is an inherent logic in the structure of the BSC. In general, learning and innovation targets drive operational measures; operational achievements generate positive customer results; and, ultimately, positive customer results translate into improved financial performance (Fig. 3.2). In the early stages of transformation, however, the specifics of this logic for an individual company are rarely apparent. Early on, leaders focus on

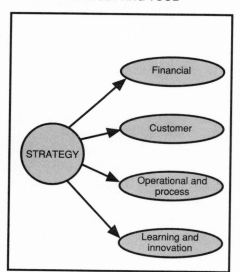
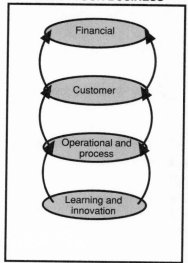

Figure 3.2. *General flow of the Balanced Scorecard.* (SOURCE: The Balanced Scorecard, *David Norton, Renaissance Strategy Group, Lincoln, MA, and Robert Kaplan, Harvard Business School.*)

defining the cause-effect connectors across high-level targets, preparing the logic for deeper probes into the corporate body.

The BSC led the leaders of Rockwater Oil Services, a division of Halliburton, to discover that operations which produced the largest number of improvement suggestions from staff were also the ones with the highest customer satisfaction ratings. Rockwater also discovered that higher customer satisfaction caused customers to pay their bills faster, thus reducing the receivables account. Lower receivables meant less capital tied up in the business, and thus a higher return on assets.

All of a sudden, Rockwater had connected the number of papers in a suggestion box all the way down to return on investment! A new theory of business was born: Stuff the suggestion box, and get rich! Well, perhaps not quite, but the firm could unleash employee involvement programs with confidence that they had the potential to improve the financial performance of the firm.

Sophisticated companies have learned to differentiate between lead and lag indicators. In medicine, high blood pressure is a lag indicator, because there is not much you can do with it unless you know what caused the high pressure in the first place. Salt intake and the number of hours spent exercising are lead indicators upon which advice and action (such as reducing salt intake) can be based.

Most companies only use lag indicators, mostly financial, which is a lot like driving a car with your eyes glued to the rear-view mirror. Few companies can even imagine what innovation or learning goals look like, yet these are often where the lead indicators are located.

Building a CIGNA P&C Scorecard

By the end of 1993, Gerry Isom was increasingly frustrated by his inability to get his specialist strategy implemented. Close to nine months had elapsed since his arrival in Philadelphia. It was all so clear to him, yet not a day went by without evidence that underwriters were still accepting the same bad risks. The remaining agents were wary of the strategy shift. The home office was another problem; support functions were getting more and more disconnected from the field. Isom wanted "alignment," and he wanted it fast.

"We had measures for everything, a thousand micromanagement measures," he says. "How could we let the situation get so bad with all those measures?" he asks, rhetorically.

He knew that simplifying the measurement system was essential, believing that a single set of high-level goals might get everyone moving in the right direction. He was intrigued by the Balanced Scorecard approach, and suggested to the President's Executive Council (PEC) that they build such a scorecard. Over the next three months, from December 1993 to early March 1994, they hammered out their scorecard (Fig. 3.3). Though skeptical at first, the PEC soon warmed up to the approach and developed the framework of targets.

In the financial area, the PEC chose four principal measures. *Shareholder value* was the primary measure because CIGNA, the mother company, was eager to see the P&C division stop destroying value in the corporate portfolio. Shareholder value was thought to be determined largely by the combined ratio. (The equivalent of return on sales in industry, the combined ratio adds up all costs, including underwriting losses and expenses, and divides them by the premiums earned during the period.) The *combined ratio* became the second measure. The combined ratio was then split into its constituents, the *loss ratio* and the *expense ratio*, and these became the third and fourth financial measures.

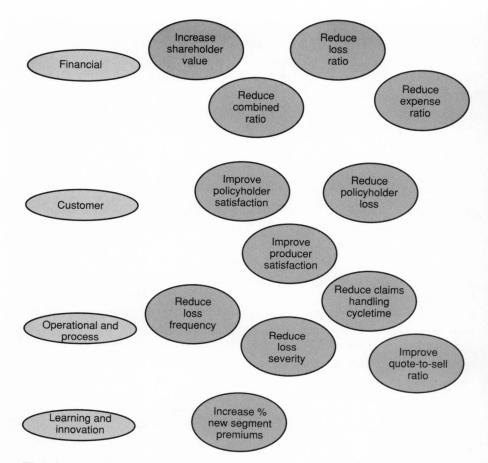

Figure 3.3. *The Balanced Scorecard at CIGNA P&C—simplified.* (SOURCE: The Balanced Scorecard, *David Norton, Renaissance Strategy Group, Lincoln, MA, and Robert Kaplan, Harvard Business School.*)

After some passionate debates about who their customer was—the agent or the policyholder—the PEC agreed that both were, and set forth three related measures. *Policyholder satisfaction,* measured by periodic surveys, was the primary one. On a pilot basis, CIGNA had begun to track how well its customers were doing as a function of losses they had (that would be subject to a claim), whether insured by CIGNA, someone else, or not at all. They called this measure *total policyholder loss,* which became the second customer measure. *Producer satisfaction* (of agents and brokers), measured through a producer survey, was the third.

The operational section focused on underwriting and claims. In underwriting, they chose the "quote-to-sell" ratio—the number of policies written over the number of policies bid for—as the primary measure. A specialist firm quotes only in the segments where it elects to compete, and wins more often than a generalist. Typically a specialist will bat, say, 20 to 30 percent, while a generalist wins only about 5 percent of bids. The underwriting target was set to reflect a specialist strategy. In claims management, the PEC chose three measures: *loss frequency, loss severity,* and *claims cycle time.*

The *learning and innovation* section was initially a source of great puzzlement. But the group promptly realized that what characterizes a specialist is the ability to continuously invent new segments on which it can, well ... *specialize.* At CIGNA P&C, the group decided to measure innovation through the *percentage of premiums generated from new segments* in the total volume of premiums collected.

CIGNA P&C now had a balanced scorecard. But it took time before they realized the importance of what they had accomplished together. On the surface, they had listed a set of high-level objectives. At a deeper level, they had begun to reconcile potentially divergent points of view, forging a consensus. The battle lines between the new guard and the old guard were dissipating, as were the walls between businesses and centralized functions. Both had been major obstacles preventing the implementation of Isom's new strategy. Now the team was coalescing and, for the first time, so was the strategy.

Having agreed on the key measures, the PEC needed to develop an integrated story. By early March 1994, they were ready to "publish" the story they wove (see Fig. 3.4).

The connections in the financial area were obvious. The loss ratio and the expense ratio clearly fed the combined ratio, and the interest that investors and stock analysts took in the combined ratio made it a good proxy for shareholder value. But what drove the loss ratio? Why, the loss frequency and the loss severity, of course.

It also appeared that the claims-handling cycle time affected loss severity, and therefore the loss ratio. After some passionate debate, they agreed that quickly settled claims pleased customers, reducing the chance of protracted litigation and, thus, potentially much higher losses. Many in the PEC had known this intuitively for a long time, but now they could demonstrate the logical connection between speed of settlement and loss severity. New connecting tissue was building, influencing the overall strategy of the firm.

The quote-to-sell ratio also was implicated in the loss ratio, because when you're the specialist in a sector, you should understand the risks better than the generalists. Understanding the risks means not taking on bad

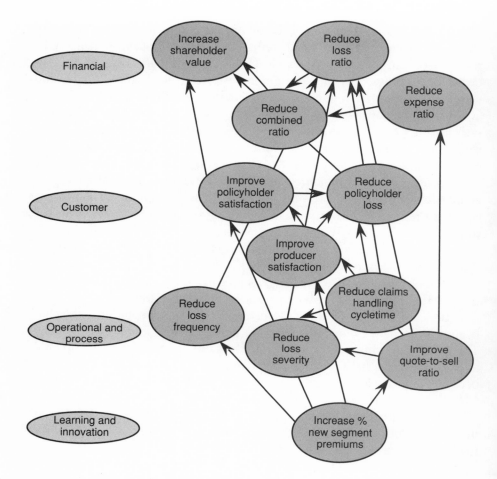

Figure 3.4. *Connected measures in the Balanced Scorecard at CIGNA P&C-simplified.* (SOURCE: The Balanced Scorecard, *David Norton, Renaissance Strategy Group, Lincoln, MA, and Robert Kaplan, Harvard Business School.*)

ones, while piling the odds on your side with those that you do. This also should translate into favorable prices from a customer standpoint. Therefore, a high quote-to-sell ratio should translate into a lower loss ratio.

Ironically, the greatest driver of all turned out to be in the learning and innovation target, the area the PEC had been most fuzzy about in the beginning. The intrinsic flow of CIGNA P&C's scorecard proved out, with learning and innovation driving operational improvement, producing customer satisfaction, and finally, translating into financial return for the firm. The *percentage of premiums from new segments* became the foundation for the entire edifice. It feeds into the loss record—if you created the segment based upon superior knowledge, then you're more likely to have a good record in it—and it results in both producer and end-user satisfaction. What better way to build a partnership with agents and policyholders than to create a new segment around the needs of a newly identified end-user group?

It took a lot of time, and talk, to agree on how the measures actually interlinked. The most interesting part of it all was the way the discussions revealed wide differences of view about how value is created in the property and casualty business. Every connector was debated, but they worked out a consensus, item by item. One member said that at the end of each session he felt "mentally drained, but smarter and closer to my colleagues."

Later, as we shall see in Chap. 6, CIGNA P&C would use the connectors it had developed in its Balanced Scorecard to map out the key knowledge flows, or *learning loops,* it needed to establish to compete. Eventually, Isom designed CIGNA's entire transformation path around the Balanced Scorecard they had created.

CONSTRUCTING A BOTTOM-UP BUSINESS CASE FOR CHANGE

Up to this point, building the measurement system has been the task of executives, built from a top-down view. While building the high-level goals and measures of the BSC is invaluable, it is the stuff of executives, not a motivator for shop floor people or customer service agents. It is often difficult for lower- and middle-level employees to see a direct connection between their actions and, say, shareholder value, or even customer satisfaction.

What gets people excited is a license to go chase opportunities in the areas they know well. Often, people in the lower ranks of the organization have been frustrated for years, seeing problems that no one from above seems willing to address. Frequently, their position in the organization has not allowed them to do much more than complain or, at best, suggest solutions. Now they are given the mandate to find ways to fix the problems themselves.

Place creative and well meaning people in the same room with some of their colleagues, give them license to think about the way things *should* be, eliminate organizational constraints, and watch the walls crumble! When they redesign day-to-day processes, especially processes that straddle several departments with little communication between them, they frequently discover exciting new solutions, and large-scale benefits to match.

To succeed, such a bottom-up effort needs the blessing of senior management. There is an inherent disconnect, however, between the executive viewpoint and the viewpoint of a grassroots-level team; executives speak the language of strategy and money, while people at the coal face speak the language of work, machines, and products. To secure the executive team's blessing, a translation mechanism is needed. Just as strategic and financial objectives must be broken down and translated into relevant goals and measures as they are cascaded downwards through the organization, so local improvement opportunities need to be translated into financial benefits that can be tracked upwards toward the top-level objectives. A bottom-up business case for change fulfills this purpose.

For example, rather than suggesting "the parts store room supervisor should keep a higher inventory of compressors to avoid stopping the production line when the compressor breaks down," the team shows senior executives the financial cost of idling a production line for several hours while somebody goes across town to buy the needed compressor. This transforms what might have been a wish list into a big stash of money, money that, as senior management knows, is very real. Given the financial justification, the supervisor of the parts warehouse can really do something about it, without even having to think about shareholder value.

The advantage of quantifying the benefits associated with bottom-up improvement lies less in the analytical rigor involved than in the motivation that it fosters. It is intrinsically more appealing to take on a task because it achieves a measurable goal than because, "It's the right thing to do." Often, a business case for change will increase in importance about one-third of the way into a transformation. When early enthusiasm has tapered off, and the leadership team begins to encounter heavy resistance, many leaders derive sustenance from their original business case.

A business case also has the advantage of giving leaders confidence that their transformation effort will have a tangible return. Rather than asking for an act of faith from senior management, a transformation team can legitimately present the cost of their project as part of the firm's investment in its future.

As the transformation process continues, however, the need for a rigorous business case tends to diminish. In the early stages, a business case focuses on quantifying and tracking short-term opportunities and benefits. By definition, it cannot capture the more significant and longer term benefits derived from large-scale transformation, such as those that arise when dealing with more strategic variables such as choice of customers, physical infrastructure, or technology base. By this time, however, there are usually enough results "in the bag" for a leadership team to relax its requirement for a precise accounting of benefits linked to every investment cost. With a high level of confidence and trust established, the initial benefits-tracking apparatus can be merged into the normal planning and budgeting process, and the goals and measures of the BSC can take its place. Now, systematic improvement has become ingrained into normal line management practice. People at all levels have come to understand the value of their actions in *business* terms.

Rolls-Royce Motor Cars Strikes Back

There is something strangely emotional in the attachment many of us have to the Rolls-Royce name, even though few of us will ever even contemplate purchasing a Rolls-Royce motor car, let alone actually own one. Perhaps it is the symbolism of the winged victory, riding high above the radiator cap, or the sheer exclusivity of the Rolls-Royce and Bentley marquees. Perhaps it is the unequaled ride, or the respect for an unmatched tradition of car-finishing with rich leather, shiny walnut trimmings, and silvery grilles. Or maybe it is the entire package, reflecting the eloquently stated vision of its founder, Henry Royce:

> Strive for perfection in everything we do. Take the best that exists and make it better. When it does not exist, design it. Accept nothing nearly right or good enough.

It seems somehow rude to discuss Rolls-Royce motor cars from a business standpoint, and not in aesthetic terms. And yet, the company came close to the precipice some three years ago, when the number of cars sold dropped by over 60 percent in a single year, driven by the 1991 recession. "As 1991 progressed," says Peter Ward, the company's chairman and chief executive, "we really did fall off a cliff." The business lost money, and its ability to fund new model development was questionable at best. Indeed, this proud company came close to disappearing altogether.

Just two years later, however, the company's position looked completely different. It was profitable again, and the new model development program was stronger than ever. The Rolls-Royce turnaround is perhaps best described as the result of two mutually reinforcing approaches: installing measures and driving a culture change from these measures.

When you ask the change leaders at Rolls-Royce Motor Cars what role measures played in their transformation, you get your answer in terms of measured achievements. The break-even volume of car sales was cut in half. The cycle time to manufacture a car was cut by nearly 70 percent. The time required to build an engine was cut from 30 days to 3. Even the time required to hand-upholster a rear seat was cut from 27 hours to just 9. Inventory turns more than doubled. The time to bring a new model to market dropped by 50 percent, as did the cost of development. Customer service, always rated as excellent, now provides the fastest query response in the world.

Faced with this avalanche of facts, you find yourself wondering how the emphasis on measures came about. We all know that pay and financial incentives are neither the exclusive, nor the most important, basis of human motivation; a sense of accomplishment in doing meaningful work is much more important. For Rolls-Royce Motor Cars, setting goals, communicating, and reporting progress against explicit, challenging objectives became a way of creating that sense of accomplishment. One of the company's directors championed each top-level objective, accepting responsibility to meet it. The operations managing director, for example, took responsibility for reducing manufacturing cycle time and for increasing productivity.

The scale of each top-level objective was ambitious. In Production, for example, the aim was to cut the manufacturing cycle time by over two-thirds, allowing the company to move from a basis of "make-to-stock" to "make-to-order." And so the change team proceeded to decompose this overall cycle time objective into a cascade of subsidiary objectives for each stage of manufacture and assembly, with annual objectives broken down into targets for specific quarterly time windows.

In the same way that the Balanced Scorecard operates at executive level, people on the shop floor develop hypotheses about how to improve operations and then test them through practical action. For every performance target ("the what"), they develop a clearly defined action or set of actions ("the how"). People at all levels are required to state how they intend to achieve their targets, even if they have only a sketchy idea of what might actually work in practice. Teams test their ideas through practical application, learning as they go. Results are tracked against key performance indicators (KPIs), and posted for all to see. To learn from progress and align initiatives, representatives from all levels of the organization participate in a framework of structured review meetings. Clearly, there is no point in having measures and targets—no focus on delivery, no motivating feedback, no useful learning—without systematic review of progress toward meeting KPI targets.

As demonstrated at Rolls-Royce Motor Cars, measures are above all an instrument of culture change. The transformation journey at the Crewe factory began as a bottom-up improvement program. Because of the emphasis on measures, targets, and open communication, it soon became a very visual business, with actions, schedules, and progress posted on wall charts throughout the plant. Through open communication and the nature of the review process, bottom-up initiatives became connected to top-down goals and measures. Now, everyone, from top to bottom, was involved in the structured review of performance improvement.

As a specialist manufacturer in today's automobile market, Rolls-Royce still faces its fair share of uncertainty. The cost of new model development, for example, is particularly challenging. But the future now looks brighter than in recent memory. There is a newly found sense of confidence in the business that is both exciting and infectious. As time passes, and as people come to reflect on the turnaround of the early 1990s, the role of measures—how they were used, the learning they triggered, and the culture change they induced—will be seen as critical to the success of the transformation.

CONNECTING BOTTOM-UP AND TOP-DOWN MEASURES

At this point, the measurement system has begun to take shape at both ends. The leadership team has sketched out a series of top-down measures, together with their main connectors. Individual teams have started at the other end, accumulating opportunities for improvement in several areas of the firm and translating them into a business case for change. What remains is the systematic linking of bottom-up and top-down measures and the implementation of structured review. This is the ultimate prize, and it deserves special attention.

To obtain maximum benefit, three interrelated components of the measurement system must be systematically linked and integrated: the measures, the improvement initiatives, and the review process. One of the most powerful ways to achieve this linkage is by building *KPI trees*. A KPI tree is a hierarchy of measures in which each indicator is derived from a key driver of organizational performance. Just as the familiar fishbone diagram traces causal factors underlying a particular problem, so a KPI tree traces causal drivers of organizational performance and improvement. If the high-level KPIs for an organization constitute its Balanced Scorecard, then the KPI trees constitute its "balanced fishbone" of cause-effect pathways that link top-down and bottom-up.

Ideally, a properly planned and resourced improvement initiative should be set against each strategic business objective, with the structured review process serving to track results and realign efforts. In the real world, however, building a framework of KPI trees and structured review is best approached like a jigsaw puzzle, starting the the most obvious and easiest moves first. The whole picture need not be in place to begin producing useful, measurable benefits. People learn by doing. As a more rigorous planning and review process gets underway, new insights and objectives arise in the light of experience, fostering continuous improvement.

Many companies struggle with "implementation problems" in the sense that they cannot effectively translate their strategic plans into coordinated action. What is needed is a systematic delivery process, a way to focus action from top to bottom on achieving the organization's key objectives. Applied in the context of an effective business management process, KPI trees and structured review provide a virtuous cycle of planning, objective-setting, achievement, and review, such that separate initiatives become a coherent, integrated whole, driving organizational learning and perpetual transformation.

Building KPI trees also enables delegation. The necessity to push accountability lower into the organization becomes more apparent, thus encouraging what one manager once called "controlled empowerment," but what others might call "guided self-determination." It also encourages independent initiative, allowing teams to identify their own priorities for action in the context of the firm's overall strategic direction.

Doing Away with the "Misery Line"

In January 1992, John Nelson was appointed managing director of Network SouthEast (NSE), the largest and busiest part of British Rail and carrier of more passengers a day than all of the world's airlines put together. Looking at the magnitude of the task in front of him, Nelson decided his first step should be to establish a comprehensive measurement system, which he hoped would give him a handle on the business and provide the motivational platform for the massive transformation effort he thought was needed. With his leadership team, he began to develop a balanced scorecard for NSE.

Not surprisingly, train punctuality was a key customer expectation, but it was more than that from a business perspective. Nelson and his executive team saw improving punctuality as an essential precursor to increasing ridership during off-peak periods. Peak travel was largely fixed by employment levels in central London, making off-peak travel the major income variable for the business. Nelson and his team set a target of 25 percent growth in off-peak travel. Reasoning that punctual, reliable service would feed this revenue growth objective, they set a corresponding target for punctuality: trains would arrive within five minutes of the published sched-

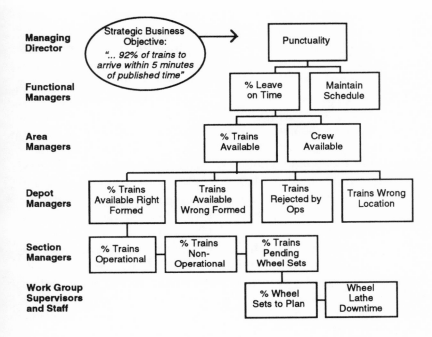

Figure 3.5. *Representative "KPI tree"—British Rail/Network SouthEast.*

ule 92 percent of the time. Following the same sort of logic, a KPI tree for punctuality was born (see Fig. 3.5).

By tracing the key drivers of punctuality, NSE was able to decompose its top-level punctuality measure down through the various levels of the organization, first backing into the percentage of trains which had left on time, then to the percentage of trains available in the right formation, eventually all the way down to a measure of wheel lathe downtime inside train maintenance depots. For the first time, wheel lathe operators at the grass-roots level, many steps removed from ultimate end-users, could see how their own performance contributed to a vital, top-level, customer-driven business objective: train punctuality.

Synapses were now connecting all the way up to NSE's brain: the system had become intelligent through the judicious use of measures. Operators could plan a course of action, actually do what they planned, and review the results of their actions, observing the impact of improvements not only in their area, but on the system as a whole. This virtuous "plan-do-review" cycle became a way of life at NSE.

But the measurement system is but one piece of the NSE story. What began for Nelson as a permanent job rapidly turned into the mother of all transformation projects when the British government decided to privatize British Rail (BR). Now the game had changed. NSE would no longer exist as of April 1994. The new challenge was not just to change operations in a public-sector environment, improving the business fundamentally, but also to anticipate the requirements of privatization. Improving the business management process became an integral component of the necessary transformation.

When it was an independent entity, NSE had annual gross revenues of $1.7 billion, employed more than 38,000 people, owned 7000 vehicles, had a train arriving in London every 11 seconds during rush hours, and was the most intensively used railway network in Europe. Operating a railway involves a complex network of fixed physical assets. Each day, there are millions of interfaces between trains, track, and signals; and because the tracks are fixed, if one thing goes wrong, everything is affected.

It would be wrong to assume it was the prospect of privatization that shocked the then state-owned railway out of its complacency. The origins of NSE's transformation, from a vicious circle of deterioration and decline into a virtuous circle of improvement, predate the late 1992 decision to privatize BR.

The mid-1980s reorganization of BR had set the scene. This overlaid the old regional structure and functional responsibilities with a business matrix, thereby creating the embryos of self-sufficient, customer-oriented operating units. In 1990–91, under the Organizing for Quality program, the two structures were fused together. For the first time, divisional directors had control of their own areas. "I knew," remembers Geoff Harrison-Mee, then director of NSE's SouthEastern division, "that everything on that patch was mine."

"Organizing for Quality did away with the regions and technical baronies, creating a real business culture," he adds.

But Nelson was himself acutely anxious about the way the privatization decision had raised the anxiety level among NSE people. "I had a responsibility to equip railway managers and train staff so they were well placed to seize the opportunities of privatization. That was my personal objective. People don't think any longer that anything is forever. Stability and security are things of the past; they always were illusions.

"We're used, now, to quite rapid, radical change. The last ten years, and particularly the last two or three, have been unprecedented. People are used to change. I'm trying to keep people busy—that removes anxiety—and the change agenda has done that. There's a lot of motivation around now."

The enthusiasm of Charles Nicholls, Infrastructure Project Director at NSE and one of the organization's senior change agents, corroborates this view. "Cars are on a downward spiral," he observes. "They're antisocial and polluting. That puts us in a strong position. When the M25 (London's orbital motorway) is so congested that people have to queue-up at traffic lights just to get on it, they will begin to regard rail as the best option. I believe there's a real opportunity for a second coming of railways."

Nicholls was not unique. There are a growing number of people in NSE who shrugged off the gloom and doom that had plagued the industry for the past 20 years and began to see the light of revival at the end of the tunnel.

Although this vision of revival—the "sense of a chance to win," as head of human resources, Bernard Williams, puts it—was a powerful motivator to top managers, it lacked the focus to inspire NSE's rank and file. Nelson knew something more visceral than the promise of a "second coming" was needed to move the whole organization. He found it in NSE's performance measurements.

In Nelson's view, the responsibility of senior executives is to set objectives and strategy, and provide the framework for delivery. If people are encouraged to take responsibility and act, he believes, that is when the real changes start happening. "But you have to take control," he warns. "The risk is that it becomes highly devolved, but unaccountable. It must be 'loose-tight.' The old system was a cross between a militaristic hierarchy, which lacked much authority, and an inefficient bureaucracy." The control has come from new attitudes, and a new measurement system. KPIs, in particular, helped ensure the consistency and rigor of Nelson's change agenda.

Nelson believes that the KPI system and the success of every change program it touched helped unpack and translate the top-level vision of change into manageable elements the organization could and would deliver. The emphasis on rigorous, structured review, to him, was essential.

"It required constant emphasis on KPIs and processes," Nelson explains. "People had been looking for meaning, but there had been no measure of success before. This approach switched them on; it's like a drug." The initial skeptics have been fast learners, but they needed to be convinced. The BR culture was always action-oriented rather than process-oriented. People were usually happiest when managing a crisis.

As change programs go, Nelson reckons NSE's must have been a strong contender for the title of the world's most challenging. The constraints at the outset were intimidating. BR's external financing limit (the money received from government for investment) had been halved, and most of the infrastructure was in need of replacement. It is hard to over-state the degree of difficulty involved just in keeping a network like this running, let alone transforming it into something so much better. Daily press criticism, particularly of service on the so-called "Misery Line" from Southend on the Sea to London, further lowered morale. By October 1991, NSE had recorded its worst ever customer perceptions and worst ever service delivery performance—"the nadir in the fortunes of Network SouthEast," as John Nelson put it.

Yet, over two years, and through the depth of recession, NSE was able to grow off-peak revenue by 28 percent, cut controllable costs by 30 percent, restructure its headquarters from 2400 staff to 52 (in under nine months), and move from significant subsidy to substantial operating profit, while improving customer perception from worst to best and raising passenger service standards for two years in succession. Even the previously critical *Evening Standard* newspaper ran the headline, "Misery Line comes to an end," promptly transferring the description to the Northern Line of the London Underground system.

NSE bettered its 25 percent off-peak revenue growth target over this two-year period, despite the recession and despite widespread skepticism at the outset. This achievement is a testament to the power of goals and measures, of forming hypotheses and testing them in practice. Again we see the power of an effective business management process—creating a Balanced Scorecard, cascading KPIs and improvement initiatives, and developing a structured review process at every level. Again we see the benefit of an executive team thinking through how they can improve their business, setting stretch targets, and backing these aspirations with properly planned and resourced improvement initiatives.

RESTRUCTURING

In human life, there is an inseparable interconnection between mind and body, ideas and action; each is impotent without the other. So it is with the biological corporation. No matter how inspiring the vision, no matter how widely and deeply mobilized an organization is to achieve it, nothing tangible will happen until the blood, bones, and muscles of the corporate body have been trained to move in the right direction. With restructuring, we now move to an exploration of the physical body of the company.

Imagine yourself taking a trip inside your own body—going down dark arteries, riding on blood cells carrying oxygen to the various organs. Observe the sudden slowing-down of your progress, where fat has accumulated close to the heart—a sign of upcoming trauma. Let the infinitely dense network of capillaries take you to new frontiers in a maze of interconnected canals. Then let yourself glide down the bone-marrow river, moving inside what appears to be a rocklike structure. Observe the massive nature of the bone system, and the complex articulation of these massive structures among themselves. Jump outside the bones, and now you're surrounded by a fiberlike structure that contracts and relaxes all around you. You are now in the musculature, trying to survive this tornado of brisk movements.

Restructuring deals with the corporate *body*, with the *physical* side of holistic health. It looks at the outward manifestations of health or illness—at the structure of the company's portfolio, the physical disposition of its assets, and the alignment of its work processes. It looks at the vitals signs of the body within—at its resource allocation system, its operations strategy, and the flow of work within processes. And it looks at the relationship of the body to the mind—how vision, mobilization, and measures guide the restructuring process; and how processes, through people, can learn to learn.

Restructuring is an indispensable dimension of a company's life. It is a necessary hygiene, without which businesses lose their ability to survive. As is true for the other three dimensions of business life—reframing, revitalizing, and renewing—the need for restructuring produces strange deformities in entities that don't practice it. Corporate bulimia and anorexia will afflict those with a deficient economic model. Scoliosis may await those who forget to take care of their physical infrastructure. And obesity will encumber those who forget to exercise their work processes.

Of all the components of transformation, restructuring is the most painful for leaders. In restructuring, the leader plays the role, not just of biological architect, but of surgeon, operating on what is often a sick patient. Inevitably, there are casualties—jobs are lost, businesses divested, and comfortable behaviors changed. Fortunately, the pain is not proportionate to the potential rewards, for if properly applied restructuring minimizes suffering, while establishing a platform for growth.

Restructuring has long been mistaken for transformation itself. It's easy to limit one's investigation to what one can physically see, thereby forgetting that there are biological principles of life behind each system. Many companies continue to confuse the mechanical rearrangment of their work processes with holistic transformation. The sirens of restructuring can be seductive indeed, with their short-term results and their illusion that those benefits will indefinitely grow. But restructuring can involve a Faustian pact, whereby immediate benefits are traded for a fate of Corporate Hell. Those who turn restructuring into a *strategy* unavoidably condemn themselves to ignominious death. Many have gone to that death in recent years.

Restructuring primarily involves three chromosomes and their corresponding biocorporate systems, which are the subjects of the three chapters in Part Two. The first chromosome, described in Chap. 4, deals with the construction of an economic model of the corporation. The economic model is to the biological corporation what the cardiovascular system is to the human body, providing the flow of resources needed to keep it healthy. It is a blueprint of how capital should flow through the system, carrying the needed resources to all parts that require them.

The second restructuring chromosome, described in Chap. 5, deals with configuring the physical infrastructure, the biocorporate equivalent of the human skeletal system. Configuring the physical infrastructure involves aligning a company's physical components—its buildings, plants, trucks, barges, machines, and other assets—both with the economic model and with the work processes they are intended to serve. Like the human skeletal system, the physical infrastructure tends to adapt slowly to the demands of the rest of the body and of the environment, often requiring painful orthopedic procedures.

The third and final restructuring chromosome, described in Chap. 6, deals with redesigning the work architecture of the corporation, the corporate equivalent of the human muscular system. It involves reorganizing work and work processes to serve the high-level goals and measures of the firm. This is partly the realm of "classic" reengineering, which can create dramatic improvements in such things as quality, efficiency, and cost. But the more fundamental and powerful effects are achieved through *bioreengineering,* which is the stepping stone to the brave new worlds of revitalization and renewal.

Once again, a reminder that the sequential presentation of the chapters is made necessary by book format, but is not intended to reflect a rigid chronology of transformation. Transformation, as already mentioned, is inherently nonsequential; at any one time, all three dimensions of restructuring are engaged, acting and being acted upon by all the other biocorporate systems. Only the leader's creativity can determine the appropriate path.

CHAPTER
FOUR

CONSTRUCTING AN ECONOMIC MODEL

As is true of people, there is a fine line between the mind and body of the biological corporation. Mental energy generates physical energy, and physical energy generates mental energy. A sense of purpose both drives and is fostered by productive work. Thoughts induce actions, and actions induce thoughts. The mind and body work together, one affecting the other in a continuous, simultaneous feedback loop. They even share the same source of nourishment—if the heart stops beating, both perish.

As the transformation process moves back and forth along the fine line between mind and body, keeping both nourished is a prime concern of the CEO. That is the function of the economic model, the fourth of the 12 biocorporate systems. The economic model is to the corporate body what the cardiovascular system is to the human body. Via the bloodstream, the cardiovascular system supplies oxygen and other vital nutrients wherever they are needed throughout the body. Via the resource allocation system, the economic model transports money, material, and people where they are most needed.

Constructing an economic model involves the systematic, top-down disaggregation of a corporation in financial terms. It is a noninvasive form of dissection, virtually painless in the doing, but not necessarily in the implications of what is revealed. Unfortunately, the economic model is almost always used as CAT scans are in medicine: as a diagnostic tool when something is known to be wrong and needs to be isolated. Usually, not just one thing, but a large set of related ailments are revealed as, layer by layer, the economic model reveals itself.

Constructing the economic model is the function of the fourth corporate chromosome. It has three genes, dedicated respectively to the corporate portfolio, the high-level value chain of the businesses, and the allocation of resources. The CEO has three corresponding tasks as genetic architect of the corporation:

1. *Managing the portfolio to build shareholder value.* Portfolio analysis techniques are a means to financially dissect the corporate body into a discrete collection of businesses, which can then be tested against high-level corporate financial goals to determine their economic value. Using this information, the CEO takes the position of corporate raider, challenging the leadership team regarding which businesses to keep, which to divest or spin off, and which to target for improvement.

2. *Encouraging the definition of a high-level value chain for each business.* It is strange but true that many businesses cannot fully articulate what it is they do. The high-level value chain is a logically connected sequence of activities that defines the tasks of a business at their highest level of aggregation. Often a strategic exercise within itself, defining the value chain provides a logical framework within which the business may be broken down by activity for the purpose of deeper economic and strategic evaluation.

In much the same way as a corporation is broken down into businesses for portfolio analysis, the business is decomposed into key activities to determine whether and to what degree they are creating or destroying value. By guiding the process of defining the value chain for each business, the leader can ensure that the imprint of the corporation remains on each business within it. This establishes a common mental and economic framework for the CEO and the leaders responsible for the businesses.

3. *Fostering the allocation of resources by activity, based on cost and service level.* Business leaders have stacks of financial reports available to them. Profit and loss statements, balance sheets, earnings reports, etc.—all provide information that is necessary for financial reporting and some degree of analysis. But the CEO, the leadership team, and all other executives and managers responsible for the allocation of resources need more than just the traditional numbers. They need to know the cost of *doing* business, and the *value* created by the work involved. They need to be able to break work down into discrete components, define the linkage between the cost of doing a piece of work and the value it creates, and then relate it all to the bottom line. This is the kind of information that *activity-based costing* (ABC) and *service-level assessment* (SLA) can provide.

Using the financial goals and measures of the Balanced Scorecard as the standard, the activities of the value chain are further broken down into key business processes, which in turn are subdivided into the activities that define them. Costs and service levels are associated with the activities using activity-based costing techniques to create an *activity cost map* for each process, and service level analysis to determine the value of each to the overall business. This information provides the basis for targeting areas to be improved, evaluating outsourcing alternatives, and exploring other strategic issues. Perhaps most importantly, it provides a more objective financial standard for allocating resources to those areas that create value for the enterprise.

Though constructing the economic model is predominantly a restructuring activity, the CEO usually begins it in the early stages of reframing. Portfolio moves, in particular, often precede the definition of the Balanced Scorecard. The deeper the economic modeling process penetrates, however, the more important it is that a consistent set of goals and measures be established at the top and cascade down through the organization. This set of goals and measures provides the gravitational pull that holds pieces of the economic model in synchronous orbit with each other, while letting components that don't belong drift into space and be pulled by someone else's sun. Otherwise, a lot of energy can be spent tracking progress along a path to Pluto, when Mars is the real destination.

The possible combinations of goals and measures are almost infinite in number. No one set is necessarily better or worse than another. They vary by industry, vision, firm, and CEO. The general rule is: use those that work for your firm and make the most sense to your shareholders. Carefully selected and properly applied, a consistent set of goals and measures makes the economic model an invaluable resource for evaluating, measuring, and tracking financial performance from the top to the bottom of the business.

MANAGING THE PORTFOLIO TO BUILD SHAREHOLDER VALUE

At night, by candlelight, driven by a ravenous curiosity and quest for knowledge, Michaelangelo defied religious authority by stealing into the physicians' morgues and dissecting cadavers. For the sake of his art, he carried out this grim, self-imposed task in musty vaults, gaining first-hand insight into the complex systems of the human body. His work, and the work of those of similar mind, slowly lifted mankind above the mystic rituals that had dominated medicine in the Dark Ages. Through their efforts, fear and superstition slowly gave way to the enlightened, rational inquiry of the Renaissance. Not just medicine, but all the sciences owe them an enormous debt of gratitude.

Ironically, many of today's corporations owe a similar debt of gratitude to an unlikely set of benefactors: the corporate raiders. Raiders such as Carl Icahn, T. Boone Pickens, Sir James Goldsmith, and Hanson Trust dug into companies' financial mausoleums and dissected the businesses within, opening the eyes of CEOs to long-standing misconceptions. Differing and, in some cases, ethically questionable motivations aside, it is corporate raiders who made the concept of "breakup value" real. They forced giant conglomerates to rethink the meaning of "value" and opened shareholders' eyes to the financial games people play. The raiders popularized concepts such as Shareholder Value Analysis (SVA), which later begot Economic Value-Added Analysis (EVA). One could even argue that the threatening posture of the raiders forced CEOs to question the meaning of numbers that had guided their asset allocation decisions for decades, and to search for new ways to examine the source of cost and profitability in their firms.

Prior to the corporate raiders, most business decisions were dominated by the sacred DCFRORAT—discounted cashflow rate of return after taxes. Generally accepted accounting principles provided the bottom line used in making most capital allocation decisions. Being "good with the numbers" was a badge of honor, the mark of an adept business thinker.

In the mid-1980s, for example, many petrochemical companies allocated capital for investments by a simple, and seemingly conservative, rule: "We will plan our capital budget around investments with a minimum 15 percent annual DCFRORAT." Their young, aggressive engineers spent intoxicating, 18-hour days running complex linear programs, analyzing and justifying investments of hundreds of millions of dollars for new refining and chemical-processing capacity. The math was exhaustive and compelling, detailing the effects of complex tax breaks, depreciation allowances, and a rigorous set of "flex cases" with respect to price trends and types of feed stocks and products.

Not surprisingly, most competitors were doing the same thing. Few questioned the strategic value of the investments as such—more was better—and virtually *everyone* justified spending more, using the same set of false assumptions: *(1) that existing accounting methods reflect the true cost of doing business;* and *(2) that end-user needs can be anticipated by evaluating price trends.* Today, the legacy of those false assumptions is millions of dollars' worth of idle reactors, distillation towers, pumps, pipe, and warehouses, rusting instead of producing a 15 percent DCFRORAT.

Perhaps more than idle capacity, the likes of T. Boone Pickens woke industry leaders up. Suddenly a corporation was no longer a collection of profit centers seeking DCFRORATs, but rather a portfolio of businesses and assets that could be broken up and sold for more than the market value of the corporation as a whole. Using various portfolio analysis tools, Boone and his compadres came armed with tough, righteous words, and the numbers to match. They dismissed board members' appeals to loyalty, telling shareholders they'd been hoodwinked out of, if not downright looted of, their just due. "We'll give you what your stock is *really* worth," they would say, virtually guaranteeing shareholders an immediate, higher return on their investments, typically on the order of 40 percent over the current stock value. Shareholders flocked to the end of the rainbow, and giants fell and splintered under their own weight. The result? Between 1980 and 1990, almost one-third of what had been the world's most powerful industrial corporations ceased to exist as independent entities.

THROUGH THE EYES OF THE RAIDER

At the height of the LBO revolution, speculative fervor started making things a little crazy. Aside from Black Monday (October 19, 1987), perhaps the greatest damper to the madness was when the more enlightened CEOs began to ask: "Why let the raiders do it, when we can do it ourselves?" They learned about SVA, EVA and breakup value. They began to look at their business portfolio through the eyes of a raider.

Today, ask any CEO for a list of priorities, and the chances are that increasing shareholder value will be number one on the list. Share price is the CEO's ultimate report card. Tell shareholders what you want about the customer, innovation and learning, or internal operations; they won't stick around for long if the stock isn't performing. And if they don't stick around, the CEO is sent packing.

Thus, CEOs can gain significant insights by adopting the viewpoint of the corporate raider and breaking their company apart on paper. It's a relatively quick way to determine where the boundaries of the corporate body ought to be. Do all the businesses legitimately belong to the corporate body? Are they contributing to the high-level financial goals of the company? Is there evidence of festering limbs in the advanced stages of gangrene that should be cut off? At minimum, are there any warts or ingrown nails that should be removed?

It is rare for a corporation not to need some form of serious surgery early in the transformation process. Initially most leaders try to avoid such radical moves, concentrating instead on process realignment and business revitalization. Soon, however, they rediscover the one huge and undeniable benefit that divestitures offer: *instant results.* Points can usually be racked up on the financial front on the day of the announcement, and often even before that (much to the chagrin of government agencies such as the U.S.'s Securities and Exchange Commission).

When there is a need to take immediate action and find resources to finance longer-term, more deeply constructive moves, the harsh reality is that amputation—divestitures—are often the best medicine. Next to administering cod liver oil to unsuspecting children, however, amputation is probably the most violent form of medicine. It is a drastic technique, but often necessary to save the entire body from infection—even death.

In general, portfolio theory drives divestitures, and its principles are widely known. There are many approaches, some elegant, some more down-and-dirty. Sometimes they come in curious garb, like the one in which the CEO is a zoo-keeper and the businesses a collection of cows, dogs, and wildcats. In the end, though, they all boil down to the same basic theme: "If a business ain't good, get rid of it."

The arrival of shareholder value–added analysis (SVA) and economic value-added analysis (EVA) techniques marked a particularly helpful new step in the development of portfolio techniques. They give the CEO an "in your face" picture of how each business adds or subtracts from the company's share price—the ultimate report card for the CEO. While traditional portfolio techniques may have garnered aesthetic or anthropological interest, shareholder value data grabs CEOs right by the wallet.

Shareholder value and economic value analyses involve the creation of a set of "What if?" scenarios, as if a company could be exploded into its component businesses and each component could become a separate entity with its own market value, equity, debt structure, and stock price. In reality, of course, there is only one stock price, and the assumption that one can assign a "market" value to just one part of a business is somewhat arrogant. But what if it were true? What would each part be worth? Would it survive in the face of the investment community? Would people buy the stock, and at what price? Answering these questions is what made so many of the raiders so successful. For the CEO, answering them is not only a necessity in terms of preventing takeovers, but also provides valuable strategic insights regarding the structure of the corporate portfolio.

SVA was the fashionable concept of the eighties, largely displaced by EVA in the nineties. Both are variations on the same theme. SVA analysis uses the well-known value curve, showing the ratio of market value to book value on the Y axis, and ROE to cost of equity on the X axis. When the businesses in a corporation's portfolio are plotted on this curve, a value of less than one shows that a business is destroying value, while anything greater than one means it is creating value. Plotted against time for any one business, the curve shows the value-creating or -destroying history of the business.

Typically, shareholder value analysis shows that 80 percent of the value is created by 20 percent of the portfolio, which unavoidably triggers the question of why the corporation bothers investing in the other 80 percent at all. In many cases, the answer is indeed that they should not. In other cases, all or part of those 80 percent are legitimately developing businesses that have yet to reach their potential.

EVA borrows from the same principle, but moves from being an "in your face" analysis to becoming a "put your money where your mouth is" technique. While shareholder value analysis deals with stock prices and differential rates of return, EVA essentially refocuses the results of the same kind of analysis on what amounts to a new definition of yearly profits; that is, EVA is the difference between operating profit after tax and the opportunity cost of the equity tied up in the business. Instead of as a ratio indicating that value is being created or destroyed, EVA is expressed in monetary terms. Obviously, that's a concept that resonates with every executive whose pay is tied to financial performance. "My division created $20 million in economic value for you, dear CEO," the division head seems to say, "so where is my corresponding bonus?"

Both SVA and EVA allow a CEO to drive financial measurements of performance, both in terms of profit and investment, to lower and lower levels of aggregation in the firm, all the way down to a product, a market, or even a customer.

Revealing Hidden Value at Sears

At Sears, the CEO, Edward Brennan, and the CFO, Ed Liddy, probably smile when they reflect on the scathing criticism of shareholder activist, Robert Monks, and the dismal analyst reports they have received over the past few years. In 1993, Sears had nearly completed what has been called the largest and most successful corporate repositioning in the history of American business, more than doubling shareholder value since 1990.

For more than 10 years, Sears had endured the skepticism of the investment community, which wondered what a retailer like Sears was attempting to do in financial services. "Does the world really need a Discover card?" was a common theme in analyst reports. "What does Sears know about real estate?" was another, as critics openly doubted whether Coldwell Banker was a viable business for Sears. Until the very moment Sears put the vote to investors, the jury was still out as to whether Sears ever should have entered these businesses in the first place.

Monks, at the forefront of the criticisms, undoubtedly credits himself for putting on the heat and forcing Sears to take action. According to Liddy, however, that heat was a lot of hot air. As he said to *CFO Magazine* in January 1994, "Each year, as part of our planning process, we do a very rigorous analysis of the values of each of our companies ... and what their value would be for a strategic and for a financial buyer." As this quote suggests, Sears in effect raided itself in 1993, increasing shareholder value by giving shareholders a chance to own some of the company's undervalued wealth in financial services, starting with its star performer, Dean Witter, Discover.

To a large degree the plan was born of frustration, the management team's sense that great value was being created but that the investment community failed to recognize it within the existing Sears structure. Meetings with financial analysts had proven insufficient to convince the marketplace, so they decided to break up the businesses and let the market decide. They would let individual investors, not analysts, decide what Sears was really worth.

In 1993, Sears sold 20 percent of the profitable but capital-intensive and undervalued Dean Witter, Discover business. The sale of Dean Witter immediately increased the public valuation of the business. It also allowed Sears to buy back some of its equity, further increasing shareholder value. In the same year, in the largest IPO in U.S. history, Sears sold 20 percent of Allstate Insurance, all of Coldwell Banker (residential real estate), and its entire mortgage company. It accompanied the financial restructuring with a dramatic reduction of operating costs, to the tune of $2 billion per year. At the end of 1994, it announced its intention to spin off all of Allstate Insurance.

It was a tough time for Sears, perhaps particularly so for Ed Brennan, the Chairman and a third-generation Sears employee. Much of the activity was alien to Sears' somewhat paternalistic tradition, especially the aggressive buying and selling of businesses and the massive layoffs of employees. An era, it appeared, had ended, poignantly marked by the day the company decided to shut down its catalog business. On that day America wept silently, and so did Sears. They could not, however, find a way to make the catalog business profitable, and although Sears still publishes specialty catalogs, the general Sears catalog—symbol of middle-American life—is no more.

Nostalgia notwithstanding, the restructuring plan proved to be brilliantly executed. In 1993 the company had its most profitable year in history, posting earnings per share of $6.13 and return on common equity of 23.8 percent (including 19 percent on continuing businesses), and achieving a total shareholder return of 56 percent. In a single year, Sears' total market value increased by $8 billion to $25 billion. Seemingly overnight, Sears image had been transformed from that of an American institution in decline to that of a role model of corporate rejuvenation.

ENCOURAGING THE DEFINITION OF A
HIGH-LEVEL VALUE CHAIN FOR EACH BUSINESS

Equipped with a clear picture of how each business in the portfolio adds value, the business leader descends deeper into each business with the economic modeling process. The attention here is focused on the high-level economic makeup of each business—the realm of the value chain.

The value chain is a logically related set of high-level activities, starting with the customer and going back all the way to the suppliers, which describe the value-creating steps required to do business. It can be thought of as the mother of all activity chains, the set of activities to which, ideally, all processes and functions contribute. Thus, defining the value chain can in itself be a strategically important exercise (see Chap. 5), but for the purposes of this discussion it is assumed that the value chain is reasonably fixed.

Consider, for example, the oil and gas exploration and production business. The managers of most oil and gas companies don't think of their business in terms of a value chain. They get caught up in their capital budget cycles, and focus on punching holes in the ground and hoping oil or gas will come gushing out. That is certainly a major part of the business, but there is far more involved, and *all* of it has strategic importance. Defining the value chain helps focus attention on each and every high-level value-creating (or -destroying) component of the business (see Fig. 4.1), and on the fundamental strategic questions associated with them.

First, there is the *acquisition and disposal* of leases. In this link of the value chain, companies bet that there is oil in one place versus another, and

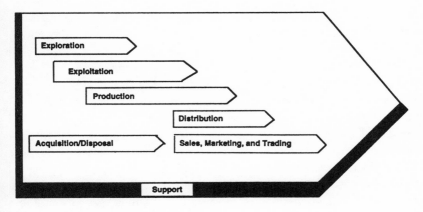

Figure 4.1. *Oil and gas value chain.*

invest significant amounts of money, often in conjunction with other partners, to acquire the rights to explore it. There is also the problem of disposing of rights, which involves selling them when the wells are dry or the hope of discovery diminishes, trading them for other properties, or deciding to hold them for exploration at a later date.

Acquisition and disposal is a complex part of the business, requiring expertise in geology and in real estate management, as well as a steady head at the blackjack table. There are no guarantees of success, and the degree and level of both investment and risk depend upon the strategy adopted by the company. Should the focus be on small, derivative plays next to known wells? Or should the firm invest in big, wildcat plays in hopes of discovering the next North Sea? Focused oil companies choose their strategy at the outset, establishing a basis up-front for their levels both of risk and of investment.

Next, there is the *exploration* activity proper: the physical process of drilling to determine whether oil and gas are in fact in the ground. This link in the value chain is driven by scientific and engineering expertise, and involves computer modeling, seismographic research, and the complex engineering challenge of drilling thousands of feet beneath the earth's surface, often below the ocean floor, and, upon a discovery, containing the fluid that is being pushed up by thousands of pounds of pressure.

Just two steps into the value chain, one can see the range of strategic options available in what, on the surface, might seem like a simple business. For example, a company might elect to buy only known reserves, eliminating both the gambling component of acquisition and the scientific expertise required of exploration. Although this might be considered a "sissy" strategy in the macho culture of oil and gas, it is a perfectly logical approach in many cases, especially for companies with a consistent habit of losing at blackjack.

On the other hand, companies exceptionally proficient in acquisition and disposal might build a business around it, trading rights for profit as opposed to being heavily involved in the more capital-intensive exploration and production activities.

The next step in the value chain is *exploitation.* The company now roughly knows where the oil and gas lie in the ground, and how much is there. It now needs a strategy for getting it out. This is less simple than meets the eye—timing and volume are everything.

The name of the game in exploitation is correctly anticipating future prices, and no company gets it right all the time, not even those like Shell that uses highly sophisticated scenario-planning tools. It is also a game of cycle management, because the cost of owning unexploited properties is high. Working capital requirements for oil and gas companies are formidable, involving complex financing issues. Large companies have millions of barrels of reserves, with each barrel representing an opportunity cost ranging between $10 and $25 per barrel, depending on the market. The more quickly a company can respond to favorable trends, the more profitable it will be.

Next in the chain comes *production*. As the name indicates, production is the equivalent of manufacturing—getting the oil and gas out of the ground as efficiently and safely as possible. The main focus here is on minimizing costs, particularly at a time when the price of oil and gas is as low as it has been since the early 1990s. Head count tends to be the focus, particularly in the maintenance and support areas.

Distribution is the next activity. It is enormously capital-intensive, requiring a complex network of pipelines, storage tanks, truck fleets, barges, and tankers. Put together, these create a tremendous capital intensity for the business—particularly when one adds the capital involved in the lease itself. The name of the game here is optimizing logistics within the network, often on a global basis. Trading—buying, selling, and swapping—products, both for profit and for efficient logistical planning, is also a crucial component, involving the complex and tricky element of extending the physical distribution network through competitors.

Sales, marketing and trading is the last element of our value chain. Since oil and gas are commodities, the ability to "move barrels" is a pretty key consideration. This raises the strategic issue of whether and to what extent an exploration and production company should invest in "downstream integration," that is, in refining capacity or in the distribution of petroleum products, most notably, gasoline. Here again, trading can make or break the results of an oil company, involving hedging production in the futures market, trading on the spot market, and otherwise buying and selling oil and gas in a high-stakes poker game.

With so many strategic options to consider, the role of the CEO is not to micromanage every step in the value chain, but rather to encourage fundamental thinking about how it should be configured and what the strategic priorities are at a high level. In our exploration and production example, the CEO's job would be to encourage reflection on what the company's acquisition strategy should be, whether and to what extent the company should be exploring at all, how to focus exploitation efforts, and so on down the value chain.

Betting on the Value Chain at CIGNA

We last left Gerry Isom, president of CIGNA Property & Casualty, in the process of a full-scale launch of a major transformation project in the spring of 1994. He and the President's Executive Committee (PEC) had established the Balanced Scorecard. A large portion of the company was mobilized. The vision was in place; the people were in place; goals and measures were in place; and he had even taken some positive, short-term actions of his own.

Now, the transformation project—known as Project OAR, for Organizational Alignment Review—is in full swing. Natural work teams have sprung up everywhere; on underwriting, claims management, producer management, home office support—no stone is left unturned, as the Balanced Scorecard helps to orchestrate the complex ballet of process redesign activities.

As part of the process, the PEC meets every Monday to review the progress of the work teams. On this particular Monday, however, an outsider walking into their conference room might think she had entered the Twilight Zone. The PEC is assembled around what looks like a casino table, hunched over a green–felted table, poker chips in their hands. There are nervous sideways glance, as each member tries to discern the strategy of the others.

The table looks somewhat like a roulette board, minus the wheel. And in place of the customary 0 to 36 numbers, the bets are being placed on the CIGNA P&C value chain, starting with the policyholder, moving to the agents, and then inside CIGNA P&C—through customer service, underwriting, claims management, loss control, information systems, support services, etc.—and back out again to the providers of medical, legal, and auto repair services. All in all, there are about 15 steps in the chain, each with a dollar figure indicated on it, representing CIGNA's current resource allocation scheme.

Each member of the PEC has been allocated 50 "plus" chips and 50 "minus" chips. Gerry Isom has invited them to place their bets on specific parts of the value chain to show where they want to invest more ("plus" chips) and where less ("minus" chips).

The "betting" is serious and the stakes high, for the power base of each executive is clearly associated with the dollars featured at every step in the value chain. A "plus" chip means more power, but a "minus" chip is a clear challenge to the incumbent's position. "You can't do this to me," one would say half-seriously, adding "if you do that, I'll hit you with all my 'minus' chips."

Once the dust has settled, the orientation of the group is pretty clear. Most of the plus chips are concentrated on the front of the value chain, to include the policyholder, the agent, and underwriting activities. Most of the minus chips are concentrated in the support services areas, especially in information systems and the financial and human resource areas. All agree that the back end of their business should be downsized, while more resources should be invested on the front end. Even the managers of the "to-be-downsized" areas have cast minus chips in their portion of the value chain.

In the claims area, one of the highest dollar-value segments of the chain, unanimity breaks down; it has a high concentration of both plus and minus chips. Isom inquires why, and two diametrically opposed viewpoints emerge. Some argue that having close to 6000 people to handle claims is way too many; they need to reduce head count. Others argue that cutting the number of claims agents would simply result in higher losses. "When you cut claims resources," a member of the plus-chip camp argued, "the only solution for them becomes to pay blindly on every claim. You will take away their ability to challenge and investigate claims. You might cut costs in the short term, but you'll pay dearly in the long term."

The discussion leads them to agreement on the path forward. They will build a claims model to simulate the many tradeoffs involved, discussing them explicitly in the process, and then abide by the model they have agreed upon. With this decided, they reach a reasonable consensus as to where they will place their bets on CIGNA's value chain. Once again they have traversed an area of potentially great turbulence, and come out more unified. Isom's legions are still growing.

Karl Gets Drawn into Big Strategic Questions

In the last chapter we left Karl, the grade-12 scheduler at Woodbridge papers, in a quandary. He is now leading the team in charge of redesigning the entire order fulfillment process. It's up to him to provide the team with a sense of direction, but the more he works and the harder he thinks, the more complex the alternatives seem to become. Until someone makes a decision about whether Woodbridge will offer a broad or a narrow product line, he's stuck.

"You look like one worried puppy," Karl's wife tells him matter-of-factly, as he sits sipping a beer after work, pondering his predicament.

On the one hand he feels scared to death. To think that they—whoever "they" are!—should ask *him*, a scheduler, to redesign the whole order fulfillment process! "Enough already!" he feels like saying. "How should *I* know whether the company should be integrated in pulp, paper, and manufacturing?" But he knows that he *must* know, if he's going to do the job right. Which brings him to the other hand. He feels honored they've asked him to do it, and if he does it right … Well, it won't hurt his career any, a career which he thought had pretty much reached a dead end before all of this happened.

But he hadn't thought it would be like *this*. He thought he would be able to carve out a neat little piece of the process, then fix it. But everything was connected—no, *tangled* was a better word. Everything he looked at affected something else, which affected something else. It was downright messy! He had tried going to the steering committee and getting them to define and limit his scope. But they just kept coming back at him, saying he had *carte blanche* to address any issue that he considered relevant. He often found himself wishing that his *carte* were a little less *blanche*.

For example, he learned that manufacturing isn't just manufacturing. It involves three steps: making pulp, then making paper, and finally coating the paper. Woodbridge competed with other companies in all three steps, but they also bought quite a bit of pulp and paper from the outside. Karl had learned that they called that being "semi-integrated." Deciding whether Woodbridge should make or buy its own paper is big-deal, strategic stuff, and he wanted no part of it. Each machine costs tens of millions of dollars, and he wasn't about to get involved in *that* kind of decision. That was the stuff of strategic planners with MBAs, not the stuff of schedulers dealing with order-to-delivery processes.

Suddenly, Karl recognizes that he's now in a double quandary. The decision whether Woodbridge should make or buy its own pulp and paper is a lot like the one concerning whether they should have a broad or a narrow product line. All kinds of issues are involved, he realizes, starting with cost. At times, in a seller's market, buying pulp and paper can kill your cost position. But when there's surplus capacity, suppliers practically *give* you the stuff. Sometimes you win and sometimes you lose.

But there are other considerations besides costs, Karl thinks, like speed of delivery. If Woodbridge decides to steadily buy significant amounts of its pulp and paper outside, then they should probably form partnerships with one or two suppliers rather than buy opportunistically from many. That way, they can put pressure on the suppliers to align their cycles with Woodbridge's, which would help cut cycle time. Could it be that the dynamics of the order-to-delivery process might actually have an impact on how integrated Woodbridge should be? Karl wonders. And if so, he asks himself, slumping more deeply into his chair, is it my place to make suggestions about such important issues?

He sees the same problem in the transportation area. Woodbridge uses contractors—has never bothered to build its own fleet. "We're not in the truck business, we're in the packaging business," the old CEO used to say. But there are important performance issues to contend with in the transportation area. Contractors are fine when lead time doesn't matter so much, but now that Woodbridge has chosen to compete on lead time, maybe they need to buy some of their own trucks.

Karl decides to go to the steering committee a second time, again with a major strategic question. The last time, he tried to get them to say whether they wanted the product line to be broad or narrow. They simply turned it back to him, asking him what *he* thought. He told them he didn't know, that he needed their guidance. Now he's about to do the same thing regarding the pulp, paper, and transportation issues. He already knows they'll just ask him what *he* thinks again, and this time he hopes to have some answers.

Taking the last sip of his beer, he thinks, "Don't they pay those guys the big bucks to answer questions like this?" But somewhere in the back of his mind, he's beginning to think that if "they" trust him to deal with these issues, maybe there isn't much difference between him and "them" after all.

FOSTERING THE ALLOCATION OF RESOURCES BY ACTIVITY, BASED ON COST AND SERVICE LEVEL

The devil is in the details. Leadership teams can't afford to get lost in the details, but they must encourage managers and employees *to live in them*. To find the biggest alligators, you usually have to wade into the weeds.

Whether for internal or external purposes, the lifeblood of the corporate body flows through its resource allocation system. In most cases that system is not a *system* at all; it is a hodgepodge of misleading financial measures, creative accounting, tradition, and good old-fashioned salesmanship. The result is the all too familiar business unit that spends to justify its budget each year, or the bloated bureaucracy of internal services that just won't seem to go away.

Creating or reconstructing the resource allocation systems involves moving down one more level of aggregation in the economic model, focusing on targeted business processes within the value chain. Each process, in turn, is broken down into the activities that define them. One can associate costs with each activity, using activity-based costing techniques (ABC) to create an activity cost map for each process. Each activity map is linked to a decomposed version of the firm's expense and capital structure, providing the means to monitor process performance and the impact of changes in activities within each process.

Process mapping and ABC techniques give in-depth knowledge about the key activities that drive value and cost in the business. Using ABC techniques, it is possible to identify which processes drive value creation—by product, by customer, by market, and by business—and which activities drive value creation within those processes. It is also possible to ascribe real costs to those activities, rather than shroud them behind the conventions of generally accepted accounting principles.

More often than not, however, ABC is applied at a level of detail that is beyond the immediate concern of the business leader. What matters to the business leader is the philosophy of activity-based costing, and the clarity of thinking that it fosters. Another concern is establishing a connection between the work of the business, the high-level value chain, and, ultimately, the high-level goals and measures of the firm. The goal is to produce an objective and aligned set of standards for allocating resources throughout the organization. The leader's role is to develop those standards by encouraging valuation by activity at all levels of the organization.

One very effective way of doing this is to select a business for a pilot application to demonstrate the insights and financial benefits that can be generated using activity-based costing (ABC). A successful pilot not only serves as a showcase, but also may spark a healthy bout of internal competition, as each business unit strives to shine in bringing newly found value to the table.

ABC, THE WORLD'S LARGEST SPREADSHEET

Traditional accounting approaches do not reflect the real world. For starters, they rely on a dubious distinction between fixed and variable costs. There are several sweet illusions built into the fixed and variable cost scheme.

As most CEOs know, there are three fundamental, albeit revised, laws of accounting when it comes to fixed and variable costs. First, variable costs become fixed when volume decreases. Second, proportionally variable costs become geometrically variable when volume goes up, often triggered by complexity. Third, fixed costs become variable when the volume goes up. Aside from these three minor points, the distinction between fixed and variable costs is clearly a rigorous one.

What matters, of course, is not whether a cost is fixed or variable, but whether a manager can do anything about it; specifically, whether he or she can help to reconfigure the work to reduce the associated cost, while increasing, or at least maintaining, the value created for the ultimate customer.

A second major problem with traditional costing methods is that they apportion costs to a customer or against a profit center in a way that fails to reflect what is actually going on inside the business. Consequently, the manager cannot isolate the cost culprit, much less accurately measure the effects of any improvement initiative.

By connecting costs directly to tasks, ABC resolves the problems of conventional accounting, allowing managers to understand the true cost of doing business by customer, by product, by market, and by business. At the end of an ABC effort a plant manager knows, for example, that he spends $5 million on palletizing a product; that he uses a million pallets a year; and that each of them eventually costs $5. He, together with the marketing team, can then think about the value of the palletizing process: "Is it really worth $5 per pallet? How much do our competitors spend on it? Right now, we shrink-wrap each pallet; is that really necessary? What would happen if we changed the palletization process, perhaps used smaller pallets that could be handled with a manual cart rather than a motorized forklift?" Although ABC does not, in itself, provide the answers to such questions, it does provide a real-world picture of costs by activity, allowing room for creative rethinking of the processes involved.

A CEO cannot be worried about whether to shrink-wrap pallets or other such details. Rather, the CEO's concern is to develop an organizationwide discipline that allocates costs to activities at the operational level. Not only can such a discipline foster company-wide cost reductions, it can also trigger alternative approaches to work that may prove to be a source of competitive advantage.

A big problem with ABC is knowing where to start and how deep to go with the analysis. There are literally millions of activities in a large corporation, and it is theoretically possible to capture all of those activities on the world's largest spreadsheet. But it is also theoretically possible to cut down the Amazon Forest with a machete. ABC has received a lot of bad press, particularly in America, because it was applied mindlessly by inexperienced practitioners.

The CEO and business unit leaders usually play a key role in deciding where to apply ABC. In making the decision, a few rules of thumb are helpful:

Pick an area where costs are high, where there is a good chance of generating savings far exceeding the cost of the effort.

Go where you expect foul play in traditional accounting systems; that is, where you expect that generally accepted accounting principles distort the true cost of doing business. Production areas with a broad product line and a mix of large and small volume runs are usually good candidates—the large volume products usually subsidize the lower volume ones.

Areas with large chunks of "indirect costs" are good prospects, and correctly realigning those costs can often transform the entire profitability picture of a business.

Choose areas where the costs are discretionary. It probably won't be helpful, for example, to carefully evaluate the cost per report in the regulatory compliance area, when each of those reports is required by law.

Given a starting point, how deeply do you take the analysis? It may not be very helpful, but the best answer is perhaps: to the level of detail necessary. The truth is, there's a lot of art to the practice of ABC. People who have been practicing it for years can spend a few hours with an executive team and focus right in on where to target the effort. The key is to go in with a hypothesis of what you're going to find. Cheat a little at the beginning by predicting the outcome, and use the rigor of the process to prove yourself either right or wrong.

SIFTING THROUGH COMPLEXITY AT MONSANTO PLASTICS

A few years ago, Monsanto Plastics had 1200 different-colored products in its product line. In the plastics business, color matching is a way of life. If a customer shows up in your backyard and asks you to duplicate a particular color, the code of honor of the plastics industry dictates that you should try. When you're good, you often succeed at matching that color. Monsanto Plastics was understandably proud to be one of the best color matchers in the business.

There was one problem, however. The firm really didn't know the cost of maintaining this fantastic rainbow. In reality, a rigorous analysis of sales by product showed that about 600 products accounted for 99 percent of sales. In other words, the firm was maintaining over 600 products to capture 1 percent of total sales. The profitability was what one would expect from such a profile.

The first temptation was to cut the apparently profit-eating 600 products. But Monsanto was concerned that their best customers might be purchasing these products, and cutting them might mean completely losing their business. Some of the apparently unproductive color matching, they reasoned, is probably done for large, profitable customers, perhaps as a service to maintain the customers' loyalty. So they looked at profitability by customer, finding that 33 customers were destroying the profits generated by some 200 others.

To obtain the information needed to redesign its product, pricing, and customer strategies, the next step involved disaggregating the value chain into a set of 23 key activities describing the business, with their associated cost drivers. The analysis showed that the sheer complexity of handling such a diverse product line drove the costs of key activities straight up. For example, sustaining the product line (maintaining bills of materials, setting cost standards, and maintaining the product line) proved a nightmare of complexity. Changing over equipment (for product runs and packaging) also suffered extraordinary costs due to the uncontrolled proliferation of the product line. Storage and several other activity costs also stood out like volunteers for reform school.

The analysis did not imply any single, clear-cut answer such as dramatically cutting the product line, dropping certain customers, or changing the value chain fundamentally. And yet the company was able to generate significant improvements simply by optimizing along those three dimensions simultaneously.

In the end, Monsanto Plastics did achieve some benefits by trimming its product line, but the bulk of the improvements were derived by adjusting price to order size, pattern, and the level of customer service provided. At the same time, the firm optimized the deployment of its production facilities against customer mix, changing its production planning, production policies and procedures, changeover time, and scrap handling approaches.

SERVICE-LEVEL ASSESSMENT

For almost every CEO, "overhead," like homelessness and polio, is something that should be eliminated. In fact, however, some degree of overhead is necessary. It shouldn't be a dirty word, not if it provides the support services required to operate a company, and not if the work processes involved are aligned to provide only necessary services at a minimum cost.

Service Level Assessment (SLA) is a tool that measures the degree of alignment of support work activity to the needs of the business. It does so by mapping the costs incurred by the *service provider* to the value gained by the *service receiver*. If ABC is the yin, SLA is the yang. Together, they represent cost and value assessments on flip sides of the same coin—the corporate work structure—activity by activity.

Applied to a product, ABC gives insights into both cost and value— cost being determined in the analysis, and value being reflected in the price of a product. But when applied to support services, ABC can lead to such dramatic conclusions as: "So what?" What difference does it make if a manager knows that it costs $5 to palletize a product, if he or she has no idea what value that service offers to the receiver, and therefore to the business? The idea behind SLA is to provide a means of measuring value in the eyes of the service receivers, making them the equivalent of a paying customer for analytical purposes.

In SLA terms, the ideal "customer" is one who directly experiences the output of the process. In assessing the value of shrink-wrapping during the palletizing process, for example, the receiving clerk on the customer's dock might be in the best position. In other cases, "customers" may be found only within the corporation's walls. For example, customers rarely can provide helpful input on the value of, say, a budgeting or cost-accounting process. In many instances a profit center, or the general manager of the business, can effectively play the role of the process customer.

In lieu of monetary valuations, SLA customers assess the importance and effectiveness of the *process output*, which is rated on a numerical scale through focus groups, interviews, surveys, or workshops. When the evaluation is complete for all key processes, both the ABC and SLA components are integrated to provide a model tying together process performance from the service receiver's standpoint, and activity costs within the process. The result is a complete model of all service transactions within the firm, including an indication of both their true activity costs and their value rating according to the service receivers (Fig. 4.2).

Consider the ammunition this gives the CEO. Viewed from the perspective of the business as a whole, it provides the basis upon which to prioritize process improvement initiatives. Obviously, the targets to shoot for are the largest spheres (the highest costs) in the lower right quartile of the activity map (the most important and least effective services from the service receiver's standpoint). Once a process has been selected for improvement, the breakdown into activities, associated costs, and impact on expenses provides the tools to analyze alternative process designs, monitor the financial impact of process changes, and measure process financial performance over time.

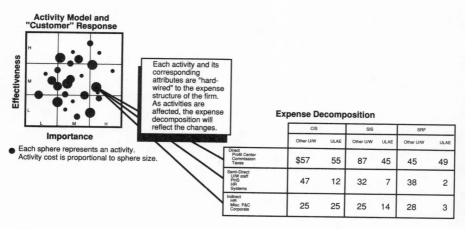

Figure 4.2. *Activity cost model for home office SLA at CIGNA P&C.*

It is now the summer of 1994, and Gerry Isom is relentless in his request that home office activities become aligned with the new strategy. Everyone knows that means too many people are doing things nobody cares about anymore. Two members of the President's Executive Council (PEC) have been appointed as leaders of the "home office alignment" stream of work. But there's still more rhetoric than action.

The heads of the three main business divisions are particularly frustrated, and have started digging into their cost structure, looking for places to cut. Every day they battle ferocious competitors who have lower prices. But as they turn their view inward, they find a complex maze of allocated costs that have been set by accounting. In periodic outbursts, they all leave together for weekend retreats with their detailed P&L statements, only to find a financial labyrinth so well designed that no human has ever emerged alive at the other end. As the weeks pass and their costs remain the same, they can feel the heat rising.

Support costs are the object of their particular focus and irritation. They can sense the fat; they know that the services rendered just can't be that valuable, and competitors look lean and mean by comparison. It feels wrong, but they can't pinpoint the sources of the error.

For example, there have been no significant new applications in information technology for several years, and yet the IT bill seems to be dragging their businesses deeper and deeper below the surface. There are lots of actuaries doing lots of reports, but no one seems to know exactly why they're doing them. The human resources function appears to be getting bigger and bigger, yet the skills inside the firm don't seem to be improving.

"We need to do something," is the carefully crafted diagnosis the business heads finally come up with.

They have tried to make their case to the managers in charge of the support functions, and both sides have displayed remarkable good faith in trying to clarify ambiguous areas. The managers have done their best to align the services their groups provide with the needs of the businesses, but the improvements have been minuscule. The problem isn't one of will, but of lack of information. Before negotiation about cutting costs or services can occur, everyone needs to understand what the actual costs are, and exactly what services are required, and at what level.

It's a conflict with no villains, a dialogue of the deaf without the benefit of sign language. They talk in such generalities that no action is ever possible. The business heads have little tolerance for details. They advise the systems department to quit spending money on the maintenance of old systems. "Focus on the new stuff," they say. "Help us build new applications for our newly designed claims and underwriting process. Don't focus on the old legacy systems."

But while they look to the future, the rank-and-file claims managers are begging the systems people to keep the old system coughing, at least long enough so that they can pay their claims. Though less visible from the top, the systems people understand that claims and underwriting will collapse without those legacy systems. This puts the head of the systems group in the rough spot of having to dance on the upper deck with the new technologies, while patching up holes in the boiler room.

The result is deadlock. The deadlock spawns irritation, and the irritation, radicalism. Radicalism can be a good thing, but only when it is the outgrowth of a carefully reasoned process. In this case, it clearly is not. People start making poorly thought-out suggestions, like outsourcing the entire systems development and legal services departments. Others start advocating across-the-board headcount reductions—every department is to suffer equally, regardless of the value it provides. Rumors of the different scenarios spread along the grapevine, and the rising fear within the organization threatens to halt Gerry Isom's mobilization strategy in its tracks.

To build a constructive, if occasionally confrontational, dialogue between both sides, Isom calls for a cooling-off period, which will be used to develop a clearer picture of their situation. He encourages the development of a detailed activity-based costing model, accompanied by a service-level assessment of each activity. It takes close to three months to develop, but the information it provides is exactly what intelligent dialogue requires.

The discussion becomes focused. Line item by line item, both the business heads and the managers can review the cost and value of information technology programs under way, and make an informed decision regarding whether to continue funding them. The same process applies to all support functions. Though the decisions are informed, they are neither easy nor painless. The generalities are gone. Their hearing restored, the leaders work together as professionals to decide what support functions are really necessary to run the businesses, at what cost, and with what expectations of value.

The next step is for each leader to rise to the challenge and make the necessary cuts. This proves more difficult. To this day, Isom feels that they have a long way to go in aligning the home office with the new strategy. "But now it's a question of leadership, not a question of ignorance. At least we have made some progress," he adds with a wink.

CONFIGURING THE PHYSICAL INFRASTRUCTURE

In administering an annual physical examination, a good physician checks the patient's physical alignment: the curvature of the back, the alignment of the hips, the squareness of the shoulders, the mobility of the joints. With a trained eye, the doctor looks through skin and muscle at the skeletal system, making sure that the "knee bone is connected to the leg bone," as it should be. It is an important part of the exam, for the skeletal system is more than an elaborate coat-hanger for muscles and organs. It is, for example, the housing for the delicate central nervous system, and the manufacturing center for oxygen-transporting red blood cells. Improper alignment can either be symptomatic of an array of ailments, or may in itself cause severe pain and illness.

In much the same way, the configuration of a corporation's physical infrastructure is one of the most visible and telling measures of the overall health and strategic direction of a company. Physical infrastructure is the corporate equivalent of the skeletal system; it is the network of facilities and other assets—plants, warehouses, trucks, barges, machines, etc.— upon which work processes, the muscles of the business, depend. Like bones, the physical assets of a company are relatively fixed and rigid, resisting movement beyond their design. Some are like the spine: When they fall out of alignment, they pinch vital nerves, causing pain and partial paralysis. Others may fracture under stress, immobilizing whole sections of the corporate body and requiring mechanical realignment for the healing process to occur.

The human skeletal system provides the governing framework for movement. A corporation's physical infrastructure provides the governing framework for the physical process of value creation. This includes such vital strategic attributes as mobility and flexibility, as well as reach into and interconnectedness with the external environment of vendor, supplier, and customer networks. The configuration of the physical infrastructure largely determines the structure of a business's supply system; that is, a company's physical assets must be aligned to support the work and relationships involved in value creation, beginning with suppliers, moving through the company, and finally through distributors to reach the ultimate consumers.

The fifth chromosome of the corporation determines that alignment. Its function is to *configure the physical infrastructure* of the corporation. Four key genes govern the design of the physical infrastructure, implying four corresponding tasks for leadership:

1. *Formulating an operations strategy.* Configuring the infrastructure is a problem of aligning a company's physical assets with its operating requirements. Operating requirements, however, are not fixed; they depend on the strategic objectives of the company. The purpose of an operating strategy is to translate strategic objectives into operating requirements and, consequently, into goals and policies used to align the physical infrastructure.

An operations strategy is formulated within the context of the high-level value chain. With strategic priorities established, as described in Chaps. 3 and 4, the high-level activities within the value chain are translated into a set of principles defining how the corporation will compete through its operations. Those principles act as the basis for defining operating goals for all parts of the infrastructure: each plant, warehouse, research laboratory, retail branch, or check-processing center.

Given these goals, the organization's leadership can evaluate whether the current disposition of physical assets is consistent with the strategic objectives of the company. For a manufacturing facility: Is the plant's physical layout consistent with the strategic objective of a shortened cycle time, or is it still configured for broad-based production to achieve economies of scale? For a bank: Are checks processed according to type for customized service, or is check processing still set up like an old-style paper factory to minimize per-item processing cost? A company's *operations strategy* embodies its basic principles of value creation, serving as the standard upon which to base the many tradeoff decisions involved in building a supply system. The CEO's task is not to manage infrastructure, but to ensure that it is managed according to a properly crafted operations strategy.

2. *Developing a network strategy.* An operations strategy provides the logic for linking individual components of the physical infrastructure to the strategic objectives of the company. But facilities and other physical assets don't exist in isolation; they are linked together in a *facilities network.* Upstream plants supply downstream plants; warehouses serve manufacturing plants; and service centers serve retail outlets in hub-and-spoke configurations. Just as value creation occurs in a continuous flow throughout the value chain, so the components of the physical infrastructure interact continuously, each affecting the others. The operations strategy, therefore, must be integrated within an overarching *network strategy.*

Without a network strategy, companies fall into a number of familiar problems. Companies organized into SBUs, for example, often divvy up plants and equipment, independently using them in response to the needs of their individual markets. Unavoidably, because what is good for one SBU may be bad for another, this creates tension when corporate objectives and business unit objectives collide. Driven by the CEO and other senior leadership, a network strategy eliminates this sort of conflict by ensuring that corporate and business unit (or regional, or plant, etc.) objectives are aligned.

Unfortunately, few companies have the luxury of being able to create their physical infrastructure from scratch. Most corporations are victims of their own history, wearing enormous financial, social, and environmental shackles that restrict their range of options. The network strategy, therefore, reflects a balance between the "as-is" and "should-be" facilities network, involving careful renovation of existing infrastructure combined with prudent construction of new facilities.

3. *Aligning individual facilities.* Within the context of the operations and network strategies, individual facilities must themselves be aligned, which often requires extensive rethinking of the existing order even at the local process level. Large, vertically integrated plants originally designed for economies of scale, for example, may need to be divided into smaller "plants within a plant." Many considerations come into play, such as capacity policy, equipment selection, physical layout, allocation of machines to product segments, control systems, plant organization, and so forth.

When it comes to aligning individual facilities, the level of detail is far too great to be of concern to the CEO and other senior leaders. Their job is to encourage initiatives at the individual facility level, while fostering the development of a process in which plant-based goals, measures, and improvements are mapped against the overall strategic targets and measures of the company.

4. *Articulating a sourcing strategy.* Sourcing strategy sets policy for managing the external supply network: suppliers, vendors, distributors, etc. Following value-chain logic, a business can be considered as a component, or subset, of an industrywide value chain. Viewed from this perspective, each business is unique in terms of its scope and its role within that chain. Some companies may focus on the supply end, others on manufacturing and service, others on packaging and distribution, and still others may attempt to be integrated across the entire chain.

A business strategy defines what that role is. A *sourcing* strategy defines where the starting and end-points of internal operations are within the chain, and establishes the standard for managing the upstream, or supplier, relationships. Sourcing strategy deals with how those relationships are managed, for example, with questions such as whether to doggedly pursue lower prices with suppliers or to form long-term, mutually advantageous relationships.

Together, these four genes determine the unique configuration of the flow of value through the corporate body and its external environment. The CEO's role is to develop the basic framework of *operations strategy* and to enforce policy standards designed to keep the goals and measures of the firm aligned from top to bottom.

FORMULATING AN OPERATIONS STRATEGY

CEOs are rarely shy, retiring types, yet many of them shy away from the more technical, engineering dimensions of operating problems, including the highly technical areas of R&D and information technology. They seem to believe that if they can't contribute to the debate at a technical level, they can't contribute at all. Perhaps this is why so many CEOs leave key operational decisions to their technical staff, who then become frustrated by a lack of strategic direction from the top.

In general, engineers and technicians are trained to solve specific problems at the lowest possible cost. Of necessity, their focus is specialized. Without the guidance of an operations strategy, they simply do not have the context needed to weigh the many tradeoffs involved in making key operating decisions. Consequently, their decisions tend to favor efficiency and cost, while failing to reflect the strategic objectives of the company. The extent to which top leaders relegate key decisions to them is the extent to which they stunt the development of the biological corporation, preventing the development of metabolic pathways that could open new doors to competitiveness, or even to entirely new business opportunities.

The engineering and technical perspectives are important, but limited. Engineers enjoy figuring out how to make machines and reactors and pumps produce more, better, and a greater variety of things. And the most influential of technicians today—computer experts—love their applications, and revel in breaking down complex processes into discrete, mechanistic parts that can be modeled and controlled by silicon, zeroes, and ones. Their respective achievements are marvelous. But relatively few engineers or other technical specialists have the generalist perspective needed to recognize and define the set of tradeoffs that must be made to create and deliver value to customers.

A company's leaders need not be technical or engineering experts, but it is their role to establish and drive an operations strategy through all levels of the organization. In most cases this doesn't require detailed technical or engineering expertise, but it does require a general knowledge of what engineering and technology make possible, and at what cost. It is this kind of knowledge that gives them the true generalist perspective required to chart new pathways of value creation for their businesses.

Of Mini-Mills and Mighty Bucks at Nucor

The well known story of Nucor, a steel manufacturer based in Charlotte, North Carolina, exemplifies how a creative operations strategy can explode the paradigm of an age-old industry.

In 1967, F. Ken Iverson was a vice president of a nearly bankrupt conglomerate called the Nuclear Corporation of America. Taking the helm of a division that shaped roof joists for small developers, Iverson reversed the fortune of the company by deciding to make it a steel producer. His strategy could, and still can, be summed up in a single hyphenated word: *mini-mills.* Iverson knew that mini-mills could do the same thing as big mills, only faster and without the management layers, allowing for quick decision making. Translation: strategic and operational flexibility.

He entered the steel market when the U.S. giants were succumbing to their more efficient Japanese competitors. Although Iverson's approach would allow production at five times the labor efficiency of the Japanese, he never intended to compete with the big boys. The plan was to make steel the small way, in small quantities for niche markets. He would locate the mills in rural areas, where the land was cheap and people wanted to work. Unskilled workers—farmers and sharecroppers—

were hired for the job at wage scales significantly below the industry average, but an incentive program was designed to bring them much higher if the business was profitable.

The company almost went under during the startup, but after two years (in 1971) earnings had soared 140 percent, rising another 70 percent the year after, when the company's name was changed to Nucor. Four more mills were opened, and the big steel makers largely dropped out of the roof joist business, unable to compete with Iverson's bargain-basement prices. By the late 1970s, Nucor had become a $42 million company.

The mini-mill strategy didn't go unnoticed; copycats popped up. Iverson's answer was to bet the company on what the best steel minds in the world considered a futile pursuit. He would build a continuous process mill that could cast, flatten, roll, and coil still hot metal into a product ready for shipping. In 1986 he found a caster in Germany that he thought would work, one that had been turned down by every major steel company in the world. In 1987 construction started on the new mill in what had been a corn field in Indiana. To save time, the plant was designed as it was being built.

It was completed faster than any other steel plant before it, and set another record by becoming profitable within its first year of operation. By 1990, Nucor was a $1.5 billion company, and it is still growing.

The essence of Iverson's strategy has never changed: small plants, few layers of management, speed, and niche markets. That strategy has driven an entire set of policies that are the envy of the industry:

Plant location. Inexpensive, rural locations with a small pool of motivated workers.

Labor. Unskilled workers are trained, promised a portion of profits, and to the extent possible, guaranteed life-time employment.

Rewards. Base wages are below union rates, but profit-based bonuses make Nucor steelworkers the highest paid in the industry. (Bonuses reach as high as 150 percent of base salary.)

Span of control. As high as possible. There is an unbelievable 300 to 1 ratio of production workers to managers, and only four layers of management within the entire organization. Less than 30 people constitute "overhead" at corporate headquarters.

Raw material. Nucor's favored feed stock is scrap, which has the advantage of not requiring smelting, the most energy-intensive and therefore costly part of the steel production process. As volume increased, the company built an ore treatment plant and perfected a process in which treated ore is combined with scrap, still bypassing the smelting process.

Culture. The culture is what Iverson calls "equalitarian": everyone wears the same color hardhat.

There are many more distinguishing features of Nucor's operating strategy, and none of them is intrinsically technical. When competitive pressures threatened to thwart the company's growth, however, a general knowledge of technology proved vital. To beat copycat competitors, Iverson asked, in effect, "Is it possible to build a continuous, rolling mill?" and sent out his best minds to find out. When facing a shortage of raw material, he asked, in effect, "Is there a way that we can augment scrap metal with ore?" and he put qualified people to work on the project. Nucor's technology is pioneering, even revolutionary, but it is the servant of the company's operations strategy, not its master.

BUILDING AN OPERATIONS STRATEGY

The logic of building an operations strategy is deceptively simple. The corporation's high-level goals and measures are established using the Balanced Scorecard, which in turn drives the definition of the high-level value chain, which in turn drives the choice of key performance requirements such as cycle time, cost, responsiveness, service, product line, and quality. The latter are the drivers of an operations strategy.

The logic is deceptively simple, because it belies the creative process— and often the sheer guts—involved in making decisions at each step.

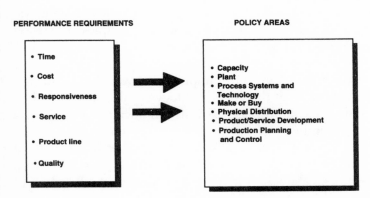

Figure 5.1. *Building an operations strategy.*

Choosing a positioning in the industrywide value chain, defining the strategic focus of a business's high-level value chain, and matching key performance requirements to that focus, all involve making choices within a virtually infinite array of tradeoffs and possibilities. The most important delimiting factor in making those choices is market and customer focus—meeting the unique requirements of specific customer segments—as will be discussed in Chap. 7. The operating strategy both reflects market focus and delineates the range of options available.

Frederick Smith, for example, built Federal Express (now FedEx) on the simple operating strategy of providing guaranteed overnight delivery of small parcels. He put together a blueprint for his would-be overnight delivery business in college. His professor gave him a C, perhaps because he considered bringing all shipments to a central distribution center to be impractical. The capital investment in planes and trucks seemed outrageously high, the professor probably judged.

Smith, however, knew that none of the commercial airlines was reliable enough to provide the service needed to make good on the overnight guarantee. In his mind, the only way was to own the airport, trucks, planes—everything—and create an unprecedented standard of service reliability. Smith sketched out the facilities network, then worked with his investors to implement it. Once he even made payroll by gambling petty cash in Las Vegas, but the company's remarkable history of growth and performance speaks well for Smith's choice of facilities network.

A CREATIVE EXPLOSION WAITING TO HAPPEN IN PROCESS INDUSTRIES

Iverson and Nucor broke the mold in the apparently mature and evidently unprofitable steel industry, throwing out the orthodoxy of economies of scale and replacing it with the new logic of customer service and innovation. We expect that other industries will see a similar explosion of their current operating molds over the next few years.

It's already happening in some manufacturing areas. The once monolithic semiconductor plant, for example, has given way to smaller, more agile units, with state of the art technology capable of responding quickly to the industry's rapid pace of design innovation. Albeit at a slower pace, the auto industry also is moving away from huge, integrated assembly plants, toward leaner and smaller units that rely more and more heavily on operator skills and supplier partnerships. In both cases, Japanese competitors catalyzed the change, usurping a decades-old operations model.

Process industries, however, are lagging behind, perhaps because they have not yet felt the fetid breath of global competition on their necks. Consider the oil refining industry, for example. At one end, small refineries are closing every month, unable to compete with larger, more efficient ones. A lesser known and arguably more important fact, however, is that larger refineries are, in general, not doing particularly well. As trade association data corroborates, economies of scale remain important, but the correlation between size and profitability is steadily growing weaker.

It seems the medium-sized refineries are doing as well as, and in some cases better than, the very large refineries, compensating for their scale handicaps with service and focused production. Their ability to be flexible with feed stocks (to process high- or low-sulfur, foreign or domestic crude oil) and to vary their product mix (to change the relative product volumes of gasoline, aviation fuel, home heating oil, etc.) seem to be becoming more important. Continuous, daily optimization of the input and output cocktails through process control technology and operating skill seem as important as size, and may soon become more important. As the more macho among the refining culture might put it, it isn't the size of the instrument, but how you use it that counts.

Given these trends, one would expect engineers who are drawing up plans for the next capital expansion to at least *consider* smaller units, favoring operating flexibility and customer service over economies of scale. It is doubtful that they will, however, because they all went to the same school, the one where they learned that if you don't build a "world-class" unit—meaning one bigger than the last one built—you die a rapid death. To them, "capacity increase" automatically translates to "the bigger the better." They are locked into the operating model of economies of scale.

There is often great merit in studying the history of operations across industries. A case in point is the comparison between the commodity chemicals industry, specifically ethylene production, and the industrial gas industry. The two industries clearly are cousins, if not sisters, and the products of both industries clearly are commodities; that is, the ethylene molecules produced by competitors in the chemical industry are identical, as are the molecules of oxygen, nitrogen, or hydrogen provided by industrial gas companies.

Despite their similarities, however, there are dramatic differences in the profitability of the two industries. Profitability in the ethylene industry is sporadic, typically marked by one or two good years within a seven- or eight-year cycle. Because there is so much production capacity, the price spread between feed-stock and product prices is rarely favorable, but because industry producers have invested so heavily in large-scale production facilities, it has become more economical to run them at a loss than to shut down completely during unfavorable periods. Consequently, major producers such as Texaco, Shell, and Union Carbide have difficulty sustaining an acceptable return on equity throughout the cycle.

By contrast, the industrial gas industry is quite profitable. Air Liquide, Air Products and Chemicals, Praxair, and British Oxygen all do well, and the market doesn't exhibit the wild cycles of the ethylene industry. What accounts for the difference?

The conventional wisdom might say that the industrial gas industry is free from the cyclical nature of feed-stock prices—its raw material, after all, is air, which is free and in abundant supply virtually anywhere but Los Angeles. But that advantage doesn't free the industry from the prospect of a price war due to product oversupply, which is the essence of the commodity chemical industry's problem. The real explanation rests with a difference in operating strategies: the industrial gas industry got smart, the commodity chemical companies did not.

In the late 19th century, the German chemical engineer, Karl von Linde, perfected a method of liquefying, separating, and compressing air, giving birth to the industrial gas industry. From about 1900 until about 1920, the gases were distributed to users in steel cylinders much like large scuba tanks. Then Linde patented a process for the liquefication of gases, making it possible to produce and ship the products to industrial users in large, bulk containers. Through the late 1940s, the operating philosophy behind industrial gas production and distribution was similar to that in the commodity chemicals industry; gases were produced in large volume at centralized facilities and distributed in bulk to its customers.

In the 1950s, however, Air Products pioneered the concept of building smaller production facilities on-site with large users. For example, they built plants next to steel companies, supplying them directly and bypassing the logistical complexity of distribution. This approach also allowed them to develop long-term supply and service relationships with customers, forestalling the possibility of a commodity price battle. The rest of the industry followed suit, and the operations strategy for the industry as a whole was a mix of centralized and on-site production until the middle-to-late 1980s. Then the advent of membrane separation made it possible to build small, compact, and highly efficient air separators. No longer was it necessary to liquefy the gases and ship them in pressurized trucks at all; the gases could be produced on-site, on demand.

This time, Praxair led the way in changing the operations paradigm. They began marketing the mini-gas plants to their users, charging a fee for the product used and offering a complete service package. They built, installed, and serviced the plants, guaranteeing a supply in return for a long-term purchasing agreement from the user. The strategy proved enormously successful, and many producers followed suit. Not all of them, however; some, especially in Europe, sell the small plants instead of the product and associated services. Others work on long-term lease agreements. In short, instead of standardizing to a single operating philosophy, the industry now competes based on a myriad of operating philosophies tailored to unique customer needs.

Why didn't the ethylene industry do the same? Those in the chemicals industry will say that there are fundamental differences, that industrial gas companies don't need to worry about locating feed stock next to their plants, and they don't face the same environmental restrictions. While these arguments are true, there is growing evidence that locating ethylene plants next to the feed stock may not be the best choice. For example, because ethylene oxide, one of ethylene's major derivatives, is so explosive, transporting it is increasingly being restricted, even outlawed entirely in some countries. If transporting it becomes outlawed entirely, which is probable in the long term, then the only option will be to produce it right next to the customer in an "over-the-fence" agreement, perhaps next to one of Procter & Gamble's surfactants plants, for example, which uses it to create the foaming effect in its shampoos.

Whether from tighter regulation or the pioneering efforts of a revolutionary thinker, change, we believe, will trigger an explosion of the time-worn operating strategy of commodity chemical and other process industries.

DEVELOPING A NETWORK STRATEGY

The configuration of physical infrastructure and the facilities network deserve special attention for a single reason: They cost a lot of money. Once acquired and in place, facilities become almost immovable, as if in defiance of their inevitable progression toward obsolescence.

Think, for example, of the facilities hand John Smith was dealt when he recently was appointed CEO at General Motors. Saturn is certainly a good card, but it is one of the few. Most of GM's plants are located in the high-cost Detroit area. The level of horizontal integration in parts manufacturing is still too high, making entities like the Automotive Components Group and GM's $26 billion parts business a millstone around its neck.

Unions are heavily represented in every major plant, pushing Smith for wage and benefit concessions at every turn. Despite recent progress, the relationships between design engineering, plant engineering, and purchasing remain difficult. If the game were draw poker, Smith undoubtedly would trade in the bulk of his hand. But he's stuck with the hand he was dealt, and folding isn't an option.

Smith probably dreams of small, agile production units, run by employees with the wisdom and power to make key decisions in a collaborative environment, their attention firmly fixed on customer needs. But he is bound by GM's history, which is embedded in its physical infrastructure. He must pay the price for the limitations of Alfred Sloan's dream of a command-and-control organization that relies on scale economies for its competitive advantage.

Existing facilities definitely impose limitations, but this "prisoner inside one's own facilities" argument can be overplayed. Usually there are more opportunities to reconfigure an operations network than people realize. It may require some creativity, including violating a few deeply-held beliefs about what can be done, but in most cases the limitations are figments of the imagination, not attributes of the bricks and mortar. It's like turning a 17th century building in downtown Paris or London into an exciting, functional office building. In the beginning, it feels like it will never work. The ceilings are so high that the heating costs will be prohibitive; there are no rooms large enough for meetings; and there is nowhere to put the elevator shaft! Yet in the end, a clever architect and a smart interior decorator can marry the elegance of the old and the functionalities of the new.

The alignment of the facilities network is of critical strategic importance. The location of plants, their interaction, their size, their relationship to the distribution network—all of these represent choices that determine a company's range of strategic flexibility. At the production floor level, for example, the physical layout equipment and machines can fix between 60 and 80 percent of the production costs. Extrapolate that to an entire plant, and then to a network of plants, distribution centers, and service centers, and before long you're talking about a lot of bananas.

A Network Play at Woodbridge

In the last chapter we left Karl, the reluctant team leader in charge of redesigning Woodbridge's order-to-delivery process, in a double quandary. Once before, he had approached the senior leadership team, asking for their guidance about how to shape the product line. Then he realized that many more elements were involved as well, including whether to buy trucks for deliveries and how to manage supplier relationships in the pulp and paper end of the business. Having been burned by his own ignorance at the first meeting, he has resolved to come prepared for the second.

At this juncture, Karl and his team have developed an integrated solution to the double quandary. This is the day that he presents that proposal.

"It's brilliant!" The CEO clapped his hands once in excitement. "A major breakthrough!"

Karl is having a great day. He can't wait to pass the good news along to the team after the meeting, and to his wife tonight.

In a two-month process, the team had come up with a new manufacturing concept for Woodbridge. They called it *Focus*. It wasn't that big a deal, really, except that it could save the company millions of dollars. It was really quite simple. Woodbridge had six plants throughout North America, which were managed regionally, meaning that each plant produced the company's entire product line for its region. Their idea was to change that, to focus each plant on a limited set of products that would be produced for all of North America. That was it, short and sweet.

By simulating the costs involved, the team had shown that the new approach would generate tremendous benefits. Their cost model demonstrated that transportation costs had always been overstated, while the cost of changeovers—switching from one product to another on a machine—had been dramatically underestimated. The whole logic of the regional operation was built around minimizing transportation costs, but the team's simulation had shattered that logic.

It had taken a little while to get there. The activity-based costing thing, which Karl initially had been suspicious of, was tedious and time consuming, but enormously helpful. Without it, they would never have known how much money was tied in setup cost, a number never before known in the plants. As a good scheduler, Karl had intuitively honed in on that process as a target for the ABC effort. From watching the machines run, he'd long known that during a changeover, the machine produced waste until the colors from the previous paper had been purged and the thickness of the paper had stabilized within tolerance levels. That often meant several hours of production time, and as the cost model demonstrated, that added up to a lot of man-hours, paper, and dye, which meant millions of dollars per year across the country.

The results had astonished him. The ABC analysis the accounting folks pulled together showed that 20 percent of the capacity of the machine was tied up in changeover. Twenty percent! That translated to a machine-and-a-quarter being idle at all times—in their plant alone! It was numbers like that which had spawned the idea of focus in the mind of one of the team members. "What if we dedicated each machine to a single product?" she had asked. When someone had pointed out that they didn't have enough machines to go around at their facility, Karl himself had suggested: "We would if we dedicated different product lines to different plants!" From there, the entire team had taken off with the idea.

So there he was, in front of the CEO and the leadership team, and they loved the idea. But he wasn't quite prepared for the barrage of questions and comments that came flying at him.

"What will this mean in terms of production cycle time?" asked the newly appointed VP of Reengineering.

"There's no way we can supply California from the Northeast with a 10-day lead time," said the VP of Manufacturing.

"Won't this require a complete reconfiguration of our distribution network?" shot the head of Logistics and Planning.

"How will this help us against Mountain View? And what about our sales organization?" demanded the president of Marketing somewhat curtly. "We'll have to completely reorganize and retrain our sales force."

The balls came shooting at him—some of them warm, supporting soft balls, others hard, breaking fast balls, low and inside. But Karl the slugger was unstoppable. Some of his answers were foul balls, but he knew that the Focus play was right; it would yield a better cost and service tradeoff than any approach previously used by Woodbridge. Out of the corner of his eye, he saw the CEO's smile. And at the end of the meeting, he heard his simple words, "We'll go with the Focus concept."

Champagne, everyone.

Configuring Marketing Centers and Claims Offices at CIGNA

In the last chapter, we left CIGNA with the transformation process rapidly migrating to all areas of the business. Process redesign activities were in full swing in claims, underwriting, and even in the home office support area (more on this in Chap. 6). Although many of the decisions had been painful, slow progress was being made, and Gerry Isom was feeling a little better.

We rejoin Isom as many of the process designs have entered the pilot stage. The all-important underwriting pilot, led by a talented underwriter from headquarters, Ward Jungers, is getting high marks in the field. At long last, it looks as if claims and underwriting will actually share their knowledge effectively, supporting the specialist strategy. As Yogi Berra might have put it, CIGNA's future is different than it used to be.

There are still many problems to contend with, however, in this fall of 1994, such as how to deal with the old environmental and asbestos claims, "the runoff" as they call it, which might better be termed a leak in a dam, because it has the potential to drag the whole company under. But Isom can do little about that now, short of segregating the liabilities and hoping for some improbable regulatory relief. There is also the unanswered issue of what to do with the old legacy systems. Finally, there is the question of the company's physical facilities.

It isn't an urgent issue for Isom, but one against which he wants to tee up a resolution process. Most of the ongoing work concerns work processes; no one has yet fundamentally challenged the organization's physical layout. And yet tremendous costs are tied to the physical facilities they own or lease throughout the country, and how they are arranged dramatically affects the level of service they can provide. Industrywide, companies are pruning their facilities, much as banks have culled their retail networks. Insurers are moving away from small, local marketing and claims offices toward hub-and-spoke configurations, attempting to reap the service benefits of customer proximity while attaining economies of scale. Isom ponders the benefits of such a strategy for CIGNA's marketing centers and claims offices.

A small, early anecdote conveyed his concern about physical infrastructure to his staff. CIGNA's corporate real estate group came to advertise its services to him, and was perhaps a little less critical of its own performance than was warranted.

"Why are we paying $55 per square foot for the home office?" he asked nonchalantly. "Isn't it a lot?" From then on, all knew that something had changed.

Shortly after his arrival, Isom also shut down the Philadelphia marketing center. CIGNA P&C now has three left. The marketing centers house the sales and marketing people, who work with the local agents and are the receiving and processing centers for new requests for proposals, as well as for contract renewals and amendments. There are also some underwriters and claims people at some marketing centers.

Shutting down the Philadelphia marketing center sent a powerful signal. Symbolically, Isom immediately reallocated the twelfth floor of the shut-down marketing center to the transformation team. CIGNA change agents, symbols of the new company, were now sharing elevators with laid-off employees attending career-counseling services. One of those change agents even remembers gallantly offering help to a young lady carrying a heavy box of papers, and triggering the response: "Yeah, if you don't mind. These are the layoff notifications we're about to send out today. You should know something about that."

Each marketing center is a profit center. There is a natural tension between the sales and marketing people, who are always eager to generate more business, and the underwriters, who are quite selective about the risks they're willing to take on. In addition, sales and marketing people take the cross-divisional perspective of agents, who routinely deal with multiple business units within CIGNA P&C and occasionally with other CIGNA divisions. The underwriters, by contrast, look at things from a specialized, transaction-based perspective.

There have been periodic discussions about sending as many underwriters as possible into the marketing centers to relieve some of the tension through co-location. Before Isom they even attempted to develop specialists for each major segment right inside the marketing center, but soon realized there wasn't enough talent available to make the decentralized concept work. Though a laudable goal, making partners of underwriters and sales and marketing people by locating them in the marketing centers seemed impractical.

What to do with the claims offices is an even bigger question mark in Isom's mind. There are a lot of them throughout the U.S., each a small paper factory in its own right. Their locations are largely independent of the marketing centers, the result of a historical compromise between economies of scale and proximity to policyholders and major service providers (doctors, lawyers, and hospitals, for example).

There are various schools of thought about how the claims facilities ought to be configured. Many say the claims agents should be located with the sales and marketing people, arguing that agent satisfaction went up when they could see that their customers—people with claims—were handled with care. If they were in the same office, the sales and marketing person could simply walk down the hall, check the progress of a customer's claim with his colleagues, and call his customer to say, "I just personally checked on it, and your payment will be mailed no later than Friday."

The second school advocates assigning some claims personnel by business, possibly moving them within the offices of the business's underwriters and managers to create solidarity between business management, underwriting, and claims. A good idea, Isom thinks—a team atmosphere between claims and underwriting is critical to his specialist strategy. At the same time, however, the claims people would give up their ability to provide personalized local service.

The third school believes that physical infrastructure is almost irrelevant; information technology could integrate everyone, irrespective of his or her location. With the right information technology tools, they argue, CIGNA P&C can enjoy both the economies of scale and the lateral flexibility of an office-based infrastructure. Moreover, by linking the average agent to a desktop support system containing the combined knowledge of true specialists, he or she could operate at a level close to that of expert. Technology, therefore, would provide the best of both worlds: low cost *and* specialized expertise.

Gerry Isom had attempted several times to broach the issue of physical infrastructure, but failed to build consensus on how to proceed. He was particularly careful concerning the marketing centers, because of the turmoil in recent years. He was also wary of claims, because disruptions in that area could cause losses to escalate rapidly.

He decides to put the physical infrastructure problem on hold while other pieces fall into place; the firm isn't ready for it yet, and that's okay with him. After all, they have corrected the most urgent problem with the shutting down of the Philadelphia marketing center. He will wait for the new producer management, underwriting, and claims processes to fall in place, then come back to it. Sometimes transformation is a game of patience, he thinks.

ALIGNING INDIVIDUAL FACILITIES

Once a facilities network has been laid out, each plant must become an expression of the will of the corporation.

A facility—whether manufacturing plant, distribution center, or clerical unit—is the creature of a complex array of decisions about capacity, location, equipment, layout, flow, and logistics. In theory, the available options are infinite.

As with network decisions, the best way to start paring down the options is to focus on the interface between customers and operations. Pure engineering clearly has a role to play, but every CEO knows that what makes facilities great is not the technical infrastructure, but their alignment with the company's business objectives. Operations become truly effective when they start walking in the shoes of their customers.

Physical facilities often are quite old, their layout reinforcing an outmoded operating paradigm. The huge plants of yesteryear must mutate dramatically to adapt to the much smaller scale model born of the modern need for focus, nimbleness, and flexibility. Making the change is possible, however; some of the world's highest-performing plants are inside GE's and DuPont's huge old sites, or "Works" as they used to be called.

A Fight for Survival at DuPont's Circleville Plant

In 1988, DuPont's Mylar® division was surrounded. On one side, Korean manufacturers were encroaching on the low-end market for packaging applications. At the other end, Japanese competitors were challenging

DuPont's position in thin and ultra-thin films, used to coat capacitors. Even the middle market, consisting of industrial and reprographics applications, was under siege by other American and European manufacturers. The profitability of the Mylar® division was marginal, and its leaders feared that, like the cellophane and other film businesses before them, it might be divested by DuPont.

The Circleville, Ohio plant was one of the three key units of the DuPont Mylar® network, making a wide range of products, varying from the very technical capacitor films, selling at close to $8 a pound, to the $1.50-a-pound packaging applications. It was a multistage plant. In the first stage, polyethylene terephthalate, or PET, was produced in a large, classic chemical reactor, complete with a complex set of manual and automatic controls, requiring constant operator adjustments to maintain temperature and pressure. In the second step, the PET was extruded into film on five parallel lines—much like a paper mill—surrounded by stretching, drying, and rolling machines. In the third step, the films were cut to width and length in an operation called "finishing." In the fourth and final step, many of the films were taken to coating machines for specific treatments such as lamination.

Circleville's production managers focused on meeting quotas set by headquarters, and had never needed to be concerned about aligning production to the requirements of the various businesses. The plant layout was typical: organized by areas, with superintendents for chemical, extrusion, finishing, and coating. Engineering, maintenance, and quality control constituted the other three major departments, and the seven departments converged at the plant manager's level. Few area heads were aware of the differing needs of the businesses or the trouble that some of them were in.

They did know, however, about problems with making the various products. The capacitor film, for example, was a huge pain in the neck. Thin and ultra-thin films had a tendency to break, and each time that happened the extrusion machine had to be reset in a complex and costly operation. Further, the films bruised easily, making them difficult to cut. Worse still, they were very light, so they didn't do much for the production figures, which were measured in pounds. Operators would slave for days on the stuff and get credited with just a few hundred pounds, making it impossible to break the production record displayed prominently in the cafeteria.

From the business's perspective, the capacitor business was quite profitable. They faced competition, mostly from Japan, but it was nowhere near as intense as in packaging, where literally dozens of firms were fighting for the business. In the capacitor business, DuPont wasn't selling pounds of material, it was selling high-performing square inches. It was a great product, and they didn't understand manufacturing's hostility toward it.

Manufacturing people enjoyed making packaging film. It had a nice, thick gauge that held tight throughout the production process. Changeover costs were low. Better still, it fed the production numbers with pounds by the ton load. But from the business's point of view, packaging's profitability was marginal at best, particularly now that the Koreans were keeping them under constant price pressure. It had become a commodity product, subject to price wars.

By 1988, Harry Canfield, the Circleville plant manager, could see the writing on the wall. There was no way the plant was going to make it through the nineties unless production was aligned to business needs. A veteran of the DuPont manufacturing system, and approaching retirement, he was a warm, caring leader who wanted his plant to survive and to continue to provide employment for the community, where he planned to retire.

A reluctant trip to corporate headquarters convinced him that the life of the plant was threatened. On his return, he turned the plant upside down. He went to school on his customers, and encouraged his "troops" to do the same. He also encouraged deeper involvement in the recently formed, cross-functional "business teams," which had been dutifully attended by manufacturing people, but without significant contribution. He invited salespeople and their customers to visit the plant, a practice that previously had been discouraged for fear of leaking production secrets. As a result, Circleville operators began to develop a working dialogue with operators in customer organizations.

Canfield found some early, concrete evidence of progress when, one evening, while leaving his office, he spotted a group of people gathered around a large table covered with electronic instruments, next to casting line number 5. He recognized two quality control engineers and the line operator and they were talking passionately. Wondering why the quality control guys were there (their stations were half a mile away), he approached and asked what they were doing.

"We're moving quality control to the line," the QC engineer said tentatively, "so we can test and provide results with a minimal delay. That way, we'll cut three or four hours from the testing turnaround time."

Seeing the pleased expression on Canfield's face, the operator added, "They're showing me how to run the test any time I want. So if I have a doubt about a setting, I can test and correct it right away, or stop the run if I need to. It'll eliminate all kinds of waste."

It was a great moment for Harry Canfield. Not only had he never thought about putting the QC testing right on the line, he probably would have recommended against it, given what he perceived as the embedded distrust between hourly and salaried workers. But here they were, working together.

Encouraged by such early wins, Canfield personally led an effort to reconfigure the layout of the plant. Each casting line became dedicated to a product: Line 2 to capacitor film; Lines 3 and 4 to industrial and reprographic applications; Line 5 to packaging. Line 1 would be the "swing line." Operators would serve dedicated markets, and constantly work to minimize changeover time.

Influenced by Japanese manufacturing principles, the layout team moved machines that had been bolted to the same floor for decades, improving the flow of product through the plant even though it meant sacrificing some scale economies in casting, finishing, and coating. Over a period of several months, the team moved selected finishing machines to the end of the casting lines, and dedicated them to the production of those lines.

Eventually the floor layout reflected business needs, and changing the organization seemed a natural outcome. They reorganized by business, discarding the old functional orientation. Instead of area superintendents, business teams represented by operators, engineers, quality control inspectors, and managers guided floor operations to meet customer requirements. Their line of responsibility followed a dotted line right to a divisional manager at the corporate level.

The results were spectacular. Inventory fell and quality and service went up, and the team spirit fostered by this new plant layout produced unexpected benefits, such as machine operators keeping an eye on the master rolls, and warning their team mates in casting of potential problems. This new little "wrinkle" solved a long-standing problem of wrinkling, which had cost the casters countless hours of wasted time, and the company thousands of pounds of wasted product.

Changing the plant's management organization seemed a natural corollary of the line specialization gambit, so they swapped their extrusion, finishing, and coating superintendents for capacitor, industrial and reprographics, and packaging *teams.* They also dedicated engineering and quality control people to each business team with a "dotted line" to the functional heads.

Harry Canfield finished his tenure at Circleville, confident that the Circleville plant would survive.

ARTICULATING A SOURCING STRATEGY

In most businesses, raw materials and other supplies are the largest contributors to cost. Cost, however, is only part of the reason sourcing strategy is so important to the CEO. Perhaps the most important reason is that it is integral to the operations strategy.

Tradeoffs are as important to developing successful supplier relationships as they are to aligning individual facilities and facilities networks. Facilities are managed within the value chain of a business. Supplier relationships are managed within the value chain of an industry.

In its simplest form, a sourcing strategy falls somewhere on a continuum between total focus on cost on the one end, to vendor partnerships or exclusive vendor arrangements on the other. In most cases, the nature of the material or part being purchased drives the sourcing behavior. The more commodity-like the part or material, the greater the focus on cost, and the greater the advantage involved in inviting a large number of suppliers to bid on the business. Conversely, the more specialized the sourced item, the more desirable it is to build long-term partnerships with a limited number of suppliers.

In recent years, more and more companies have discovered that how they acquire virtually any material or part may contribute to creating competitive differentiation in the final product or service. In many cases, it is not the intrinsic qualities of the sourced item that count, but the package of services that accompany it. This is why partnership arrangements are gaining market share as the preferred method of sourcing strategies. It is a trend we believe will continue, one that could expand to the point where the lines between businesses blur, and proficiency in business network management will itself become a key source of competitive differentiation.

Tough Purchasing at General Motors

While every other major automotive company was moving toward partnership-based sourcing strategies, General Motors (GM) swam against the tide. Under the leadership of its purchasing head, J. Ignacio Lopez de Arriortua (formerly of GM's European operation, and now departed for Volkswagen), GM played hardball with its suppliers.

Lopez installed a system he had designed himself, Purchase Input Concept Optimization with Suppliers (PICOS)—a classic cost-cutting sourcing strategy. He threw out existing supplier contracts and demanded renegotiation, or auctioned off contracts with as many as 10 bidders for each one, organizing several rounds of bidding to get the price down.

The reaction from suppliers was predictably negative. Some of them undoubtedly felt betrayed. Former recipients of the GM Targets for Excellence quality awards were tossed out just for being slightly underbid. Stories started to circulate about senior executives from GM's major suppliers who had waited for months to get a meeting with Lopez, only to be psychologically "roughed up" when they did.

Although few could afford to walk away from GM's business, some did, like Rockwell, which withdrew from GM's electric car program. Others backed out more subtly, quietly reducing their investments in product development and their levels of customer service support. A few even suspected GM of leaking proprietary drawings to rival suppliers to obtain lower prices.

Lopez also built a team of GM production and sourcing experts who were dispatched to key suppliers and charged with finding additional opportunities for "joint savings." Some suppliers called Lopez's team helpful, but others felt that they were the moral equivalent of industrial terrorists. Lopez's characterization of the team members as "warriors" did little to defuse such charges, nor did the teams' practice of wearing their watches on their right hands to symbolize "new ways."

But GM certainly got results from PICOS. When Rich Wagoner took over from Lopez in May 1993, he claimed that the savings realized in 1993 (compared to a 1990 base) amounted to $4 billion, roughly equivalent to GM's 1992 losses! So no one was surprised when he said he would continue the policy.

Lopez's strategy is questionable. The issue is whether the tough negotiation style initiated by Lopez has undermined the trust of suppliers, and whether the short-term results will prove sustainable. Trust is a fragile thing, and suppliers may find it difficult to forget what happened if GM comes back and tries to involve them in long-term engineering developments.

REDESIGNING
THE WORK
ARCHITECTURE

Muscles are the vehicles of human life. They are workhorses of the brain, turning ideas into action and allowing response to the external environment. They are complex creatures that work in teams, continuously adapting to demands placed upon them while they animate the bones, circulate the blood, and induce other such teams to keep on working. If properly trained and if properly conducted by the nervous system, muscles work together to produce a symphony of motion so fluid that evidence of the individual players all but disappears.

Work processes are the vehicle of business life, the biocorporate equivalent of muscles. Processes translate ideas into chains of activity that support the vision and purpose of the business. They animate the physical infrastructure and determine the *actual* flow of resources through the business. Like muscles, they can be considered in isolation, but are in fact so interconnected that a change in one may affect them all. Also like muscles, they must continuously adapt to the demands placed upon them, or atrophy from lack of stimulation. If properly configured and aligned, and if properly orchestrated by an integrated set of goals and measures, they produce a symphony of value creation so fluid that process boundaries seem to disappear.

Biocorporate muscles have two distinct advantages over the human variety. First, they can be rearranged. Work can be reorganized to achieve radical improvements in efficiency, quality, service level, or a variety of other product or service attributes—a process otherwise known as *re-*

engineering. Second, and far more importantly, work processes have intelligence—they can *learn.* Biocorporate muscles are governed by people, not electrochemical impulses, and people not only can apply knowledge to continuously improve processes, they can identify the critical points of intersection between processes and exchange knowledge across them in a series of continuous *learning loops.*

A corporation's complex network of work and work processes is its *work architecture,* generated by the sixth of the 12 corporate chromosomes. Three genes govern the configuration of the work architecture, implying three, stepwise tasks for the corporation's leaders:

1. *Aligning individual processes for "early wins."* Aligning a process is the reorganization or rationalization of work within a process—the central element of "classic" reengineering. It typically involves improving an operation by mapping it out as a process flow; evaluating it; designing an improved, or "to be," process flow; and then implementing the new design. To be effective, this usually requires deep involvement from a multidisciplinary team representing all of the functions and disciplines involved in the process.

The team acts as the core of a bottom-up mobilization process in which individual work steps and the flow of work are redesigned, while corresponding changes are made in the measures associated with that process and in the roles and responsibilities within the organization. The desired outcome is "early wins," including cultural improvements that boost the company's confidence in its ability to change and financial benefits that help to finance more ambitious redesign activities in the future.

The critical role that the CEO and senior leaders play at this stage involves promoting the alignment of individual processes, highlighting accomplishments, and reassuring employees that the effort isn't a disguised attempt to reduce head count.

2. *Fostering complete alignment of individual processes.* Processes don't exist in isolation; each affects and is affected by all 12 of the biocorporate systems. Individual process alignment focuses on creating the early wins needed to sustain the change effort, involving only four chromosomes: mobilization, work architecture, measures, and organization. This stage, a natural progression from the first, adds a new order of complexity to process reengineering, involving the interplay of possibly all 12 chromosomes and their corresponding biocorporate systems.

The company begins to use less direct, and often more costly, change levers, such as new technology and changes in physical infrastructure. It begins to broaden the scope of individual process redesign, bringing in the customer view and perhaps introducing the possibility of growing new businesses. Many firms, such as Xerox, Merck, Ford, and Motorola, have managed to improve their performances significantly in this way.

At this stage the CEO and other leaders become more deeply involved, for the very genome of the corporation may begin to change. They communicate the scope of the effort, remove roadblocks to progress, and perhaps most importantly, begin to look at the effort in the context of the Balanced Scorecard they are developing. In the first step, strategy and the investment base were assumed as a given. No more; now everything is negotiable.

3. *Generating learning loops.* Drawing from the work of the first two steps, this step elevates reengineering into a new realm: *bioreengineering.* Processes react not only with the systems of the corporate body, but also with each other. They are connected at many and various points within the 12 biocorporate systems. Moreover, new points of intersection can be created. The trick is to locate or create the strategically important *connectivity* points, then build cause-effect connectors between them to generate *learning loops.*

Early and secondary wins have paved the way, but the design logic changes here. The company now sees itself as a complex system of interwoven processes that must be redesigned concurrently. The goals and measures of the Balanced Scorecard represent the yardstick of the company's success, providing the logic for measuring the success of each process. But the metabolic link between process success and corporate success is complex, if indeed it exists at all. Building, growing, and nurturing those metabolic pathways is what generating learning loops is all about.

At this stage, senior leadership's role becomes intimate. Their objective is to ensure that process performance feeds corporate performance by linking the top-down, corporate goals and measures of the Balanced Scorecard with bottom-up, process goals and measures. Hypotheses are formed about where the critical connectivity points are, or *should* be, between and across processes, and are then tested at the process level. Through examination of cause and effect, through both logic and gambling, the links gradually are generated, forging metabolic pathways that create learning loops. And through those loops, vital information and knowledge flow to and from processes and systems, feeding them with the vital information required to act and react, often transforming the fundamental nature of the processes involved.

Although the logic of reconfiguring the work architecture may appear neat and sequential, the reconfiguration process seldom is. It may start as a small, site-based initiative to improve productivity, migrating slowly to other facilities and then exploding into a corporatewide effort that finally captures senior management's attention. Conversely, it may start as a directive from senior management to cut costs, maturing into a full-fledged work redesign as the connectivity between processes is revealed.

No matter what the starting point, the leader's task is to encourage migration of the small into the big, and the big into the small. The goal is to align processes with all 12 biocorporate systems and with each other in ever increasing orders of complexity, but in such a way that the flow of work, value, and knowledge is continuously simplified and improved. Early wins provide the fuel, measurements the motivator, and learning loops the metabolic pathways needed to fundamentally reconfigure the work architecture of the biological corporation.

ALIGNING INDIVIDUAL PROCESSES FOR "EARLY WINS"

Aligning individual work processes falls into the domain of what is now called *reengineering*. Reengineering is a hot topic these days, and when methodologies get hot, they unavoidably draw both zealots and detractors. Some say reengineering is a pathway to the new economic order. (A "manifesto." Really?) Others say it is little more than a warmed-over quality movement, with a few added ingredients thrown in. As usual, the truth probably lies somewhere in between.

Reengineering involves the reorganization of the work of a business, with work processes as the focal point of analysis and improvement. When work processes change, so must the organizational roles and responsibilities that accompany them, so that too is part of reengineering. In this sense, reengineering is very similar to classic industrial engineering practices, and even more similar to the Japanese *kaizen*, a business philosophy of continuous improvement. What makes it different is the radical nature of the redesign proposed.

The term *reengineering* first appeared in the early 1990s, in Michael Hammer's *Harvard Business Review* article "Don't automate, obliterate." Hammer further elaborated on the concept in a book. Essentially, he discarded the old notion, "If it ain't broke, don't fix it," replacing it with the more ambitious, "Let's make it the best in the world." It's a helpful approach, especially in its reframing dimension—it helps people break the mold when redesigning processes. Any radicalism, however, ends there; the methodology of "classic" reengineering is quite pedestrian.

Individual process alignment is the first component of classic reengineering. A cross-functional team drives the alignment effort, using a bottom-up mobilization process to get more and more people involved, as described in Chap. 1. Their task is to develop a flow chart depicting the existing process work structure; identify problems; design the new process; establish new measures; redefine the accompanying organizational roles and responsibilities; and then put the new process and organization in place. Thus, four of the twelve corporate systems are involved: *mobilization, work architecture, measures, and organization.*

Typically it begins by bringing together as many of the people involved in the process as possible, and getting them to map the chronological flow of work. The focus usually is on analyzing "a day in the life of" something, such as an order being processed, a product being made, or a complaint being handled. This exercise in *process mapping* is very helpful, because it often reveals glaring inefficiencies that can be corrected quickly to produce bottom-line results—the "early wins" needed to pay for the more ambitious redesign work of the second and third work architecture genes.

Because most companies are organized into discrete functional slices, people rarely get a view of the whole process to which they contribute, much less discuss possible disconnects with colleagues from other functions. Suddenly, an order entry clerk sees that a seemingly small error in coding a customer address sends a delivery truck aimlessly wandering through a distant neighborhood; or a machine operator discovers that loading palettes differently makes room for one extra palette on the truck; or the IT department realizes that the apparently silly, redundant updating of data (which, of course, rarely gets done) puts customer service agents in a position to accurately tell customers whether the item they want is in stock.

Discovered errors like these add up, and when collectively corrected, yield significant benefits. The disconnected pieces can be put back together and the redundant steps eliminated, directly impacting the bottom line through cost reduction, improved cycle-time, and increased service effectiveness. The alignment of previously disconnected pieces alone often generates savings significantly greater than the cost of the effort.

Thus, the key to "classic" reengineering is less the analytical method used than the effectiveness of the team-based mobilization process. If mobilization does its job, people get involved and generate insights worth a lot of money. Effective meetings, rigorous problem-solving frameworks, and a proper understanding of the dynamics of individual change are more important at this stage than creative representation or the true redesign of processes.

Picking Low-Hanging Fruit at Woodbridge Papers

We last left Karl and his team basking in the glory of their successful Focus play, the redesign of their network of plants and production within them. But even before that had all come about, they had had to wrestle with the more mundane issues of the order-to-delivery process. In fact, it was in the mundane that they first found something they could really sink their teeth into. Here we step back to the time before they developed their grand scheme, when they were still involved in looking at the nuts and bolts of the process.

Karl was sitting in his office, looking at the large map of the order-to-delivery process they had put together. It had been quite a process, getting everyone involved together to map the whole thing out. Now that they were done, he really didn't need to look at the map anymore. Every detail was in his head, he himself could draw it from scratch, and he delighted in showing everyone what was wrong with it. When he told the story, he could barely conceal the pride he felt at having uncovered such shameful secrets.

"First," he would begin, "look at the number of mistakes we make entering orders—wrong product codes, delivery dates, and addresses. Now that those people understand the role they play, they'll be more careful, especially since they've met the people who suffer the consequences of their mistakes. But we need to do more than that. What we need to do is make them responsible and accountable for being accurate, build a feedback loop somehow, and measure them on it. Our team is working on that now. Cutting those numbers by 90 percent may not make the company rich, but it's a start."

He could go through the whole process that way. The next step was credit checking. Right after the order was entered, they were supposed to verify that the customer was in good standing with Woodbridge. The problem there was that credit clerks quit at 3:30 in the afternoon, while the order entry clerks worked until 5:00. Orders entered after 3:30 got left for the next day, wasting a day of cycle time. With Mountain View stealing customers through shorter delivery times, one day was a lot of time on the production calendar.

Karl's team had devised a simple solution: align the hours of credit checking with those of order entry—everybody goes home at 5:00 P.M. A small subteam of the credit checkers were investigating more radical ideas, such as checking credit only on large orders, which potentially could reduce 70 percent of the workload.

The biggest problem of all was that at each stage of the process there was lag time. Karl and his team discovered that of the 30 days of lead time they quoted to customers, only two were used to "move the ball forward," as Karl put it. Most of the time the order was simply in a queue, waiting idly for something to happen. One of the worst cases of this was right on the production line. The single biggest wasted chunk of time resulted from waiting for enough orders to accumulate to justify a production run. And the reason they waited was that changing over could eat up one or two days, as the additives and dyes from the prior run purged through the system. They couldn't think of any quick fixes for that one, but the discovery had helped spark the idea for their Focus approach.

They could find a way to reduce changeover time, however; they were determined to. So they launched a subteam with the manufacturing folks, who discovered that there was a lot that could be done, such as adopting a "changeover team" concept. The idea was so simple that Karl couldn't believe they weren't already doing it. Previously, it had been every operator for himself when it came to changing products on the machine. But since the machines don't require constant attention while running, all available operators could pitch in on every changeover. They might not get as many trashy novels read on the job, but it would probably make their job a lot more interesting.

FOSTERING COMPLETE ALIGNMENT OF INDIVIDUAL PROCESSES

The first stage of redesigning the work architecture brings only 4 of the 12 corporate chromosomes into play: mobilization (Karl's team), work architecture (should we do credit checking, and how?), measures (how do we measure the performance of the order entry clerk?), and organization (how do we make the order-entry clerks responsible and accountable for accuracy?). Complete alignment, however, requires involvement of the other eight as well, and offers far more spectacular results.

Bringing in the other eight is far more complex than the first four, however. The first four are essentially free, and the results they produce are more than enough to pay for the relatively nominal costs involved. Nor did they require much attention from top management (Karl and his team did just fine on their own). But when the whole corporate genome is involved, the reach of the alignment effort grows broader and deeper, the resource and cost commitments are larger, and the timeline for achieving results extends further into the future. The company's leaders, therefore, need to be involved, not just because of the size and the scope of the commitments, but because the "biological essence" of the corporation may begin to change. To completely realign a process, both bottom-up and top-down involvements are required.

Since both top-down and bottom-up initiatives are involved, measurements become much more critical at this stage. If the Balanced Scorecard or some similar set of goals and measures hasn't been established, this is the time when leaders must turn their attention to building them. From the top-down perspective, goals and measures are needed to prioritize the many alignment initiatives under way, to decide upon the resource commitment to each, and to track performance along the way. From the bottom-up perspective, goals and measures are needed for the same reasons, but on a localized, initiative by initiative basis.

The trick in aligning top-down and bottom-up initiatives is to build an integrated measurement system, which is the leader's responsibility. It can be accomplished by linking the Balanced Scorecard to KPI trees, and making periodic adjustments to it through a structured review process, as discussed in Chap. 3.

Plugging the Leaky Pipes in Telephone Service Activation

A good example of the complexity involved in complete process alignment is service activation in phone companies. Most of us have suffered through the aggravating experience of getting new telephone service. Someone has to be at home, the person on the phone tells you. No, they can't say exactly when the installer will be there—either morning or afternoon, take your choice. Then the installer gets there, only to inform you of some problem. He'll try to get to it today, but he doesn't have the right materials in the truck. In the end, it eats up nearly two days of your work week.

But then again, many of us have had the experience of calling the phone company, giving them the new service information, and within five minutes or so the customer service representative tells us, "You will have service by 5:00 P.M. this evening." When you go home, you pick up the phone and hear the lovely sound of a dial tone. What makes the difference? Why can't it always be the second scenario?

The answer is "leaky pipes," but not of the water or sewer variety.

Most phone companies scramble with "leaky pipes." In an ideal world, you'd call for service, and everything would happen electronically. The customer service agent would enter everything you want into a computer; all the physical infrastructure, from the exchange to your house, would be in place; the electronic circuitry would create the necessary connections; and you'd be in business.

There's a small problem, however. The electronic pipe has leaks every-where. It leaks because the customer service agent makes a mistake when entering your order. It leaks when there's a problem with the line to your house, or with one of the switches outside your house. It leaks when the soft-ware handling the electronic switching of your home has a bug in it, or when the database of records is incorrect. It leaks if there have been problems in updating the billing system. And every leak requires a plumber—a time-con-suming intervention, whether of the physical or the electronic variety.

On average, fewer than 30 percent of orders flow through the service activation process without leaks of one kind or another; that is, some man-ual intervention is required in about two out of three cases. When the elec-tronic pipeline *doesn't* leak, the phone company makes a profit on the installation. When a "plumber" is required, they make less profit, or may actually lose on the transaction. Therefore, the central alignment challenge in service activation is to minimize leaks.

Many of the leaks can be plugged using the standard process-mapping and alignment techniques described previously, with the goal of aligning policies, procedures, and measures across departments and functions. For example, suppose someone has asked for service, but there's a faulty line or connection outside the house. The customer service people want that switch fixed, pronto, because their priority, and their measure of perfor-mance, is happy customers and a reputation for excellent service. The people in installation and maintenance, responsible both for installations and repair, share a desire to fix the leak, but may be driven by a different set of priorities. For example, if their primary goal is to minimize the total cost of sending trucks and technicians across the service area, then their work schedule will be set up that way, resulting in lengthy delays in impor-tant service orders and leaving the customer *and* the customer service people frustrated. Putting the mobilization system to work can fix those kinds of problems.

But the mobilization system can do only so much; first-level reengi-neering is only part of the answer. Many other biocorporate systems must be brought into play to make a telephone company a top performer in ser-vice activation.

Technology plays a key role. Telephone companies are effectively "managed by wire"; that is, their entire operation is managed electronical-ly. Ideally, everything is infinitely reprogrammable and interconnected. The ideal scenario runs like this: You call and decide you want "call wait-ing"; the service representative changes your electronic file; through a chain of electronic events, you have the new feature; and the telephone company starts billing you for this additional service. In outstanding tele-phone companies, it actually does work like that.

Advanced telephone companies have connected or combined their databases, and can get the customer service, the repair and maintenance, the network, and the invoicing databases to function interactively. On the high-tech end of the spectrum, some companies are installing "soft-dial" technologies, which allow new residents to place the order for new service by plugging in to the very line they want activated (they can connect only to the local phone company)! The leaders are forging ahead, while less well managed companies are bogged down with problems caused by legacy (out-of-date) systems, patching the leaks because the older systems cannot be effectively connected to one another.

Physical infrastructure also plays a major role in the effectiveness of the service activation process. Each year, telephone companies have to make costly decisions about their network. First, they face major technological choices; for example, whether to stay with conventional cable or convert to fiber optics. Second, the location of network facilities is critical, requiring investment in large, expensive "chunks." Before a company can decide where to place these chunks, it needs a vision of how it ought to deploy its network across its franchise area. Traditionally, companies have opted for large, standardized central offices. More and more they are moving toward smaller, "hub-and-spoke" arrangements, investing in technology that can be better tailored to the customers' needs within a small geographic area.

Another option for preventing leaks is to have a large, over-built network of physical facilities, increasing the probability that whenever a customer calls, the physical infrastructure will already be in place. But clearly this is a costly option, involving major tradeoffs between the investment cost and the cost of sending trucks on an as-needed basis.

Phone companies also need an *economic model* to guide them in the allocation of service activation resources. Like those in many other industries, telephone customers want tailormade, flexible products and services. Some residential customers may want a single line with rotary dialing, period. Others may want four lines, with a portfolio of options that rivals that of a fairly sophisticated business. A small business, on the other hand, may want nothing but a pay phone. A large corporation may want a phone company to build its entire internal network. In other words, some orders are simple and others are complex, and often it does not break down neatly into consumer versus commercial segmentation schemes.

Most telephone companies fail to recognize this distinction, and treat all orders in the same way. The result is cross-infection: Basic customers fume about high service charges, because of the high cost of the standardized service activation process, while complex customers complain about not being able to find a single person who can help them with all of their needs; and both bemoan how long it takes to get connected. Activity-based costing and service-level assessment, both part of the economic modeling process discussed in Chap. 4, can be helpful in resolving these issues.

Market focus is another vantage point critical to resolving the diversity of customer needs. It may be helpful, for example, to elevate some customer service agents to the level of consultant for complex customers, developing them into experts (*individual learning* comes into play here) who can help a customer design a system to meet the needs of *its* customers.

Karl's Team Gets More Ambitious

The champagne bottles have long been empty; Woodbridge Papers is planning to reorganize and realign its six plants in North America; and Karl's team is still far from finished redesigning the order-to-delivery process. Encouraged by its early success, Karl's team is now expanding its horizons further, venturing into all corners of the organization that touch the order-to-delivery process. They are doing it with management's blessing, and for good reason: The initiatives launched by their team have realized close to $20 million in cost reductions, not counting the future benefits of the "Focus play," and most of those will recur annually. The organization is starting to take them seriously, and the time is right to make a bid for additional resources.

They have two ideas pertaining to physical infrastructure. The first is a derivative of the Focus initiative, and has to do with getting products to the California market from the northeast region. They want to build a warehouse. It won't be cheap, but no matter how they look at the problem, it's clear that's the only way they can reach customers in California within 10 days. They have considered shipping from the Midwest, the nearest set of plants and warehouses, but they would have to allow four days to reach the hinterlands of the West Coast, which doesn't leave enough for order entry, scheduling, and manufacturing. Inelegant though their solution is, there appears to be no viable alternative.

The second idea is to make hot-slitting standard in all plants. Manufacturing is now pushing hard to get slitting machines installed at the end of the paper manufacturing line, arguing that if you slit the paper hot, you get lower work-in-process inventory, higher productivity, and less waste. It would be a major step, involving a fundamental rethinking of the factory layout, but the economic model projects benefits too good to pass up.

"I can't believe this modest idea from the Chicago plant has traveled this far," Karl thinks.

Technology also is raising its head slowly, which is ironic, considering Karl's almost innate aversion to it. The team is kicking around the idea of installing SAP nationwide, the very system Karl used to say was appropriately named. It's an integrated production software program, such that an order entry would automatically post scheduling, transportation, billing, and other transactions that rely on the same data. That would eliminate all the time wasted in trying to reconcile the various small databases and systems throughout the company. Karl, once the strongest disbeliever of them all, has been converted by seeing it in operation at other companies.

In the credit area, they are tinkering with the notion of automating the process with a new computer application that could bring up the credit status of the customer while the order is being taken. Finance isn't keen on the idea, because the credit clerks are worried about their jobs, and the managers aren't sure the order entry clerks could be trained to become credit analysts. It doesn't feel great thinking about changes that might mean lost jobs, but better to do it now, Karl thinks, ahead of the competition, than be forced into it by the competition and not have the resources available for training.

Organizational issues also are growing in importance. For example, the tension between scheduling and transportation isn't helping much. Karl, as former combatant, knows firsthand what is involved. In another twist of fate, it's his idea to put scheduling and transportation under the same leadership, perhaps to create a Vice President of Materials Management, or some such equivalent. Neither he nor the team feels confident making such a sweeping recommendation, but then again that was what they felt about the Focus idea.

They also are becoming aware of the key role played by the reward system. If there is one silver bullet, this had to be it. The way things are, nobody cares much about the cycle time involved in the order-to-delivery process. Scheduling people and transportation folks, in particular, worry about the cost of changeovers and the cost per mile transported, for example, but never consider their contribution to the order fulfillment's cycle time to be particularly relevant. If they were measured and rewarded by lead time, too, then a lot of the needed changes would happen by themselves.

The team is considering a lot of things in a lot of areas, but the biggest and still unresolved issue on Karl's mind is the same one that reared its ugly head many months ago: to cut or not to cut the product line.

In the absence of a carefully crafted set of integrated goals, Karl is still on the fence. Marketing has said that Mountain View, with its 10-day lead time, is killing them, because theirs is 30 days. Or *was* 30 days—now it is 20, and falling. By this view, his mission is clear—*cut lead time!*—and if they prune the product line, he knows he can get there faster. Of course, marketing then will make noise about the disappearance of those exotic products. But what do they know about manufacturing? If they had it their way, they would have their cake and eat it too: the world's broadest product line, and the world's shortest lead time. Get real, marketing!

Streamlining would help in order entry, for example, where lots of mistakes are made because the clerks or the customers get confused by the sheer number of selections in the catalog. It also would help in billing: Accounting wouldn't have to search through reams and reams of paper just to find the right price, if the right price was available. When the price sheet isn't updated, it causes endless invoicing errors and arguments with the customers. Fewer products would mean fewer prices and fewer updates; translation: fewer errors, and less wasted time.

The real boon would come in manufacturing, however. He is a scheduler, and he knows: It's a *nightmare* trying to fit small-quantity products into the production program. No matter what they do with the plants, there's still the problem of interrupting long batches and gearing up the machines for a batch of stuff that takes just a few hours to make. The changeover time takes longer than the actual run! It's like driving a Ferrari wide open, but having to stop periodically to let a couple of donkeys cross the road in front of you. Get rid of the donkeys, and let the Testarosas *vroom*!

That's it! He will recommend pruning the product line. But then again, what if marketing is right...?

The Metamorphosis of Union Carbide

Less than a decade ago, Union Carbide was a vulnerable, wounded animal, all but written off by Wall Street analysts. Today, it is among the Dow Jones Industrial's star performers.

Through 1984, Union Carbide was a huge, dispersed conglomerate, struggling to achieve consistently acceptable shareholder return. Then, in 1984 and 1985, it was dealt two such staggering blows that its very survival was questioned. First, a disastrous gas leak occurred in its Bhopal, India, plant, resulting in the deaths of more than 2000 people. Although the evidence ultimately pointed to sabotage by a disgruntled Indian employee, Union Carbide immediately assumed moral responsibility. Nevertheless, the Indian government protracted the litigation process, and a torrent of bad publicity shook the Carbide culture to its roots.

The second blow was a hostile takeover bid, led by Samual Heyman of GAF Corp. Although the timing certainly was no accident, the thrust of Heyman's logic had little to do with the disaster in India. Heyman's argument was simple: Carbide had grossly undermanaged its assets. The bidding battle that followed brought the firm to the point of surrender, but it survived in the end by auctioning off its profitable and popular consumer products businesses, which boasted Eveready Batteries, Glad Bags, and Prestone antifreeze, among other products. In the aftermath, the company was a shadow of its former self. From being on a par with Dow, DuPont, and the big German chemical conglomerates, it had become a second-tier player on the chemical stage.

Today, Union Carbide is a lean, focused chemical company that nearly quadrupled shareholder value between December 1990 and December 1994. In April 1993, Merrill Lynch stated, "Union Carbide was the best performing stock in the Dow Jones Industrials last year, largely due to a massive cost reduction and restructuring program, which included the spinoff of the industrial gas division." Said Paine Webber about the restructuring effort, "Some companies talk a good game when it comes to total quality, employee empowerment, and value creation, but Carbide is writing the book on it." Carbide again led the Dow in 1994.

How did they do it?

It started with leadership, with Carbide CEO Robert Kennedy and Bill Joyce, now Carbide's president. To Kennedy, the past was full of issues, but as he has said, "Companies don't run on issues, they run on values." A lifetime employee, Kennedy valued Carbide. First and foremost, he believed the firm had to find focus and become what to him its name implied, a world-class chemicals company. The problem was how.

Kennedy, Joyce, and the leadership team took a contrarian approach. While all major chemical companies were placing their bets on specialties—chemicals whose value lay predominantly in the application engineering and marketing knowhow of the firm, not in the economics of its manufacturing—Carbide decided it would take its stand as a commodity chemicals company. It was a case of unconventional wisdom. While competitors focused their investments on product research and development, some of them even venturing into pharmaceuticals and biotechnology, Union Carbide invested in scale, process technology, and its raw materials position, with the goal of becoming the world's leading supplier of ethylene, polyethylene, and their derivatives. They would do so through scale economies and technology leadership. Skeptics abounded, seeing the strategy as tantamount to Bill Haley and the Comets trying to make a comeback when grunge rock had become the rage.

But Union Carbide proved the merits of its approach. Today the firm is an uncontested leader in the production of ethylene-based products. The ethylene chain includes a long list of chemical products with technical names that a musical friend of ours refers to as *monochlorotrombone* and *polychlorosaxophone*. More seriously, ethylene and its derivatives are among the raw materials for a vast array of products, including automotive antifreeze, polyester (used as a blend in many different textiles, and as the sole fabric in suits worn by the archetypical car salesman), and soaps, to name a very few. The company also has become one of the leading suppliers of polyethylene, a plastic made from strings of ethylene put together and used to make garbage cans, squeeze bottles, toys, car parts, packaging products, and a list of other products too numerous to mention.

Union Carbide also has a position in solvents and coatings and even in specialty chemicals, but the remarkable thing is that virtually everything it does is built upon the chemistry of the ethylene molecule, which no one knows better than Union Carbide. That makes it difficult for anyone to find a chink in their chemically coated armor.

But reaching its position of preeminence didn't come easy. Articulating the strategic vision was only the beginning. Then they had to deliver on the promise.

Carbide Pioneers Reengineering Before the Term Is Coined

In late 1990, Carbide launched what would become, and what remains today, one of the largest and most conspicuously successful reengineering programs ever undertaken. Under the corporatewide banner of EQ:AI (Excellence through Quality: Accelerated Improvement), the company proceeded to redesign all of its key processes worldwide. No stone was left unturned, but that doesn't imply that EQ:AI is a thing of the past. As Kennedy and Joyce would be quick to point out, it is a way of life at Union Carbide.

The origins of the effort date back to 1988, when each of the four chemicals and plastics divisions had begun to focus management attention on a work process critical to improving its performance. Polyolefins was concerned about new material and in-plant logistics; Industrial Chemicals was concerned about upgrading maintenance; and Solvents and Coatings Materials was learning how to improve its customer-related processes. The broadest initiative, however, was that of the Specialty Chemicals Division (SCD).

Under the new commodities orientation, SCD's position was somewhat precarious; after all, it was in the specialty chemicals business. This was especially alarming in light of the recent sale of the polyols unit, a significant part of Carbide's portfolio, to Arco Chemical. In addition, SCD's two plants in South Charleston, in the Kanawha Valley of West Virginia, were suffering from the loss of several high-volume production units. The president of SCD, Joe Soviero, recognized that the very survival of his division might hinge on whether it could be, not just profitable, but one of Carbide's star performers. Soviero decided to launch a major improvement initiative, one unlike anything Union Carbide had ever seen before.

The project was to focus on sales effectiveness, managing the business portfolio at the divisional level, and "work simplification" (AKA, reengineering) at the Kanawha Valley plants. SCD's initiative proved to be a significant advancement for Union Carbide's existing corporatewide quality program known as EQ (Excellence through Quality). It would also prove to be a pilot for the entire corporation.

By mid-1990, the program had been so successful, particularly at the Kanawha plants, that Soviero pushed for an analysis to identify more opportunities for improvement across the entire division.

In late 1990, Soviero brought his proposal to the chemicals and plastics presidents council, which consists of the five divisional presidents. Just when it was about to be approved, however, Bill Lichtenberger, then Carbide's president, made a fateful statement: "If we go that route with SCD, why can't we mount an enterprise-wide effort that encompasses initiatives from all divisions?"

Carbide had long encouraged each president to run his division as a separate business. The meetings of the council were intended as a forum for the exchange of information, and as a means of keeping the high-level objectives of each division relatively aligned. They could sense that that was changing.

Each president committed to lead at least one initiative for the total chemicals and plastics business, not just his own division. Every division in Union Carbide was now in the reengineering dance. Kennedy supported the broadened set of initiatives and, recognizing an emerging new operations paradigm within the company, endorsed the birth of EQ:AI.

The plan called for each division to pick a target process and then design and implement it. If the therapy was successful, the division would be responsible for migrating the program to other divisions (Fig. 6.1). For example, the Specialty Chemicals Division took on accountability for developing a new production management process, as well as a worldwide business management process. The Industrial Chemicals Division offered to pioneer the development of the future maintenance process. The Polyolefins Division assumed ownership of logistics. The Solvents and Coatings Division focused on outbound logistics, the process of moving product to the customer. All the divisions signed up. It was the corporate equivalent of the unification of Germany in the nineteenth century, when, after centuries of rivalry, all provinces joined to become one of the most powerful nations in modern history.

The idea behind the council's plan was simple, but powerful. Ideally each initiative, if successful, would spread like wildfire across the whole corporation. In practice, each initiative was predominantly successful, but the migration process met with resistance. The wildfires hadn't caught on. What they needed was an engine to drive the fires throughout the organization.

That engine came in the person of the newly appointed COO, Bill Joyce, now Union Carbide's president. Joyce was relentless, driving cost-reduction goals that no one thought they could reach, and driving their achievement ahead of schedule. When they were reached, he and the division presidents set the goals even higher, continuously stretching Carbide's performance standards. Under Joyce, division heads could still run their organizations independently, but only if doing so served the vision and values of the corporation as a whole. Joyce gave the presidents council some teeth. His management style was fair, but tough. He set forth goals and objectives, then let each leader decide how to achieve them. Joyce was implicitly saying to each of them, "It is your responsibility; you decide. But if you don't take responsibility, I'll make the decision for you."

Among his many other leadership attributes, Joyce understood the importance of some healthy internal competition. If Specialty Chemicals can knock tens of millions off of its production costs, why can't you, Industrial Chemicals, or you, Solvents and Coatings, or you, Polyolefins? What are they doing right that you're not? At the same time, he had to encourage sharing of the knowledge to knock down the walls between divisions. He did that by fostering the practice of using teams represented by multiple divisions to guide the planning and implementation of projects. This gave each division the legitimate right to destroy the ramparts of its neighbors, with the clear understanding that their neighbors would be doing the same to them.

One of the most challenging and important tasks the multidivisional teams faced was getting the leaders and managers of each division to "sign up" for a set of benefit targets. When Kennedy announced the initial $200 million chemicals and plastics cost-cutting target (which, when delivered ahead of schedule, was raised to $400 million by Joyce and the presidents, and later even higher), the question remained open of how much Specialty Chemicals, Polyolefins, etc. should be responsible and accountable for, and why.

It was a difficult challenge, which required the development of an enormous amount of trust from the division heads. They were being asked for a solemn commitment to bottom-line improvements, but had no direct control over many of the reengineering resources involved. It took almost a full year to clarify the targets and the portion of the targets each division would "own." But in the end, the discipline of this process forced each division to develop a business case for its process alignment efforts, providing a set of targets and responsibilities that were aligned to the high-level cor-

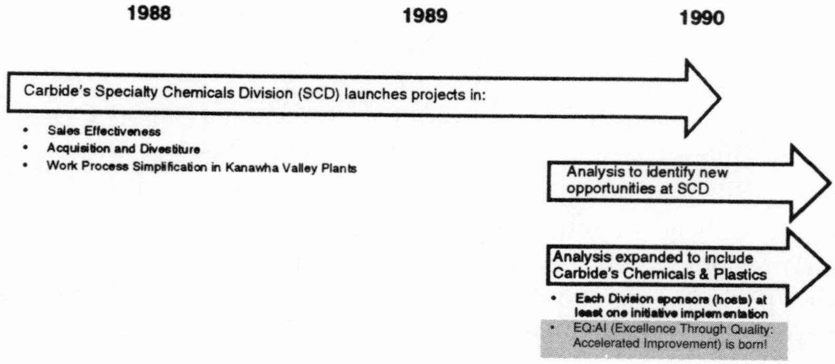

1988   **1989**   **1990**

Carbide's Specialty Chemicals Division (SCD) launches projects in:

- Sales Effectiveness
- Acquisition and Divestiture
- Work Process Simplification in Kanawha Valley Plants

Analysis to identify new
opportunities at SCD

Analysis expanded to include
Carbide's Chemicals & Plastics

- Each Division sponsors (hosts) at
  least one initiative implementation
- EQ:AI (Excellence Through Quality:
  Accelerated Improvement) is born!

Figure 6.1. *Project Migration at Union Carbide.*

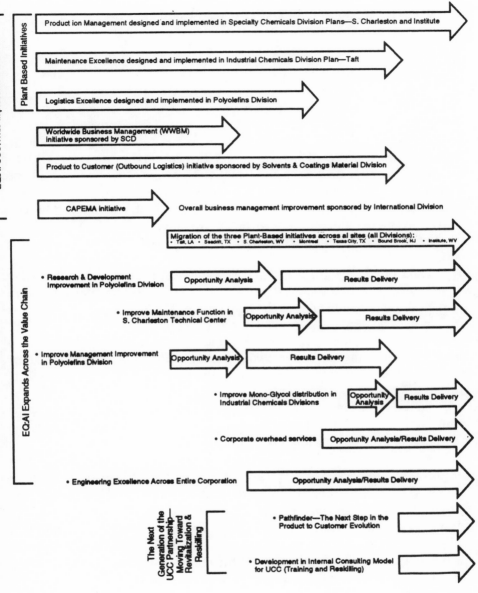

EQ:AI-UCC-Wide Improvement Effort

1991 1992 1993

Plant Based Initiatives

Product ion Management designed and implemented in Specialty Chemicals Division Plans—S. Charleston and Institute

Maintenance Excellence designed and implemented in Industrial Chemicals Division Plan—Taft

Logistics Excellence designed and implemented in Polyolefins Division

Worldwide Business Management (WWBM) initiative sponsored by SCD

Product to Customer (Outbound Logistics) initiative sponsored by Solvents & Coatings Material Division

CAPEMA initiative   Overall business management improvement sponsored by International Division

EQ:AI Expands Across the Value Chain

Migration of the three Plant-Based initiatives across al sites (all Divisions):
• Taft, LA • Seadrift, TX • S. Charleston, WV • Montreal • Texas City, TX • Bound Brook, NJ • Institute, WV

• Research & Development Improvement in Polyolefins Division   Opportunity Analysis   Results Delivery

• Improve Maintenance Function in S. Charleston Technical Center   Opportunity Analysis   Results Delivery

• Improve Management Improvement in Polyolefins Division   Opportunity Analysis   Results Delivery

• Improve Mono-Glycol distribution in Industrial Chemicals Divisions   Opportunity Analysis   Results Delivery

• Corporate overhead services   Opportunity Analysis/Results Delivery

• Engineering Excellence Across Entire Corporation   Opportunity Analysis/Results Delivery

The Next Generation of the UCC Partnership—Moving Toward Revitalization & Reskilling

• Pathfinder—The Next Step in the Product to Customer Evolution

• Development in Internal Consulting Model for UCC (Training and Reskilling)

porate goals and against which its performance could be measured. Clearly, belonging to the new Union Carbide meant much, much more than simply reigning supreme over one's own division.

Full-Scale Migration

Under Kennedy and Joyce's leadership, both top-down and bottom-up measures helped EQ:AI take hold, and the wildfires started to spread across Carbide's entire value chain. The first two projects, in particular, provided the early wins needed to get the corporatewide effort off the ground. The first one, sponsored by SCD, involved turning around the production management process of its ailing plants near South Charleston, Virginia. The second, sponsored by the Industrial Chemicals Division (ICD), was a maintenance improvement initiative in Taft, Louisiana. Both were hugely successful, producing model processes that would be rolled out to the entire corporation.

The impact of the Kanawha Valley and Taft initiatives was dramatic. The early wins they achieved were of huge proportions, and the entire organization took notice, with the help of a corporatewide communications program. The process alignment projects produced not only results but heroes, and the winning spirit was infectious. Suddenly other maintenance departments in the Carbide network started inviting the Taft maintenance team to come to their plant, in spite of the fact that it would unavoidably result in manpower reduction.

Armed with these early successes, Chairman Kennedy, supported by Bill Joyce, decided it was time for a major cost-reduction effort across the corporation. In 1991 he announced what seemed then an incredible stretch target of $275 million in cost reductions, including a 17 percent reduction of fixed costs to be achieved by 1993. Moreover, Kennedy made it clear that across-the-board layoffs were unacceptable; he wanted the reductions to stem from work simplification. As Bill Joyce once put it, "We can't deliver the performance required to be world-class, if we're bogged down with obsolete systems and processes. We must simplify the work we do." In 1992, when empowered teams throughout the company made it clear that there were many more savings opportunities, the cost-reduction goal was enlarged to $575 million and extended for a year. By year-end 1994, the program was a complete success.

Driven by the cost-reduction target from the top, and the impetus of early and ongoing wins from the bottom, the reengineering effort took off, involving not just manufacturing processes but also areas such as the entire engineering operation across the corporation, the distribution of mono-glycol, corporate support services, and R&D. Virtually every segment of the value chain was touched by the reengineering program. Carbide employees in every part and at every level of the company—management and hourly, union and nonunion—made contributions to its success.

The effort was not, however, focused solely on cost-cutting. The spin-off of Praxair, for example, was a premier example of improving share-holder value through inventive portfolio management. None of the other gas companies such as Air Liquide, Air Products, and British Oxygen was affiliated with a major chemical firm, and all of them carried higher multi-ples than chemical companies. Spinning off Praxair, Kennedy thought, would unleash its hidden value. He was right. Shortly after its flotation in 1993, the combined prices of the two stocks was double that of the origi-nal Carbide shares. (Carbide shareholders were granted an equal share of Praxair stock as part of the offering.)

Thus the Union Carbide of today is an integrated, focused, commodi-ty chemicals company, bearing little resemblance to the sprawling con-glomerate it was just a decade ago. And it is well on the way toward mak-ing its vision a reality.

Having "written the book" on reengineering, the challenge for Union Carbide is to master Revitalization with similar speed and skill. We are con-fident that it will.

GENERATING LEARNING LOOPS

As the Union Carbide story illustrates, redesigning the work architecture by "classic" reengineering principles, as governed by the mobilization and visioning systems, can produce remarkable results. In stage one, the involvement of only four biocorporate chromosomes often is enough to create the early wins needed to advance and broaden the scope of the effort. It is predominantly a bottom-up effort, requiring very little direct involvement from a company's leaders.

Stage two brings more chromosomes and more senior management attention to bear on the individual process. As the Union Carbide project migration process illustrates, it is far more challenging and complex to manage, but also promises benefits orders of magnitude greater than stage one. Though the leader's role may be significant—communicating the vision, establishing overall goals, removing roadblocks, allocating resources, tracking performance, etc.—he or she has little to say about the design effort itself, which remains focused on individual processes. In that sense, stage two is also a predominantly bottom-up process.

The third stage of redesigning the work architecture—generating *learning loops*—deals with something quite different than the other two. It builds upon "classic" reengineering, but only in the sense that it addresses its fundamental limitations. In this form of redesigning the work architecture, most of the logic of the first two stages is discarded, and what remains is turned on its head. In fact, a newly configured learning loop could actually demolish the tidy structure of a freshly aligned process.

"Classic" reengineering has at least two fundamental limitations. The first could be termed "process tunnel vision." Locked in its focus on individual process, classic reengineering provides no analytical framework for linking the redesign to the corporation's high-level goals and measures, or to the systems that affect them. In other words, classic reengineering lacks the top-down, holistic perspective needed to examine the interplay of systems and processes.

The second limitation, closely related to the first, might be characterized as "the clockwork syndrome." By definition, a process is a chronological sequence of work steps, with such things as technology, buildings, and roles and responsibilities attached to the steps of the sequence. It is locked into this mechanistic view, creating an inherent restructuring bias. Like LEGO® toys, the work steps can be rearranged to make what's there—cost, cycle time, etc.—better, maybe even the best in the world. But while having the lowest cost or the shortest cycle time is great, it won't help much in the areas of revitalization and renewal, where the real promise for both human and business growth lies.

The drivers of growth are seldom found within a chronological series of work steps; they arise when critical, strategic cause-effect relationships are connected across systems and processes. In other words, learning loops are the springboards of revitalization and renewal.

For any organism, including the biological corporation, learning loops drive adaptation to the external environment. A learning loop has four functional components:

1. *Observation*—the ability to sense data from both the internal and the external environments

2. *Orientation*—the ability to interpret that data within a specific context

3. *Decision*—the ability to select a response based on that interpretation

4. *Action*—the ability to execute the response

The biocorporate equivalent of an observation might be a measurement that affects eight different processes, a work step shared by three processes, a competitor's shift in strategy—virtually any event that affects a system or process.

Consider, for example, a complaint. Depending on the orientation of people, systems, and processes the complaint touches, the interpretation of that complaint will be quite different, as will be the response selected in reaction to it. In turn, the action taken to execute the response will depend on the range of capabilities that can be called upon, which are in turn affected by other loops, and so on.

There is virtually an infinite number of existing and potential learning loops within a corporation, so generating them can get pretty messy. The idea is to focus on defining learning loops within and across processes that have a positive impact on the measures tied to the Balanced Scorecard. This adds several new dimensions to redesigning the work architecture. For example, the focus is no longer just on individual processes, and the emphasis has moved from chronology to cause and effect. Work redesign has entered a new realm, which we call *bioreengineering*.

FROM LEARNING LOOPS TO BIOREENGINEERING

Bioreengineering is built upon pioneering work done by Harry Lasker and David Lubin of the Renaissance Strategy Group in Lincoln, Massachusetts. Lasker and Lubin have spent a lot of time building processes that feature learning as the key performance driver. The idea is to link learning to process performance, and process performance to corporate performance. To build such a model, an integrated set of high-level corporate goals and measures is needed as the design basis. The obvious fit of the Balanced Scorecard (BSC) drew them to David Norton, one of the two authors of the BSC model. The fit became one of the conceptual foundations for their firm.

Bioreengineering builds on Lasker's and Lubin's thinking, adding a few twists. The approach differs in at least five fundamental ways from "classic" reengineering:

1. The focus on individual processes is abandoned, replaced by a focus on generating and configuring learning loops within all twelve biocorporate systems at once.

2. The mechanistic focus on work steps is replaced by a focus on the system of cause-effect relationships that drive the underlying purpose of the work.

3. The vantage point for the design is top-down, that of the leader looking through the lens of the BSC.

4. The method is to build connectors to the cause-effect pathways leading both to and from the measures of the BSC.

5. The goal is to generate and configure the learning loops to have the greatest positive impact on the measures of the BSC, thus driving corporate performance.

In bioreengineering, the once centrally important process becomes a subset of learning loops, a way to link and categorize components of related loops chronologically. Learning loops become the relevant unit of design, with the BSC providing the core set of design principles.

The BSC attempts to capture an overall set of cause-effect relationships that are the logic of the health of the company. In the same way, learning loops capture the logic that accounts for the behavior and health of the corporate body's systems, organs, and other constituents. The challenge of bioreengineering, then, is knowing which loops to focus on, how to develop them, how to reconfigure them, and how to interconnect them to support the logic of the BSC. Like transformation itself, meeting the challenge requires a mix of artistry and alchemy.

In almost every sense, bioreengineering can be thought of as a microcosm of Business Transformation. As in transformation, all 12 biocorporate systems are always at play; as in transformation, the leader's role is that of genetic architect; as in transformation, vision and high-level goals and measures are required to focus and direct the effort; and as in transformation, the outcome may be so profound as to fundamentally alter the nature of the corporation. In virtually every respect, bioreengineering *is* Business Transformation, but a bounded version, limited by the narrower perspective of the work architecture chromosome.

WHERE TO START WITH BIOREENGINEERING

With respect to figuring out where to start with bioreengineering, there are a few helpful hints.

First, you don't have to wait until you've mapped out all your high-level goals and your learning loops—classic reengineering, which is quick and to-the-point, can take you a long way. As much as possible, though, try not to commit to things you will greatly regret later when the more advanced bioreengineering approach kicks in. Experience is the best teacher in managing this duality between classic reengineering and bioreengineering.

Second, remember that the Balanced Scorecard provides a context within which to consider, judge, and test your options. In many ways, the Balanced Scorecard defines the higher-level loops to consider. It's helpful to think of the learning loops you need to find as "in there somewhere." Once they have been discovered, simple logic will open the door to many opportunities. Cause-effect relationships are nice to work with, and logic is all you need to understand them.

Third, remember that, when it comes to learning loops, exhaustiveness may be your worst enemy. No matter how you cut it, there is a virtually infinite number of learning loops to choose from. Focus on the main ones, those you deem to be of strategic importance to your transformation. The most fruitful loops usually are those that deal with relationship to the external environment. This is where growth and renewal usually lie.

Fourth, the key to successful bioreengineering involves running experiments to test the hypothesis against real-world conditions. Process modeling, including the tools of systems dynamics, can be used for this purpose. In addition, a detailed simulation of the impact of the hypothetical proposition on the measurement system can help anticipate the results of the experiment. If the experiment doesn't prove out, then either there is a fundamental flaw in the logic of the hypothetical learning loop, or some parameters of the functional components of the loop need to be changed.

To adapt, corporations must adapt to every significant change in the environment, whether a technology change, the emergence of a new competitor, a strike, new regulations, or competitor moves. Ideally, an organization's learning loops can "observe" those events and carry the information to the right places in the right systems and processes, such that the corporate body resonates constantly with processes, systems, and the learning loops themselves.

Bioreengineering at CIGNA P&C

When Gerry Isom took the position of President at CIGNA Property & Casualty in March 1993, it became clear to everybody that underwriting was due for a victorious comeback. By early 1994, when the Balanced Scorecard had laid the groundwork for the entire transformation, underwriting, as predicted, had become the heart of Isom's specialist strategy.

The first pass at redesigning the underwriting process had been quite successful. It was driven by Ward Jungers, a talented underwriter whose personal itinerary is described in more detail in Chap. 11. First, Ward and his team developed a decision model, drawing upon their considerable knowledge to determine how it should work. Process mapping at the decision level revealed numerous opportunities for improvement.

For example, many of the interfaces between the marketing centers, which received requests for bids, and the underwriters, who provided the bids, were deficient. The service centers sometimes failed to notify the underwriters when a request was urgent, and the underwriters lost the opportunity to bid on the business. Sometimes the loss record of existing customers looking for new policies wasn't available, and the underwriters were operating in the dark when claims should have been able to provide the necessary information. Business was being lost.

Those kinds of problems were being fixed, however, and now it was time for a more ambitious, second wave of redesign. The operational problems revealed in the first wave paled in comparison to the fundamental problem in underwriting: to implement Isom's specialty vision, while simultaneously reducing the overall losses due to an ill-begotten underwriting strategy and ineffective underwriting practices. Over the years, CIGNA P&C had lost focus and become a commodity underwriter. Basically, the firm had attempted to underwrite anything that generated premiums, sometimes with almost no consideration of the risks. This approach boosted revenues, but increased the volume of claims even more, and with disastrous consequences to the division's bottom line. Solving this problem was at the very heart of their challenge.

The decision model was largely complete, and it offered valuable help. It didn't answer the fundamental question, however. Progressively, the team quit looking at semi-chronologically connected decision steps, and instead began to follow trails of cause–effect relationships that started with the loss number in the Balanced Scorecard and ended up in the guts of the underwriting process. Their guns were loaded and cocked as they traced those paths, for when they found the cause of the losses, their orders were: "shoot to kill."

They started weaving a complex pattern of root causes, identifying deficiencies in the policies and manuals, in a lack of underlying discipline, and in the information technology itself. They embarked on a discovery journey in which the 12 biocorporate systems all conspired to reveal alternately remarkable or shameful practices. They started building "bubble charts" showing which causes produced which effects, creating newer learning loops. These learning loops connected the different parts of the underlying process, and, progressively, also the world of claims, the world of the agent, and eventually the world of the policyholder. The higher the altitude they reached, the more they realized how CIGNA P&C could compete differently. "Shared learning" had arrived in the world of CIGNA P&C, opening up new horizons.

"From up there, I can invent a brand-new company," a team member once commented in front of what appeared to be a picture of a neural network in a human brain. "And it's pretty darn exciting; much better than fixing the handoff from sales and marketing to underwriting."

When the underwriting redesign team followed the trail of the learning loops, it found a big hole at critical knowledge nodes. Over the years, as CIGNA P&C had slid into its commodity underwriting position, its specialty knowledge had drained away. There were a few underwriters with good specialist knowledge—Ward Jungers, a leader in the redesign, was one of them—but not enough of them to go around. There were huge databases in the old legacy systems, but no one knew how to extract knowledge from them. The team figured out what it had to do now: close the learning loop.

In the course of discovering the critical underwriting learning loops, CIGNA P&C ended up touching most of the 12 biocorporate systems. It first redesigned its underwriting process, injecting more triage in the front end of the process to reflect the new specialist strategy (work architecture). To improve the skills of the underwriters (individual learning), it developed underwriting review sessions in which underwriters would share their experience (organization development), as well as learn about newly developed guidelines, policies, and procedures aimed at better assessing risk (work architecture, again). And the key to closing the knowledge loop would be a desktop support system (technology) that would make a virtual specialist out of almost any underwriter.

The MIS department, in collaboration with an outside vendor, developed a learning system, the heart of the learning loop concept, which guided the rookie specialist through a menu-driven underwriting support, providing expert coaching from the resident expert along the way (see Chap. 9). The coaching consists of the real experts' answers to the most common questions, which are recorded and loaded into the database. When answers aren't available, the rookie can ask for advice on-line in the forum section of the application, posing and answering questions to experts and other colleagues hooked into the system. The system also makes all relevant forms, news bulletins, and technical information available on-line. As of this writing, CIGNA P&C is in the midst of implementing this learning system throughout the entire underwriting organization.

To help fill the knowledge void more quickly, CIGNA P&C has also brought in new leadership from the outside, recruiting underwriting talent into the firm (organization development). It also changed its compensation system (rewards), to reward underwriters *only* for taking on "good business," basing bonuses on premium volume *and* associated loss ratio, rather than simply on premium volume, as had previously been the case.

Each change was linked to an associated set of measures, which were connected to the learning loop just described. For example, they started measuring how often the underwriters consulted with the experts; how many reviews were held; how much of their business fell within the targeted areas; how often they decided to offer a quote when asked; how often they won the quote within the targeted segments; and so on, all the way to the measure of loss-frequency ratio at the top of the Balanced Scorecard.

As we shall see in the ensuing chapters, CIGNA P&C didn't stop with underwriting. The company went on to build bigger and bigger learning loops, progressively connecting underwriting, claims management, and the outside agents.

THREE

REVITALIZATION

To better understand the process of revitalization, let us sneak into the maternity ward of a hospital and visit a mother discovering her newborn baby girl, a few hours after the birth. Such a tiny thing she is, awaking to the universe around her! First, her eyes won't come into focus, and roll around aimlessly, making the mother smile down on the precious little creature. Then the little hands reflexively wrap around the parental finger, bringing tears to the mother's eyes.

It has taken so long, though, to get to this magic moment. Even now, the pain of the birth is still with the mother, as she hobbles along the halls of the hospital to the baby ward, supported by a nurse. The mother remembers her first meeting with the baby's father a few years back; their tentative relationship; the highs and the lows; some of the economic hardship; all the way to the decision to have a child together. And then the pregnancy, with the little body growing inside her, making her sick, and transforming everything she liked about her own body into grotesque shapes. Little had been pleasant about those past experiences; it was just a turbulent river she had had to cross to get to the other side. And it is going to take so much dedication and nurturing in the early years: the diapers, the feedings, the first teeth, the pediatricians.

But look at the baby now. She is already figuring out all sorts of things, beginning to connect things together, like the fact that if she cries, she gets changed, fed, or cuddled. She's also starting to understand that sucking on round pink things can produce food, even though she sometimes gets confused and sucks on her little pink ball.

Over time, she'll learn to move her head from one side of her body to the other to breathe better or to avoid a light. She'll begin to understand that she has a body with limbs and a head, and that all are linked together. Before long, she'll know how to define the boundaries of her own body, and where she fits in relation to the world around her.

Revitalization is similar to giving birth and developing a child. It is about bringing new life into an organization; developing existing businesses and inventing new ones. It is about how the corporate body relates to its environment, but above all it is about *growth*.

The Western business world, in particular, has largely forgotten how to grow, and has exhibited an unfortunate proclivity in recent years for restructuring rather than growing. As a result, companies have taken defensive stands vis-à-vis their environments, trying to minimize their losses and forgetting to invent their future. In this section, we invite corporations to move beyond restructuring, and, like the baby girl, start claiming new knowledge and new space.

There are three main components to revitalization. In Chap. 7, we observe how the corporation uses market focus as its senses. By watching itself through the eyes of its customers, the company can define itself in such a way that it can first survive, then thrive. As with the baby girl, it will take a bit of experimentation for the company to figure out how to get the food, the attention, and the nurturing, but eventually it will get there. If it doesn't, the company will remain handicapped, perhaps blind, deaf, or dumb, struggling to survive in an unfriendly world where business predators abound.

Chapter 8 is dedicated to the invention of new businesses, the equivalent of the human reproductive system. New businesses are born not from chance, but from the deliberate cross-fertilization of capabilities within and across firms. As is true of our baby girl, a new business requires unfailing nurturing before it is able to sustain itself. Even then, the strength of the newborn business will remain an open question until much later, and many will not survive their childhood disorders.

In Chap. 9, we see how information technology acts as the nervous system of the corporation, linking all the pieces together inside the body and often connecting the body to the outside. Progressively, as the body grows and matures, the function of each cell becomes more and more specialized, creating a need for some central coordination of information and knowledge across those cells. This is what the nervous system does for humans, and what information technology does for corporations. For biological corporations, as for humans, the ability to pass on knowledge quickly and efficiently from one end of the body to the other, and in many cases across *several* bodies, becomes a sine qua non of survival. From the rich complexity of these connecting pathways, a stronger corporation will arise.

Revitalization is what distinguishes the strong from the weak. It also is what distinguishes Business Transformation from mere restructuring. Although corporations will be tempted at times to focus on restructuring first, *then* turn to revitalization, they should be warned that restructuring has a tendency to drive out revitalization. Like the children that it will eventually generate, revitalization itself requires care and feeding in its early years.

ACHIEVING MARKET FOCUS

In the human body, maturity is the point at which aging begins, when the cells and tissues of the body can no longer reproduce and regenerate fast enough to replace the dying ones. In the corporate body, maturity is the point at which its systems and processes stop regenerating themselves fast enough to adapt to the changing market environment. In both cases, the demise of the body begins when it stops growing. In the case of the biological corporation, however, reaching that point is not inevitable, and if it *is* reached, the aging process is reversible.

In the biological corporation, the equivalents of cell and tissue regeneration are systems and processes that rapidly adapt to changing market conditions. The outcome is the company's ability to stay ahead of its customers and competitors with its product or service portfolio; to keep them fresh, different, and unique; to avoid letting them become something horrible: dime-a-dozen *commodities.*

According to the prevailing wisdom, the way to do this is to "focus on the customer," or alternately, "focus on the market." Now, virtually every corporation and every business claims to be customer-focused or market-focused. The problem with these concepts is that their meaning appears self-evident, when it is not. Focus on the market? Yeah, absolutely, nobody can stay in business without paying attention to the market! Focus on the customer? God, man, we *love* our customers; wouldn't be where we are today without 'em!

But market focus means a lot more than "paying attention," and customer focus *does not* mean giving your customers exactly what they say they want. There is a term in black, South African culture, *ubuntu,* which explains it well. Roughly translated, it means, "I can see myself only through your eyes."

That is the essence of market focus. The market focus chromosome picks up a company's unique knowledge of itself, steps outside the corporate body, and examines its relationship with the market from the perspective of the customer. But which customer or customers? One customer, or many at a time? How far down the downstream chain? Grouped into what types of segments? In the approach suggested here, every company's variety of market focus will, by definition, be unique.

Market focus is to the biological corporation what the senses are to humans; it provides information needed to relate and adapt to the external environment. The market focus chromosome consists of three genes, implying three corresponding tasks for the genetic architects of the corporation:

1. *Requiring the development of value propositions.* Every business is characterized by a value proposition—a definition of what *benefits* it intends to provides its customers, and at what price. Customers judge the value propositions of several competitors, and pick the one providing them with the best combination of benefits offered and price charged. A benefit represents an emotional end state. It may be defined as one or more products and/or services that help the customer solve an irking issue, that causes the customer to perceive his or her life as somehow better. The best way to identify benefits is to spend a day in the life of one's customer, and to imagine what the company can do to solve some of the problems that customer faces.

Three rules are helpful when developing a value proposition. First, creativity requires that you pick customers as far down the value chain as is practical. The immediate customer often screens companies from more creative downstream plays.

Second, working on one customer at a time allows insight development that no group approach can provide. Intimacy is the key to market focus, and there is no such thing as intimacy with a large population.

Third, creative value propositions come from companies that never abdicate to their customers the task of defining their own value proposition. They listen to their customers, but don't rely on them to tell them what to do.

Companies have value propositions, whether they know it or not. They may be mixed and contradictory, but they are there nonetheless. To operate without clearly defined value propositions is like walking through a jungle in a sensory-deprivation suit; you may make it through, but only if you're lucky.

Therefore, in addition to defining the high-level strategy, the role of leaders is to require each line of business to develop a set of value propositions. Ideally, the sum total of a company's value propositions forms an integrated set, supporting the corporation's ultimate strategic intent.

2. *Segmenting the customer base by benefits.* In a perfect world a company would have a separate value proposition for each and every customer, but typically that's not a practical approach. Consequently, corporations need to build aggregations of customers, or *customer segments.* Homogeneous expectations of benefits and prices (i.e., similar value propositions) constitute the standard for grouping customers together.

Often, companies mistakenly group customers into demographically-based units, such as industry, region, age group, product, or service. Unfortunately, these traditional ways of divvying up the customer base make it difficult, if not impossible, to effectively deliver the benefits offered by a value proposition.

Following a benefits-based segmentation strategy offers many advantages. In addition to providing focus and direction for the high-level strategy, it changes the standard of customer satisfaction from "selling products and services" to "making the customer's life better." The former tends to lock companies within their existing portfolio of products and services. The latter encourages creative thinking about how to recombine capabilities, products, and services to make customers' lives easier. It is the difference between stagnation and growth. The leader's role here is to sell the corporation on the merits of benefits-based segmentation.

3. *Guiding the design of a value delivery system.* Putting the concept into practice carries sweeping implications for the other biocorporate systems. Benefits-based segmentation typically implies the need to reorganize marketing and sales, change the manufacturing strategy, make corresponding changes in physical infrastructure, and so forth. Ideally, all biocorporate systems are designed around the benefits the company intends to provide. When all systems have been aligned with the business' set of value propositions, the company has created a *value delivery system.*

The need to align all systems around the value proposition of the firm produces a formidable logistical challenge. Every work-related decision is linked to the set of benefits the company intends to provide. To keep all systems aligned, the natural tendency of biocorporate systems to run in different directions must be overcome. The role of the CEO and other top leaders is to guide and orchestrate the realignment effort to create the new *value delivery system.*

Until just a few years ago, the leading thinkers in business strategy cast the customer in a passive, secondary role. It is a great paradox, but for almost

30 years, strategic thinking has been dominated by economic approaches, yielding the experience curve, portfolio management, competitor analysis, and shareholder value theory—everything but *the customer*! Those approaches showed that business was about creating value, but they never recognized that it is *the customer* who determines what has value and what does not. Michael J. Lanning and Dr. Lynn W. Phillips were the heretics who plucked customers out of the chorus line and placed them on center stage, making them the starting point of strategy, as they should be.

REQUIRING THE DEVELOPMENT OF VALUE PROPOSITIONS

Companies exist to create value for customers. To create value, they provide customers with benefits; that is, things customers perceive as making their life better. Those benefits are delivered at a price that allows the company to be profitable. A value proposition is *a description of the benefits offered and of the price charged.* The name of the game is to maximize the (conceptual) spread in the customer's mind between the benefits provided and the price charged.

A product or service is a benefit only if the customer perceives it as such. A benefit induces a positive emotional end state, or at the minimum a change in the customer's state of mind toward a problem he or she has. Identifying a benefit involves imagining the customer's life in a simple "before and after" video. Before, the customer is struggling with his daily lot, trying to resolve some irking issues. After, the customer has resolved several of those issues and is a happier person. Benefits are the magic wands that produce the happiness.

In the simplest competitive terms, the company with the best value proposition wins. Contrary to the popular belief that companies can win only if they are either low-cost providers or fully differentiated competitors, there can be as many value propositions as there are creative combinations of benefits and prices, allowing for an enormous range of strategic flexibility and business growth, with room for many winners. The key, again, is to have an "out-of-company" experience, to look outside-in through the eyes of the customer, while retaining the unique context of the company's genetic makeup. In practice, this requires detailed knowledge of, and close relationships with, customers. In market focus terms, therefore, the company with the most intimate knowledge of its customer's problems and desires will own the customer relationship, and the company that owns the customer relationship, wins.

EXPERIENCE A DAY IN THE LIFE OF YOUR CUSTOMERS

The best way to develop close knowledge of customers' problems is to live through them, to experience both the rational and emotional elements firsthand. In other words, experience a day in the life of your customer; smell the scents, taste the flavors, and take in the colors. Analysis alone won't do it. True understanding takes compassion, sometimes even passion. Ultimately, business success is more artistry than analytics; your head lays the framework, but your heart and your guts get you there. Anyone in business knows this firsthand, but it's easy to forget that customers feel the same way.

The customers' world comes alive by empathizing with them and gaining insights from their perspective. Adopting their viewpoint is the source of new ideas about how new technologies might solve their problems; about how they will react to new products and service offerings. It is these kinds of insights that inspire new strategies and feed the free-wheeling imaginations of people throughout the organization, where ideas to reinvent the business are born.

Visionaries like Bill Gates, Chuck Knight, Fred Smith, and Sam Walton created their visions around a deep understanding of people's needs and feelings. Too often, however, after building successful businesses, founders lose that kind of understanding, that *feel* for what the customers need. *They stop taking personal responsibility for looking at, listening to, and touching their customers.*

Instead they rely more and more on linear, mechanical, institutionalized processes and layers of bureaucracy to acquire, digest, and interpret "customer data." Ask most CEOs about their customers, and they will reach for a file, or bring up a computer screen filled with customer satisfaction indices, market-share data, productivity benchmarking results, inventory turns, and product-development cycle times. It is as if the CEO were on a gurney, tubes inserted into every possible orifice, down which are being pumped all manner of informative liquids. The whole system is fed by monitoring devices designed to capture every metric known to modern management science. For good measure, electrodes are attached to the patient for the periodic delivery of the latest management fads.

In this sanitary, isolated environment, how can the executive's natural senses not become dulled, how can a leader not lose the compassion and empathy required to respond intuitively? While these management tools clearly serve a real purpose, they are no substitute for the corporate leader's own sense of the market.

Executives also need to continuously translate new or evolving insights about customers into the processes and systems that serve those customers. They need to rethink and reshape the company's objectives, structure, processes, and systems to match their changing perspective of the company's customer base. As the customer's view changes, the company changes, while at the same time attracting new customers and creating new businesses and new markets.

The alternative is the stagnation that occurs when competitors all are scurrying to do and become the same thing, creating a *downward spiral of commoditization*. The downward spiral of commoditization is a self-inflicted wound and a self-fulfilling prophecy. It starts when companies in the same business focus on each other, constantly reengineering, benchmarking, mimicking each other's best practices, and consequently driving prices down and products toward uniformity. Once in the spiral, the momentum is strong, making the fall seem like an inexorable, unalterable reality. There are no winners—everyone is weakened—but often there are losers; many companies have died before they could step off the ride.

Failing to observe and listen to customers carefully and with an open imagination creates an unintended bias toward reducing service levels, streamlining product lines, and driving product designs to uniformity, when market needs point toward distinct, heavily customized segments. An even stronger bias, again unintended, is created to reduce costs, which is further reinforced, because when you don't know your customers intimately, it's hard to build a convincing case for improvement based on growth. Instead of building multiple processes around customer segments and the benefits they seek, companies trapped in commoditization drive each other toward a single, generic process producing like benefits. In the systematic application of market-blind methods, the corporation goes out in style, looking better and better until the very bitter end.

The airline, steel, and insurance industries are just a few examples of commodity industries. Typically, companies in those industries consistently destroy shareholder value, recording large losses at the bottom of their industry's cycle and making money only one year in seven or eight. Even reputed low-cost producers follow this pattern, enjoying the marginal advantage of destroying less shareholder value than their competitors, but still not achieving a decent return for their shareholders over the long run.

Within most of these industries, however, are a few market-focused players, dismissively referred to as "niche" players by the "major" competitors. Southwest Airlines, for example, has consistently created value, while American Airlines, Delta, and United Airlines keep struggling unprofitably through waves of restructuring and consolidation. Unlike the others, Southwest Airlines doesn't think in terms of economies of scale and load factors; it thinks in terms of the needs of the family, or the student traveler, catering to those who are willing to forego the amenities of business traveling for a convenient, low-cost approach to transportation. Southwest's infrastructure is geared for short hauls. It has no reservation system, offering seats on a first-come, first-serve basis. And it has limited, no-frill service on-board.

Nucor, discussed in Chap. 5, is another example of a successful niche player. A few years ago it realized that the traditional success factors in the steel industry—size, utilization rates, cost of labor—had become less important than an ability to serve customer needs through first-rate application engineering and service. By listening to its customers, Nucor has made light of its apparent scale disadvantage and has won its battles against much larger foreign and domestic mills.

In the life insurance business, Northwest Mutual Life built its strategy on a unique understanding of the upper-income population, transforming its agents into financial planners with a unique understanding of that group's career and family aspirations. As a result, Northwest Mutual's agents are able to talk to their customers about broad-based needs extending far beyond life insurance, creating an advisory relationship within which life insurance is successfully nested. As a result they have had by far the lowest lapse rate—the percentage of people who stop paying their life insurance premiums—in the industry, and have had an outstanding investment performance, largely stemming from their ability to invest with a long-term view, given the stability of their premium stream.

Air Products Relieves the Orderly's Plight

The story of Air Products & Chemicals' helium business provides an illustration of market-focused creativity.

Some 20 years ago, the first MRI machines (Magnetic Resonance Imaging) appeared in American hospitals. General Electric was one of the pioneers. MRI was a technological marvel, another proof of Western innovation. Hospital administrators were both enthusiastic and skeptical. On the one hand, the medical staff was in love; the diagnostic was more accurate, the pictures clearer, the treatment potentially more effective. The patients would benefit greatly. On the other hand the machines were notoriously unreliable—and incredibly expensive. Hospital administrators had been shown the machine; they had heard stories from their pioneering colleagues at various university hospitals; and they didn't trust the idiosyncrasies of the beast.

Orderlies and lab technicians were particularly fearful. The machine was cooled by a weird substance: liquid helium. Liquid helium is very expensive, and extremely hard to handle. In gas form, the material is harmless: We happily let children kick around helium-filled balloons at birthday parties. But keeping it a liquid requires that it be stored under high pressure in tall cylinders. And those cylinders have to be moved as if there were nitroglycerine inside. Let the container fall, and the valve on top might break off. Under that much pressure, it would probably shoot through a couple of walls and hit someone. Orderlies didn't like to mess with the stuff, and acted accordingly; the tanks didn't always get changed over on time.

From GE's perspective, this was one of the hardest issues to resolve. The service technicians of General Electric Medical Equipment had done their best to train lab technicians and orderlies, but it hadn't worked. They had tried coordinating the handling of difficult situations with their supplier, Air Products and Chemicals, but that hadn't worked either. GE's people were electronic and mechanical specialists, not chemical engineers, and that was that.

Air Products and Chemicals had an idea. Knowing they were better equipped than anyone else to deal with liquid helium, they offered to build their own service business for MRI machines in hospitals. They would handle all the liquid helium, even inside the hospital, through their service representatives, and guarantee hospitals that they would never run out of the cooling agent.

This removed one the greatest reservations hospitals had had about the technology, and they began opening their doors to the MRI. The orderlies were delighted, too. General Electric Medical Equipment was so pleased with their supplier that they signed a long-term supply agreement with Air Products.

The story even has a nice ending. To this date, some 20 years later, Air Products and Chemicals still dominates the liquid helium market.

Air Products was able to build an entire business on *one* insight: the fact that hospital personnel were struggling with the handling of helium. What was the source of this creative move? The experience of a day in the life of a hospital orderly. A classic market research approach would have led Air Products to ask questions like "How do you like your liquid helium?" or "What are the attributes of service in the liquid helium business?" Instead, sympathetically experiencing the customer's problem told Air Products that it had a profitable business just waiting to happen.

There are hundreds of businesses out there just waiting to happen. They happen when a company generates unique, customer-based insights, and then converts those insights into a value proposition it can deliver upon.

Three Simple Rules

Following three simple rules will help you become market-focused:

1. *Choose the right customers, through the entire value chain.* This is no trivial matter, for often there is an infinity of customers to select from. First, there's the issue of which stage of the value chain to focus on. Generally speaking, the most creative plays are those farthest away from the company's immediate business. Conversely, the farther one ventures from one's immediate business, the more difficult it becomes to identify what the company can actually do to have an impact that far down the chain. The further the company ventures away from its immediate customers, the higher is the potential return, but also higher is the risk of striking out.

Once the stage of the value chain has been chosen, typically there are multiple possible customers at each step. So which one should the company focus on? Experience is the best counselor. The size of the potential segment clearly is an important consideration. The complexity of the application is also critical. The more complex the environment in which the product or service is used, the better the chance to create a truly original value proposition.

2. *Take one customer at a time.* Becoming market-focused requires a great deal of patience. Identifying the benefits a customer will respond to requires an intimacy that, by definition, can only be created one customer at a time. While the economic pressure for shortcuts is always there, no group approach can succeed in matters of market focus. Segmentation is the key, and segmentation needs to be based on benefits, which are the result of intimacy.

Without detailed knowledge of individual customers, many companies jump to what they think is the next-best thing: demographically-based segments. But trying to conquer a demographically-based segment is tantamount to broadcasting a love declaration to an entire regiment over a public address system. The chances of gaining any real intimacy through such an approach are slim, and the economic results often are disastrous.

3. *Don't rely on customers to do your job.* It's important to listen to customers. But it's equally important not to let your customers define your strategy for you. Customers can give you ideas, but they don't know your business as well as you do—if they did, they would have moved into your territory a long time ago! Their counsel is always helpful when they are talking about their own business and the utilization they make of your products. But when they try to do *your* job, they often become naive or idealistic. They will suggest approaches that make good sense from their perspective, but that will generate no profit for you. Use their input, but never abdicate your own responsibility to define your own strategy.

Nalco and Betz Escape the Chemical Paradigm

The well known success story of Nalco and Betz, two chemical companies (Nalco prefers to call itself a service company), illustrates the power of a creative strategy rooted in a market-focused insight. The two companies focus on water treatment problems, mostly for large industrial plants. Their financial performance is spectacular by all standards, particularly when one compares them with other chemical companies. How do they do it? And how have they escaped the commodity syndrome, given that there is nothing terribly distinctive about their products?

The answer is deceptively simple: They are both acutely market-focused.

Nalco and Betz are both manufacturers and distributors of polymer-based products that are used in the treatment of effluent waters in industrial processes. Had they chosen the commodity approach, they, like many chemical companies, would have dropped bulk shipments of their chemicals off at their customers' plants and competed, like everyone else, on price, quality, and service.

Nalco and Betz discovered, however, that industrial users don't want to deal with water treatment problems. The maintenance departments of utilities, for example, want to focus on boiler and steam problems, not water problems. They don't want to go to water treatment conferences, nor do they have the time to read the manuals involved.

The people at Nalco and Betz knew their customers well, understood their frustrations. They also knew that they had the internal know how—in engineering, sales, and customer service—to take the problem off their users' hands. After all, they made the chemicals and knew more about using them than almost anyone else. "Why not manage our customer's whole water treatment process?" they asked themselves. Instead of just offering a range of polymer-based chemicals, they developed a service-based business, assuming responsibility for the entire water treatment process at customers' plants. For a monthly fee, they guaranteed "best-in-class" handling of water treatment problems, and left customers free to concentrate on their core business.

How did Nalco and Betz hit upon this lucrative business idea? Did a utility come up one day and say, "I wish you would take my water treatment off my hands, and let me concentrate on my business"? Clearly not. The Nalco and Betz people spotted a potential benefit not currently provided—the peace of mind of the manager of the water treatment area, developed the concept themselves, and the business they created turned out to be hugely profitable.

The Hall of Market-focused Fame also includes data-processing firms such as EDS (founded by former presidential candidate Ross Perot), Service Master, and ADP. These companies weren't built on insights generated by survey research or declarations from customers about what they wanted. All insights were gained through observation, listening, imagination, and thoughtful action.

SEGMENTING THE CUSTOMER BASE BY BENEFITS

Simple native cultures in Africa have three numbers: one, two, and many. This accurately describes the approach one should use when expanding a value proposition to an entire segment: first one customer, then a second, then an entire group.

The trick is to go "bottom-up" rather than "top-down," at least in the initial stage. Market-focused companies first develop the value proposition for the single customer, then use that customer as a pilot site to discover how many customers share similar problems. After testing the proposition in the real world, they make modifications until the product or service becomes sufficiently appealing to a large enough customer segment to justify building a business around it.

Only when the contours of the segments become apparent does classic market research become helpful. If the hypothetical segmentation stands the test of a series of workshops and interviews, then large-scale surveys, telephone interviews, and polls begin to make sense. It is now time to employ the statistical apparatus of market researchers: regression analysis, cluster analysis, and conjoint analysis. The focus shifts away from building the contours of the segments, toward analyzing what is inside each segment. In particular, this is when companies determine whether they can build an economic model to address the needs of any particular segment.

Customer Awakening at CIGNA Property & Casualty

By the middle of 1994, Gerry Isom has become worried that CIGNA P&C is still too internally focused. On one hand, there has been much progress on many (mostly internal) fronts, as evidenced by "the numbers," which are progressively getting better. On the other side of the ledger, though, the strategic plans being developed by the business units strike him as largely uninspired. They read like a bureaucratic exercise, with neither the fire in the belly nor the epic flair that Isom wants to see.

"The profit centers need to start taking accountability for their own bottom line and growth," he stresses. "I also want to see evidence of a true understanding of your markets."

There are 16 profit center leaders, and Isom's insistence on independent responsibility was new news to them. Historically, they had lived in the shadow of giant functional organizations and had not thought of themselves as being accountable for anything vaguely resembling a bottom line, or even a customer group. Most had regarded themselves as low-key marketing or underwriting advisors to a line organization. Most feel excited about this new responsibility, but quite scared at the thought of "owning" a bottom line. Consequently, meetings are an interesting mix of chest-pounding and draft-dodging.

Driving into each profit center the notion that customers matter to the business is Isom's first challenge, and he resorts to his favorite medium: mixing it up in the trenches with the people who matter.

"Who is the customer?" the flip chart asks.

Isom is relentless in his belief that the company has to abandon its commodity approach to the business and adopt a specialist strategy. But to inculcate that belief in others, he must convince the rest of the division's leadership, particularly the profit center managers, that it really is the way to go. What that requires, he realizes, is a new view of customers. That is the goal of this meeting of selected profit-center managers. But Isom has one view of the customer, some members of the group have another.

His opposition is defending the company's existing commodity orientation.

"You can try anything you like," they say, "but at the end of the day it's a question of price. Every new piece of business generates a request for seven or eight proposals on the part of the agent or broker, and it boils down to price. All this stuff about differentiating ourselves by specializing in target segments is a pipedream. We don't call the shots, the agents do. They're our customers, and they buy on price. That's why they get bids from six or seven carriers on every policy for their customers. They call the shots, and there's not much we can do about it."

Isom disagrees. "The true customer is the policyholder, not the agent," he asserts. "I agree that the agents and brokers are key, and that we can't afford to ignore them. But if we focus on satisfying the needs of the people they take care of, it will reflect positively on their reputation, which will translate into more business for them, which will come right back to us."

Many members groan inwardly. It's the specialist argument again.

But there's no avoiding it. Isom is determined to convince them that they can break out of the commodity trap, so once again he reviews the framework of the specialist approach. Like most leaders, he has to repeat the same message again and again. Sometimes the man seems like a piece of artillery, wearing you down until you surrender.

"As a specialist, you select the types of risk you want to underwrite," he explains, yet again. "Specialists focus on end-user groups whose risks they uniquely understand."

Sometimes he has to refrain from going into "automatic," he knows his text so well. But every audience is a new audience, and he has to keep displaying great conviction.

"You manage your relationships with agents and brokers, drawing them in to become partners in serving those end-user groups," he continues. "Right now, we have no focus; we bid on everything, relying on agents to manage our risk for us. But they aren't concerned about our risks; they're concerned about taking care of their customers to get repeat business. So, if we take great care of a select group of their customers, but in such a way as to manage our own risks, agents will flock to us with their business in that segment."

"Now think about costs," he continues, hoping that he's reaching them. "Say you know everything there is to know about movie theaters, about what can go wrong. That gives you the ability to go to a theater and assess their operation and make recommendations that reduce the risk of those things happening. If they agree to make those changes, then you have effectively lowered the probability that a claim will be made. Fewer claims translates to a lower loss ratio than commodity-oriented providers. That means you can charge slightly lower premiums while still running at a higher margin. The bottom line is, if you want to compete on price, the way to do it is to become a specialist."

A few nodding heads mean he's getting some support, but others still look skeptical.

"Once loss-control services enter the picture," Isom states, "the entire nature of the game changes. The value proposition isn't simply limited to providing insurance coverage for a premium anymore. It involves minimizing all losses for the client, ideally by taking preemptive steps to eliminate every possible mishap. That requires having an intimate understanding of policyholders, which requires developing a close relationship with them. Many can play the commodity game, but only a few can provide high-quality loss-control services to different segments."

Isom explains how Progressive Insurance made money in automobile insurance by focusing on "hard-to-insure" cases. For example, they had examined the records of drivers who had been convicted of driving under the influence of illegal substances. As it turned out, offenders with two or more children had a remarkably low rate of repeat offenses, making them a good underwriting risk. Had they gone by the conventional wisdom that all such offenders are a bad risk, they never would have have identified this profitable segment. CIGNA, Isom argues, should use a similar approach in its target industry segments.

On the conceptual level, his logic was unassailable, and many surrendered to it. But on the practical level, that logic was far from translating into new underwriting practices in the trenches. Commodity underwriting had spread through the division like a cancer, and it would take time to remove all of the malignancy. But Isom was determined. He would be back, as often as he had to be, until new cells were growing where the old cancerous ones had been.

Of Freshness and Exotic Produce at Idlywilde Farms

There's a great little produce store in Acton, a suburb of Boston, that caters to a unique set of customer needs. It is called Idlywilde Farms, and one of us occasionally buys produce there. He could buy produce at the large local grocery store, where he does his other grocery shopping, and where the produce is of fairly good quality and significantly cheaper. So why is he willing to make an additional stop and pay a lot more money for produce? The answer lies in peeling back the onion of benefits.

First of all, everything is fresh and neatly stacked at Idylwilde Farms. It looks better. The apples are redder. He can get Brussels sprouts on the stem. Where else can you get Brussels sprouts on the stem? They have mini-pineapples for decorative purposes, and those small ears of corn for salads. He can buy mangos, guava, and fruits with names that no one can spell, let alone digest. And he likes it in there; no shelves cluttered with baby diapers and toilet paper and dog food. It's smaller. He can park at the door. And when you need something, there are plenty of people there to help. When they're not helping you, they're restacking oranges to maintain a pyramid shape for effect—*that* must eat up a bundle of labor cost. Also he can get *cornichons* there. Cornichons are French-style pickles, and he hasn't been able to find them anywhere else in the Boston area.

According to traditional strategic thinking, these sorts of features are "operational," a code name for irrelevant. Because traditional strategists like to think in high-level abstractions, they try to boil everything down to a few key principles. "Surely," they would say, "you don't believe that Brussel sprouts on the stem have any strategic value?"

"Yes," many customers would retort, "they surely do." Within the context of Idylwilde's overall value proposition, built around fresh and exotic produce, the Brussels sprouts take on a strategic dimension. Sprouts on the stem are an integral part of what attracts customers to the store.

In offering its value proposition, Idylwilde has made many tradeoffs, not all of which are to this customer's liking. It doesn't provide the "one-stop shopping" experience for example, and he's a very busy person. The high prices bother him a little bit too, but he understands that that's what it takes to provide such fresh and exotic produce. At the same time, however, he does value convenience and low price, so the large local store gets most of his business. But nothing's perfect. The art of designing a value proposition largely consists of finding a recipe that works. Theirs seems to be working just fine.

GUIDING THE DESIGN OF A VALUE DELIVERY SYSTEM

A good value proposition is like a swan gliding elegantly across the water; each hides what is going on beneath the surface. Just as the swan's apparently effortless trek belies the frenetic paddling underneath, so the apparent ease with which a good business provides benefits to customers belies the complex value delivery system that makes it possible.

A value delivery system is the unique set of capabilities required to create and deliver the benefits of the value proposition to the target customer segment. It represents a cross-section of all 12 biocorporate systems, brought to bear in a carefully crafted set of processes and learning loops. For example, the selection of the value proposition is a representation of the vision; building the value delivery system requires mobilization; creating the products and services needed has implications for physical infrastructure and organization; and information technology is almost always involved.

In bringing all the systems to bear, however, none is more important than the work architecture. The benefits offered by the value proposition will materialize only if the processes and learning loops within the biological corporation start mutating, extending themselves, and creating new metabolic pathways to reach the newly set goals.

Consider, for example, what would be required to create the business of Idylwilde Farms from scratch. Assume, for example, that their full value proposition is the following:

Idylwilde Farms offers uniquely fresh merchandise and exotic grocery products at a premium, in a comfortable, customer-friendly and rustic atmosphere, with easy access from the western suburbs of Boston.

In terms of generating the work architecture, creating the value delivery system would require the following steps:

1. Create the store concept.
2. Select the merchandise.
3. Grow or purchase the merchandise.
4. Store and warehouse the merchandise.
5. Display the merchandise for sale.
6. Collect the money from customers.
7. Manage the customer relationship.

Supporting processes would be required as well, such as managing the store personnel and managing the farm's financial and accounting functions.

The value proposition acts as the design standard. Without it, each design step would be dictated by functional knowledge, with no common context for alignment. If, for example, every step were entrusted to functional specialists, each, acting on his or her own best judgment, would unavoidably step out of alignment. Even if each was striving to contribute in good faith to the overall strategy—and typically there are deviationists by intent—the system would have a tendency to work itself out of alignment, because each of us behaves according to his or her own version of the ultimate goal.

The second law of thermodynamics states that the degree of disorder, or "entropy," of an isolated physical system always increases. One only need look at a neglected car or house to appreciate the truth of the law.

The same is true of a set of corporate systems and processes. Whether in the design of the value delivery system or in full business operation, a system or process that is left to its own devices will tend toward chaos. The check against business entropy is an actionable value proposition. The work architecture cannot live independently of the market focus chromosome.

Consider the myriad of micro-decisions involved in each of Idylwilde's work architecture design steps. The first step, "Create the store concept," involves decisions about the number of square feet inside and outside the store, the layout of the parking lot, the amount of refrigerated shelf space, the layout of the shelves, the width of the aisles, and the decor. Each decision either reinforces or diminishes the customer's perception of the Idylwilde value proposition. If the parking lot is too small and customers have to wait, there goes the claim of "comfortable." If it is too big, there goes the "rustic" quality. The way to resolve such dilemmas is to consult the value proposition and interpret it in functional terms every step of the way.

The same applies to the next step, "Select the merchandise." Should the store carry *cornichons* or not? How about cheese or fish? Here again, the two claims of "freshness" and "exotic products" should be the guiding lights. Brussels sprouts on the stem reinforces both claims. A great cheese or fish counter will be consistent with the quest for freshness, but Campbell soups and canned tuna are inappropriate, because nothing in the value proposition resonates with such items.

The problem with most reengineering efforts is that they don't proceed from a clearly articulated value proposition. Without at least an implicit understanding of the value proposition, imagine the predicament of the person responsible for "displaying the merchandise for sale" (the fifth design step). If freshness is a key part of the value proposition, it will make sense to have employees rearrange the shelves several times a day, to remove damaged produce, stack oranges in neat patterns, and shine lights on the merchandise to make it look attractive. But if the value proposition is fuzzy, our display specialist will be tempted to gravitate to the lowest-cost solution. When you don't know what benefits to provide, you tend to minimize costs, by default. So out go the people stacking oranges, out go the lights above the tomatoes, and soon Idylwilde Farms looks and feels just like any other grocery store.

It Begins to Fall into Place for Karl

We last left Karl, the scheduler at Woodbridge Papers, puzzling about whether to cut the product line. In his role as leader of the team responsible for redesigning the order-to-delivery system, he has discovered that cutting the product line will allow them to quickly and dramatically cut lead time, perhaps even to a level below that of their competitor, Mountain View, which currently quotes customers a 10-day delivery time. But a gnat buzzing around in his subconscious has prevented Karl from making a decision. We rejoin him shortly thereafter, participating in something called a "market-focused" workshop.

Karl can't quite figure out how he got involved in this customer workshop thing. His days are so full now, that sometimes at the end of the day he can't remember everything he did. It worries him sometimes, but his wife assures him that no, he isn't showing symptoms of Alzheimer's, he's just busy.

The idea for the workshop was conceived after one of their best customers, a printer in Chicago, had made an offhand comment at a dinner with the head of marketing: "Mountain View Papers can now deliver in a week, and I'm thinking of switching," he said. "We find Mountain View can bail us out when our big soup manufacturing customer runs out of packages during its promotions. As a matter of fact, we've switched about 40 percent of our business from you to them already."

The meeting has been convened by Woodbridge's CEO, who had the idea of bringing together the Chicago printer and the soup manufacturer to talk about the problem. The vice president of marketing had protested that they already had plenty of customer data, quoting surveys, focus groups, and touch-and-feel tests. The CEO wanted none of it, and somehow it fell to Karl, as the person in charge of the redesign of the order fulfillment process, to organize the customer workshop.

The soup maker's delegation consists of the VP for gazpacho, the buyer of packaging products, and the plant superintendent. The Chicago printer is represented by its owner and CEO, and Woodbridge has a team of 10. Karl, much to his dismay, has been appointed "facilitator." He has protested vehemently, "I'm a scheduler, not a damn meeting facilitator!" but to no avail. He isn't looking forward to it, not one little bit.

He's been given some hints by the marketing department about how to lead a workshop. At first it looks like the soup manufacturing people are taken aback, when the questioning focuses on soup manufacturing and marketing rather than paper making or printing. The Woodbridge people are curious about what problems the soup maker has, what major issues *they* face, and what would help them to increase *their* profit.

"One of our problems is in handling promotions," the gazpacho VP volunteers. He's not sure why he should bare his soul in front of a supplier who is two-steps removed from his business, but he's doing it anyway. "We never know how successful we'll be until the product hits the grocery stores' shelves. When the promotion's successful we stock-out, which costs us big money in lost sales and margin, not to mention wasted advertising dollars."

The soup plant's superintendent shoots back, "But a lot of the time you guys forget to tell us when you're going to run a promotion. Without knowing ahead of time, there's no way we can plan ahead. It blind-sides our schedule." To Karl's amazement, the two seem to be discussing the problem for the first time.

The gazpacho VP confesses his guilt, but adds, "But even when we do notify you, we don't always hit the sales projections right. Then the problem's made worse by the fact that no printer can print packaging fast enough to get us out of trouble. We still lose a significant amount of sales that way."

"That's true," the Chicago printer grants, "but we're not the problem. It's Woodbridge, with its three- or four-week lead time. We've got old presses we could use for rush jobs, if we could just get the paper fast enough."

"Is that why you like Mountain View's 10-day delivery time?" Karl asks, intrigued.

"You got it," the printer and the soup people say in unison.

During a break, Woodbridge's VP for manufacturing approaches the Chicago printer when both are using the men's room. He says, "You know, we've got an old paper machine we don't use anymore. It would work fine for the occasional rush job. It's not the fastest or the most efficient machine on the block, but it could help in stock-out situations." They sketch out on a bathroom towel how such a "rush system" might work.

There are other surprises in store when the workshop resumes.

"The key to the soup business is taste, taste, and taste," the VP for gazpacho begins. "But the other trick is to make your soup stand out on the shelf. The soup business is becoming very complex. We need to tailor our recipes and packages more and more to regional tastes through the distribution system. For example, they like gazpacho spicy in the Southwest but bland in New England, and we're finding that bright colors help in export markets. Holland likes bright red cans. France likes a picture of a vegetable garden on a dark green background."

The soup plant manager groans. "Don't remind me," he says. "All that fragmentation is a nightmare. France is a six-hour run every six weeks, Holland a two-hour run. Each time, we have to reset the machine, switch the recipe, find the packaging, run the order, and then clean up."

"It's the same with us," Karl adds. "Our shiny vermilion—I suppose that's for your Dutch cans—is very hard to make, and so is the shamrock green, for your French market."

"Actually, we're thinking of dropping those particular lines," Woodbridge's financial controller reveals, "because we're losing our shirt on them." His colleague from marketing glares at him from across the table, and for some reason the controller suddenly reaches down and starts rubbing his shin.

"If you did that, you'd be just another supplier to us," the soup company's VP of gazpacho warns them sternly. "If you can't get us those colors, we'll just go to the lowest bidder with the shortest lead time. If you and the printer could get your acts together, maybe we could review prices for these low-volume items and make them profitable for you." This time it is the VP of gazpacho, sitting across from the VP of purchasing, who rubs his shin.

Karl can almost physically feel the revelation coming on. Several months ago he put the two statements on his flip chart, one about cutting the product line to cut costs and lead time, the other about broadening the product line as a way to competitively differentiate the company. He had been leaning toward cutting the product line, but now he has his answer, and he knows it's the right one.

Not only is their fat catalog of products valued by their best customer's customer, it is vital to the company's entire strategy. Now he knows what his order-to-delivery team should be doing.

The challenge is to somehow deal with the complexity, not eradicate it by pruning the product line, and Karl sees three things they could do right away.

First, they could get out that old Woodbridge paper machine for rush jobs, align it with the printer's "in times of trouble" printing press, and integrate the rush scheduling all the way down to the soup manufacturer. The soup guys have already expressed a willingness to pay premium prices in such situations. Karl will call this the "rush order" system.

Second, Woodbridge could dedicate its smaller Canadian plant to the smaller volume specialty runs, including papers for export markets. They would make to inventory during promotional campaigns. He will call this the "hard-to-make" system. It will fit really well with the Focus idea they've sold the CEO on.

Third, Woodbridge could dedicate the rest of its machines—now freed from small-batch duties—to large-volume items, running them in tandem with the printer's high-speed presses and the soup maker's automated packaging plants. It really is conceivable, Karl realizes, that this streamlining will allow Woodbridge to cut its lead time from 30 days to somewhere close to the 10-day target set by the CEO. There again, this is remarkably consistent with the Focus idea they have devised separately. Later, when they run the numbers, Karl's team also will discover that the proposed three-part paper manufacturing system could cut inventory by 75 percent and thereby save $300 million of working capital.

Even beyond the issue of immediate savings, Karl feels that all the elements are falling into place. A strange peace is replacing his previous moods of anxious intellectual torment. Decisions have become easy, nearly self-evident. Somewhere up there, the great god of business alignment has a new disciple.

INVENTING
NEW BUSINESSES

M any people feel connected to the future by their children. All too aware of their own mortality, both the physical and spiritual attributes they impart to their children give them a sense of continuity and represent an enormously important component of their legacy. In much the same way, corporations take great pride in the children they spawn: the new businesses they create. Although a corporation need not die, it often happens that, in a sort of corporate rite of passage, the structure of the parent company is overtaken by the form of its children. Over time, the very essence of the parent company passes on, its name and legacy carried forward by a new corporate body. Conversely, if a company cannot invent new businesses, it will most likely die a long, protracted death, the memory of its contribution to the world fading into oblivion.

Inventing new businesses is the biocorporate equivalent of human reproduction. Like human reproduction, it involves moments of great excitement and pleasure, but also carries enormous long-term challenges, risks, and responsibilities. What is at stake is the future of the entire company, and the time horizon is from 3 to 20 years. This is the stuff legacies and legends are made of, and because nothing worth doing is without risk, CEOs must often come to terms with personal failure.

In Chap. 7 we examined how market focus links the customers to the corporate body from the outside in, ensuring continuous regeneration and new growth of processes and systems. In this chapter we combine the outside-in with the inside-out, examining how the unique capabilities of a company can be combined to create whole new organizations with new purposes and new goals. It is no longer enough just to find better ways to compete: leaders now look to become the next Ted Turner, inventing CNN; Sam Walton, creating Wal-Mart; or Akio Morita, building Sony.

Inventing new businesses is the job of chromosome number eight. It has three genes, implying three corresponding tasks for the genetic architects of the corporation:

1. *Fostering the cross-fertilization of core competences.* Core competences represent the very essence of a corporation; they are the unique, bundled sets of resources, skills, and abilities upon which its businesses are built. They represent core relationships across the 12 biocorporate systems. They also are the reproductive organs of the firm, which when combined or cross-fertilized, give rise to new business opportunities.

Cross-fertilization of core competences involves bringing the market-focused perspective back into the corporate body and unleashing it to feed the collective corporate imagination. The goal is to reveal points across competences that, when connected, generate new ways to provide customers with the as yet unfulfilled benefits they seek. It calls for an act of creation and discovery that cannot be programmed or planned. The leader's role, therefore, is to foster an organizationwide understanding that combining competences can create growth opportunities, and to maintain an environment that encourages and rewards experimental probes into the realm of new business creation.

2. *Building alliances.* In many cases, a corporation doesn't have the internal competences it needs to capitalize on new business opportunities; "fresh blood" is needed if the corporation is to develop the genetic characteristics required. By forging alliances, a company can reach beyond its body, extending its boundaries by cross-fertilizing its competences with those of other companies, but in a limited, controlled way.

The leader's role is central in building alliances. The challenge is to create agreements that allow the free exchange of knowledge and capabilities in fertile areas. Each company's competences feed and play off the others, such that key process and system boundaries disappear. At the same time, however, there's a danger of "giving away the store." Each company keeps its unique identity, retaining control and ownership of the core competences that distinguish it from other companies. Cultural clashes, too, can be a major pitfall. No matter how elegant the theoretical strategic fit, the alliance will amount to little if the people in the respective companies neither share a common mental framework nor work well together.

3. *Making acquisitions.* The most ambitious, challenging, and risky way to create new businesses is to combine core competences through mergers or acquisitions. Acquisition is like marriage, bringing an entirely new genetic blend to bear in the corporate offspring. Sharing competences is no longer sufficient; the idea here is to meld them, creating whole new competences that can be leveraged to generate unique new benefits for existing and new customer segments.

Successful acquisitions require careful management from the top before, during, and most importantly, after the event. Both parties have to live with "the morning after," regardless of the level of cultural compatibility.

FOSTERING THE CROSS-FERTILIZATION OF CORE COMPETENCES

The concept of core competences has been taking the business world by storm. According to Gary Hamel and C.K. Prahalad, the originators of the concept, a corporation's strength rests on its portfolio, not of businesses, but of core competences. New businesses, they say, are spawned by leveraging core competences in new business segments, by taking what you do well *across* businesses and creatively applying it in new, unexplored industries.

This thinking has turned generations of strategic and organization thinking on its head. It has shown the chief pitfall of organizing the corporation into strategic business units (SBUs): the strangulation, rather than the nurturing, of new business growth. Understanding this phenomenon requires defining this crucial concept of core competence.

A core competence is a *related set of skills, capabilities, and technologies that makes a company uniquely adept in an area or field that has applications across businesses and industries.* Honda's core competence in engine design and manufacturing, for example, is what enabled it to expand from the motorcycle business to automobiles and trucks, to lawn mowers and power equipment, to industrial compressors. Canon leveraged its optical and mechanical expertise to expand from the camera market into copiers, now competing side-by-side with the once dominant Xerox. A focus on core competences is one of the driving forces behind the emergence of Japan as a major industrial power. In fact, it is the underlying principle that has spawned most large industries.

Consider, for example, what propelled the rise of DuPont as a major power in the chemical industry. It was their unique mastery of certain catalysts, such as hydrogen cyanide, hydrogen fluoride, and others. These are among the most toxic and difficult chemicals to handle, yet they drive key chemical processes and represent the foundation for DuPont's chemical empire, the inner sanctum of the firm, the roots of its chemical tree. The public knows about and buys nylon, Lycra®, Corian®, and Kevlar®, but few would want to handle cyanide in their garage. Thus, *process catalysis* is one of DuPont's core competences.

By contrast, SBU dogma fractures, not builds, empires in industry. The concept originally was developed by General Electric, Shell, and McKinsey, and was perfected by many generations of management thinkers. Its conceptual underpinnings were formed in the day of the distended corporate conglomerate, and in that context were far from all bad. In the 1950s, 1960s, and 1970s, corporations grew into huge, unfocused collections of businesses, and managing the portfolio was the dominant rule of the day. This meant centralized management that focused on broad financial indicators, not the strategic or operational imperatives of the individual businesses.

What was needed, said the logic of SBU thinking, was to make each business a stand-alone enterprise, to give them the strategic and entrepreneurial flexibility to operate on their own. This would give each business focus and much needed autonomy from the slow-moving central management structure. In many ways, the thinking worked. But the remedy was found to have some severe side effects.

Focus is the intent of SBU thinking, and focus is the outcome. But sometimes the line is a fine one between focus and wing-clipping. Within an SBU framework, imagine the motorcycle unit of a manufacturer suggesting the development of a lawnmower or a power tool, as Honda did. "Unthinkable! Stay focused!" would be the likely response. SBU thinking locks in a mindset focused on a single business within a single industry. But most opportunities for new business growth occur at points of intersection *between* industries and, therefore, between divisions of multi-business corporations. It is core competences that provide the connectors across businesses and industries.

A corporation's strategic architecture can be viewed as a tree, with core competences as the roots, businesses as the fruits, the trunk representing core systems shared across businesses, and the business-specific systems as the branches. In DuPont's case, for example, process catalysis would be a root of the tree, and Lycra® and Nylon fruits.

The historical approach to managing businesses is tantamount to injecting water into the fruits instead of watering the roots and letting the businesses draw the sap. The first approach may create a deceptively juicy-looking fruit in the short term, but the yield is likely to drop year after year. And if by chance a bolt of lightning should strike, the once hallowed oak may reveal its hollow core. By contrast, the company that focuses on core competences nurtures a healthy trunk and limbs, making it a prime candidate for the experimental grafting of new branches to grow altogether new and exotic fruits, rich in nutritional content.

Many companies have missed major opportunities to grow businesses through the cross-fertilization core competences. Most large Western corporations have enjoyed a real annual growth rate, excluding acquisitions, of around 1 or 2 percent over the last 25 years. For example, one could argue that General Electric, although heralded as a model firm, had a chance to become the American version of Sony, but blew it by failing to bring cross-fertilization to its repertoire. With its RCA components, its television appliance business (later sold to Thomson of France), and its "content" arm in NBC, it had all the ingredients to be an 18-wheeler on the electronic superhighway.

While we in no way wish to detract from GE's prodigious and often pioneering achievements, it does seem true that if it hadn't pursued a policy of stand-alone success vis-à-vis its individual businesses, and had it not sold what might have been key components of its competence portfolio, it might now be a major player in the media revolution, rather than watching it from the sidelines. Even the greatest companies have their Achilles' heels.

DISCOVERING COMPETENCES THROUGH ACTION

"It sounds appealing" many companies thought when the concept of core competences first emerged, "but how do I identify these competences and extract growth from them?"

The analytical quest to discover core competences has disappointed many a company. More often than not, such attempts yield a fairly trivial model of the firm's strategic architecture, providing neither the insights nor the actions that were hoped for. One problem is that the process can be quite boring, involving long lists of technologies and capabilities to which are applied many tests. The attempt to generate exciting ideas dies due to lack of interest. So what's the key? How do you unleash the power of core competences?

It is predominantly a behavioral, not an analytical problem—the answer lies in the approach. Create interdivisional *projects,* rather than interdivisional *reflection.* Get people excited and talking to each other, and the insights and actions often will jump to the surface. The essence of the approach is "design as you go"—strategy in action. Pick a couple of initiatives requiring the cross-fertilization of capabilities across multiple businesses, and run with them. Let people discover for themselves the value of sharing knowledge and information across organizational boundaries.

Mixing Stocks and Socks at Sears

The retailing giant, Sears Roebuck and Company, demonstrated that growth from cross-fertilization can indeed be derived from high-level strategy. In Chap. 4, we showed how Sears rocketed shareholder value through the spinoff of several businesses. The real secret of this success was a fundamental shift in the company's strategic thinking; specifically, its decision in the early 1980s to build a presence in the financial services industry, what has been dubbed Sears' "stocks and socks" strategy.

The leadership team went about it quite systematically. From Sears' original platform in retailing and insurance (insurance through Allstate, formed in the early 1930s), they rapidly branched into real estate through Coldwell Banker, brokerage through Dean Witter, and mortgage banking through Sears Mortgage Banking. For close to a decade, business analysts were quite skeptical, if not downright critical. What did a retailer like Sears really know about financial services?

But Sears had a clear mental picture of what it was doing. Through its retail operation and its catalog business, it had a unique understanding of its customer base: *all* of Middle America. In its relationship with Middle America, Sears had discovered both its own core competence and an emerging market discontinuity. Middle America was becoming more affluent: it needed mutual funds; it needed more insurance; and it needed to buy a new house. The executive team deemed these to be "Sears' kind of businesses," and the stocks and socks strategy was born.

At Sears, there is a religion of the customer. Eliminate the very rich and very poor, and you have defined Sears clientele: 60 to 80 percent of America. More importantly, the company's knowledge of these customers is intimate. With its huge base of credit card holders, Sears knows these people's names, plus a lot more than that. If they buy a lawn mower, they probably own a house; which means, they could use mortgage, insurance, or real estate services. If they buy baby clothes, they probably have children; which means, they could use an investment plan for the children's college education. And if they buy Craftsman tools, they're probably do-it-yourselfers, which makes them likely candidates for a home equity loan. Sears knows their credit history, can infer probable income, and it knows how to target a full range of services within a huge customer base. This was the conceptual essence of the socks and stocks strategy.

Within the context of the stocks and socks strategy, the introduction of the Discover card marks one of the most successful examples of the creation of a new business at the intersection of several existing businesses.

Like stocks and socks, the launch of the Discover card was criticized, if not laughed at, by business analysts and competitive credit card companies. Sears, the critics eagerly pointed out, was suffering from delusions of grandeur, the same malady that had been the downfall of conglomerates in years gone by. It was a very decentralized company, in which divisional executives enjoyed great freedom of action. There was no way, they said, that cross-divisional cooperation would work. And besides, they argued, who needed *another* piece of plastic?

What the critics didn't comprehend was that, in spite of its decentralized structure, the leaders at Sears understood core competences, and what it would take to make the new card work. Intimate knowledge of the customer base was the starting point; the target market for the Discover card was Middle America. In addition, it was able to prequalify potential card holders through its existing portfolio of charge-card holders and financial services customers. By offering the preapproved, no-fee Discover card to millions of people at the same time, it established an overnight customer base for the new business. In its retail and financial services operations, it had more transactions-processing skill than it would ever need. It had the banking facilities of Greenwood Trust Company to serve as the sole issuing and acquiring bank, eliminating the need for costly interbank transaction fees. This enabled Sears to undercut the competition in terms of the transaction fees it charged merchants. If merchants could save a point or two on Discover card sales, what did they have to lose? Finally, Sears had the ability to sell insurance and financial services directly to the card holders. In these capabilities it had the roots of a powerful tree, whose fruit Sears' leadership hoped would be a thriving credit card operation.

As Sears built the Discover card business, the critics continued to scoff. After three years, Discover had lost a whopping $230 million. But then a few of the smarter analysts began to prick their ears, for the Discover card operations already had accumulated $3.8 billion in receivables. To put that in context, First Chicago had just paid Beneficial National Bank $247 million to get $1 billion in receivables. In addition, Sears' integrated strategy resulted in economies of scale that have made the Discover card the low-cost provider in the marketplace. Its annual operating expenses per active account average 12 percent below the industry average, allowing it to continue offering the card with no annual fee, not to mention offer a rebate program that builds customer loyalty much as frequent flyer programs do for the airlines. Viewed within that context, the $230 million loss may represent one of the cheapest investments in the history of the credit card business.

The proof of the pudding, however, is in the bottom line. By 1992, Dean Witter, Discover reported earnings from its credit services of $207 million, a 20 percent increase over the previous year. Some 90 percent of that profit was attributable to the Discover card. Discover accounted for nearly 7 percent of all credit card transactions worldwide, 15 percent of all credit card customers, and 8 percent of outstanding balances. Nearly 40 million people held Discover cards.

And what about stocks and socks? Well, the strategy has now played itself out, with Sears' leadership deciding to move out of the financial services business, primarily to allow the financial markets to value the various components of the company. Now Sears has spun off its interest in Dean Witter and Discover. It has sold the Coldwell Banker Residential business to the Fremont Group, Sears Mortgage Banking to PNC bank, and has announced its intention to spin off to shareholders the remainder of its Allstate holdings. Sears is getting back to being what it used to be: a retailer.

And the results are quite impressive. Sears has received $4.2 billion from all of those transactions. Over the 10 years Sears was involved in financial services, the revenues from those businesses tripled to nearly $30 billion and assets quadrupled to nearly $90 billion. Between 1990 and 1994 the Sears stock price more than doubled, and it close to tripled if one includes the Dean Witter stock dividend granted in 1993. Sears, over a span of 10 years, demonstrated how the cross-fertilization of core competences is a mighty engine of growth.

A Farfetched Idea at Woodbridge ... Or Is It?

We last left Karl emerging from a customer workshop, having gained the insights that he needed to solve his dilemma about the product line. There was no doubt about it now, Woodbridge's broad product line was a source of competitive advantage. They would keep and maybe even expand their product line, while reconfiguring their production facilities, machine utilization, and price structure to solve their customers' problems.

The success of the first workshop has spawned many more of them, and now they've taken on a life of their own. Whenever their customers let them, Woodbridge videotapes the events, then edits them to produce snappy "customer focus" tapes that are distributed throughout the firm. Even the CEO looks at those tapes with his wife and kids in the evening. What an exciting life he must lead!

There's a room where they accumulate all the workshop data on the walls. Customer by customer, they synthesize what customers are looking for, and group the customers in segments according to the benefits they seek from Woodbridge. One of the plants' engineers, who strongly disapproves of this unscientific approach, calls it "ocular segmentation." Scientific or not, it's catching peoples' eyes. They wander into the room, curious to learn what the world out there wants from them.

Karl has become quite an apostle of the market-focus faith. He talks with the zeal of the newly converted, insisting that the firm is too inwardly focused. "You need to find out how our customers provide value to *their* customers, and their customer's customers, all the way to the end of the value chain," he preaches. His associates think he may have popped his lid—can this be the same Karl who used to send customers packing when they inquired about the status of their order?!

"Only idiots never change their mind," Karl is fond of saying. "I've always believed that—and will never change," he loves to add with a wink.

Today the workshop is with a German manufacturer of printing equipment. He has been invited, because they've heard he has developed some innovative technologies.

Karl is outside, taking a much needed coffee break. Thus far, the session has been awkward and tiring. The German visitor's accent makes him hard to understand, and he's having trouble picking up on the vernacular subtleties in their questions. It's the middle of the day, and about two-thirds of the audience has given up, drifting away from the conference room. Karl is right outside, feeling a little guilty for leaving, but not too guilty. He's learned a lot in recent months, but his global instincts are still limited at best. He's never spoken any foreign language—his three years of high school French were for naught—and he has little sympathy with foreigners trying to express themselves in broken English.

He sees, however, that Woodbridge's R&D staff still is clearly intrigued. Fortunately, one of them speaks fluent German, acting as translator when necessary. The German guy is on to something, they seem to think, and the dialogue has turned technical, full of references to pressure, temperature, and tensile strength. As Karl drifts back into the conference room, he can see that they're diagraming an oven and talking about a cooling unit.

Just the three people from R&D are left on the Woodbridge side. Out of embarrassment, Karl sits down. He doesn't want Woodbridge to appear impolite to their German guests. His eyes roam around the room.

At first, he's not sure what he's looking at on the flip chart. But step by step, from it and the slow-moving conversation, he begins to put the pieces together; at least he thinks he does, for he can't quite believe his eyes and ears. They're talking about a fully integrated paper-making and printing machine! Yes, sir, that's got to be it! He recognizes the distinctive pulp vat at the front end of the line, all the motors driving the process, the oven; hmm, yes, a cooling unit, and then an attached printing press. It's a strange looking duck, this integrated paper-making and printing machine.

His first thought goes to scheduling, of course. Ignoring the 20 technical miracles it would take for this machine ever to see the light of day, it sure would solve a bunch of scheduling problems. This would go beyond just-in-time, it would be *simultaneous production*! They wouldn't have to worry about work-in-progress or paper inventory anymore. Going directly from pulp to printed packaging—man oh man, what possibilities!

But oh, the headaches it would create! He sees a million different problems. Who would own the machine? Woodbridge? Their printer customers? Or even the soup company? It would force a complete redesign of the entire supply chain. Wow, that's pretty scary stuff!

But never mind—it will never, never work. Look at it! Can you believe the audacity? Hey, the paper is so fragile when it comes off the paper machine. It needs to cool first. No cooling unit will get it to the right temperature that quickly. And for cost reasons, the paper machine output needs to be very, very wide; while for print layout reasons, the width of the printing machine needs to be much, much narrower. Besides, you can't expect the printing industry to learn paper-making, nor can you expect paper-makers to learn that much about printing. No, of course not, it will never work.

And yet ...

The research and development folks are now so pumped that Karl can feel their energy. They're rolling around the idea of building a prototype. Karl, the old fox, has an idea: He knows of a small, single-line Wisconsin manufacturer that's just gone out of business, and they should be able to buy his machine dirt-cheap. Perhaps the integrated paper-making and printing prototype could be built off that machine.

A few days later, the CEO and the head of R&D summon Karl to the CEO's office. He already knows what's cooking, even before they speak. Yes, he'll be glad to undertake responsibility for following up on the prototype idea. No, of course he doesn't mind. Yes, it is compatible with his 80-hour-per-week workload. Yes, he's delighted that he and his team are becoming the main driver of transformation for the firm as a whole.

Karl's worried about two things. Selling the idea of more madness to his wife, and avoiding a brain meltdown. If he dodges those two obstacles, he knows his life will never be the same again. And he's beginning to like it.

Regaining Corporate Citizenship at CIGNA P&C

CIGNA P&C has been the black sheep of the CIGNA family of businesses for longer than most CIGNA executives care to remember. With its bottom line beginning to improve, however, it's earning a new reputation. At long last, CIGNA executives can view the P&C division as a potential vehicle for growth. And in this spring of 1994, Gerry Isom is wondering how to respond to the new corporate initiative.

The firm is toying with the idea of creating a new, integrated offering across the Healthcare, Pensions, and P&C divisions. It would be known as "24-hour coverage." CIGNA would target medium and large companies, offering them a tailor-made package covering all three areas. Rather than negotiating separate coverage with each division, customers would negotiate with a single CIGNA representative for all of their insurance needs.

It's a beautiful idea for at least three reasons. First, corporate clients are getting tired of the complexity of insurance. There are too many carriers, too many policies, and far too many relationships to manage. Second, most corporate customers see health and pension coverage as connected, because both are integral components of compensation and benefits packages. In addition some P&C policies, such as professional indemnity, are perceived as part of the larger benefits "whole." Third, Healthcare and P&C could share a network of providers, including doctors and hospitals. The managed-care network of the Healthcare Division offers interesting cost-reduction possibilities for P&C.

Perhaps the most attractive feature of the idea, however, is that CIGNA is one of the few providers strong enough across all three businesses to make the offering a reality. The barriers to entering the insurance business are relatively low, which means that there are many competitors within individual business areas. If CIGNA could get "24-hour coverage" off the ground, it could offer integrated packages to companies that were now dealing with three or four different providers. CIGNA would create economies of scale, making it difficult for niche players to compete. Most importantly, it would make customers' lives so much easier that they were bound to find it appealing. CIGNA would consolidate many customer segments into one new, much larger segment. In so doing it would significantly raise the barriers to entry, giving the firm a good shot at "owning" it.

In spite of its conceptual elegance, "24-hour coverage" will prove much harder to implement than to articulate.

Gerry Isom is wondering how fast he can go. He's been slaving for more than a year to break down the functional walls within P&C, and is barely rounding first base. Now he's going to ask people to collaborate *beyond* the boundaries of P&C. It is, no doubt, a great strategic play, but will it overload his team? Will pushing for cooperation with CIGNA's stronger divisions jeopardize the success of his team-building efforts? Is it just too much to ask?

A more practical concern is systems. They have enough problems with their own legacy systems, without having to merge claims, underwriting, and producer files across three divisions. Then again, why not take care of both problems in one fell swoop?

In spite of his concerns, Isom is convinced that the best growth opportunities lie between businesses, not within them, and he doesn't have that many internal opportunities for revitalization. And there's P&C's status within the CIGNA group to consider. He has momentum now, and needs to capitalize on it. The other two divisions may have liked the idea of "24-

hour coverage" before, but they wouldn't be taking it seriously had it not been for the recent achievements of P&C. If he were to send out the message that P&C is too embroiled in its own problems to cooperate, it could set back the division's reputation for years.

He can't risk that, so Isom becomes a willing, if somewhat apprehensive, partner in the "24-hour coverage" project.

BUILDING ALLIANCES

Companies can spawn new offspring by cross-fertilizing competences across businesses, but inbreeding alone can lead to a stale genetic pool. Alliances provide a way to revitalize the corporate genome selectively, by blending skills and capabilities across companies to generate new competences and new businesses upon them.

The last 10 years have been marked by an explosion of alliances, and increasingly they are of a global nature. Alliances may be viewed as existing on a continuum in increasing orders of complexity. At the simplest extreme, alliances are merely *opportunistic,* formed because it is more economical to acquire know-how from other companies than it is to develop it internally. At the other extreme, alliances may represent the emergence of a new economic order in which businesses are nodes within networks, and in which the ability to effectively manage networks is the new measure of success. This second view may be termed *the Big Bang theory of alliances.*

Two primary factors drive the need for alliances of the opportunistic variety: the *proliferation of technologies* and the *globalization of markets.*

It used to be that businesses drove technological advancement within their own industries. Now it's more the other way around: Technology drives business advancement across various industries. It is rare for the leading players within an industry to have a monopoly on technological innovation. In fact, keeping up with the pace of technological innovation forces companies to seek alliances with creative partners, swapping access to their strong business position for access to innovation. There is evidence that R&D spending is increasing globally, and that the proportion of cooperative R&D spending within that total is also increasing. Individual companies can't go it alone anymore, not even giants like IBM or NEC.

Merck, the very successful U.S. pharmaceutical company, is a prime example of a company that has committed to literally hundreds of alliances. In its agreement with DuPont, for example, Merck was willing to entrust some of its products to a more dedicated, and somewhat starved, detail sales force at DuPont, allowing its own sales force to remain focused on its "big gun" products. Conversely, DuPont had promising technology that it hoped Merck would help bring to market.

Globalization of the business world is the second factor behind the growth of alliances. True global companies rarely exist. Consequently, gaining access to markets around the world often requires partnering with other firms that have a stronger foothold in various parts of the globe. The trade involves exchanging strong manufacturing, technology, economies of scale, or other business positions for market access.

For example, in the search for global access, 12 global electronics companies—LM Ericcson of Sweden; Digital Equipment, IBM, Honeywell, and Texas Instruments in the United States; Siemens in Germany; Seiko in Japan; Plessey and Thorn-EMI in the United Kingdom; Matra and CGCT in France—allied themselves to exchange knowledge and standardize switching technology. Similarly, to gain access to the European aerospace industry, General Electric has teamed up with SNECMA of France to manufacture aircraft engines. Pilkington relies on subsidiaries wherever it has a strong presence, but builds alliances to reach other parts of the world, often with competitors: Nippon Sheet Glass in the United States, Mexico, South Korea, and Taiwan; and Saint-Gobain in France, Argentina, and Brazil. Merck has allied with Johnson & Johnson, trading its pharmaceutical knowhow for Johnson & Johnson's consumer marketing skills. British Airways and USAir have allied themselves with the goal of building a global airline network.

But alliances can be cumbersome. Two heads aren't always better than one. Alliances often generate cultural and operational conflicts that a company acting alone can avoid. They may produce more and better value, but since the proceeds must be shared, they had better create *a lot* more value. Upon entering into an alliance, each company steps into the other's territory, which may mean exposure to new competitors. Perhaps the greatest risk of all is the chance of giving away core competences. The world of alliances is far from perfect.

THE BIG BANG THEORY OF ALLIANCES

The motives of alliances are often quite simple, based on opportunistic goals such as improving a cost position, acquiring a new technology, gaining access to a market, or distributing risk. There is one motivation, however, that deserves special attention: *the desire to learn from one another.* The ability to learn is rapidly displacing physical assets, market share, technology positions, and patents as the most critical success factor in many industries. The ability to quickly acquire knowledge and to parlay it into products and services is emerging as the principal driver of success. Since most knowledge exists outside a company's boundaries, the ability to build knowledge-based alliances is becoming a major competitive weapon.

Japanese firms are particularly skilled at learning through alliances. Ampex, for example, was the original innovator in the development of the commercial VCR, but JVC and Matsushita became the winners by driving the adoption of the VHS standard. The television industry illustrates the same basic pattern: American innovators licensed their know-how to Japanese firms, who ended up dominating the market.

If knowledge is to become the fundamental driver of business success, then the ability to manage the flow, acquisition, and application of knowledge will become a far more relevant measure of a company's value than the auction price of its asset base. As companies develop webs of alliances, equity perimeters between firms are becoming increasingly loose and ill-defined, making the ownership contours within industries more a relic of the past than a relevant measure of competitiveness. Consequently, the somewhat frozen, albeit rapidly thawing, structure of companies as we know them—as represented, for example, by listings on The New York Stock Exchange or in the performance reports of *Fortune* and *Business Week*—is bound to explode in an economic "Big Bang." One can envision, after the Big Bang, strings of former competitors locked in a cosmic embrace, joined together by the sharing of related sets of knowledge.

Without venturing that far, there is growing evidence that strategic *networks* are already developing. Some are driven by industrial policy considerations; Sematech, the association of chip manufacturers, is one such example, albeit a struggling one. Others are produced by the convergence of technologies. For example, the various "electronic highway" projects linking semiconductor manufacturers, electronic appliance companies, computer firms, and telecommunications companies with the so-called "content" companies are already here.

According to the Big Bang scenario, alliances will become much more than opportunistic; perhaps they are destined to become galaxies, with companies as the solar systems within them. We once thought the Earth was the center of the universe, around which danced the sun, the moon, and the stars. We now know it is a speck, the dynamics of its movement governed by millions of other bodies in the universal dance of gravitational force. Alliances may become the gravitational force of the new business universe, with the dynamics of individual companies being governed by the interplay of alliances. For the foreseeable future, the individual company will remain the focal point of performance, but increasingly its fate will rest in its network of alliances, and depend upon the strength of the galaxy within which it associates.

Nowhere is evidence of the Big Bang so clear as in the global telecommunications market. Driven by privatization and the emergence of the EEC, growth in international telecommunications has become explosive, averaging 20 percent per year. Large multinational corporations represent the largest and fastest growing segment, and 80 percent of their voice traffic is contained in less than ten countries, including the United States and the United Kingdom. There is a true dog-fight under way for the business. In fact, within the industry and the financial community there is general agreement that, in as little as a decade, there probably will be only three or four major global telecommunications companies in the world.

There is also agreement that no one, not even the mighty AT&T, can go it alone. The result is an explosion of alliances. The capital costs involved are huge, and alliances provide the means to spread the funding and resource requirements. International networks are only as strong as their weakest link (i.e., a country's weakest network), and alliances represent a way to get access to the best. Regulatory hurdles, especially in the voice business, are very hard to clear, and alliances provide local inroads to speed the process.

What is emerging is a three-cornered fight among complex networks of fiercely competitive alliances. In one corner is AT&T, with its WorldPartners consortium of owner companies and fee-paying member companies (KDD, Singapore Telecom, Unisource, etc.). In the second corner is a proposed alliance, code-named Phoenix, recently struck between Sprint, France Telecom, and Deutsche Telekom. In the third corner is Concert, a joint venture company formed by BT (formerly British Telecommunications) and the international long-distance carrier, MCI. Concert is the competitor we focus on hereafter. Nippon Telephone and Telegraph, the major force in Japanese telecommunications and a potentially powerful partner, is a guest conspicuously absent in this global party.

At present, WorldPartners and Concert appear to be the major contenders, with Concert emerging as the clear victor in round number one. The race is on for the lucrative market called virtual network services (VNS). VNS allow corporations, from within their own networks, to make calls over publicly switched lines as if they were linked in a private network. Using VNS in a multi-national firm, for example, a person in New York can dial a three-digit code to ring an office in London, Paris, or Rome. In addition, users can operate an internal e-mail system or an internal knowledge-sharing application such as Lotus Notes over a virtual network. About 50 percent of major US corporations use VNS domestically, compared to a mere 16 percent in Europe. The growth potential of this market is mind-boggling, and BT/MCI's Concert is almost six months ahead in the battle to capture it.

Concert, as already mentioned, is a joint venture between BT and MCI. It was conceived in mid-1993, officially born in June 1994. By November of 1994 it had released its first voice product, Concert Virtual Network Services (CVNS), available initially in eight countries. On the day Concert announced the release, AT&T reluctantly announced that it wouldn't be able to offer similar services for at least six months. There are reports that AT&T's executives are miffed at having been beaten to the punch, and are redoubling their efforts to get their own product out.

Concert was formed to combine the complementary competences of BT and MCI, as well as to address MCI's customer base in North America and BT's customer base in the UK (and its growing base throughout Europe and the Asia Pacific). Both firms formed Concert to develop global, seamless communications solutions, or products, to be distributed solely by MCI and BT. The idea is to make Concert a noncorrespondent (single-contact) provider, such that a multi-national company would use it as sole provider of all its communications needs. This is in contrast to AT&T, which has alliances with correspondent countries but doesn't have control over them, meaning that they independently market their products to companies. Concert believes its approach will allow delivery of communications services worldwide in a way that other more loosely formed alliances cannot hope to.

In Big Bang fashion, the ownership structure of Concert is complex. For legal reasons, it started as a wholly-owned subsidiary of BT. BT subsequently agreed to purchase a 20 percent stake in MCI for $4.3 billion (foreign carriers can own up to 25 percent of a U.S. domestic carrier). In spirit and in operations, however, Concert was a 50-50 joint venture between the two firms from the outset.

Concert's spectacular achievement in being first to the market masks, however, the tumultuous and somewhat painful process that led to the launch of the CVNS offering. The leaders at Concert had to overcome personality and cultural conflicts at many critical junctures.

Staffing was one such juncture. As the alliance was being forged, MCI and BT developed independent binders of processes and roles and responsibilities within their firms, but neither assigned people or groups to work with Concert. Shortly after being appointed leaders of the new venture, Concert's executive team members realized they would have to staff the company from scratch, and fast. Concert, according to the plans drawn up, was to deliver major, complex products, CVNS among them, by April of 1994. By comparison, the company had acquired its first employees in

June 1993, only 10 months earlier! This was beyond cycle-time reduction—more like acrobatics!

Chris Ernshaw, formerly of BT and part of the initial negotiating team with MCI, was appointed designate CEO immediately following the initial conception of Concert in mid-1993. He quickly appointed an executive team from a variety of backgrounds in the two companies. Kathleen Flaherty, from MCI, became responsible for marketing and product management. Tom Rowbotham, from BT, became responsible for product development. Mike Read, from BT, became responsible for operations. Roy Nash, from MCI, became responsible for finance. Senior executives from one of BT's U.S. subsidiaries, which was merged into the Concert venture, became responsible for human resource and legal functions. Together, this executive team knew it was sink or swim.

As CEO, Chris Earnshaw's first and most challenging duty was to be a peace-maker and a team-builder. He had to get to know his team, yet he had to make strategic decisions right away. He gave marketing responsibility for profit and loss, but technology and operations easy access to capital. This ensured an even distribution of power during the culturally rocky start-up phase, and gave a kick start to the development and investment programs.

With only a limited commitment of resources from the parent companies and no human resource processes in place, the leaders had no choice but to look back within their previous organizations for people. This presented a very real danger that staffing plans for particular functions would be skewed to one parent or another. In addition, convincing likely recruits to join Concert proved to be no easy task. There was the question of benefits. There was the minor matter of leaving a secure job that would definitely be back-filled, for about the same money, to work twice as hard, to be part of a firm that might not even survive! Concert discovered the hard way that questions like "Where will my BT pension go?" and "What about my MCI stock option plan?" needed to be answered in a hurry. Sometimes the spirit of adventure isn't enough to lure talent, the venture learned.

Concert struck a compromise with employees—known in the culture as "secondees." Employees would initially join Concert for two-year stints. Thus most Concert employees describe themselves as either an MCI or a BT employee, particularly if they saw their futures as back with their parent companies. But now that Concert has made a splash on the market scene, the sense of cultural identification is beginning to develop, and employees increasingly refer to themselves as Concert employees. In the space of just 12 months, the company grew 100 fold, from 9 to 900 employees.

Those staffing hesitations had taken their toll on the schedule, however. The launch of CVNS initially had been targeted for April, then was moved to August, and finally was rescheduled for November. Even then, few were confident that the deadline could be met.

By June, the SVPs of marketing, technology, and operations had gotten together with Earnshaw and selected other officers to discuss how to resolve this destructive trend of delaying release dates. Flaherty, in particular, had had it with delays. A product of the MCI culture, she believed in aggressive marketing, and felt she had been embarrassed one too many times by being forced to retract the target dates she had promised to customers. Something had to change, and everyone knew it.

But because accountabilities weren't clear among the leadership team, they debated for weeks on how to proceed, then finally brought back a question to Earnshaw: "Chris, who gets fired if we don't get CVNS out by November 1?" Earnshaw looked at them solemnly and said, "Tom, you do—followed by Kathleen Flaherty and Mike Read." While Tom was to head the charge, the message was clear: if one failed they all failed.

Tom Rowbotham and his technology VPs had long felt that divvying up the development between separate MCI and BT functional teams was culturally expedient, but technically inadvisable. They needed a faster, more integrated approach. In early July, Concert launched a new approach, appointing a task force for the new product's development. It was comprised of 35 cross-functional team members from Concert, MCI, and BT, all fully dedicated and accountable for releasing CVNS on November 1. For the first time, they were mixing blood in earnest at the operational level.

Tom Rowbotham was the executive champion of the team, but called on his two senior colleagues each week to review progress and resolve critical issues. He appointed Ron Hilton as the task force leader, saying to the team, "I've got one bullet left, and I've saved it for Ron in case he doesn't make the goal. But I've given Ron some weapons of his own to help us win the race against the November 1 deadline. And that's *you*, folks. You're the best of our respective firms, and, working together, you have 100 days to release CVNS. I'll do all I can to remove roadblocks in your path, but most of the work must get done by increasing your levels of communication and coordination."

Enthusiasm was high in the beginning, but soon began to wane, as team members learned they were largely starting from scratch. Ron Hilton, the task force leader, proved to be the perfect pick to lead the team to the seemingly impossible goal. Originally from Texas, he has a soft-spoken southern drawl and the Texas charm to match. With a strong engineering background, he knew CVNS better than anyone else. Over the years he also had woven an impressive web of contacts within MCI, BT, and Concert, which he now used to advantage. Because he could remove obstacles by sweet-talking people on the telephone, he became affectionately known as the "tele-cowboy."

Predictably, the BT and MCI cultures clashed on the task force. BT task force members, mostly operations-oriented, tended to take a serial view of how activities were to be performed, insisting that the technical solutions and low-level designs be in place before detailing their functional processes. Wearing their operations hats, they insisted on the highest quality design, no matter what the time constraint. MCI task force members tended toward the other extreme: rushed planning practices and activities designed on the run. "Ready ... shoot ... aim!" seemed to be their motto, and they liked it that way.

With necessity mothering invention and a few bullets emerging from the "tele-cowboy's" pistol, the cultures began to merge within the team, becoming a prototype for the entire Concert organization. The team tested the product with three companies. The three companies were, in effect, a part of the alliance web, winning a period of free services for letting Concert use their companies as "beta sites" for the new product.

Concert met its November goal, and the three companies are now customers. CVNS was launched, perhaps with fewer features than originally planned, but still significantly ahead of competition. In the celebration that followed the successful product launch, Ron Hilton was fitted out by his colleagues with the full tele-cowboy regalia, complete with new cowboy hat, sheriff's badge, and cowboy boots, but, much to his dismay, no horse.

Concert intends to keep moving forward at hyper-speed, building a full portfolio of products in several communications areas. It hopes to rapidly build audio and video conferencing capabilities on the CVNS platform, as well as further develop its data products. In all likelihood, Concert will become a multibillion-dollar company within a span of five years or less.

If it does, many on the task force will remember that Concert's first performance was more an improvised jam session than a carefully crafted piece of counterpoint. But when you *win* and when you learn so much, aesthetics matter so little....

MAKING ACQUISITIONS

The most ambitious, challenging, and risky way to create new businesses is to combine core competences through mergers or acquisitions. There are no more trial periods here. Also, remember that there are no prenuptial agreements when it comes to acquisitions. Watch your assets!

Acquisitions involve paying a premium in the present for growth in the future. The acquiring company typically pays a premium for the acquired, betting that synergies exist that will create organic growth in the future. In the pre-deal phase, considerations of shareholder value prevail, and many companies are highly adept at the pre-deal work.

Efficient market logic cannot explain why most acquisitions take place at a significant *premium* over the current value of businesses. Why, after all, would the value of a company suddenly shoot up, even double or triple, in an efficient market? The explanation probably is more closely tied to the feeding-frenzy instinct, triggered by the first drops of blood. But is it economic value, or some sort of corporate ego contest that triggers the auction process now so common in acquisitions?

Studies have repeatedly shown that acquired companies benefit from acquisitions, while most acquirers do not. There are exceptions, of course. There are cases when the fit between two companies is so uniquely *right* that a premium price is warranted. Nevertheless, acquisitions remain, first and foremost, a high-risk gamble.

In the post-deal phase, the main challenge is to implement the intent behind the pre-deal work, and it is in this phase that most acquisitions fail. Experience shows that companies tend to focus more on the pre-deal phase, less on the post-deal assimilation period. While a company can fail at either stage, post-acquisition failure is far more protracted, painful, and costly.

But what makes it so difficult? On the surface, acquisitions seem to be the simplest form of expansion. A company has the competences you need, and you buy it—what could be simpler than that?

Acquisitions, however, involve a fundamental, and sudden, altering of a company's gene pool, making them an inherently complex vehicle for growth. Many acquisitions are inspired by the hope of triggering new growth for the core business through gaining access to expanding industries. Companies that find themselves stuck in low- or no-growth environments place calculated bets by acquiring firms on higher growth trajectories. Witness, for example, two recent acquisitions in advanced materials: Hitco, by BP, and Beatrice Composites, by BASF.

The world of post-merger management is far less glamorous than the world of pre-merger deal-making. Yet, the true value of acquisitions emerges from these more pedestrian post-acquisition processes.

A Unionist and Nationalist Marriage in Ireland

Business occasionally provides a role model for society as a whole. If a business deal ever achieved that status, it was the acquisition of the

Northern Ireland Division of Trust Savings Bank (TSB), a major Northern Ireland and U.K. clearing bank, by Allied Irish Bank (AIB), the most profitable bank in the Republic of Ireland. TSB in Northern Ireland was traditionally associated with the Unionist community, while AIB was firmly seen in the Nationalist tradition. The merger was the brainchild of three AIB executives: Brian Wilson, Eamon McElroy, and Dan Harvey.

Looking at it from the outside, one might have expected the acquisition to die in the pre-deal phase. The political backdrop was one of frequent terrorist acts in Northern Ireland, and bringing together a Nationalist and a Unionist institution might almost seem a bit like a provocation.

So the cultural challenge was as daunting as the political one. The Northern Ireland division of TSB had been vigorously built by a tough and effective Northern Irishman, Brian Johnston. It was a working man's banking operation, lean and profitable, catering to a predominantly working class, Protestant base. Johnston knew the figures for every branch, knew each branch manager by name. He ran the bank with a rod of iron. It was practically *his* bank, with his personal stamp all over it.

As was true of its leader, TSB's strengths lay in its operations. Its per-check transaction cost was substantially less than that of AIB's. It had strong information systems, a good and profitable product portfolio, and a tightly woven financial measurement system.

AIB, by contrast, was positioned predominantly in the south, with only a limited presence in Northern Ireland. Its customer base was strongly built on middle-class Catholics and small businesses.

The team of AIB, however, was unphased by the magnitude of the challenge. In TSB, they saw the opportunity to establish a competitive market share in the Northern market. They also saw a fit of related competences. AIB was a "relationship" bank, with a very strong customer base of small businesses and middle-income families and professionals. It had a strong competence in managing the human resource components of banking, particularly in developing strong branch managers. It had spent a lot of time building human resource competences, supporting its people through MBA programs, sponsoring advanced management courses, and developing finely honed management practices.

There were areas of overlap in terms of geographical coverage and product offerings, but the potential synergies outweighed these by far. Strategically, it was a good fit.

From the perspective of the TSB parent company, the sale of the Northern Ireland division represented a much needed opportunity to mend some financial wear and tear. It had gotten itself into some financial trouble in the acquisition of Hill Samuel and another firm, Target Leasing. Selling the Northern Ireland division would release some shareholder value. Furthermore, its Northern Irish operation was no longer a great strategic fit with its core banking group.

Brian Wilson saw the acquisition of TSB as an opportunity to build market share and acquire the foundation for a growth program. Very much hanging his career hat on the move, he personally pushed hard for the acquisition.

Implementation got off on the wrong foot. For example, Brian Johnston was not informed until after the event. One can imagine how he must have felt, as well as how easily he might have spoiled the probabilities of success if he had chosen to. What turned out to be the key to the success of the acquisition was a firm commitment made to Johnston that he would be given a "level playing field," that the great things he had built in TSB would not suddenly be displaced by new policies handed down from AIB. The post-acquisition process was designed integratively, with cross-company teams focusing on migrating best practices to create a new consolidated enterprise. The choice of a new name, First Trust Bank, was far from accidental; it was a symbol of a new, unified firm.

There were of course tensions, conflicts, and some degree of pain, as there always are during the post-acquisition process. AIB's vision, however, proved itself a good one, and in the end the Protestant versus Catholic issue turned out not to be a factor. According to McElroy, the outcome has exceeded expectations in all ways. First Trust has increased the volume of its business, gained customer and market share against competitors, and successfully merged many of the best practices, and it is becoming a learning platform for the entire industry.

CHANGING THE RULES THROUGH INFORMATION TECHNOLOGY

Together with customer needs and core competences, information technology completes a trinity of elements leaders can combine to create market opportunities through revitalization. In fact, this element is so powerful that a company's leadership can *change the rules of the game through technology.*

Technology is to corporate life what the *nervous system* is to human life. It connects the various parts of the body in an integrated network of information sharing and decision making. It "wires" together disparate parts of the organization, allowing them to progress together toward a common goal rather than remain hopelessly disjointed. It can improve speed and efficiency, for example, through the automation of slower and error-prone human tasks.

Even more importantly, technology provides the wiring and programming needed to build connectors across corporate boundaries into the lives of other organizations, giving birth to new corporate communities. This is why technology belongs to the revitalization section of our transformation framework, even though it can also be used for restructuring. For example, technology allows a company to build direct electronic links between itself, its customers, and its alliance partners, thus providing a conduit to extend the reach of the firm's core competences.

When otherwise inert information feeds active learning, the possibilities for creative growth become endless, and technology becomes the competitive weapon par excellence. Perhaps most important of all, it provides the means to link and integrate the knowledge held by individuals within and across corporations. This is perhaps the most interesting application of technology in transformation. The new economic order is becoming more reliant on the knowledge worker and less on the industrial means of production and distribution. Consequently, the role played by technology in increasing the amount of knowledge, or accelerating the dissemination of skills within and across firms, is becoming strategic. This is where technology truly becomes transformational, where technology strategists and business strategists become one, integrated breed.

Following the framework first offered by N. Venkatraman, the technology chromosome has five genes, corresponding to five levels of business operations, in increasing order of ambition and complexity: isolated activities or tasks, linked or integrated sets of related tasks, business processes, intercompany networks, and the scope of the business as a whole. The CEO has the following five corresponding tasks as genetic architect:

1. *Sanctioning technology for localized efficiency improvements.* The most apparent and widely applied advantage of technology rests in its ability to automate information-intensive (and formerly paper-intensive) transactions and services. These are the more traditional applications that tend to be locally or functionally based. Payroll, order entry, customer support, CAD/CAM, reservation, and JIT inventory systems are but a few examples here. Most companies recognize and use such systems, achieving remarkable increases in efficiency compared to days gone by. Yet most companies are still plagued by unnecessary processes and layers of management that were created before the era of "bit magic."

It is the CEO's job to disallow such waste, to encourage and sanction the deployment of technology capabilities in high-leverage areas. Why, for example, have hundreds of people answering thousands of phone calls and making hundreds of mistakes, when a voice-response system can do this task more efficiently and virtually error-free? CEOs with a good command of technology not only keep a finger on the pulse of such opportunities and make sure that the company capitalizes on them, but also recognize that no system is generic. They ponder every decision to deploy technology within the broader context of the company's strategic direction.

2. *Inducing technology-based integration of internal business processes.* Common information is the central component of business process integration. Payroll information affects benefits administration. The information taken in the order-entry process affects, or *should* affect, marketing, production planning, order fulfillment, inventory management, accounts receivable, and so forth. Today's technology makes it possible to build an electronic "Main Street," where related business processes are linked through shared information on a common IT platform. This in turn requires the integration of organizational roles and responsibilities needed to use that shared information.

This sort of Main Street is a company's electronic equivalent of its physical infrastructure. As with physical infrastructure, designing and deploying a technology infrastructure is a highly strategic choice, involving many options and tradeoffs. It is the leadership team's job to set the high-level direction upon which a consistent set of policies can be built. And setting that direction involves not only looking at comparisons of the efficiency and effectiveness of internal options, but also taking an outward view to ensure that Main Street connects easily with the tributaries and highways that link the company with suppliers, customers, and other members of the supply chain.

3. *Promoting technology-enabled reengineering.* Connecting processes by putting them on the same technology platform is a launchpad for exploring brave new worlds of business process redesign, entering the realm of bioreengineering. This is where radical change begins, where the "ought" starts becoming the "is." It is where old process and organizational lines become very blurry, linked by the ordered chaos of free-flowing information within an organization. It is how Lands' End takes your clothing order by phone in less than a minute, and has it sitting on your doorstep within three days.

It is no longer enough to design a process, then overlay technology to simplify it. Now companies simultaneously look at what technology can do and design systems and processes accordingly. For the technophobic among today's business leaders, it seems an alien approach. It is the leadership team's job to make it the new standard of reengineering.

4. *Leading the development of technology-enhanced business networks.* If technology-enabled reengineering leads to brave new worlds of business process redesign, then technology-enhanced business networks transport a company into whole new galaxies. Many companies already are forming more closely knit relationships with their suppliers, distributors, retailers, and customers. And while politicians are talking about building an "information superhighway," some corporations are constructing their own, opening new strategic frontiers by sharing not just information but what was once considered proprietary knowledge.

As we approach the "Big Bang of Alliances" (see Chap. 8), CEOs of successful companies are leading the way in growing networks of alliances and partnerships with other firms, creating mutual benefits for all. This means more than just developing appropriately interconnected technology systems. It means that the CEO is creating the cosmic glue, developing the spiritual bond of mutual interest and trust that will allow intercompany systems to collapse space and time, blurring the lines of process, not just within a business, but across systems, companies, and continents.

5. *Redefining the scope of the business through technology.* As companies advance their business processes and networks through technology, the very act of doing so expands or even fundamentally alters the scope of the business. In other words, "bit magic" does to some corporations what automobiles did to buggy whips, or what desktops did to mainframes. The preferable course is for a corporation to outmode *itself* with innovative applications of technology, while leveraging that innovation to redefine its business.

Using technology to expand a business's scope or redefine it altogether is perhaps the CEO's greatest revitalization challenge. It can feel like being weaned a second time—altering or discarding the very source of growth that has nurtured a company for decades. Few leadership teams accept the challenge, fewer still have surmounted it. But like Mount Everest, it is *there*. *Unlike* Mount Everest, meeting the challenge is not merely a personal option. Mastering technology has become a requirement of business survival.

Rhetoric about change can ring hollow and become tiresome. In the realm of technology, however, change means something. In the areas of both hardware and software development, the world seems like one great big R&D department run amok, creating newer, better, faster, and more sophisticated capabilities far more quickly than any individual or business can assimilate and apply them. One end of the spectrum has been captured on T-shirts: "He who dies with the most toys, wins." At the other end is the philosophy: "I'll wait 'til next year, when everything is cheaper and better." Whichever your attitude, creativity is no longer hindered by the lack of technological options.

This fact fundamentally alters the relationship between leaders and technology. Historically, leaders have had to know a lot about technology to conceive of creative technological plays. Today, leaders can safely assume that if they can write a technological sonata, someone can play it. Therefore, they shouldn't worry about rapid prototyping, relational databases, and parallel processing, any more than they should worry about what's under the hood of their BMW. Business creativity is what's needed, not nerd magic.

Most CEOs remain strangely shy about technology, as if the old technology-constrained paradigm had left a permanent imprint on their brain. Yet the most successful among them have freed themselves from such thinking. In so doing, they have realized that they have the humbling power to change the rules of biocorporate life.

SANCTIONING TECHNOLOGY FOR LOCALIZED EFFICIENCY IMPROVEMENTS

Information technology can make life easier, or harder, depending on how you look at it. Now you can complete a document in London, fax or e-mail it to New York, Frankfurt, and Tokyo, and have a videoconference about it within the hour. No more three-day grace periods while you wait for the mail. Technology compresses time and space, which makes it possible to use time more efficiently. It is easier logistically, but more demanding personally. You must do more in less time to keep up. These days, back-to-back meetings pack a lot more punch.

The business world is replete with examples of using technology to achieve localized efficiency improvements: ATMs replacing live tellers, automated approval of credit card purchases, and bar-code scanners, to name but a few. These are applications that streamline work within a process or function. The focus is generally on cutting costs and saving time. At times, however, efficiency can prove to be of critical strategic importance.

Consider Citibank's Mortgage Power Plus program, for example. Member mortgage brokers can tap into the system from their office PCs, and apply on-line on behalf of their clients. The system runs a credit-decision model, and checks the client's credit from a number of sources. More than half the time, the system sends back a binding mortgage commitment. On the surface, this may seem just another case of efficiency gained through electronic wizardry. In reality, however, home buyers with mortgage approval in their hands bid more aggressively and therefore get the house more often. In addition, the first bank to issue a mortgage commitment is most likely to get the business, even if its interest rate is slightly higher than a competitor's. The result? Once brokers have joined the Power Plus program, they book 20 to 30 percent more of their business through Citibank.

But if Citibank can do it, so can other banks. The strategic advantage will fade quickly over time. Still, if Citibank plays its cards right, the high leverage of this local application of technology can pave the way for the next level of integration, in both financial and strategic terms.

It is in developing this sort of technological succession plan that the CEO plays a critical role in sanctioning the localized exploitation of technology. This means driving the leadership team to identify areas in which new technological capability can be applied quickly and with greatest possible financial benefit. It means recognizing that even technologies targeted for efficiency improvements may have strategic implications down the line. Should the company buy a generic system? Or should it design the local system with a view to its becoming part of a broader, differentiating technology infrastructure?

ERAM, or a Computer Hiding Inside a Shoe

The French shoe manufacturer, ERAM, knows a lot about improving process efficiency through technology. The company makes and sells a lot of shoes, grossing approximately $1 billion in sales annually, from approximately 700 stores. It has 12 manufacturing plants scattered throughout Europe and specializes in small lots, catering to fashions by segment at a price affordable to the masses. One of the biggest reasons ERAM hasn't lost its manufacturing base to the cheap labor markets of the Far East is that it has used technology as a competitive weapon.

To stay on the leading edge of fashion for the masses, ERAM must maintain low prices; but it also needs to be quick, turning out six or seven assortments of shoes every year. Fashions started to change quickly in the 1960s, and they still do today. In fact, ERAM has made this fast rotation a blunt instrument of war vis-à-vis its competitors. "Try to keep up with me," the company seems to say, tauntingly.

ERAM has been making technology moves for the last 30 years. The company installed its first computer in 1964, practically at the birth of the Communications Age. In 1966 it installed data-gathering cash registers in all its stores, allowing the firm to collate sales data quickly and send it back to headquarters, thus accelerating manufacturing response time. In 1969 the firm installed its first interactive systems, dramatically simplifying purchasing and accounting systems. In 1977 it installed the first distributed computer, enabling several users to access the computer at the same time. In 1980 the company installed desktops throughout the company, automating the order management and production systems.

Given its PC-based network, ERAM recently was able to solve one of its longest standing problems: developing a new catalog six or seven times a year for hundreds of shoes that differ by region. Imagine, if you will, the high quantity of errors certain to arise due to ordering from outdated catalogs, or from simple transcription errors. When the ISDN system was adopted in France, which enables picture transmission by phone line, ERAM seized the opportunity to make its catalog electronic. Now retailers can page through the catalog, look at the shoes, and place their order online, with virtually no possibility of error. Typically they receive their orders within just a few days. Thus they have the best of all worlds: a paperless catalog that is never out of date, and a system that supports the store's need for speed and flexibility. For ERAM, technology is the means to support its fast-paced, multiple-segment strategy.

"Karl, Get Us a New Scheduling Package, Will You?"

Back at Woodbridge headquarters, Karl is savoring his recent victories. He never knew he could have such an impact. The focused manufacturing program is now in implementation mode. All agree that the product line should remain broad, should perhaps even be expanded to make it harder for competitors to duplicate. He is more than on-track with his original project goal: lead time is now just 16 days, and still shrinking. There are new partnerships developing with customers, triggered by the workshops he's helped to organize. Now his attention is returning to what marked the beginning of this great adventure: scheduling.

Karl is talking with a software vendor, looking at the possible implementation of a new application they call The Cut-sheet Optimization Program. To Karl, the application represents a potentially important step toward improving their scheduling effectiveness, and it could help to further reduce the order-to-delivery cycle time.

While it may look like a simple problem, those who have tried to solve it by hand know that it ain't that simple. It involves fitting as many customers orders as possible, orders that usually come in all sorts of widths and lengths, inside the very long rectangle of paper constituting a master roll. Yeah, it looks like kids' stuff at first, cutting small rectangles inside a large rectangle and doing it in such a way as to minimize scrap. That used to be part of Karl's job, and he had developed a few rules of thumb that worked well, until it dawned on him there had to be a better way. Now the software vendor is peddling a package that does the optimization automatically, utilizing "an algorithm." Karl knows he's in trouble when they use words like that on him.

If the program can beat Karl, even by a small margin, it will quickly pay for itself in reduced scrap. Karl is curious. He's eager to compete with the machine. He's ready for a simulation game, man against machine. He feels like Anatoli Karpov testing the latest chess computer program. The software vendor is visibly nervous, wondering whether his program can beat the crusty scheduler at his own game. Karl stares the vendor down as intimidatingly as he can, hoping that just as in chess, he can scare his opponent into submission.

The first game goes to the machine, by a large margin. Karl is crushed. He wins the second game in overtime, though, and regains hope. The third and fourth games again go to the machine, again by a landslide.

Game, set, and match. Karl, while a grumpy loser, recommends buying the software nonetheless. The software vendor is happy. Woodbridge will install the new Cut-sheet Optimization Program.

A few minutes later, Karl is staring at the computer screen, lost in his thoughts. It's not that he's sore; it's just that he's reflecting on the fact that he's gone full-circle in the last two years. Cut-sheet optimization is where it all began. Karl can still see the head of manufacturing coming into his office, asking him "to fix scheduling because it takes too darn long." He vividly remembers the recommendation of his boss: "Change the way orders are accumulated, and let's get on with it. There's gotta be some computer program that can help. Karl, get us a new scheduling package, will you?"

Karl, the good soldier, even remembers going from supplier to supplier, each of them advertising a particular program. He also reminisces about how he didn't want to purchase any of them until he'd figured out the bigger picture. And the flak he's taken for holding on to that belief! The "Karl, what are you waiting for?", and "Karl, if you can't solve the problem, we'll find someone who will!" still resonate in his head.

And what a trip it's been, from humble beginnings, trying to identify the new scheduling "algorithm," to figuring out how wide the product line ought to be, whether they should be integrated in paper and pulp, and redefining the entire production scheme across the six plants of the firm. No wonder he found it difficult at the outset to pick a software package. He had to work across all those other issues and involve hundreds of people before he could make an intelligent choice.

And now that all those issues have been settled, he can finally address the issue of the scheduling algorithm. Now that he knows which products are expected to be produced on which machines, he can indeed use a piece of software that might help. He shivers at the thought that he might have listened to his boss and simply purchased a piece of software. He knows exactly what he would have done: He would have installed the SAP production management module, and by golly, it would have produced some good results. But then the company probably would have missed out on some significantly larger opportunities, like the Focus play. Today they'll install the SAP module, but modified with the Cut-sheet Optimization Program that's just beaten him in the scheduling duel.

Karl is feeling good about himself today. It doesn't even matter much that the silly machine was able to beat him three times out of four, implicitly shattering the legacy of his 20-year scheduling career. Deep in his heart, Karl knows he's much more valuable than the machine. After all, he has proven that he operates at a much higher level of contribution than simply optimizing the cut sheet.

"Technology is the best and the worst of things," he mutters, new-wave philosopher that he's become.

INDUCING TECHNOLOGY-BASED INTEGRATION OF INTERNAL BUSINESS PROCESSES

While most leading companies take advantage of technology within processes, many companies are only now launching initiatives to link their processes through technology. They are attempting to build an electronic and digital infrastructure that will act as Main Street for interprocess transactions across the business. The idea is to have a common pool of data and information that is input once and then automatically flows to the point of need in every affected process. And as new information is generated within processes, it too must enter the pool and find its way to the processes it affects.

In principle, it sounds simple. In practice, it never is. Many corporations have been burned by the go-go spending of their MIS departments' internal application developments in recent years, so they have resolved to buy standard packages from outside vendors. SAP, originally developed in Germany, is perhaps the best recent example of such an application, and MRP played the same role in the previous generation. While many such programs are well built, their implementation raises two major challenges.

First, the arrival of a new, powerful, integrated software package often causes the reengineering river to reverse its natural flow. While the application should be tailored to the processes it is supposed to serve, many process owners, in practice, become intimidated by the software and start to fit their process to the technology. Second, process owners look for the same benefits in the same areas, usually the inventory, cycle time, and service areas. This is the stuff that disasters are made of, because the same software package is rolled from competitor to competitor, leveling the competitive floor. In the end, the software vendor ends up as sole beneficiary of the effort, having successfully led entire industries to competitive parity by selling each member the same expensive weapon.

Other firms, rather than jumping to a new integrated software solution, prefer to migrate their existing systems to the new world. This involves different challenges. There are old, mainframe legacy systems to deal with. There are existing, local systems that can't "talk" to one another. And there are intangible cultural walls that resist cooperation and fear the consequences of integrated systems. Some people know that the new system will displace them. Why should they help build a system that will cost them their jobs? And then there's training, thousands of man-hours of training, and generally not enough high-quality suppliers of training services for the new software packages. For example, SAP implementers currently are in extremely rare supply the world over.

And yet if you *don't* integrate your processes through technology, one of your competitors *will*, and will then beat you. Successful CEOs subtly induce internal process integration through technology, for it is upon this logic that the detailed technological and organizational decisions will be made. The more advanced technology-based process redesign and business network integration are impossible without it.

Zeneca Uses Systems as a Trojan Horse for Change

Zeneca, a U.K.-based, $7 billion agricultural chemicals and pharmaceuticals company, provides an interesting example of transformation through technology, one that we will follow throughout this chapter. The firm was created in 1993, when it "demerged" from the worldwide chemicals company, ICI, to release shareholder value perceived to be "hidden" inside ICI's portfolio. One outcome of the demerger was that Zeneca would eventually have to run on different information systems than ICI.

The short-term solution was a lease-back agreement, according to which ICI would provide services through year-end 1994, leaving Zeneca with two years to develop systems of its own. Zeneca headquarters decided to standardize its worldwide supply chain and financial support with the SAP integrated software package. With SAP, transactions posted in one area automatically generate related transactions in other areas. (For example, shipping an order may generate a reduction in inventory, create an invoice, and post accounts receivable.) Zeneca's individual businesses were left on their own to develop their business systems from the SAP platform.

Bob Woods, the president of Zeneca Agricultural Products in the United States, saw the systems challenge as a unique opportunity to concurrently reengineer the business's processes. Woods mused that Zeneca might do even more than that by changing the rules of an industry generally thought to be as conservative as the farmers it serves. The concurrent systems development and reengineering program could, he thought, be a Trojan horse with which to fundamentally change the company.

In his view, Zeneca's competitive position was a mixed bag. The product portfolio was well balanced. Net sales per sales representative was the highest in the industry. But there was also a downside. Zeneca was fifth or sixth in overall market share. Sales growth was variable relative to years past, but costs still were on the rise. Return on net assets (RONA), the number he himself had to answer for, was unacceptable.

Before Woods could ponder changing the agricultural industry through technology, he had to backtrack one step. To make a difference in the marketplace, he would first need to energize a team inside his own company. This became his first priority.

His biggest problem here was resistance to change. The organization had been built around functions, not processes, and as often happens, walls between functions had been erected over time. This made it difficult to mobilize people across different functions. Woods wanted every employee to be "on-board" for the transformation journey.

Woods appointed a full-time change agent from within Zeneca, Jerry Quinn, an expatriate American who had been on assignment in England. Quinn is a veteran in the ag-chem business, and as he started tackling the enormous transformation agenda, he quickly learned that getting employees behind the program was going to be a challenge.

Both Woods and Quinn recognized that the role of the leadership team would be critical, which meant developing a shared understanding of the vision. The central component of that vision was "creating customer enthusiasm," which implied a new definition of who Zeneca's customers were. By the new view, Zeneca's customers were not just the distributors and dealers who bought their products directly but also *their* customers: dealers, applicators, pest control operators, and farmers working their fields. Zeneca henceforth would focus not so much on selling products as on solving the farmers' problems, working with distributors and applicators to make everyone's business life better.

Other parts of Woods' vision pertained more directly to the information systems. When Jerry Quinn first took on his new role, Woods told him, "I want velocity … and I want paperless processes. Get rid of all non-value-added activities. Redesign the entire business if necessary." Woods knew what he wanted, even though he wasn't sure how to get it.

The transformation effort was formally launched in April of 1993. Ostensibly, the initial focus was on implementing the SAP software system inside the firm, although the leaders of the firm knew that the agenda really was much larger. Over the next several months, process-level natural work teams designed their "to-be" processes, working closely with each other and with an IT team to develop an integrated design that utilized the SAP platform to its fullest potential. At the same time, Zeneca's leadership team was developing a Balanced Scorecard, looking ahead to the development of a singular vision of where they wanted the business to go.

They decided to concurrently redesign processes and systems, in spite of the pressure put on them by an absolute requirement to have the systems up and running by the end of 1994, the end of the lease-back period from ICI. The reengineering effort was focused primarily on the redesign of supply-chain processes and the implementation of SAP within them.

Woods and the executive team knew, however, that it was only a beginning....

PROMOTING TECHNOLOGY-ENABLED REENGINEERING

This is where technology becomes fun. It's where revolutions are started, where new ideas take root and spring to life. The more mundane first and second leadership tasks have created a stage, the launchpad. Now the CEO begins to create the play, to ignite the thrusters. Forget about process boundaries. Abandon rigid process frameworks. Invent new processes! Let creativity explode!

Technology-enabled reengineering involves more than simplifying traditional process redesign through technology. It involves a fundamental rethinking of what work must be done, why, and by whom, in the context of what technology makes possible and with special emphasis on creating learning loops and enhancing knowledge sharing. It is bioreengineering (see the last part of Chap. 6) with a heavily weighted technology component.

In bioreengineering, the goal is to create learning loops within and across the processes that move the company toward its goals. In the context of bioreengineering, technology often can help one interpret, decide, and act upon that data. The real art of utilizing technology in bioreengineering comes as the last step in a three-part process:

1. Identifying the critical learning loops that drive performance toward the goals established in the Balanced Scorecard.

2. Defining the key cause-effect connectors—the metabolic pathways—among the learning loops.

3. Deciding how and to what extent technology can inform the learning loops and create their connection to each other.

All three components of this process are of critical strategic importance. It is often the last one, however, that determines the degree of a business's strategic flexibility and the nature of its competitive differentiation. No matter where technological innovation takes us, ultimately it is the human factor—the ability to act upon knowledge and create a different perception of reality—that is the ultimate strategic weapon. Technology often is the only way to creatively link "many to many." Ultimately, technology is but a means allowing individuals to gain and leverage knowledge for competitive advantage.

Technology-enabled Claims and Underwriting at CIGNA

From the beginning, Gerry Isom knew that playing the specialist game required knowledge; specifically, underwriters with specialized knowledge of different market segments. He also knew that that was exactly what CIGNA was lacking. He needed a *staff* of them, not just a handful. Nor did he have the time or the resources for classroom training in specialist techniques. That wouldn't have worked anyway—the best training for a specialist is experience. He had to get maximum leverage out of the specialists he had. With an unshakable faith in the power of technology to address knowledge problems, he chartered a technology team to find a solution.

"I had used learning systems in the past with great success," he remembers. "When you don't have enough talent to go around, technology can often help."

Let's now rewind the tape to a technology workshop in the spring of 1994. It's "make or break" day for the technology team. They are gathered backstage, pacing, shuffling, and cracking their knuckles as they wait to make their presentation. Members of the MIS department, a few underwriters, and an outside firm have teamed up to design a desktop learning system for the underwriters. They have been working for six weeks developing the prototype, and now it's time to unveil their product.

"Don't worry, they'll like it," the project leader says, trying to sound reassuring. "They" are 30 underwriters, the people who will actually use the learning system. These 30 essentially have veto power over the project. If they don't like it, the project is dead. It's as simple as that.

The unveiling has been carefully staged. It's a two-day affair, designed to give the underwriters many technological options to consider. The session begins with a series of demonstrations showing how the competition uses IT in underwriting. Several outside vendors have been invited to show off their wares. The internal team is given equal time to present its system: two hours at the end of the first day.

"Ladies and gentlemen," the moderator announces, "we now hand the podium over to our internal MIS team."

The lights dim and attention focuses on the screen. The presenter holds his breath, praying that the software will "boot" as planned. It has worked the 17 times he's tried it in the last half-hour—but you never know. The expected image comes up, and he breathes a little easier.

"Our team has been working on this prototype of the Underwriter Performance Support System, or PSS for short," he begins. "We want to show you where we are, and to let you tell us what you like about it and what you don't, and whether you think it's worth pursuing. We'll also ask you to steer our efforts by suggesting features and functionalities that would be helpful to you."

He sits down, handing the microphone to one of his team members, an underwriter who describes the system while his MIS partner sits at a nearby table, clicking the computer mouse and changing the screens as the presentation progresses. It doesn't hurt to have one of their own making the presentation to the underwriters.

"Let's assume we're being asked to underwrite a child care center in South Carolina," he begins. "Here's what the underwriter would see." Up on the screen comes a diagram of the underwriting process, depicted just as the underwriters themselves had recently designed it, but with the specifics of the hypothetical problem hung upon it. Seeing their own process inside the machine produces a noticeable rustle in the audience— somebody, somewhere has been listening after all.

"Let's start with the big exposures," he goes on. "The first question is whether you're in an earthquake zone. Well, as you can see, the answer is no. You also have to ask if it's a tornado area, and in this case the answer's yes. Now that raises a whole lot of questions, doesn't it?" He has their full attention now.

"Let's assume you want to know more about tornado-related risk," he continues. "What you would do is move up to the tutorial about wind damage and click on it, like this." A multimedia package kicks in, complete with sound effects, pictures of houses after a tornado, sketches of what happens to walls and roofs in a tornado, and a checklist of preventive measures, with assessments of their risk-reducing impact.

"This is as good as having Winslow on your team," one of the underwriters comments. Winslow is the uncontested expert in the firm on wind damages.

"Winslow helped us design this section," the presenter says with a grin, "and if you want to swap notes with him, here's the window to do it in. Winslow has promised to answer all questions within 24 hours."

Winslow acknowledges the commitment by raising his hand and saying he's also available for informal coaching. He adds: "If you folks don't mind, I'd love to have access to your work, not to judge what you're doing, but so I can learn more about wind-related risks. That way, I can update our manuals, grids, and pricing databases to reflect our latest experience."

A new picture of how they could work emerged for the 30 underwriters in the audience.

The new performance measurement system was embedded in the PSS, and all necessary forms and policies were built in, so there would be no more intermediate paperwork and files to process and go through. With this system, the underwriters in the audience realized, they could concentrate their energy on problem solving. The real value, though, was that the knowledge of the expert was built into the system, and where it wasn't, there was an on-line connection to the expert. Moreover, as questions would be asked and answered, they would be accumulated, becoming a part of the learning system.

There are now 15 hands in the air, and a rolling fire of questions.

"Will we be able to access claims files on-line?"

"Eventually. We're developing a similar system for claims, and we'll connect it with the underwriting system, if we decide to proceed with both."

"Who will have access to my work? I'd love Winslow to look over my shoulder, because I know he can help, but I would *not* like my boss to do it."

"We'll have to work together on that," the presenter says. "It's still too early. All we have is a prototype. We still have to define the organizational and human implications. For today, all we want is to know how you feel about it, and where you'd like to take it."

The vote was 29 in favor and 1 abstaining, and the internal technology team left with pages and pages of suggestions on where to take the next iteration. They hadn't just won the order—they'd blown the competition out of the water. At the back of the room, Gerry Isom allowed himself a smile.

LEADING THE DEVELOPMENT OF TECHNOLOGY-ENHANCED BUSINESS NETWORKS

Here, the CEO extends the bounds of process and technology outside of the safe walls of the individual company. It is fertile but murky ground, where shadows lie, where proprietary lines are hard to discern. But it is also *rich* ground that is being explored, settled, and cultivated through a new form of colonialism in which vision and knowledge, not might, rules.

This is CEO territory par excellence, because it involves both a vision and the creation of strategic alliances. It means working with other businesses to build new capabilities and to create new market discontinuities, building and supporting an infrastructure that allows controlled information and knowledge sharing. It involves linking one's own business's learning loops with those of other businesses. The benefits to be gained range from reduced costs to increased effectiveness, to doors being opened to entirely new businesses. It involves applying the principles of technology-enabled reengineering to the supply chain as a whole.

The business world is replete with examples of network applications. In the mid-1980s, for example, Robert Haas, Chairman and CEO of Levi Strauss & Co., was the first in the garment industry to introduce EDI-services through the LeviLink system. LeviLink offers services such as electronic purchase orders, advance shipping notices, financial services, electronic funds transfers, and some specialized programs. Today, almost 60 percent of Levi Strauss's U.S. purchases are handled through this fast and efficient system. Levi's, like many others, uses its system to form tighter bonds with its suppliers and customers.

This kind of network building goes beyond information sharing into the realm of building networked *learning systems*. In every business, there are opportunities to build interconnected learning systems. Building them will increasingly be the key to gaining the next generation of sustainable competitive advantage. And as we shall see in the next section, creating such connectors often leads to redefining the business altogether.

Zeneca Leads Industrywide Change Through Technology

Every now and then it's helpful to change not only yourself, but your entire industry. Such is Bob Woods' philosophy at Zeneca, and that's why Zeneca is part of an industry task force, leading the way in forging new information standards for its industry.

But why bother? What's in it for Zeneca, if all this technology simply raises the water level for all boats? "Because the customers need some help," is Zeneca's first answer. But Zeneca's leadership isn't entirely altruistic. Zeneca understands that if it can lead the entire industry to a higher level of information sophistication, there will be plenty of opportunities to create competitive advantage for itself along the way.

"The advantage isn't in the infrastructure," Woods likes to say. "It's in how you use the information. And we're pretty good at that."

In much the same way that JVC saw the benefit of having one, world-wide VCR standard, Woods believes his entire industry will benefit from standardizing its electronic transactions platform. Standardization will accelerate the availability of information, and when that information becomes available, the opportunities to implement real innovation will begin.

Zeneca's drive originates from customers' frustrations with the existing way of doing business:

Growers are demanding more flexibility and higher performance in products and services.

Inventory- and distribution-related processes can be inefficient and costly.

Regulatory compliance is increasingly difficult and costly to everyone in the supply chain.

Working capital levels are too high, largely due to over-stocking and proliferation of product packages.

Through ACPA (the American Crop Protection Association, formerly the National Agricultural Chemicals Association), the industry has developed a shared, five-year vision to address the problem. They have agreed on what they term a *pull strategy,* meaning that growers will dictate what is produced and shipped by basic manufacturers. This common vision is based on four propositions:

1. The entire supply chain should be electronically linked on a common EDI-based standard, enabling real-time product-movement data and JIT inventory practices.

2. Growers eventually will be provided with *smart cards,* similar to banking cards, allowing them to purchase products electronically.

3. Dynamic forecasting practices can provide real-time inventory levels and production forecasts to minimize stagnant inventories.

4. Technology-enabled, flexible manufacturing techniques will minimize manufacturing lead times, and allow the production of products closer to the season. (Right now, many agricultural chemical companies "level-load" their plants throughout the year, even though the selling season is extremely short).

Implementing this vision requires that the entire industry be electronically linked. ACPA has appointed a task force in charge of project RAPID (Responsible Agricultural Product and Information Distribution) to move the industry in that direction. Co-chaired by Jerry Quinn, this task force is an industrywide reengineering team, its mission being to develop the industry's technical network infrastructure and to design standard processes around it.

One of the task force's first challenges was to develop a common, EDI-based set of standards for the industry. Many businesses in the industry were already using EDI and bar-coding systems on a limited basis. The problem was that operators, manufacturers, distributors, and retailers were using different definitions and policies. One system, for example, might define inventory as "product in the warehouse"; another system might define it as "warehouse stock, plus purchases made but not yet received"; and still another as "warehouse stock, minus product committed for sale within the coming two weeks." If the systems were to talk to one another, they would need a common language. Over a six-month period, the task force agreed on the new standard.

But the team went far beyond establishing the EDI-based standard. It developed a three-phase design to be implemented over a five-year period. By mid-1994 the team also had redesigned six integrated processes involving manufacturers, distributors, and retailers. They include order management and logistics for packaged and bulk products, container tracking, regulatory compliance, inventory management and forecasting, and financial reporting.

As of this writing, the new processes are being piloted at over a dozen sites industrywide. In addition, distributors, dealers, and retailers are embracing the vision. The signs of improvement already are visible, with product availability and manufacturing flexibility on the rise, while inventories and working capital levels are decreasing.

Zeneca intends to lead its industry in climbing the systems pyramid it has helped design, reaping as many benefits as possible along the way. And while the technology component is an integral part of that climb, it is not the central focus—the central focus remains on the customer. "Eventually," Quinn predicts," a grower will come into a dealer to buy a Zeneca product, knowing that it is the best. The grower will make the purchase using his smart card, which posts the purchase into the industry-wide system. But instead of receiving the product and an invoice, every aspect of the transaction will be handled automatically, including the filing of required regulatory forms. Because the grower buys from Zeneca, he'll not only get a great product, he also won't have to waste time with a bunch of paperwork."

"And one day," he adds, "there will even be a nationwide performance support system in there, coaching the farmer on what to use given his field, his location, and even the prevailing weather conditions."

REDEFINING THE SCOPE OF THE BUSINESS THROUGH TECHNOLOGY

Ultimately, technology can help corporations fundamentally change the nature of the game. This is what successful CEOs have done in numerous industries, as in the invention of homeshopping, the birth of CNN and of cable stations and operators, and the advent of the videogame industry and on-line information services. There's one problem, however: These stories show only the shiny side of the coin.

For each of them there's a victim on the wrong side of the fence. Classic retailers are trembling in their boots, wondering whether customers will still come into their stores when they can order customized merchandise electronically. CBS, NBC, and ABC haven't exactly been paragons of profitability in recent years, threatened not only by CNN and its global, satellite-based network, but also by the proliferation of cable channels eating away at their advertising revenues. The old manufacturers of fruit and pinball machines are struggling against Sonic the Hedgehog and SuperMario Brothers. And now daily newspapers and magazines often are competing against on-line services for the right to provide news and customer information. Even if it's for defensive purposes alone, leaders benefit from technology issues.

Almost without exception, we find that leaders who have revolutionized their industries through technology aren't particularly knowledgeable about technology. They are at heart creative strategists, with an interest in the role of technology in business and a quiet confidence that technology, like infantry, will follow their lead. They are students of technologically induced market discontinuities, but they aren't fountains of knowledge about what can and can't be done with the bits and bytes. This gives them the mental latitude to think without constraint, to freely connect pieces of knowledge across disjointed pieces of the value chain and let their imagination wander (and wonder).

When Taxis Go High-tech

Who among us hasn't had a terrible experience with a taxi? You call, and get put on interminable hold. Finally, a dispatcher speaking in muttering code answers. You tell him where you're going. On hold again. Then he comes squawking back to tell you a cab is on its way. When will it arrive? Somewhere between 15 and 30 minutes. If it doesn't get there, call back.

Five minutes have now passed since you first dialed, and you hang up, nervous. It better get there, or you'll be late for your plane. The cab arrives 25 minutes later. For the last 10 minutes, you've been wishing you hadn't quit smoking. The cabby asks for your destination again, then groans at the prospect of fighting airport traffic. Somehow, you make it. Dripping with sweat, you take your seat in the plane, wondering how long it will be before the cocktail cart arrives.

Now imagine this. You call the cab company, and a pleasant female voice greets you, politely asks your name, location, destination, and, if you're a corporate customer with a G7 relationship, the name of your company. "One moment, please," she says. Within 15 seconds she's back on the line, telling you the cab will be there in 10 minutes. Astonishingly, she gives you a description of the car, and the cab's number! The cab arrives on time and the cabby steps out, greeting you by name as he helps you with your luggage. Inside the cab he confirms, not asks, your destination, and tells you that your fare will be billed directly to your company, including a standard 15 percent tip, and you're on your way.

"Yeah, right," you may be thinking, "maybe in 2010." But in fact this is what a long-established, Paris-based taxi company, G7, has recently implemented. G7 has elevated its service level to that of private limousines, but at the more economical fares of taxis. Each cab is equipped with a box that is linked to the central dispatch system. The dispatcher enters, or if it's already there, reads the customer data. The system, which continuously tracks the location and status of all on-duty cabs, notifies the nearest vacant cab, or a cab soon to be vacant in that area. In the cab is a display indicating the customer's name, location, destination, and promised time of pick-up. By pressing a button, the cabby confirms that he is en route. If he or she turns down the fare, it automatically migrates to the next-best available car, and the first taxi loses his or her turn in the queue.

Not only is it a wonderful system from the customer's vantage point, it also helps the drivers. To the driver, the system reduces the stress of listening to CB voice traffic all day, and does away with the previous system that involved jumping onto the response button whenever he heard the dispatcher list a fare he wanted, and beating his fellow drivers to the punch. Granted, a few drivers, perhaps feeling that Big Brother was watching, preferred the old system and moved to other companies. By and large, however, the experiment has been a great success. The net result is not just higher levels of customer satisfaction, but higher levels of cab utilization. Translation: more money for the company, and more money for the drivers, who operate on commission. It's also a clever way of injecting scale dynamics—or at least network dynamics—into what is otherwise a cottage industry.

Zeneca Changes the Rules

Springtime is planting season, and it's a hectic period for agricultural chemical dealers. For weeks on end there's a rush to get chemical to customers, fill out paperwork, comply with regulations. Employees work overtime.

Everyone gets exhausted. A day's worth of work is scribbled on note pads, on the back of business cards, or on yellow Post-its™ on the bulletin board. Sometimes it takes days to get it all put onto the books, and during that time, transactions can get lost or misplaced, inventory records go out of date. Inevitably, there are stockouts. Sales are lost. The bottom line is affected.

Or, the dealer gets so busy that he lets an inexperienced worker fill some bulk containers. The wrong chemical gets into the wrong container, and cross-contamination occurs. Hundreds of gallons of expensive chemical are lost. And it means filing a report with EPA to get special dispensation for disposing of the chemical.

Understanding how hard this period is for dealers, Zeneca decided to do something about it. They teamed up with Fillrite, a division of the Tuthill corporation, a world leader in the development and manufacturing of fluid-handling technology for the petroleum and chemical industries. Zeneca worked with Fillrite to develop a system that could help dealers handle their bulk inventories more effectively: prevent shrinkage, provide immediate information to eliminate lost sales, prevent cross-contamination, reduce paperwork, and make compliance with federal regulations manageable. They wanted an approach so simple that anyone could learn how to use it in a matter of minutes. The solution they came up with is called Chemdata™.

Chemdata™ is an integrated, bar-coded, card-activated system designed to make the dealer's life a lot easier. It's a combination of hardware and software, installed at the dealer's site. But the dealer pays only an annual fee for the use of the system, plus a nominal, one-time fee for adding non-Zeneca chemicals to the system.

A typical transaction works like this:

Bill the farmer shows up at the counter to pick up a small bulk load of Eradicane®, an herbicide used for weed control. Sam, an employee of the dealer, pulls out Bill's card and slides it through a sensor. As a result, a screen appears on the computer displaying everything Sam needs to know about Bill as a customer: credit arrangements, special licenses, and so forth. Entering the order into the system, Sam immediately finds out if he has any prefilled containers to meet the customer's order. If not, the systems tells him which empty containers on-site are authorized for use with that chemical. In this case there are no prefilled containers, so through a few key strokes Sam sets up the system for bulk dispensing, and the two agree to meet at the loading dock.

Outside, Bill the farmer pulls his truck up next to the dispensing pump, and Sam puts the container onto it. Then he places the pump nozzle in the container, selects the chemical with a switch on the pump, and scans the bar code on the container to activate the pump. Nothing happens. Sam has inadvertently selected the wrong chemical. Since the transaction has been preset, the system allows only the right amount of the right chemical to be pumped into the authorized container. Sam resets the selector, scans the container again, and the pumping begins. The system automatically shuts off when the preset amount has been pumped, and a bill is printed, much like those provided at credit-card-activated gasoline pumps.

There are numerous benefits generated by this system:

Real-time inventory tracking.

Complete transaction documentation: date, time, chemical dispensed, how much, by whom, into what container, for what customer, and on what terms (cash or credit).

Bar coding protects the customer from cross-contamination and the overfilling of containers; it also facilitates container tracking for retrieval and regulatory purposes.

Reports customer purchase history and product requirements.

Automatic compliance with regulatory requirements, and generation of regulatory documentation.

The system was designed before the ACPA standards were agreed upon, but Zeneca and Fillrite are quickly moving to adapt it such that all information generated by the system can be fed directly into other ACPA-standard systems.

From the dealer's standpoint, the system removes all the headaches that once were associated with bulk dispensing systems, while simultaneously reducing costs. Dealers using the system conservatively estimate that it has added at least 1 percent margin to their bottom line, a sizable increase in a notoriously narrow margin business. In fact, Zeneca guarantees that the system will reduce dealers' operating costs.

From Zeneca's standpoint, the real advantage lies in feeding the information gathered at the dealer site right into its own information systems, extending the tentacles of its own learning loops in sales, marketing, and manufacturing. Chemdata™ gives Zeneca the ability to learn more and faster about what's happening at the dealer's site, giving it the opportunity to distill that information into meaningful knowledge for its own strategy and operations.

RENEWAL

U ltimately, human life is more than its biological makeup; beyond a certain point, it can no longer be described as an aggregation of nuclei, cells, and bodily systems. The brain becomes mind, the neuro-transmitters jumping from synapse to synapse become thoughts, the DNA code becomes a trace of one's family history, and the body gives way to an abstraction, what we often call a personality, with its richness of emotions and aspirations. The individual, in particular, becomes an expression of interactions with other people. It is to the *people* inside the corporation that we now turn our attention, not to their flesh and blood, but to their spirit.

For *people* are the spirit of a corporation. Reframing was the kingdom of the rationalist; restructuring the field of the surgeon; revitalization the domain of the ecologist. Renewal is the terrain of the spiritualist. As is true of people, we don't often think of companies as spiritual creatures. We prefer to think of them in terms of their products or services, or as an expression of the processes and systems they utilize. Yet more often than not, companies evoke emotions for us: the joy of a child playing with a Macintosh computer; our warm trust in our financial adviser at the bank; the pleasure of driving a new car home. Each of these emotions is rooted in the spirituality of the offering firm, and triggers similar spiritual responses on our part. The Macintosh computer, for example, embodies everything that Apple Computers means to us; perhaps the image of a fast-growing, imaginative company with whom we have grown, producing, in this case, a pleasant feeling. Watching one's child play with a Macintosh incarnates the spirit of Apple, and connects that spirit directly to that of the proud parents of the child.

Spirit is a difficult word when used in a business context. It is redolent of philosophy and other intellectual wanderings, and doesn't readily marry with the pragmatic world of offering goods and services for profit. And yet, spirituality is a key component of successful corporations. Without spirituality, there can be no transformation. The spirit of learning and growth is what animates all great people and all great corporations. This spirit exerts itself through the building of bigger and bigger networks of connected nodes. It is what constitutes renewal.

The world of renewal starts with rewards, described in Chap. 10. Rewards appeal to the sense of gratification in all of us. This is the lowest level of spirituality, the simplest form of human connectivity. Working for a company, the individual expects to be compensated in some fashion for producing an effort, at a minimum, a just material return for one's labor. Even in a more spiritual context, people seek material rewards, offering their love and respect for their respective gods, in the hope of receiving some worldly relief.

But at some point, individuals are no longer motivated simply by rewards. The relationship between the individual and the environment seems to reverse itself; the individual stops looking at the corporation as the provider and begins assuming responsibility for his or her own development. In so doing, he or she has entered the realm of individual learning, stepping to the next higher spiritual plane by becoming both a student of the world and a more active participant in it.

It is a matter of adopting the business version of John F. Kennedy's famous challenge: "Ask not what your country can do for you, but what you can do for your country." People stop defining themselves in terms of expected material rewards, and begin to define themselves in terms of the impact they can have on the people and the world around them. Their connections to people and things become more dynamic than static, a state of constant, design-each-other-as-you-go interaction. The boundary between self and the external environment becomes blurred, with the self expanding into the environment and the environment entering the self.

Ultimately, the individual's quest for spiritual freedom finds its best expression in a shared search. Individual pursuits give way to organizational learning, the topic of Chap. 12. This is the most advanced form of spirituality, where groups of like-minded individuals search together for new connections that can be made with others. The connectivity becomes one of "many to many," rather than "one to many" as before. Rather than being a hermit, the individual now draws energy from others and finds that group-based quests yield the best answers. The solitude of the monk yields to the warmth of the ecumenical parish.

Renewal is by far the hardest form of transformation. Many companies have perfected reframing and restructuring. Some are on their way to revitalization. But few can legitimately claim to have conquered renewal. Nonetheless, the ability to get a large number of people to behave in a mutually supportive fashion, and to strive together for renewal, is ultimately the only form of advantage the corporation can attain.

DEVELOPING THE REWARDS SYSTEM

W hen people fundamentally change, what changes about them is their behaviors. But at a deeper level, what changes is the benefits or *rewards* they reap, or hope to reap, as a consequence of what they do.

Whether held implicitly or explicitly, consciously or subconsciously, each person has adopted a unique mental system of rewards. And whether internally consistent or not, that reward system is what motivates one on a day-to-day basis. Because rewards are psychologically rooted, they take many forms. In particular, they are derived from the desire to attain pleasure or the need to avoid pain.

A CEO may adopt a less autocratic style, discovering that a more participative approach is more likely to help turn an ailing company around enabling him or her to make a mark. A saleswoman may redirect her priorities and start advocating the more complex product she had heretofore shied away from, to increase her commission. A formerly resistant middle manager may suddenly take a corporate cost-cutting effort seriously, realizing for the first time that the company's future, and therefore his or her ability to provide for family, may depend on its success. An alcoholic may quit drinking, prodded by the counseling of a peer group and scared by the rehabilitation center's ominous prediction is that he will die a lonely man unless he changes his ways.

Though the desire to attain pleasure and the need to avoid pain drive our perception of rewards, the problem is that there is no guarantee that what we perceive as pleasurable is inherently productive, or conversely, that what we perceived as painful is inherently destructive. We subconsciously hold values and beliefs that act as the filter of the reward system.

Consequently, the efficacy of the rewards system is the result of the "objective" mechanisms put in place by the corporation and the "subjective" filter of each employee. What leaders aim for isn't always what they get.

In the biological corporation, the rewards system caters to the human *sense of gratification*. Just as an individual's reward system drives his or her behaviors, so a corporation's rewards system drives the way the people of an organization work. The rewards system is the connector through which people decide whether to make the goals of the corporation their own, personal goals. The corporation bares its soul through its rewards system, implicitly inviting people to accept or reject the very essence of the organization.

Developing the rewards system is the work of the tenth biocorporate chromosome. It has three genes, implying three corresponding tasks for the genetic architects of the organization:

1. *Fostering alignment of rewards to the goals and measures of the organization.* A corporation's goals and measures are inextricably linked, and rewards are the glue that binds them. Ideally, rewards reflect the goals of the corporation, connecting people to multidimensional measures that drive their own and the organization's performance. In most companies, however, achieving this linkage is a major challenge, for their reward systems rely predominantly on financial incentives indexed to the company's financial performance. In reality, financial performance is only one of many drivers of success, which is why many forward-looking companies are developing reward systems based upon a balanced perspective of goals and measures.

The Balanced Scorecard provides a helpful framework for building and aligning measurement and reward systems. Just as corporations can use the four broad categories of measures of the Balanced Scorecard (financial, customer, operational, learning) to build their measurement system, so they can use the same categories to build their reward system. In both measurement and reward systems, the key is to connect the measures and rewards to an integrated "story" about how the corporation intends to transform itself. The role of leaders is to foster the alignment of measures and rewards, and to maintain the integrity of the interrelationship between them.

2. *Extending the reward system beyond corporate boundaries.* As companies extend their connectivity networks outward into the businesses of their customers and suppliers, the rewards system must adapt accordingly. This involves working closely with customers and alliance partners to align the different companies' rewards systems at key points of intersection. A manufacturer, for example, may need to shift its rewards systems to reflect customer satisfaction instead of reaching production quotas. Suppliers may need to become integrally involved in a company's performance measurement system, even to the point of adopting it as an integral component of their own.

It is the leader's role to cement supplier relationships, and to build the levels of trust needed to integrate rewards systems. As the Big Bang of alliances (see Chap. 8) draws ever more near, the ability to align measures and rewards may prove to be the key gravitational force that holds galaxies of alliances together.

3. *Allowing people to determine their own rewards.* At least implicitly, every organization offers a pact to its people, which serves as the basis of their participation in the corporate organism's life. We call this pact the *psychological contract.* The dominant psychological contract was once the paternal, "Give us a dedicated 40-hour week year after year, and we will give you the security of lifetime employment and a comfortable retirement." It then evolved to the raw "People are like physical assets, to be used and disposed of as the company sees fit." Today, a more human psychological contract is emerging in successful firms: "You are an individual, responsible for your own life. Give us your dedication to growing and bettering the company, and we'll enhance your opportunity to grow and better yourself."

A corporation can't avoid expressing a view of human life through the rewards it offers to its people. The emerging view of life in successful companies recognizes the sanctity of the individual as prerequisite to corporate success. Consequently, formerly rigid and hierarchical reward systems are giving way to systems that provide structure, but flexibility, such that individuals can discover their own motivations and create their own development path within the corporation. The most effective systems offer tangible rewards—involving formal recognition and financial incentives for achievement—as well as intangible rewards, such as letting people own and follow through on the ideas they generate. Above all, they promote learning and knowledge-sharing, not just for the organization, but for the individual as well.

FOSTERING ALIGNMENT OF REWARDS TO THE GOALS AND MEASURES OF THE ORGANIZATION

One of the strongest metabolic pathways inside the biological corporation is the one linking measures and rewards. Many successful managers concentrate most of their personal actions in those two areas. These leaders understand that *not* aligning measures and rewards is like ignoring internal hemorrhaging and hoping for the best.

Most leaders agree that the most difficult challenges of transformation emerge around cultural conflicts. But as veteran transformation leader Jerry Stead said to *Fortune* magazine, "Ninety percent of what people call cultural conflicts exist because of conflicts in measures and rewards." (Jerry Stead, the successful leader of many transformations, currently is CEO of AT&T's Global Information Solutions [GIS], the $7.3 billion company that AT&T formed when it acquired NCR, merged its own computer division into it, and then grafted on Teradata, a producer of massively parallel computers.)

The implication is obvious: Align measures and rewards, and you've solved some, if not most, of your most significant transformational problems. As measurement systems become more complex, however, that becomes a difficult challenge in and of itself. When measurement systems were primarily financial, the alignment was relatively easy. Most rewards systems were based on return on investment, return on sales, sales growth, net income, or more recently, shareholder value. The only real complexity involved striking the right balance among these elements.

As discussed in Chap. 3, effective measurement systems reflect a complex web of interrelated measures that reflect the major cause-and-effect relationships inside the corporation, interlocking, in the case of the Balanced Scorecard, goals and measures along financial, customer, operational, and learning lines. The rewards system consequently needs to reflect those four families of goals, while still feeling relevant, or "real," to employees.

Although Lloyd's Bank addressed (to various degrees) all the components of the Balanced Scorecard, it unequivocally selected shareholder value as the main driver of its highly successful transformation effort

Driving Change Through Shareholder Value at Lloyd's Bank

When Brian Pitman (now Sir Brian Pitman) became CEO of Lloyds Bank in 1983, the bank's vision, to the extent it had one, reflected the British banking industry's conventional wisdom. Everyone assumed Lloyd's should be a big, international player, but no one could explain why. If anyone dared to ask, they were rewarded with a pitying "If you don't already know, I can't explain it" look, supported by some vague reference to the need for balance between domestic and foreign business and a challenge to name one major U.K. bank without a large international business. No matter that the international business was weak and that a number of foreign acquisitions had turned out badly; all of this was excused by the assumption that Lloyds would somehow be vulnerable without its international business.

Based on Lloyds' inadequate performance in producing shareholder value, Pitman launched an attack on the conventional wisdom. He had come up through the domestic business—the bank's principal profit generator—and had later been moved into the international arena. He had thus seen the foreign business in sharper focus than most top managers, and he couldn't understand why the international people were treated like golden boys when they performed like deadbeats. He also observed that all of the bank's employees acted more like civil servants than bankers. They were paid simply for showing up, and were under no pressure to perform.

Recognizing the need to frame a new vision for the company, Pitman organized a series of meetings with leadership and tried to get them to face reality. The process was emotional, full of denial, and more than a little bloody. The head of the international business steadfastly defended the old way, right to the day of his "early retirement."

"I tried to make the management team face reality," Pitman remembers. "I was always asking them, 'What constitutes success?' I focused, in particular, on the reality of shareholder value. No one could say we'd performed well for shareholders. I used our failure in this area to challenge the prejudices of my colleagues. I asked them, 'Will this particular business, plan, or policy create shareholder value?'"

He announced that Lloyds would no longer operate under the assumption that if it did business in one area, it had to be in another. Henceforth each business, such as the international division, would need to supply a reason for its existence; the burden of proof would be on those who wanted to stay in business, not on those who wanted to withdraw. For instance, no one could tell Pitman what was special about the Lloyds business in California. "We had to face the fact," he recalls, "that we couldn't be the best as the number seven or eight in this market, and I felt that if we couldn't be the best in a segment, we should get out."

It sometimes seemed that Pitman's approach was to identify which way the herd was running, and then go the opposite way. Early after his arrival, for example, a question arose as to whether Lloyds should be a gilt dealer (essentially, a government securities broker)—an opportunity created by deregulation that other London banks, both U.K. and foreign, were salivating over. There was a strong feeling within Lloyds that their company would not be considered "legitimate" if it failed to become a gilt dealer.

Pitman ordered a review of the option, which revealed only a slim chance of profiting from gilt dealing. He decided against it, which proved to be a wise business decision as well as a strong, symbolic act.

Conversely, Pitman took Lloyds into arenas where other banks dared not tread. Lloyds was the first U.K. financial services group to invest in real estate agencies, and the only one to make money from it; the first bank to buy a life insurance company; and the first to bid for a building society (essentially, a savings and loan company, in American terms).

While the top level of management was gaining a new sense of purpose, rigid bureaucracy and lack of motivation were still evident at the lower levels. "Employees were not aware they had to perform," Pitman recalls. "There wasn't enough excitement or involvement." People believed they were paid to do what they were told, nothing more.

So despite the outraged indignation of the bank's more conservative elements, Pitman instituted a performance-linked compensation scheme. The reaction? Shocked silence, followed by a rapid deployment of entrenched defense mechanisms. "You can't do that in the branches!" some said, scandalized. But Pitman was adamant. "We linked it all to the drive for shareholder value," he says, "and it ultimately changed the whole culture of the bank."

"We began with top management," Pitman recalls. "We devised a way of paying them based upon theirs and the bank's performance. Then we moved to our 30 general managers, and they sold the plan to their direct reports." Within three years, 1000 people were on performance-related pay, with key people and groups persuading others of its merits. Now, a decade or so later, all employees are on performance-related pay.

"In a performance-related system, pay rises aren't automatic and inflation doesn't drive compensation," Pitman explains. "The unions opposed it, but we communicated directly with the employees. The key thing was to get everyone involved in people management."

In addition, Pitman introduced a program that allows employees to invest in bank stock in lieu of cash compensation. "When we started," Pitman remembers, "no employee held Lloyds Bank shares. Today [summer of 1994], 28,000 employees are shareholders, and many have done very well with it. Our share price has doubled every 3 years for the past 10 years. Because they participated in our performance as shareholders, some employees are retiring with money they would never have dreamed of having previously."

The pay-for-performance compensation scheme has four major components:

1. *Profit sharing.* In an egalitarian, across-the-board profit-sharing plan, approximately 5 percent of the group's pre-tax profits go to employees in the form of stock or cash (the employee's choice). In effect, those

who elect stocks roll their share of profits back into an investment in the company's future, enjoying the benefits of equity ownership. In addition, under the British government's Save as You Earn (SAYE) scheme, they enjoy a tax advantage if they hold their stock for five years or longer.

2. *Incentive allotments.* On a more individual level, employees receive additional payments if they meet certain performance targets. These payments are expressed as a percentage of base compensation, and they vary according to the employee's position in the company. The range is broad, varying from as high as 60 percent for the CEO to as low as 3 percent for the clerical staff in the branches, with performance targets set according to level and type of work, usually based on a standard of team performance. In a retail branch, for example, payments are set in terms of customer service measures. In general, the more senior the employee, the more customized the targets. In theory all performance measures are related to the bank's overall objectives, but the nature of the beast requires constant fine-tuning.

3. *Performance-based base salary increases.* In 1993, Lloyds introduced an even more individualized component to its merit pay program: performance-related increases in base compensation. Automatic or collectively negotiated raises now are prohibited, making managers responsible for annual decisions about the rewarding of every employee under them. Managers are given a pool of money to allocate as they see fit. Employees receive a full explanation of the scheme, the thinking behind it, and how their pay has been linked to their performance.

4. *Executive incentives.* Senior executives participate in a fairly conventional, incentive-based stock option plan, which is tied to key, high-level financial measures.

The remarkable part of Lloyds' transformation—one of the most spectacular to be seen in the last 20 years across the world—is its simplicity and elegance. No fancy footwork here, just a quiet focus on measures and rewards.

Tchibo, or the Death of an Operational Paradigm

At Tchibo, the Hamburg-based coffee manufacturer, it was an accepted axiom that salespeople should receive a large bonus based on their individual sales volume. "We don't want our salesmen spending time by the pool instead of calling customers," management used to say. Tchibo managed its sales force with financial incentives. It was one of those deeply held values, like the black, red, and gold of the German flag.

The company was created in 1949, and, in becoming the second largest coffee roaster and distributor in Germany, it became a household name for many German families. In 1992, however, Tchibo decided that it had a problem. Its sales force appeared to be increasingly ill-suited to the modern requirements of coffee distribution. While greatly successful overall, Tchibo knew that something had to change in the sales-force area.

First of all, there was the issue of randomness. Salesmen received a significant bonus, close to 50 percent of salary on average, as a function of their coffee sales. While originally intended to build sales volume, the bonus system had become lottery-like, hanging on the volatile swings in global coffee prices. "Why should the Lower Saxony salesman be penalized or rewarded for a bad crop in Brazil?" Tchibo legitimately asked itself.

But the problem went deeper than that. Being a coffee salesperson was becoming more and more technical. In the old days, small neighborhood merchants were the predominant coffee distributors, and the salesman's ability to build friendly rapport with customers drove sales. Tchibo's salespeople were great at that. Over time, however, the distribution shifted to large retailers such as Marktkauf, whose sophisticated buying committees were looking for in-depth product information, quality and service assurances, and promotional assistance. They wanted Tchibo to manage their coffee shelves for them, complete with an interconnected EDI platform and inventory optimization across both firms.

Attracting qualified college graduates to those jobs—a logical answer to the emerging new business requirements—also was a problem. College students were hesitant to take a job in which the starting salary was comparatively low and most of the rewards took the form of a hypothetical sales bonus. It wasn't easy for a freshly minted *Diplomkaufmann* (graduate) to assess the financial odds of selling a ton of coffee for Tchibo.

Further still, Tchibo wanted to create lateral career flexibility. It wanted its salespeople to think of themselves, not just as functional specialists, but as aspiring area managers and sales managers, perhaps even with the potential to take on responsibilities outside of sales later in their careers. Given the existence of four sales channels, each with a different salary structure, incentive plan, and earning prospects, creating this flexibility was a significant challenge.

Upon deeper internal investigation and benchmarking of the best practices in the industry, Tchibo concluded that its bonus system had lost its incentive power. While veteran salespeople *expected* the bonus (making it a natural extension of their salary), it frightened young recruits away. In addition, most consumer goods companies were moving away from bonus-based systems, either capping the amount of incentive compensation—for example, Iglo Langnese, the manufacturer of frozen products, capped them at 10 percent of salary—or doing away with bonuses altogether, as had Procter & Gamble, Germany.

In considering the options, Tchibo's conservative element argued that the disappearance of the bonus system would result in Apocalypse Now through the demotivation of the sales force. Another group advocated getting rid of commissions and bonuses altogether, painting a picture of bright young graduates strolling through the countryside with their elders and learning from them.

Wisely, Tchibo's management concluded that a compromise was in order. Rather than abandon its bonus system completely, it deciding to set a target of a 15 percent average bonus, while raising salaries significantly. It is now in a position to recruit young college graduates who can be developed to deal with supermarket managers as peers. Also, Tchibo now is able to rotate its salespeople through sales channels, loosening the rigidity that had plagued its human resource systems.

Small though this change in the reward system at Tchibo may appear, it is often a succession of such small changes in a reward system that yields success in aligning the rewards system as a whole. The foundation of the entire edifice, however, is a system that rewards learning—the fourth component of the Balanced Scorecard. We will defer discussion of that component to the next two chapters, which are in large part devoted to a more detailed discussion of learning and innovation.

EXTENDING THE REWARD SYSTEM BEYOND CORPORATE BOUNDARIES

The logic of aligning rewards to the measurement system applies equally to customers, suppliers, and alliance partners. External members of the supply chain may be viewed as employees of a different type. Like employees, they provide products and services for a price, based on varying sources of motivation. Like employees, they may be more or less motivated as a function of how they are treated. And like employees, they usually want more out of the relationship than just financial security.

But unlike relations with employees, it is difficult to extend other than financial rewards to them directly. Within the firm the reward system is quite transparent, taking the form of a paycheck, a direct compliment or thank-you, or a promotion. The communication of a reward to a customer, a supplier, or an alliance partner is by definition more subtle, more indirect. It may take the form of a price reduction, an award, or inclusion in a meeting or celebration, among many other possible gestures.

Extending Corporate Boundaries Through Shared Destiny Relationships at Unipart

When it comes to extending reward systems to customer and supplier networks, few companies do it as well as the Unipart Group of Companies (Unipart) in Great Britain, headed by John Neill. In Chap. 2, we briefly examined Unipart's unique constituency-based vision, which states the company's commitment to lifelong customer relationships, to suppliers as stakeholders in the company, and to interdependence with the community. What is behind that vision is Neill's belief in an emerging business paradigm.

To Neill, there are two kinds of companies: "Model A" companies, those wedded to the short-term, adversarial relationships that characterized the industrial age, and "Model B" companies, those that favor *shared destiny relationships.*

In Neill's view, Model B is the one to follow. In a shared destiny relationship, a supplier relationship, for example, is created with acceptable margins built in at the start. This allows both parties to focus on creating greater value at the same or lower costs. When forged across what he calls the entire "demand chain," this creates a shared drive to improve efficiency and quality and constantly reduce costs. In effect, he argues that a tightly integrated network of producers, suppliers, and customers, if properly maintained and managed, is less vulnerable to competitive threat than a single business on its own. On a more pragmatic level, he points out, "It costs five times more to get new customers than to keep the ones you have."

Despite the benefits, shared destiny relationships aren't always cozy. Self-interest, by definition, requires an outward view. In the struggle with competing demand chains, every member of a demand chain must constantly strive to ensure the survival of the whole, which means constantly looking for ways to improve and cut costs in its own backyard. Ultimately that responsibility rests with the people in each firm, which to Neill means "knowledgeable and empowered employees who can work together with stakeholders to eliminate waste and non-value-added activity."

Non-value-added activity ranks high on Unipart's public enemy list. Neill claims that 65 percent of human activity in Western manufacturing companies is unnecessary, non value-added activity; that 30 percent is necessary, but non-value-adding; and that 5 percent is value-adding. He can list 72 business activities that don't add value, including errors, inspection, maintenance, and storage. If the U.K. auto industry as a whole earned 3 percent on sales in 1993, he asks, "Isn't it better to get rid of the 65 percent of waste, than to fight over the 3 percent of margin?" And if you choose to get rid of waste, he argues, you rarely have to eliminate people. "It's a virtuous circle," he says, claiming further that "practice delivers everything the theory predicts."

According to the Unipart philosophy, the tradeoffs involved in Model A relationships between customers and suppliers are inimical to the stakeholder concept. "The tradeoff is rooted in the traditional economic model, where costs level off," Neill explains. "If that thought got you—that costs level out—then for someone to win, someone must lose. But costs can go down forever, so it's possible for everyone to win. This is capitalism moving forward. These relationships aren't cozy, they're enormously demanding; but if you believe costs can go down forever, then it's possible for all stakeholders to win by working together."

In 1993, Unipart embarked on the second phase of "'Ten-to-Zero," a supplier relationships initiative launched in 1988. The program is taught at the "U" (Unipart's "university," described in more detail in Chap. 12) and is supported by videos and literature used in presentations to suppliers.

It measures joint rather than just supplier performance, and injects a powerful dynamic into supplier relationships. Performance is measured against 10 criteria, of which the following five are common to all divisions:

1. Zero lead time
2. Zero delivery errors
3. Zero defects
4. Zero transaction costs
5. Zero logistics

In this rating system, a "perfect 10" is perfectly awful—a zero is the best possible score for each criterion, with 10 being the worst. With 100 as the worst possible starting point, the idea is to progressively reduce one's score in all ten areas. Theoretically a perfect zero is impossible, so continuous improvement (Japan's *kaizen*) is the natural way to go.

For example, Electronic Data Interchange (EDI) is now an integral part of Ten-to-Zero. If suppliers say EDI is all mumbo-jumbo, they score a 10. If they say "it's interesting, we'll see what we can do," they score 9. If they accept an order through EDI, they score 8, if they send confirmation by EDI, they score 7, and so on. A "perfect zero" score would reflect a zero transactions cost with the supplier—theoretically impossible, but the ultimate benchmark of performance.

The Ten-to-Zero system provides a clear, quantifiable method of rating shared destiny relationships with suppliers. It has proven so effective that some Unipart divisions are planning to make supplier appointments conditional on participation in Ten-to-Zero.

"Even if we're world-class," Neill explains, "if anyone else in our enterprise chain isn't, then we all lose out to the best chain. Ten-to-Zero is transferable: We can teach our suppliers to teach their suppliers. Eventually, you will have large numbers of people talking a common language."

An important implication of the shared destiny relationship is that all stakeholders should be treated fairly. Unipart seeks long-term, fair returns, because it believes that trusting, long-term relationships reduce costs and improve quality faster, while dampening the income swings inherent in the business cycle.

"If you treat everyone equally," Neill insists, "you will get superior, long-term returns. That's the mental model in the company; the thought that's got us."

Neill explains, for example, that Unipart wanted employees to buy shares in the company, not so the company could privatize, but so they would truly feel like stakeholders. "It was driven by our values and our belief in the free enterprise system. I have always thought that communism is actually in conflict with the human spirit. We wanted individuals to have the opportunity to end their working days having generated more wealth than they had expected as a result of being shareholders in our company."

It involved risk, and Unipart made it clear that there would be no free shares or discounts, going to extraordinary lengths to communicate the scale both of the risk and of the opportunity. "So far," Neill reports modestly, "it has worked well."

That's an understatement. Shares bought for 0.5 pence each in 1987 were changing hands for 130 pence each at the end of 1993 (a gain of 26,000 percent!).

Karl Makes Friends with Transportation

Karl is engaged in one of his old-time favorite tasks, arguing with the transportation folks and their carriers. Yes, he knows that he's now an important person and that he shouldn't be doing things like this anymore, but it's a deep-seated tradition within Woodbridge Papers that schedulers don't like transportation agents, and vice versa. He also knows that Bob, the transportation supervisor, has been looking forward to their scheduled jousting for a couple of weeks, so he doesn't want to disappoint him. Bob has invited Mr. Gundersen, the head of Gundersen Van Lines, to join their discussion. Gundersen is one of the local carriers that is working with Woodbridge during their transformation, so that they can stay in touch with "the real world."

"What will it take for you to get goods to the destination faster?" Karl asks Gundersen impatiently, as a way to get the debate rolling. "Two weeks ago, it took seven days to get a shipment to California. Seven days! The paper could have hitch-hiked its way faster than you guys got it there. Hell, we can make the stuff a whole lot faster than you can carry it!"

Bob, the transportation supervisor, feels the need to stand up for his supplier.

"It's fine and dandy, all your talk about cycle time and getting the products to the customer fast, but the fact of the matter is that road transportation is what it is, and it takes a while to drive to California. If you want your stuff air-shipped, let me know. I'll get you one of those DHL flying trucks—you know, the kind you've seen on TV—but it's just a tad more expensive," he finishes sarcastically.

Karl is not amused. He's trying to get cycle time down to 10 days, and 7 of those 10 days, in this one instance, have been gobbled up by transportation. But he's learned a few things about dealing with people, and he decides to "process them" just as he has many times before.

"Let's map out what happens," he starts, moving nonchalantly to a flipchart. This is something novel to the holy alliance of transportation, and Gundersen feels that he may be getting set up. But Karl is relentless, drawing boxes, detailing each step in the process, from the moment when the paper is manufactured to the moment it is delivered to the customer's dock.

"So what do you do when you receive the paper, all packaged and ready to go?" Karl asks Gundersen. Bob pleads with his eyes for Gundersen to take the fifth amendment, but it's too late, he's already answering.

"We wait for enough freight heading in the same general destination to accumulate so that we can economically justify the run," says Gundersen. "We have a software package that optimizes container loading and routing. Once the container is full, we ship it. Sometimes there's no wait at all. Other times it can take three or four days, especially for West Coast destinations. We do most of our business in the East and Midwest, so California usually takes longer."

"If I asked you really nicely to send the stuff to California immediately, rather than wait for a full truck, would you do it?" Karl asks in a wooing tone, trying hard to look like the clever lawyers he sees on television.

"Well, I would, if you were willing to pay for LCL [Less than Container Load] versus FCL [Full Container Load]," the supplier answers. "In fact, I've offered it before, but your guys in transportation turned me down because of the price difference."

With a malevolent smile on his face, Karl turns to Bob. "So, dear Bob," he asks, "why is it that you won't consider LCL, particularly for destinations like California, where geography plays against us? Yes, it would cost a little more, but it would protect us against competitors who are eating our lunch on service out there."

Bob now remembers why he likes the new Karl even less than the old Karl. With the old Karl you could at least have a nice, irrational argument, and there was some comfort in the inevitability of a draw at the end of the exchange. The problem with the new Karl is that he can actually *win* the battle. Bob hates that.

"Well, we're being paid to minimize cost, and that's what we do," Bob explains. "In fact, that's how our budget is built. Like Gundersen, we have a computer simulation that models transportation costs, optimizing our cost per mile. That's our budget number. The game after that is to stay within budget, and going LCL is not the smartest way to do that."

Now it's Gundersen's turn to bail his transportation colleague out of trouble.

"Frankly, I would gladly give up your California business," he volunteers, "and exchange it for some other east coast or Midwest business. We're not strong in California, and other carriers will do a better job for you there. But I'd love to get your Boston and Philadelphia business, because I have great backhauls from both destinations and I could give you both great service and a good deal."

By the end of the day the three parties have redefined the allocation of business to Gundersen Van Lines and have rewritten the rules of engagement. FCL shipment will remain the norm, but Woodbridge will use LCL whenever meeting the 10-day cycle time looks like a challenge. To cover the remainder of the year, Karl will allocate some of the project money to create an allowance for occasional FCL shipments, thereby allowing transportation to do the right thing without being penalized. Karl also will help transportation to build their budget for the next year so that it includes some FCL transportation, and will help to redefine the department's reward system to accommodate more process- and less cost-thinking. For the first time, all three parties leave the meeting on a high note.

Karl and Bob clap each other on the back. But already, they both miss the old days....

ALLOWING PEOPLE TO DETERMINE THEIR OWN REWARDS

THE SWINGING PENDULUM OF THE PSYCHOLOGICAL CONTRACT

Like people, corporations can't help but adopt a "sense of life," a view of what human life is about. And like people, the real view corporations hold is often not that which is explicitly expressed. For an individual, a "sense of life" represents a subconscious, psychological estimate of the relationship of the world to oneself. For a corporation, a "sense of life" represents the organization's estimate of its relationship to the people within it. The prevailing view a corporation has of its relationship to its employees, as seen through *their* eyes, is the essence of the psychological contract.

Beginning after World War II and lasting until the 1980s, the predominant psychological contract was paternal, offering lifetime employment and a paid retirement for a dedicated life of work for the corporation. Companies expected dedication and loyalty from their people, and a solid day's work. In return, employees knew that "the company" would provide for them and their families. Many European countries passed labor laws enforcing this paternalistic pact, making it very difficult to lay off workers. In Japan, lifetime employment became not only a universal corporate practice, but also an integral part of Japanese culture.

In the past 15 years, however, the pendulum of the psychological contract has swung dramatically. As company after company has succumbed to downsizing, economic realities have made the lifelong work-for-security contract impracticable. People learned that even companies like IBM and General Motors were financially vulnerable. Companies began to state explicitly that they could not offer lifetime employment any longer, and that the people within the corporation must be willing to put their jobs at risk. The promise of security was forsaken. From paternalism and loyalty, the pendulum swung to asset management in its rawest form, and with that swing came the unavoidable sense of spiritual loss. People started to ask, in effect, "Where has *my* corporation gone?".

The trend, however, may even now be reversing itself again. In many companies, the pendulum is already swinging back, looking as if it will come to rest somewhere between the two extremes of paternalism and Darwinian capitalism. More and more companies are realizing that, while they cannot offer a cradle-to-grave security blanket, they have a responsibility to create an environment that nurtures the individual's ability to grow and thrive; and that, given the right environment, people will give their all for the company, not in an altruistic way, but because it benefits the team, the company, and *them*.

Consequently, the concept of "incentives" is taking on new meaning to many business leaders. Ask many of them what motivates people, and money will almost always come up, but so will things like encouraging people to drive new initiatives based on their own ideas, prodding them to "own" the results of their work, making them directly accountable for their team's output, and giving them the freedom to take risks, even if that means failing occasionally.

A new, more enlightened view of the psychological contract is emerging, which assumes individual self-responsibility as a given, while recognizing that the corporation has an important social role to play. The roots of capitalistic society rest on the premises of Enlightenment thinkers such as the British physician and political philosopher, John Locke, who proposed that the right to own property was an extension of the individual's inalienable right to life. In Locke's terms, property is simply the product of one's own effort, and the right to property is the freedom to use and dispose of the product of one's own effort as one sees fit. Therefore, he argued, the right to property is the very essence of individual liberty and the fountainhead of an individual's sense of pride.

Based on Locke's thinking, property rights have been sanctioned to varying extents throughout the Western world, but especially strongly in the United States, where Locke's definition of property rights became the basis for most law. The corporation, by this view, is nothing more than a legal framework for a distributed form of property ownership. Ironically, however, this new form of distributed ownership removed the *fact* of ownership from the direct work experience. Nevertheless, just as corporate employees feel that they own their work, so they feel a sense of ownership of the company. The fact that shareholders are technical owners doesn't change the basic fact that the leaders and employees of a corporation enjoy an immediate sense of ownership of the corporation, with both the worries and the pride which that entails.

Unfortunately, however, most corporate leaders have adopted a view of people as merely automated parts of the corporate machine, and have designed work processes accordingly. The employees' property is their paycheck and what they buy with it—nothing more. People become psychologically disconnected from their work output, and learn to work strictly for their paycheck, supervised by managers who make sure they do what they are told to do. To a large extent, the ability to achieve a sense of gratification has been removed from the workplace, and achieving financial security and leisure time has become the focus of the employee's motivation.

There has been far-from-silent rebellion to this mechanistic view. Management and labor became antagonistic constituencies. In labor unions, people found an outlet for their frustrations as well as the power to bargain for security and leisure time. Largely due to the influence of labor unions, corporations adopted the paternalistic approach, becoming the providers of security, comfort, and leisure time, but still failed to address the more deep-seated need people have to feel a sense of ownership in the output of their work, with both the pressure and the sense of gratification that entails.

In the pendulum swing from paternalism back to economic mechanism and now toward a middle ground, some corporate leaders are beginning to address the essence of the problem. They are building multifaceted rewards systems that reflect the individual's fundamental need for a sense of pride in ownership, within a context flexible and adaptive enough to tap the diversity that comprises the motivation of its employees. They are developing a psychological contract offering not security, but an environment of opportunity.

Ward the Underwriter Gets Involved

"I'm shocked!" Ward suddenly erupts. "How can you draw such a conclusion from this one observation?" The tone is emphatic, nearly vindictive. The 30 people on the change team stop dead in their tracks, watching Ward's victim freeze like a deer in the headlights. For two or three seconds, there is an eerie silence, everyone bracing for the crash. But instead Ward hits the brakes, and the tires screech to a halt just before impact.

"You just shouldn't say things like that when you don't have the facts," he says, apparently calm again. There is a notable sigh of relief from the change team; the meeting can proceed. But many shake their heads in disbelief, thinking that Ward has done it again.

Meet Ward Jungers, the underwriter. Ward is a tall Californian, smart as a whip, impeccably groomed, with a large mustache and a commanding presence.

Ward can be difficult to work with, full of adamant statements about what should and should not be done. Some folks are annoyed and love to "coach" him behind the scenes on his antisocial tendencies. Others understand that he's a diamond in the rough, the keeper of both a new and an ancient flame for CIGNA P&C. It has become apparent to everybody that Ward is a linchpin when it comes to the transformation effort. If Ward joins Isom's legions of transformation, many undoubtedly will follow. It will be a symbol of the possible redemption of the talented, but frustrated, people of CIGNA P&C. If he doesn't ... well, there's no telling what will happen.

We are back in October 1993, six months into Gerry Isom's tenure. Ward has been drafted into Isom's change army, and he's a somewhat reluctant inductee. Ward is the very senior Vice President for

Underwriting Services, in charge of developing underwriting policies and monitoring compliance.

"I've always been an underwriter," Ward Jungers states matter-of-factly. "That's all I've ever done."

Saying that Jungers has a passion for underwriting is an understatement. To him, underwriting *is* insurance. From his 1966 graduation to now, he's always been an underwriter, first with the Travelers, then with INA, which in 1982 merged with Connecticut General to form CIGNA. He talks about underwriting the way Carl Sagan talks about the cosmos.

"I like the discipline of underwriting," he states, looking you straight in the eye. "Always have. I like its objective side, its deceptive simplicity. I'm not a relationship-driven person. Not even a people person. I'm an impatient analytic."

It's now a year later, and Jungers remembers being quite skeptical about this boat he had suddenly found himself on in the fall of 1993.

"I had a basic uneasiness about the new environment," he remembers. "Before this started, I had a nice office on the thirtieth floor, and a secretary whom I'd known for four or five years and was quite fond of. All of a sudden everything was gone. I had a chair and a telephone inside a cubicle, and was surrounded by 40 people interrupting me all the time. Except for one lady who was my peer, all the other folks were more junior than I was."

Although he's not an emotional person, he can make you feel the pain. He pauses for a while, a wrinkle forming on his forehead.

"It was a time of great confusion," he reminisces. "I had told my boss, Rich Franklin, that I wanted to be involved in this transformation effort, should it start, but I had no idea what I was getting into. Nobody knew much about it. For example, I didn't know it was going to require full-time participation, abandoning everything else. And I didn't know when it would start. When it did, I was given twenty-four-hour notice. Also, I thought I was going to provide expert consultation to the group. Instead I was told I'd be one of the folks doing lots of things besides underwriting. I was quite resentful, and I made it clear."

Isom's arrival caused him great apprehension.

"His arrival was a huge deal," he remembers. "Nobody knew him. I was worrying about job security, like everyone else. My first encounter with him was in the cafeteria. He looked really great, professional, reassuring. I was introduced to him as 'the one responsible for underwriting quality.' He commented that 'it's a very important job.' I remember feeling better about Gerry after that little exchange. I guess everything you say is important to somebody when you're the boss."

But there was also anxiety, a great deal of it.

"Isom, after his arrival in Philly, disappeared in the field. There was a vacuum. He also starting bringing in his own folks, people like Dick Wratten, my boss two steps removed. I started wondering whether there was room for us old CIGNA people. It took me a while to get to know Wratten and to discover his views were close to mine. Rich Franklin, my boss, did feel comfortable with him, though, and I trusted Rich's judgment."

When Isom launched project OAR, the second phase of his transformation effort, Jungers found himself enrolled, working as part of a large group of people trying to identify what needed to be done.

"We were analyzing what I already knew," he remembers. "There were lots of meetings, overly structured meetings. Some people were quite naive about the business, others didn't have a clue, and yet all were venturing opinions, which annoyed me. Over time, I discovered that my knowledge of underwriting allowed me to influence things disproportionately, and it gave me hope. In particular, I was able to steer the group toward considering a fundamental recasting of underwriting, rather than simply aligning some functions at the home office, as had originally been considered."

Nowhere is Jungers more eloquent than in describing the dialectic involved between the discipline of underwriting, which demands the merciless selection of business based on risk-management criteria, and the sales-development imperative, which calls for relaxing some of these constraints in periods of hardship. There is little doubt where Jungers stands on this one, and he describes it as a straight battle of underwriting good versus sales evil. "When you ignore guidelines and start showing a lack of respect for the underwriting discipline, it doesn't take long before you start paying a price on your bottom line," he points out, somewhat ominously.

At the end of 1993, as Isom was urging the team to move toward implementation of some of the early findings of project OAR, Ward remained remarkably circumspect. "We all had dinner with Gerry close to Christmas time, " he comments, "all ten of us involved full-time in the effort, and nobody was volunteering for implementation. I personally still had my doubts about the commitment of the organization. I was also still weighing whether my old job offered a better platform than the project. But Gerry was determined and pushed hard. His personal pronouncements made a big difference. He saw underwriting as the key, and I let myself be seduced." In a reflective mode, he even adds, "And I couldn't think of anybody who could redesign underwriting as well as I could." Strangely, the statement doesn't sound immodest, just factual.

By early 1994, it had become clear that Ward Jungers was a man on a mission. Isom and the President's Executive Council had begun to take notice, and Ward had occasionally been invited to present the views of his team to the PEC.

The first activity of Ward's team after Christmas involved the development of a charter and objectives for the underwriting process redesign team. Assembling the necessary resources was also one of the team's early tasks.

"It was a strange experience, and we went through all the stages of team-building I had been warned about," he comments. "You know, the bit about storming, forming, norming, and so on. We had a senior officer from claims, a manager from systems, a senior underwriter, a systems application person, and a facilitator. There again, nobody had told me I was going to lead. But I was the most knowledgeable about underwriting, so I naturally became the driver of the effort."

Jungers knew that the key for the team was to broaden involvement and to start setting up additional relays in the field. He set up five major natural work teams, largely dividing the process into pieces such as "triage," "roles and responsibilities," "technology and underwriting desktop," and the new-wave-sounding "shared learning," which was chartered to capture the linkage between underwriting and claims. The team also set up several other ad hoc teams and organized numerous phone conferences.

"Recruiting the right people was probably the hardest," Jungers adds. "We had a few volunteers, but these, by and large, were not the right people. We knew who were good and went after them. We were astonishingly fortunate with the people we got. We didn't pick the people we thought were compliant. Perhaps people more like me, occasionally rambunctious, but with a good view of the business and a heart in the right place. We also got tremendously helped by the barrage of communication from Isom and the PEC. By then, being part of the effort had clearly become politically correct. This made our task much easier."

The first victory was at hand. The underwriting team was rapidly becoming known as the one running out in front, and Ward Jungers was emerging as a transformation leader of the new era.

"By March 1994, we had the first outline of the new process," he remembers. "Field people 'owned' the work, saying 'it basically makes sense.' We had lots of partial unveiling. But the crowning moment was the presentation to the PEC, when we showed them the new process. We got an incredibly positive response."

But it was only a beginning. The team had to move to the next level, filling the model with details. It proved a much more demanding job, and required the setting-up of a second-generation team. The team worked throughout the summer. Technology, increasingly, was becoming an important part of the redesign.

"My personal attitude is that technology should be the support, not the driver of the redesigned process," Jungers states. "I deliberately was slowing the technology effort down at the beginning, because I wanted us to understand the process first. The systems folks were raring to go, and I know I occasionally drove them wild. But systems and underwriting were a real partnership. The systems people were involved in the design of the process from day one. One of them now talks like a true underwriter."

Jungers talks about technology with the zeal of the newly converted.

"Technology will end up being quite important," he states. "It will make the implementation of the new process real. We've installed it in four pilots already. The technology is rolled out two or three months behind the new process, and will eventually touch 12 different sites."

When asked what he has learned from his one-year tenure as a transformation agent at CIGNA P&C, Ward sits back in his chair. "I've learned I can make a real difference," he says. " I know I picked the right road. I would never have been able to do what I did in my previous job. I feel good about bringing the discipline to what we do, and helping our results. I have a slide I use all the time. It says 'Our problem has been dumb underwriting, not dumb underwriters.' We're proud again."

Interestingly enough, his rewards seem to have been far more of the spiritual than of the material kind.

"I've gotten a lot of recognition, more so than rewards," he points out. "I'm not making more money than before. Perhaps it will come at some point. But more importantly, I've been acknowledged by the top management. I've gotten exposure to the PEC. I'm a missionary. Five years from now, I hope external people will point to CIGNA and recognize we have sound and imaginative underwriting. As for my contribution, I hope my colleagues will say about me, 'Frankly, we couldn't have done what we did without him.' That would be nice; real nice, indeed."

BUILDING
INDIVIDUAL
LEARNING

The New England Aquarium in Boston presents daily sea lion shows in which children and adults watch with delight as the sea lions toss balls, clap their fins, jump over hurdles and through rings, and splash the front row on cue. With every trick, the crowd roars and the animals are rewarded with fish. Through their trainers, they have made the association: No trick, no fish. Conversely, they know their just due and protest loudly, to the further delight of the crowd, if a nice jump doesn't immediately win a fishy prize. The system works well, and several generations of sea lions have proven quite reliable in front of an audience. The system has a limit, however: No sea lion has yet been known to develop new tricks spontaneously.

To a significant extent, most corporate rewards systems are based on a similar Pavlovian model. And to that extent, they constitute the weakest form of renewal. Money, banners, trophies, and other symbols are held out as carrots to stimulate motivation in the pursuit of specifically defined objectives. Employees and managers learn to expect certain returns for certain behaviors, each of them operating in their assigned slot. The model remains predominantly paternal, authoritarian, and reactive in that top management "provides" and the firm's personnel receive the various forms of compensation made available. The problem is that the clearly defined rewards produce expected results, not the creative, unexpected, and dramatic outcomes that comprise the very heart of renewal.

Individual learning represents a more advanced stage of renewal. It builds the individual's sense of self-esteem by enhancing his or her store of knowledge, thus promoting an increased level of competence and efficacy in approaching work-related problems. More importantly, it creates the opportunity for people to experience perhaps the most fulfilling of all rewards, a sense of *self-actualization*—the pride of recognizing the output of one's mind in the external reality of the workplace, and the sense of purpose, productivity, and participation that comes with such achievement as part of a collective quest.

By promoting individual learning, the corporation recognizes the individual's responsibility for his or her own personal and professional development, while accepting its responsibility to create an environment of opportunity in which all can thrive. As greater numbers of high-self-esteem individuals unleash their creativity, they reshape the contours of the firm. The corporation comes alive as employees continuously adapt and improve the way they do their work, and constantly redefine their roles and interactions. Rather than dealing with a machine-like firm, leaders become conductors of the biocorporate symphony, orchestrating the organic growth of the firm as the cells and organs of the corporate body adapt, change, and reproduce.

Too often, corporate leaders lose the perspective of seeing employees as a collection of individual human beings, each one with unlimited potential. In an organization that fosters individual learning, these individuals shine forth as a living resource, by far the corporation's most valued and irreplaceable assets. The formerly inert organization comes alive—constantly learning and adapting—defined by human wills and passions. Squashing these wills and passions through rigid organizational principles is a terrible waste, both to the organization and of the individual human spirit.

Instead of matching an organizational chart with a description of each employee's skills, the new leader now deals with a rapidly accumulating set of capabilities, planting seeds of innovation and creativity by moving key people and teams to points of need inside the corporation, animating the organization with an eagerness to discover new horizons. Rather than dealing with the cold facts of each employee's track record and skills, the leader uses the energy of the individual to pursue key objectives. Heptagon and rhomboid designs replace round pegs and square holes. Palpitating hearts displace industrial motors and pumps. The CEO observes the genesis of new cells within the corporate body, watching the cells divide and grow as people define their own jobs to serve the purposes of the body as a whole. The respective definitions of *job* and *project* become blurred. As a result, the boundaries of skills and innovation in the corporation themselves expand, allowing the firm to conquer new spaces.

There are four genes associated with the chromosome of individual learning, implying four corresponding tasks for the genetic architects of the organization:

1. *Committing to the development of the individual.* The value created by a firm resides in the accumulated knowledge of the people within it, expressed in the form of products and services sold. A firm succeeds by building capabilities in its people *first.* Only then do capabilities begin to translate into more efficient operations, more satisfied customers, and higher levels of financial performance.

Advocating a commitment to individual development is the responsibility of the corporate leader. In many corporations, individual development is entrusted to a disempowered human resource function, displaced from the focus and attention of leaders. Perhaps the best way for the CEO to communicate and demonstrate this commitment is to urge executive leaders to participate directly in development activities as a natural extension of their line responsibilities.

2. *Creating mentor-guided, life-forming projects for high-caliber individuals.* People learn best on the job, especially in the execution of ad hoc projects, often self-defined by individuals with a passion for a particular area. Authorizing and helping to design jobs and projects for high-potential individuals is therefore a key responsibility of the leadership team. It allows individuals who can make a difference to develop new skills and achieve higher levels of personal and professional fulfillment, thus enhancing the individual's life, while also injecting new life into the biological corporation.

The selection of the proper mentors for each high-caliber individual is another vital responsibility of the leadership team. Mentors are senior executives with the flair and patience for developing less experienced executives, and they are tasked with providing guidance and directing learning throughout the project experience.

3. *Identifying critical skills and designing an education strategy.* The principal sin committed in most training programs occurs when they become disconnected from the core business, taking on a life of their own. To be effective, such programs need to be rooted in a model of the individual and organizational skills that need nurturing. Skills modeling is a complex exercise, requiring the selection of a few key capabilities directly tied to the transformation agenda of the company. Once key skills have been identified, high-performance corporations often find it advisable to develop their own educational facility, with programs focused on "real-life" problem-solving in their business.

The role of the corporation's leadership is to emphasize the role of education in individual development, and to personally utilize the education strategy as a vehicle of transformation.

4. *Balancing the supply of and demand for skills inside the corporation.* Company leaders have long recognized the business inefficiency and the ethical quandary involved in laying off large pools of qualified people in some areas, while aggressively hiring and training large numbers of new specialists in other areas. In some countries, particularly in Europe, the ethical problem has been translated into labor legislation that all but prohibits companies from using layoffs as a cost-cutting tool. Consequently, large companies throughout the world are experimenting with new ways to enrich the learning experience and to deploy people to match skills to business needs.

The behavioral and psychological dimensions of changing jobs are proving to be the greatest obstacle to the success of redeploying people. In some cases, technology provides the critical link allowing people to identify their learning requirements, gain access to the knowledge they need, and connect themselves and their skills to emerging opportunities in the corporation.

The role of the leadership team is to experiment with new ways to enhance learning and to match individuals and their skills to the needs of the organization; to pilot new programs that open doors to individual opportunity, while reshaping the corporation's skills portfolio.

COMMITTING TO THE DEVELOPMENT OF THE INDIVIDUAL

The value of a firm consists first and foremost of the knowledge possessed by the individuals that comprise it. When we buy software from Microsoft, we buy the collective knowledge of the people at Microsoft who developed it. We don't buy their headquarters in Redmond, Washington, or their sales and distribution network, or their patents. We purchase the collective ability of a group of several thousand people, expressed as a software program.

Misguided by traditional accounting practices, companies have long measured their value in terms of the auction price of their underlying "hard" assets, almost completely discounting from their financial decisions knowledge, and the people who hold it. Witness how bankers insist on collateralizing only hard assets, arguing that land, buildings, and machines cannot walk away at night, whereas employees can. It is true that people's attachment to a firm can be fleeting. That doesn't imply, however, that only the inanimate can retain its value over time. Assets may be more permanent, but that is also their downfall: They become obsolete proportional to the rate of innovation, and therefore proportionally irrelevant to the value of a firm. Conversely, people are the source of innovation, and they can grow and adapt with it. The company that can attract, develop, and retain high-caliber individuals guarantees the continuous replenishment of its knowledge base, ensuring a continuous increase in the firm's value-creating capacity and, therefore, its performance.

Consider how great sports teams sustain their enterprises. Every sport on any continent has teams that waste their considerable resources and teams that do much more with much lesser means. In French soccer, the Olympique de Marseille has long had a history of acquiring internationally reknowned star players at extraordinary premiums. Every few years they rush to the top of the French, and more recently, the European championships. Those spasmodic rushes to the top, however, are interspersed with periods of nearly complete oblivion—the team often doesn't even play in the major French league anymore. All in all, the club has never managed to balance its finances through these huge peaks and valleys, relying on municipal subsidies to survive.

Conversely, for the last several years the A.J. Auxerre soccer club has consistently ranked in the top four or five clubs in France, and has qualified for the various European cups nearly every year for the last 15 years. Auxerre is a mid-sized town, one that doesn't have anywhere near the stadium attendance of Marseilles at its peak. The key to Auxerre's success? Its soccer school and development program. The club spends considerable time identifying young, promising players all over the country, offers them scholarships in its junior teams, and develops them into competitive professional players. Auxerre often finds it difficult to hang on to its players once they have achieved greater fame, but the team gets compensated for those transfers, and the club considers watching its best players achieve greater wealth in richer European clubs a natural outcome of its commitment to player development.

The same is true for corporations. But how many corporations have Auxerre's commitment to the development of individuals inside the firm? When we think of fostering the growth of individuals, we immediately think of recruiting, training, career path building, succession planning, and other related processes. Too often we tend to aggregate all of those critical processes into one big lump: human resource management. Making it all the job of HR seems a tidy solution, and allows us to return to our somnolence.

This attitude is but another outgrowth of a perverted logic that has permeated our thinking for many years. If one thinks back to the four sets of goals in the Balanced Scorecard—financial, customer, operations, learning and innovation—we erroneously assume that the flow goes from setting financial goals, to creating customer goals, then establishing operational goals, and finally developing the learning and innovation capabilities in the back room to support the rest of the strategy. As a consequence, we believe that learning and innovation come last, after the corporation has defined the other three elements.

This assumption mistakes the chronology of conceptual development for the chronology of implementation. In thinking about what the firm should do, it does indeed help to follow a sequence that starts with financial goals and customer needs and then works back to the skills and capabilities required to meet these needs. In actually meeting them, however, the firm needs to start by building capabilities, and then watch as capable people produce results that ripple through operations, touch the customer, and produce the expected financial results. Like the Auxerre soccer club, sustaining performance requires building competences in the back room *first*. Individual development is the lead indicator, with customers and financial achievements lagging behind the building of capabilities.

Putting HR in charge of fostering the development of individuals involves the same mistake companies have made when they put a strategic planning function in charge of strategy, or quality czars in charge of quality. The only difference is that strategy and quality have managed to escape their functional ghetto, whereas human resource functions to a large degree have not.

Consider the sad situation most firms are in. For many firms, recruiting remains a lonely HR function, tasked by management "to find good people." Such recruiting departments are full of young college graduates eagerly trying to excite campus candidates and more seasoned applicants about the prospect of being with the firm. There's only one problem: They are human resources specialists without real field experience. Their only real experience with the firm relates to compensation grids and benefits packages. It rapidly becomes clear to potential recruits that they are merely going through "an HR screen," with the result that no goodwill gets generated in the discussion, particularly if a competitor's interview was conducted by senior line executives.

Too often, training is in the hands of mid-level managers. Their expertise often is limited to facilitation and behavioral techniques, without any real content knowledge of the business. Every year the training manager runs a survey that gets sent to all managers of the firm, asking them "what skills and capabilities they want people to be trained in." Responses, when they come, are superficial, for line managers aren't always the best judges of skills required, nor do they really trust that the training department can provide them with what they need anyway. Consequently, such courses are by and large misaligned with the needs of the business. Regardless of the firm's explicit training policy, the people of the firm regard training as predominantly optional, and last-minute cancellations are frequent. Dutifully, the training department surveys those who do attend, usually amid the

mild euphoria that sets in at the end of the session, and typically the survey shows favorable ratings. A few weeks later, however, the relevance of
the training has eroded to virtually nothing. Consequently, the training
budget is often the first to get cut at crunch time.

In such firms, career path and succession planning are little more than
bureaucratic exercises. Individuals develop confidence in their firm's ability to help them along only when they see professionals committed to their
own success, not when they see paperwork being exchanged between their
managers and headquarters. In itself, building lists of high-potential people and formally planning the succession of key individuals is of little help,
unless successful people inside the firm get involved, thereby leading the
next generation of high-potential people to believe that there is a true support mechanism at play. Absent such involvement, no career path management or succession planning effort can be successful.

The situation is perhaps not *quite* as bleak as we are painting it here.
Many corporations are awakening to the importance of developing people.
Increasingly, the human resource function is coming out of its torpor, and
some directors of HR actually play the role of second-in-command behind
the CEO. Many have discovered that success lies in transcending functional boundaries, and in getting line managers to involve everyone in the
firm in learning and people development. In some cases, human resources
directors have earned the right to influence the strategy dramatically,
spearheading the development of new capabilities for the firm.

Professor Karl, or the Birth of a Teaching Vocation

Karl, the Woodbridge scheduler, thought he had seen it all. As it turns
out, he hasn't. He's about to lead a discussion with new employees about
the ongoing transformation project. *"Me, a teacher? They gotta be kid-
ding! Why not make me wear a clown's nose or a tutu while they're at
it?"*

Well, here he is, waiting in the wings, coached by the training manager. He's brought about 200 slides with him, because he's afraid he'll run out
of things to say. For a two-hour slot, that ought to do. *Yeah, yeah, she wants
it to be interactive. Well, I'll ask them whether they have any questions,
and if they do, it will be interactive. How many folks are there in here?*
About 20, from all parts of the firm, she tells him, trying to get him
pumped up.

Karl doesn't even know where to stand as she's introducing him. *Gosh,
they look so young! The fellow in the front row looks downright prepubes-
cent. And it says on his name tag that he's with sales.* Karl sure wouldn't

buy any paper from a kid that young. The new-hires are observing him eagerly, as if he were a polar bear at the zoo.

Clearing his voice, he nervously gets started. His early transparencies describe how the project came about, how the order fulfillment process needed to be shortened, and how they organized themselves to achieve that. Karl feels tense, mumbling at the screen, trying hard to forget that there's a group watching him. Only 20 minutes have gone by, but he knows he's very boring, as confirmed by the yawns he sees from some of young recruits. The training manager is attacking her nails in the back of the room, trying to smile encouragingly whenever her eyes meet his, hoping it will get better.

Mercifully, a young woman has a question. "How is paper made?" she asks with disarming innocence.

For 10 seconds, Karl looks at her, mouth open, completely aghast. He's been discussing the subtleties of scheduling and order fulfillment, but he suddenly realizes that these young folks have no clue what he's talking about. He looks at the remaining 170 transparencies, wondering how he can use them without further deepening the hole he's dug for himself. Then, inspiration strikes like a lightning bolt.

"Why don't we go across the street?" he asks. "I'll show you the plant and how we make paper. I can pretty much cover what I wanted to right by the machine."

The training manager in the back of the room looks up, thanking the powers-that-be for divine intervention. She jumps up, waving everybody to follow Karl.

Transplanted into his natural habitat, the self-absorbed, stooped silhouette that was Karl in the training center is gone, replaced by an enthusiastic manager with a confident smile and shining eyes. He gathers everybody close to him and they listen intently, in spite of the bustle surrounding them. Taking in Karl's safety instructions, they all look a little intimidated and feel a little self-conscious wearing the unfamiliar safety glasses and hard hats.

Karl leads them through the process. First, they go over to the huge pulp vats and the tossing of the magic brew with its secret additives and coloring agents. Then to the giant paper machine with its fast moving bed of pulp that dries rapidly into paper. In the heater section, the new recruits' glasses fog up instantaneously, and they have to cock their heads back to see, to the boisterous amusement of the operators who had been waiting for the moment. Then to the wind-up section, where giant master rolls are moved away by huge cranes and placed with the semi-finished inventory. Finally to the finishing section, with its huge scissors cutting the master rolls to the desired width and length.

All of a sudden, lights start to flash in the finishing section, and the whirring sound of the alarm overrides any other noise in the plant. A swarm of workers rushes to the paper machine. To the unsuspecting recruits, it looks like a scene out of *Rescue 911*.

"Don't worry, folks," Karl says reassuringly, "there's no danger. It's what we call a break. Look right in front of you, and you'll see that the paper has ripped right down the middle. What they'll now do is clear this through the machine, then start a new run."

Some excited, some scared, the new recruits move nervously, trying to stay out of the way of the workers who are trying to solve the problem. They have a million questions. What produces a break? How much does it cost? How can it be prevented?

Even as things quiet down, the rolling fire of questions continues, most of them quite naive. But it doesn't matter. Karl knows all the answers, no matter how much they push him. He never knew he was this good. There's something happening inside him, something he likes, even though he can't quite put his finger on it. He's growing fond of these bright, eager minds, looking for knowledge. It feels as if he's taking them by the hand and showing them the world for the first time, the same kind of thing he felt when he helped his daughter get through middle-school math. Much to his surprise, he finds himself—the legendary grump and misanthrope—being patient. There's pride involved as well. Suddenly, he wants to give these young folks a favorable first impression of the place they've just committed their future to.

He's getting downright pedagogical, although he couldn't spell the word if they asked him to. Back in the training class after the tour, he asks them to sketch out the production process as they remember it. It's amazing, but as he walks around the room he sees that some of them can do a pretty good job of it. He also asks them to describe what to do during a break. There again, they've evidently learned a bunch. Had he known what they could do, he really could have used a few of these bright kids on his project.

When the training manager tells him that his time is up, he feels sorry. He had so much more to say, and he can tell that his students also would have liked more time. But at least he knows some of their names, and he'll be able to greet them whenever he runs into them day-to-day. He also knows that they'll now be able to call him if they have any questions about the production process. The training manager, in the enthusiasm of the moment, gets him to promise to come back for the other entering classes for the rest of the year. It's a big commitment, but he finds himself agreeing to it, not so much because he feels it's important, but because it's *fun*.

On the way back to his office, he finds himself whistling a tune from *Snow White*, one of his daughters' favorite Disney movies.

CREATING MENTOR-GUIDED, LIFE-FORMING PROJECTS FOR HIGH-CALIBER INDIVIDUALS

Great organizations rely on more than just an elite few to manage themselves. They know how to use the people and capabilities they have to the fullest extent, creating second and third opportunities for those who have not quite made it the first time but whose values and intentions are in the right place. Betting everything on the assumption that one has hired only the "qualified" is simply unrealistic, if not naive. What distinguishes great corporations from others is their ability to inject learning into, and therefore extract more value out of, their middle- and lower-rank performers.

Of all the forms of personal development, none is more effective than learning on the job under the guidance of a mentor. Although there are many advantages to more formal training and development programs, they are usually poor substitutes for learning by doing. Many new training designs blur the distinction between formal training and real problem-solving, and most programs disconnect people from their work, inducing a sense that it's not quite "the real thing." Therefore, assigning high-caliber individuals to mentor-guided, life-forming projects remains the most effective way of accelerating individual development.

Life-forming projects are those that enrich the experience and knowledge base of the individuals working on them, while also carrying the potential to inject new energy and growth into the corporation. The major attraction of project work is that it doesn't distinguish between doing one's job and learning new things. The individual's official responsibility may be to deliver against a "line" commitment, but a clever design of the job or project ensures that the only way the individual can succeed is by acquiring new knowledge and skills.

The ability to design such ad hoc projects is one of the most valuable talents a leader can have. Few are great at it. It isn't taught in books, nor is it recognized as a discipline. Consequently, many leaders limit themselves by picking up on loosely defined, but often fashionable, themes, such as reengineering or total quality management, and designing equally vague projects around them. Great leaders focus on more specific themes, often linking the development of a new capability for the firm with a defined performance goal. Inspiration for such ad hoc programs often is provided by enterprising individuals who have a passion for something a little bit off the beaten path. Allowing people to express and act upon their passions in projects of this type can yield enormous payoffs, and the growth of many firms can be traced back to such roots.

Astute leaders recognize that the success of these projects depends on the people driving them, and therefore they start to pick talent early. After designing the project, they search for up-and-coming young individuals, able to spearhead the project independently of the constraints of the line organization. Obviously, the people who suggest the projects are the likely candidates to lead them, because their passion will carry them farther than those who have been randomly assigned. Once selected, the team leader is assigned a *mentor*, an executive with experience, authority, and the will to teach, who will provide air cover in times of trouble, and who will serve as a learning resource to the individual.

Although mentors can be among an organization's most valuable resources, most companies treat mentoring more like a hobby than a legitimate leadership role. Few career management programs list mentoring as an explicit objective, yet successful managers almost always credit one or two mentors for their success.

Mentors lead from behind. Their counsel is discrete, the antithesis of micromanagement. Often, they're warm in day-to-day contact, but they're tough when they have to be. Because they enjoy great credibility in the organization, they often act as back-channel providers of information, helping line managers understand how the project is progressing and, if necessary, suggesting what should be done to change it. The best mentors often are managers in the twilight of their careers, men and women who identify with the less experienced and younger individuals they are coaching.

Like a good parent, the good mentor allows the person they are coaching to make mistakes, recognizing that the best learning often occurs from making errors. This can be extremely difficult at times, for it's difficult for an executive to willingly see something go wrong in an organization and among people he or she cares for. The idea is to exert subtle influence, such that the damage caused by the error is minimal, while the learning from it is great. This sort of creative *error management* is an integral part of a well thought-out development process.

John, the CIGNA Accountant, Spreads His Wings

"We used to be the know-it-alls, the sharp-pencils," John Downham confesses. "We were the superstaff, not really part of the business, but checkers in charge of interpreting for corporate what was going on inside the division."

John Downham is describing the financial staff of CIGNA P&C as it existed before Gerry Isom's arrival. Downham is a friendly accountant with a keen sense of metaphor, who today carries the title of Transformation

Officer for one of the three main divisions of CIGNA P&C, Commercial Insurance Services (CIS). Until Isom's arrival he worked in the controller's area, doing expense management and budgeting, worrying about receivables and cashflow.

Downham, although he has become a leader in the transformation effort, refuses to indulge in simple black-and-white characterizations of the past and present. "Today, it's easy to dump on the old regime," he states. "But I respected my boss. He was a man of conviction who believed that insurance was a financial business that had to be run by financial people. Perhaps that was his blind spot. He wore that belief on his sleeve, and he alienated some people. But he was a man of integrity, and I often regret he's not with us anymore."

Clearly, it's hard for Downham to put the entire episode of his boss's departure behind him.

"My boss left a week after I'd signed on to become a full-time member of Isom's transformation team," he continues. "I had a sense of a terrible loss. I'm not afraid to say it, I was in tears when I said my good-byes to Howard. I first felt mad, then let down."

Slowly, Downham worked his way out of his depression, and became involved in the whirlwind of activities created by project OAR (Organization Alignment Review), the second phase of Isom's transformation effort, in the fall of 1993.

"Now, I had an open field," he recalls. "I had no sense of defending anything. I didn't have to be my boss's emissary anymore; I could use my own judgment. At the same time, that was scary. It took me a while to work out that philosophical difference."

Downham remembers the first three months of project OAR as mostly frustrating. "In this phase of work, we were mostly highlighting existing organizational problems," he says. "We also supported the discovery process with financial information. I knew it all by heart, and had to educate lots of people on the numbers. We were also running survey after survey on cultural issues, and I thought it was nonsense. One year later, I now recognize that culture is everything in a successful company."

Like Ward Jungers, he remembers the dinner the transformation team had with Gerry Isom shortly before Christmas 1993. The diagnostic phase of project OAR was now over, and Isom was trying to encourage the team to pursue the task they had initiated some three months earlier. "I was in a lousy mood," he remembers. "All 10 of us, full-time team members, were burned out. I had a sense of impending failure. It was as if we'd seen the promised land, but were unsure we could bring the rest of the organization with us."

Downham had been assigned to the "support alignment team," which had perhaps the toughest job in the effort, spearheading a dramatic personnel reduction in the home office support functions. "No more studying, it was time for action," he recalls. "It was a brand-new ball game. I started with the financial organization, since I knew it well. I was moderately successful overall, quite successful with some of my colleagues, less so with others. In that position, I rapidly learned the power of leadership. When you're dealing with leaders, you get results. When you don't, you might as well forget it."

A few frustrating experiences remain vivid in Downham's mind. "At one point, I launched a blitzkrieg of natural work teams in a number of areas, but all it left me was Magic Marker on my hands. We got kicked out of at least two departments that I can remember. But it didn't matter."

In the heat of the battle, Downham remembers losing a sense of perspective. "In early October 1994, our team wanted to write our own obituary," he states. "We assembled our team and produced a long list of reasons we thought the transformation had been unsuccessful. We got pessimistic, nearly morbid. Based on that, we generated a report and sent it to senior management."

Finally, at the beginning of the new year, Gerry Isom invited the group to a session. Much to the group's surprise, the tone was decidedly upbeat. "Gerry Isom is the one who pointed out that we'd been quite successful," Downham remembers. "He showed us things we were too close to to even notice. Perhaps our stream of work was not as spectacularly successful as some others, like underwriting, but we'd had an indirect impact on the whole business. Jim Engel, the head of claims, for example, had decided to align his big organization more closely with the businesses, and even though we hadn't worked with him directly day-to-day, he credited our work with having helped him think through the issues."

Downham remembers finding himself once again at a crossroads in late 1994. He had a choice between returning to his old job in finance or continuing in a transformation role.

"That boost from Isom got us pumped," he beams. "We started talking about what would be needed to continue the fight. It wasn't done for personal reasons. We simply wanted to make sure that we kept the flame alive. We talked ourselves right into those positions. First I felt a little like Woody Allen: 'These jobs are too important to give them to the likes of me.' Then I thought I'd learned a few things over the last year, and maybe I could help move the company."

Dick Wratten, the head of Commercial Insurance Services (CIS), offered Downham the job of transformation officer within CIS. It was a brief conversation, in which Wratten simply told him he'd like to have him as part of the team.

"I accepted on the spot," Downham recalls. "Then I went back to my old boss and told him what I was going to do. He asked me a bunch of questions, such as "Who are you going to report to?" and "What will your level be?" Somewhat embarrassed, I told him I didn't know. It hadn't dawned on me that those things could be important. I went back to Wratten and asked him whom I would report to. 'Me, of course,' was his answer. The point is, I knew what I was doing was important, and that's all that really mattered to me."

In spite of his early misgivings, Downham feels the year just elapsed [1994] has been the most important in his professional career. "I can't imagine a scenario in my old job where I could have had the same impact," he says. "What I've been through has been so unique, I can't really explain it. Sometimes people who knew me look at me as if I have three heads. I talk differently, I think differently. Yet deep inside, I know I'm just a simple accountant, trying to do this transformation thing."

IDENTIFYING CRITICAL SKILLS AND DESIGNING AN EDUCATION STRATEGY

Project assignments and mentoring are the most effective way to foster individual learning, but they can reach only a limited number of individuals. The next best thing is an education strategy involving less customization but more employees.

What distinguishes good educational programs from bad ones is not so much the level of resources committed or the quality of the facilities, but their relevance to the business. Most training dollars spent today are wasted on the ill-focused development of generic skills, usually triggered by some functional manager's personal hobby, or in response to a proposal made by a third-party training or consulting company.

The design of an education strategy cannot occur in a vacuum. A skills or competency model needs to be defined *first*; only then can skill and competency training be focused and meaningful. Building a skills model involves striking a balance between two extremes. On the one hand, having *no* skills model is clearly not the answer. At the opposite extreme, building the world's most *thorough* model is equally dangerous.

We vividly remember the case of a firm that developed a skills model so comprehensive and complex that it took on a life of its own. Millions of consulting dollars were spent on developing it to such absurd levels of detail as "tries to engage colleagues in friendly, interpersonal manner most of the time, while exhibiting the necessary firmness in emergency periods."

How would you like to be tested on such an ability? Now imagine this dimension to be one of 35 attributes, pertaining to one group of individuals among 68 groups of "key individuals." And imagine the puzzlement of the head of human resources or the CEO, trying to find the high-stakes skills he or she should invest in within this 68 by 35 matrix in which every coordinate is conceivably a development area.

Efficiency dictates that the skills model should focus on high-payoff skills. Experience shows that such skills usually are associated with the key processes and learning loops of the firm (see Chap. 6). Once again, the intertwining of the biocorporate systems prevents us from neatly isolating pockets of skills that can be individually nurtured. Skills development is an integral part of transformation, and it cannot be dissociated from the mapping of key interrelationships within the firm. Yet few firms carry their change aspirations all the way to an educational agenda, and few human resource departments have the capability to trace the firm's skill development needs all the way back to the firm's transformation path.

All educational programs run the risk of losing relevance to the core business. Even the highly regarded grandfather of all corporate education programs—the Crotonville executive training program of General Electric—once lost its relevance, in the 1970s, when it started to benchmark itself too much against other schools rather than remain focused on the specific needs of GE. It's easy for training centers to fall in love with themselves and their prestigious teaching staffs, and to start overinvesting in their bricks and mortar.

Aligning an education program to a results measurement system is the best way to prevent training centers from becoming irrelevant to the corporation. Ideally, one should be able to track the skills developed through educational programs to bottom-line results. For example, Allstate Insurance and Federal Express have been able to link an increase in customer service skills among their customer-facing employees to objective increases in customer loyalty and even revenues.

Unipart U

In Chaps. 2 and 10, we saw how Unipart, a U.K. automotive parts manufacturer and distributor led by CEO John Neill, achieved exceptional performance through its constituency-based mission and values. In particular, we looked at the firm's explicit commitment to what it calls *shared destiny relationships* with customers, suppliers, and throughout the supply chain. In Chap. 10 we delved more deeply into Unipart's external relationships, examining how it aligns measures and rewards with its "demand chain partners," as Neill might put it. Unipart is equally remarkable in its commitment to employee learning. It is *so* committed, in fact, that it has established its own university, modeled to a significant extent after Motorola's University, which Neill admires.

In September of 1993, Unipart U, the company university formed by Unipart, was formally opened by John Patten, British Secretary of State for Education. "The U has a clear mission," says Neill, "that derives logically from the group's mission: to build an enduring, upper-quartile performing company in which our stakeholders are keen to participate."

"The U reflects our intention to train and inspire people to achieve world-class performance, both within the Unipart Group and among its stakeholders," he continues. "There is a good commercial argument for the U: it's a support route to commercial advantage, and it enhances shareholder value by helping to prevent us from becoming obsolete."

Unipart's vision for the U is "to help us create the world's best lean enterprise," says Neill. "It is by working with all our stakeholders in long-term shared-destiny relationships, and by using the best learning, that we can eliminate waste and improve quality and customer service. Learning and training are fundamentally and inextricably linked with the very being of our company.

"We have therefore created our *deans' group*, consisting of the divisional managing directors. They have their own *faculties*, responsible for defining the critical success factors of their businesses and ensuring that high-quality training courses are available to meet them," he explains with pride. One envisions busy executives hastily throwing professorial robes over their three-piece suits in the backseat of a car on their way to a lecture.

"So now, our managing directors have two roles: first, as managers of their businesses, and, second, as deans of their faculties and full members of the deans' group," Neill explains. "It's through this that we share the best available learning with our colleagues. Each dean writes and presents training courses in the U, and we've all been schooled in how to teach—not only the deans, but managers and employees at all levels teach each other in the U. We're transforming our managers into coaches."

Unipart U has 10 faculties, all directly traceable to its business:

1. Commercial
2. Communications
3. Core
4. Finance
5. Industries
6. IT

7. Marketing

8. Outlets

9. Sales

10. Warehousing and distribution

The deans' group is chaired by professor Dan Jones of Cardiff Business School, a world-recognized motor industry expert and co–author of the book, *The Machine That Changed the World.* Professor Jones acts as the business philosopher and mentor of Unipart U, and lectures two days a month on "lean thinking."

There is nothing "virtual" about Unipart U. It boasts state-of-the-art facilities, 14 training rooms, a lecture theater with remote-control auto-cues and touch-sensitive controls for projection equipment. The U's library, called The Learning Curve, contains books, audio and video cassettes, reference works, maps, periodicals, newspapers, and librarians who can get anything you want through an interlibrary loan system. Laptop computers can be checked out for weekend or overnight use. The library is connected to various on-line information services. Not bad for a $1 billion automotive parts company, operating in a traditionally low-margin business!

Attached to the U is The Leading Edge, a showroom and classroom for computer hardware and software where employees can learn at their own pace, starting with basic computing skills and moving right through to the most sophisticated software. The latest software releases are on display, available for employees to test. The Leading Edge has glass walls and is deliberately placed next to the entrance and reception area of Unipart's Oxford headquarters. Neill wants everyone—existing and prospective stakeholders, tradesmen, visitors, or casual passersby—to understand Unipart's commitment to harnessing information technology in preparing for the future, as well as to think about how they might harness it in working with Unipart.

Neill believes that many of the ideas incorporated in the U could be of value to industry as a whole. "We're building physical infrastructure, a new platform to use. We've got to build it here, because it will see us safely into the next century."

He says people are still intimidated by IT, but insists that everyone must be computer literate. "We have to seduce people through the pain barrier, and we need a place for that."

Neill says the major strategic idea behind Unipart U is to make line managers responsible for training. Their time is costed at an appropriate rate, not including their opportunity cost, and programs are costed too. It takes 10 days, for example, to teach Ten-to-zero, Unipart's quality philosophy, at the U, and the course begins with a lecture on the philosophies underlying it, delivered by Neill himself.

Neill believes that many of the ideas incorporated in the 'U' could be of value to the industry as a whole. "The 'U' is a platform from which we will be able to see future possibilities in a way which might not otherwise have been possible," he says. "It has a fundamental role to play in inspiring the learning that will be essential to getting us safely into the next century."

BALANCING THE SUPPLY OF AND DEMAND FOR SKILLS INSIDE THE CORPORATION

It has long been the dream of socially minded CEOs and government officials alike that people displaced by restructuring at one end of the firm could be redeployed, often after retraining, in another end of the same firm. This generous thinking is born both of human compassion and of the belief that most firms display inefficiencies in their internal labor market. Without a doubt these inefficiencies do exist, especially in large, established corporations that are simultaneously involved in the restructuring of more mature businesses and the development of others.

The telecommunication industry perhaps best illustrates this phenomenon, with the dramatic restructuring occurring in the regulated telephone business, simultaneous with the explosive growth in deregulated markets such as cellular phones, yellow pages, and many other facets of the future "electronic superhighway."

The challenge, of course, has proven to be a practical one. Companies and governments have discovered that skills, even after making a generous provision for "reskilling," are not infinitely fungible. It isn't easy to take shop floor foremen and transform them into automation specialists, nor is it a cinch to turn repair and maintenance personnel into customer service representatives inside telephone companies. Some people *will* adapt more readily than others. Some people *can* adapt more readily than others. Unfortunately, the objective realities are bound to create obstacles for even the most generous and well intended redeployment programs.

The major obstacle, however, is psychological, and the major limitation has proven to be behavioral. Most of us carry a picture of displaced employees as rational beings who, given the chance, would welcome an opportunity to be redeployed. It is seldom that way, and the choices are seldom that clear. Many people who know that their positions are going to be eliminated can't get past their feelings of anger and betrayal. Those who have survived previous bad times may feel that their job could survive after all, so why move before they are forced to? Often the redeployment alternative is equally ill-defined, frequently amounting to a vague promise of a hypothetical future, for an undetermined compensation level, supported by an unproven program. Only now are companies beginning to understand the psychology of the displaced within the context of restructurings.

Individuals undergo a personal trauma in the transition. Self-esteem drops. Denial, anger, and depression may become factors. Employees become confused, defensive, and sometimes irrational, in turn producing frustration for the leadership team, whose members can't fathom why threatened employees don't spontaneously reach out for the hand that has been extended to them. "If I were in their place," they think, "I'd jump at the opportunity in a minute." But the threatened employee doesn't have as clear a view of his or her choices as the leadership team does, nor can he or she look at the situation dispassionately.

To add economic motivation to good intentions, many countries, primarily in Europe, have built up a high social cost around layoffs and other displacements of full-time employees. This has provided an added incentive for corporations to look for alternate solutions, encouraging internal retraining schemes and producing a flurry of experiments vis-à-vis within-company redeployment.

The results to date have been mixed at best, but a few companies are getting good at it. The key to success is the creation of the internal equivalent of market processes to match supply and demand. The companies that have done the best offer a strong behavioral support infrastructure, while simultaneously opening pathways for individual exploration of opportunities throughout the firm. They help displaced employees deal with the psychological trauma, while providing a process through which they can take action toward finding their next job.

Technology has entered the equation, sometimes with great success. Critical to the success of an internal labor exchange is a forum that can link "many to many." In corporations with tens of thousands of employees—where the potential inefficiencies are greatest due to the size of the pool involved—the simple logistics of communicating job availability can be enormous. Technology can provide that forum, and in addition can become the platform for individuals to devise skill-building and career-path planning within a corporatewide framework of opportunities.

Barclays Bank in the United Kingdom has developed such a technology. A few years ago, Barclays made the commitment that it would not lay off its large group of MIS specialists, whose skills had been built around the now obsolete COBOL programming language for mainframes. Rather than fire them and hire new employees with the requisite "modern skills," the firm invested in the development of a large-scale IT application designed initially to help the MIS people, but eventually to allow every employee in the firm to acquire new skills to ensure themselves a place within the organization in the future.

Designed for delivery through desktop systems, the program starts with a multimedia module, in which the CEO communicates the general strategy of the bank and the implications of the strategy in terms of new skills requirements for the MIS department. The program then itemizes what the new jobs are likely to be over a period of a few years, and what skills will comprise each job. Employees then are prompted into an interactive session designed to characterize their current jobs and associated skills, and to explore potential paths leading them from their current skills to the required new skills. At any point a human resources counselor may be invited to step in electronically, to offer advice or to validate the self-assessment. As an incentive for employees to log on, the program also lists all available jobs within the bank at any given time. Employees also know that their superiors look upon use of the program as an indication of a commitment to learn and grow with Barclays.

AT&T Resource Link®

Among the many experiments conducted in the area of intra-company employee redeployment, the one established by AT&T in October 1991 is one of the most successful. AT&T Resource Link® is an in-house, temporary-services unit that supplies general management and technical professionals to AT&T divisions and helps satisfy the ever-changing work-force requirements across the firm's business.

The idea was to improve the responsiveness and flexibility of the firm's internal labor market, so that talented managers, who might otherwise have left the company as a result of its restructuring activities, could be retained and developed. It is now AT&T policy that all business units and divisions must consider AT&T Resource Link® before resorting to agency temps or other contractors to fill management needs. Though assignments are temporary, "associates" retain their status as regular AT&T employees.

Since its formation, AT&T Resource Link® has developed into a vigorous, self-confident supplier of internal know-how to help AT&T manage its fluctuating skills needs, and it has acquired a clear idea of its mission and its customers.

The unit commends its services to its customers—the rest of the company—in precisely the same way as an external temp agency would. In effect, their market positioning is: "In today's competitive environment, leaders must constantly seek new and creative ways to achieve business objectives. AT&T Resource Link® can provide you with the flexibility to perform short-term project work, to temporarily back-fill a vacant position, or to support temporary peaks in workload. Our associates offer customers a variety of technical and managerial expertise and, in contrast to outside temps, are familiar with AT&T products, services, and infrastructure. In addition to minimizing 'on-boarding' costs, associates offer knowledge and experience gained in other parts of the AT&T group, offering clients the opportunity to extend their networks and enhance their collaborative efforts."

The unit is aware of the potentially negative perception of being the home for the victims of AT&T's restructuring. The basic operating premise, however, is that there's nothing intrinsically wrong with employees who have been displaced by restructurings; they just happen to have skills that were no longer needed at that particular place and time. AT&T Resource Link® screens its associates and assesses their skills, knowledge, and adaptability. Given the proper direction, they can represent a tremendous resource for other parts of the business. As of March 1994, the unit had over 400 people on contract with more than 25 different business units and divisions throughout AT&T.

In March 1994, about a third of the unit's associates were on technical assignments, and the demand for nontechnical skills was increasing. Most assignments were from 3 to 12 months, some much longer, and most assignments are extended. As a result, once a displaced employee signs up with Resource Link®, he or she spends on average less than 2 percent of his or her time between jobs, a remarkable result by the standard of the temporary services industry.

Customer satisfaction surveys give high scores (90 percent and above) on quality, ease of use, and readiness to use AT&T Resource Link® again. Associates also value the unit's responsiveness and its ability to match skills to work requirements. The following two testimonials from associates illustrate how the system is being used:

> Working for AT&T Resource Link® has been one of the most rewarding and challenging experiences of my AT&T career. It enabled me to acquire new skills and gain exposure to other areas of the company, both of which led directly to my promotion into NSD Human Resources.

> [AT&T Resource Link®] offers me the ability to increase my overall market value by giving me the opportunity to continue to develop myself and my skills set, to work within many new and existing business units, to gain a better understanding of where the BUs are headed, and to be a part of the overall growth of AT&T.

Perhaps the most remarkable feature of the whole program is the way in which an initiative that was designed to salve the wounds of restructuring and to give tangible substance to AT&T's Common Bond philosophy, is producing a new career option and a new kind of AT&T manager. A significant number of associates end up in permanent positions, and at least 15 percent of those placements are promotions. Even more encouragingly, many people have turned down permanent offers, preferring to take advantage of the variety of assignments AT&T Resource Link® offers. AT&T Resource Link® has become a legitimate career path in itself.

Over 50 percent of associates choose Resource Link® as a career move, because they see, in the peripatetic nature of the work, an opportunity to expand their knowledge of the group, enhance their skills, raise their profiles, and expand their network. These are not traumatized victims of restructuring; they are high-fliers, cruising around the group, picking up contracts, establishing credibility, and searching for the most exciting areas or the most promising routes to the top.

Reskilling at France Telecom

France Telecom faces the massive redeployment challenge of major telecommunication companies, with a double twist. First, it operates in a country whose social legislation is among the most comprehensive and restrictive, essentially barring France Telecom from using the type of restructuring chosen by its American and British counterparts. Second, its work force is strongly unionized, further restricting its freedom to adjust its work-force level to its perceived needs.

This in itself would not be of major consequence if France Telecom could continue to compete as a regional player, protected by a set of local regulations. But this isn't the case. To survive, France Telecom has no choice but to participate in the global telecommunications race; which means achieving status as a global competitor as quickly as possible. To do that, France Telecom has undertaken a massive transformation in the last few years, and today it bears little resemblance to the sleepy monopoly the French people once loved to make fun of. The company, since 1991, has a new status, partly government- and partly public-owned. It also has formed a major alliance with its German equivalent, Deutsche Telekom, to develop a global service offering (see the Concert story in Chap. 8). No more Gallic isolationism—the global war is on.

The need for the massive transformation of France Telecom is triggering an equally massive shift of skills requirements, resulting in potentially large displacements of individuals. For example, in a complete redesign of its order-activation process—the process of making a phone line available to anyone who requests it as quickly and efficiently as possible—the company has found that it can reduce manpower by a considerable margin in this area. Given the social context, however, France Telecom was puzzled as to where to go next.

The Toulouse regional district was put in charge of piloting the new order-activation process, as well as of proposing solutions to the arduous social questions involved. Of the 80 full-time equivalent people working in service activation—close to 180 people actually were involved, many on a part-time basis—it found that 14 could be made redundant (the job could be eliminated) in the new process.

Painstakingly, the managers of the Toulouse regional district proceeded to search elsewhere in the firm for employment opportunities for the 14 employees. They found needs across numerous functions, in areas as diverse as complaint management, agency-based customer service, field service, new cabling offering for large buildings, and relationship management with municipalities and developers.

With great care, they organized in-depth interviews with all 14 employees, working with them on matching their skills and interests with the available options. In addition, they jointly determined which skills the displaced employees would have to acquire. In the end, each of the 14 employees was successfully redeployed, each in customized fashion. Remarkably, the unions, traditionally perceived as fairly antagonistic, supported the program throughout.

Finding a solution to the fate of 14 people in the Toulouse region may not look like much in light of the fact that France Telecom has 168,000 employees in all! But the approach that was created sent a wonderful signal to the organization as a whole. For the first time, something concrete had been done about helping along the individual renewal of people whose future was threatened by the company's transformation. As one of the 14 testified recently with great gratitude: "It's wonderful when our bosses worry about implementation at this level of detail. Because that's where my future is, in this detail."

DEVELOPING THE ORGANIZATION

Everyone has experienced it. You're at the theater, at the stadium, or at a meeting. The curtain falls, the goal is scored, or the difficult decision is made. All at once, the emotion swells. You leap to your feet with the audience—simultaneously laughing, shouting, and crying—participating in the collective *yes!* You roar with the crowd, slapping "high-fives" with complete strangers. Or you exchange misty-eyed nods with colleagues, nearly bursting with kinship, pride, and yes, even love. It is a profoundly personal experience, you feel it physically: "This is *right!*" Yet you know all of it is greater, somehow, because others are sharing it, too.

People who share our sense of life become our psychological mirrors. We *commune* with them to enrich our own internal experience, embracing both the positive and the negative to complete our sense of identity. We experience our *selves* most profoundly in the presence of kindred spirits. We crave the company of other people, describe our need for them as a "hunger." The appetite is for a *sense of community*, obtainable only through human interaction.

This sense of community is a *need* for the biological corporation, an increasingly critical one in this information age. As knowledge displaces assets as the measure of wealth, as the division of knowledge displaces the division of labor as the measure of efficiency, corporations increasingly will need to develop internal and external communities in which individuals succeed. With so much new knowledge to master and apply, the importance of team-based work will continue to grow; but paradoxically, so will the corporation's reliance on the self-responsibility, self-assertiveness, and integrity of individuals. Companies will need to develop a family of people who can think independently and work interactively, who know how to work alone and when to work with others, who take pride in their achievements and relish the achievements of others.

The history of organizational development reflects an accelerating ascendancy of *mind* over physical labor in the workplace. Under the authoritarian industrial model, the regimented work force represented an extension of the minds of business leaders and manufacturing engineers. The good worker was obedient, fast, and efficient—like a well-oiled machine—and the military model of a command-and-control structure seemed appropriate. As technological advances led to automation, skilled labor and managing the growing swell of information became greater priorities. Functional expertise became prized, and it became more efficient to organize around functional capabilities. Organizational charts were neat block-and-wire diagrams, pyramids representing layer upon layer of management.

That trend played out as communications technology made layer after layer of management unnecessary. Many companies started focusing on optimizing cross-functional work processes, and some even began organizing around those processes. In other companies, focus on core competences became the model, and their organizational charts started to look something like a pepperoni pizza. Now, even as those models are being adopted, they tend to splinter, as if to defy simplistic modeling. As the manager-worker model disappears, as companies become more and more an integration of specialists, as mind becomes the dominant factor in business activity, it is becoming increasingly difficult to mechanically map the ever adapting organization in the two-dimensional universe of blocks, circles, and wires.

In the Communications Age, an organization needs to maintain two seemingly antithetical characteristics: being clear and focused on the one hand, while being prepared for ongoing change and adaptation on the other. Individuals need a sense of clarity for themselves, and they need to know what they are accountable for. They naturally resist ambiguity, because it's a source of confusion. As command-and-control management structures collapse, managers complain about the complexity of organizational charts and their reporting relationships, represented by a maze of solid, dotted, double-solid, and double-dotted lines. Most people agree conceptually that the neat, hierarchical model of the organization has outlived its usefulness, but as practitioners, many hearts still yearn for it.

The path forward, however, is inexorable. Every healthy organizational structure must prepare for ongoing adaptation that blurs existing organizational boundaries and fosters new organizational allegiances that defy the existing organizational chart. The very essence of human progress is applying new knowledge in new ways, continuously making the old way of doing things obsolete. Organizations don't make progress, *people* do. The organization is just a vehicle for human cooperation. Its form adapts as the needs of the people adapt, and peoples' needs change with the progressive acquisition and application of new knowledge. At the current rate of acquisition, the sum of what we collectively know is doubling every 10 years. Ninety percent of all the scientists who ever lived are alive today. There is no reason to believe that the pace will slow. To keep pace, organizations will look more and more like pools of skills, which gather and part like thoughts in the human mind, constantly developing, adapting, and improving to expand the realm of the humanly possible.

In the biological corporation, developing the organization is the job of the twelfth corporate chromosome. Properly handled, this chromosome closes the virtuous circle of the biocorporate genome, enabling the corporation to become truly transformational. The organization development chromosome has four genes, implying four corresponding tasks for the genetic architects of the corporation:

1. *Designing the organization.* There are organizational designs that work, and others that don't. Although the mode of organization shouldn't be the sole preoccupation of the leader—the way the organization evolves is often as important as the final design—the organizational design remains an important component of the life of a corporation. There are many approaches and models of organizational design: the classical functional approach; the SBU model; matrix models; and more recently, organizing around core competences and business processes (sometimes called *horizontal organizations*).

Whatever the leader's choice, no solution will solve all problems, because any organizational design can only approximate the network of skills the company needs to create. The organizational design, while important, cannot hope to encapsulate all the desirable behaviors of the firm's employees. Successful leaders use the designs to help realize a few dominant business objectives, while realizing that the richness of connected networks of people and teams is created independently of any specific model, through activities such as individual goal-setting, generating rewards, and, most importantly, through the inexplicable alchemy of individual motivation.

2. *Using teams as the basic connecting node and the driver of organizational adaptation.* Since organizational designs inevitably carry the virus of organizational immobility, leaders need to stimulate continuous adaptation through a more dynamic process. Just as ad hoc teams built around specific objectives are the best source of individual learning, so they are the foundation for organizational learning and, if successful, for the future organizational design. By unleashing teams inside their organization, leaders deliberately sacrifice a degree of clarity in the hope of discovering the nature of their future organization.

Through these teams, leaders can test the validity of their contemplated design, as well as the true ability of the people who populate the teams. When both survive in the ensuing Darwinian battle, the leadership team can install a new organization with the confidence that both the new design and the new leaders have proven their value.

3. *Creating global learning.* Only now are we beginning to understand that learning is the most strategically important activity within the corporation. Historically, companies have viewed skills and competences as something related to, and yet distinct from, corporate processes and systems, as something people are supposed to bring to work with them. Now companies are realizing that every event, within every process, within every system, represents a learning opportunity that, if capitalized upon, enriches the organization's skill and competence base. And when companies start to capture this learning, they start to compete as an integrated army rather than as an isolated battalion.

Capturing learning—becoming a learning organization—requires building a knowledge architecture, establishing a knowledge management process, and creating a technical infrastructure. The knowledge architecture creates the conceptual framework for generating an ever growing body of systematic knowledge, as well as the structure for matching knowledge to skill requirements. The knowledge management process provides the formal methodology for collecting, integrating, and disseminating knowledge. And the technical architecture, destined to become computer-based, allows every individual to gain access to the knowledge wherever and whenever it is needed.

4. *Embracing the corporation's soul and its shadow.* As organizations adapt and progress, expanding their connectivity networks, they have the opportunity to evolve from being dominant *economic* institutions to becoming the preeminent *social* institutions of the knowledge age. Potentially, corporations have a significant role to play, but they must *earn the right* to play it. Many people basically distrust corporations. Some of that distrust is philosophical, but most of it is attributable to the authoritarian heritage of the industrial age.

Like people, corporations make mistakes. Moreover, they are a composite of both the good and the bad, the hero and the villain. And like people, corporations become more whole and more credible when they embrace both the hero and the villain within themselves, both their soul and its shadow. The corporations that earn the right to help shape the future of society will be those that reflect the self-acceptance and self-responsibility of the people that comprise them.

DESIGNING THE ORGANIZATION

As we learn that the process of organizational evolution (discussed in the next two sections) is at least as important as the organizational structure that overlays it, organizational design may not seem as important as it used to be. But make no mistake: Organizational design still matters, and picking the best one remains one of the most important tasks of the leader. There are still organization designs that work and others that don't. If the lines, boxes, and circles aren't in the right place, then everybody focuses on the dysfunctions that are created. The firm turns its focus inward, it loses the market perspective, and progress grinds to a halt.

Organizational design is the area in which leaders most directly exert their influence, redefining and reassigning roles and responsibilities among the employees of the firm. Nobody can tell a CEO *not* to redesign; this is one of the few domains where his or her will can be signaled and exerted immediately and unchecked. That is why most transformational leaders use organizational redesigns sparingly. They know that they unleash raw power struggles and otherwise create formidable disturbances in the organization, so they choose their timing carefully.

The most common time for reorganization is at the beginning of a CEO's tenure, when with surgical precision the most glaring malfunctions can be corrected. Usually these moves focus on a few key functional areas, sparing the bulk of the organization from massive change. The more fundamental redesign usually comes much later, typically in about two years, after key elements of the transformation have fully taken hold and the CEO has developed the context within which to make wise choices. Often this is when new leaders emerge, those who have proven both their commitment and their ability through the transformation process.

Most leaders select their basic organizational layout from a limited portfolio of options, each with its own benefits and drawbacks. Historically, functional, SBU-based, and matrix organizations have been the dominant models. Functionally-based organizations preserve the integrity of skills, but the individual functions tend to become self-propagating over time, failing to realign according to the needs of individual businesses. SBU-based organizations allow businesses the independence needed to align themselves, but often fail to nurture the development and cross-fertilization of functions and competences across businesses, much-needed characteristics in fostering corporate growth (see Chap. 8). Matrix-based organizations attempt to accumulate the advantages of both functionally-based and SBU-based organizations, but sometimes become stifled in the ambiguity of the dual relationships involved.

More recently, core competence–based and process–based organizations (AKA horizontal organizations) have emerged on the scene. Some companies organize around core competences to encourage the cross-fertilization of competences and generate new businesses. While this has its advantages, it introduces yet another dimension in an already complex array, and often loses that ease of alignment which the best of functional and SBU-based organizations enjoy. Process-based organizations are the latest fashion, riding on the popularity of the reengineering movement. They put processes at the center of the organizational universe, solving the problem of cross-functional process dysfunctions, but they often replace the problem of functional silos with process "tunnels."

Depending on the unique nature of the corporation involved, any one of these macro organizational types may work, but the key to success depends on what happens at the micro level. The reason organizational designs and depictions are becoming more complex is that corporate leaders are learning that connecting learning and skills into a cross-corporate, integrated network is the ultimate goal. Mapping that kind of network in a simple block-and-wire diagram isn't easy. Considered from just the four-dimensional viewpoint of the Balanced Scorecard, it's impossible to visually capture that system of connectors with a sense of three-dimensional clarity, much less the two-dimensional clarity of a block-and-wire diagram. When you consider the complexity introduced by the 12 biocorporate systems, even using the most advanced computer-simulation models becomes problematic.

Successful companies understand that an organizational chart is a mere approximation of the way the system ought to work. Rather than attempt to build the organization in the image of the model, they create the framework, then build the organization organically, using goals, measures, rewards, ad hoc teams, and the spirit of individuals to generate ever-widening networks of learning loops. The organizational structure always lags behind the reality of desired behavior, but that's fine with them as long as the corporate body keeps advancing.

SPAR, or the Unification of a German Retailer

If you have traveled to Germany, you have undoubtedly seen the SPAR insignia at the top of a small neighborhood store. Redolent as most SPAR stores are of fresh meat and vegetables, there is something quaintly old-world about them, a feeling of an era gone by in which merchants were friendly and neighbors came by and discussed the weather over their daily purchases.

Beyond the nostalgia, however, SPAR is a large corporation with sales of about $9.5 billion and 28,000 employees. It has enjoyed tremendous growth over the last five years, largely due to acquisitions, most notably that of the "HO" chain of supermarkets in East Germany. SPAR is both a wholesaler to 5,000 independent retailers managing SPAR-labeled stores, and a retailer through 350 company-owned supermarkets, 70 hypermarkets (very large supermarkets), and 250 discount stores, under the NETTO brand. SPAR also owns a tremendously powerful logistical machine, with 23 warehouse centers, able to deliver food anywhere in Germany on a daily basis.

When Helmut Dotterweich, took over as the new chairman of SPAR, he knew that his main challenge was to improve profitability. In 1993, net pretax income was only 0.4 percent of sales, while German retailers averaged about 1.5 percent and best practice was around 3.8 percent. Dotterweich could easily see the road ahead: SPAR had been growing rapidly, and it was time to integrate the patchwork of different organizations developed during the rapid growth of the previous few years.

Where to start was Dotterweich's question, for he had problems aplenty. First, the company was split culturally between retailing and wholesaling. Dotterweich himself was a retailer, coming from REWE, one of the main SPAR competitors. (There was in fact some speculation that he was a REWE mole, placed there to orchestrate the subsequent acquisition of SPAR by REWE.) There were five regions in the formerly West German organization, all with considerable power derived from their wholesaling expertise and from their relationships with the 5000-strong network of independent retailers. The regions were independently suspicious of any attempt to align them behind a national strategy or organization.

The future of the independent retailers was questionable, however. Most of the SPAR stores were deemed too small to survive. The average store had only 600 square feet, and some were much smaller. Shopkeepers' age averaged 55 years, and many of them had no designated successor. The economics were quite unattractive for a young German with many other opportunities. The immigrant population, Turks in particular, were willing to accept lower income of this type, but there simply weren't enough of them to stem the tide.

There were significant questions associated with the bigger stores as well. Both EUROSPAR supermarkets and INTERSPAR hypermarkets required considerable investment, which fit neither the SPAR culture nor its cashflow. Furthermore, it was becoming increasingly hard to locate new construction sites, particularly for hypermarkets. The East German stores were a headache in their own right, and the process of integrating them into SPAR hadn't even begun. In addition, the IT system already was buckling under the weight of adding the new region.

To complete the picture of Dotterweich's nightmare, the equity structure of SPAR also was of concern, with rumors that a 28 percent owner of SPAR stock wanted to sell, opening the doors to a change of structure that might involve competitors. That owner was Bernhard Schmidt, the former chairman and now head of the Surveillance Committee (Aufsichtsrat). Finally, Germany was in the midst of one of its darkest recessions since World War II.

Dotterweich is both a visionary and an excellent communicator, a leader who quickly gained a good sense of what his organization could accept. In this labyrinth of issues, he and his team decided to focus on operational issues first, with an understanding that he would later tackle the politically loaded strategic and organizational issues the company faced. But first he initiated a series of analytical probes to uncover the true position of the business.

The leadership team was in for a few surprises. First, SPAR discovered through activity-based costing that the small stores, contrary to what it had believed, were in fact quite profitable. Dotterweich had thought he should encourage the death of smaller stores, but discovered that they were in fact a profitable channel, even though the demise of the smallest stores was probably inevitable. Regional heads were triumphant, saying in essence: "We told you so." Conversely, when service costs were properly allocated, the larger stores proved to be less profitable than originally thought. "When supermarkets require four strawberry deliveries per week, your net margin goes down rapidly," Dotterweich commented.

In addition, regional heads were not pleased when a survey revealed that their customers viewed them as something other than the epitome of freshness and service they had thought the stores projected. SPAR stores ranked in the middle of the pack, while some discount marketers without a fresh produce department and with only minimal services rated higher. Another paradigm shattered!

Dotterweich and his team began mobilizing the leadership team around these emerging facts. In workshop after workshop—there have been 16 to date—Dotterweich the communicator gathered the regional leaders around the same table to discuss the implications of the recently uncovered facts.

The first workshop was "very quiet," Dotterweich remembers, with warmth developing progressively over time. "We invented a new communication style," he says simply. "It was not a very German thing to do, but it worked."

Based on SPAR's analysis of the situation at hand, Dotterweich's vision began to gel both in his mind and that of his team.

"The biggest opportunity was associated with leveraging our collective strength," he says. "We simply had to take advantage of our size, and stop behaving like unconnected regions and stores."

SPAR discovered there was power in bigness, in two areas in particular. The most obvious was purchasing, where SPAR could use its clout to buy centrally. Today, 90 percent of the buying process is centralized, with 10 percent left in the regions, primarily for local products. Some regions resisted, lamenting the perceived loss of power associated with "giving up" purchasing. There again, the team-building effort of Dotterweich played a major role in overcoming the resistance.

The second area was in building the product line—*category management*, as it is known in the trade. SPAR discovered that aggregate volume sold or purchased is less important for bargaining purposes than "volume in the category." Under its regionalized organization, SPAR had never approached suppliers in an integrated way, offering to distribute and promote its products on a national basis in exchange for favorable terms and promotional support.

Before they could do that, however, they had to convince both the independent retailers and the regions of the merit of the approach. Dotterweich and his team presented the rational arguments: "You will get lower prices, more help from our central information services, promotional support and advertising, including from TV and radio, and this will increase your revenue." To many independent retailers, it still sounded like a loss of independence, and they were wary. In the end, though, involvement turned out to be the key, producing numerous meetings in which the categories were painstakingly defined and agreed upon. The meetings also helped the traditional SPAR retailers to focus on the end-customer's need as opposed to just supplier terms, which had been the primary object of their attention until then.

The next challenge involved the suppliers, big-league manufacturers with well known brands who would not readily play along with the new scheme. Here again, Dotterweich's talent as a communicator came into play. Dotterweich and his team organized a large fair at headquarters, invited close to 100 suppliers, and urged them to participate in joint programs with SPAR. Many came tentatively, expecting the event to be the usual pretext for a renegotiation of terms more favorable to the company.

"We want to extract neither money nor more favorable terms from you," was Dotterweich's first sentence in his introductory speech. "We want to show you our new capabilities, build a new relationship with you. And we need your help."

It was a first for this group of suppliers. They filled in questionnaires, participated in workshops, and developed recommendations for SPAR. Many were so visibly excited by the approach that they were gushing with praise.

"It's the first time a retailer got us together without beating us up," one supplier commented.

In its transformation, SPAR learned that its primary competence rests more in wholesaling and logistics than in the actual running of company-owned stores (with the exception of NETTO). Therefore they are now focusing on developing two types of independently owned stores, while progressively downplaying the importance of company-owned stores. The first is a convenience store, typically located in small villages and neighborhoods, acting as a convenience grocery but also offering postal services, a bank automatic teller machine, and perhaps lottery tickets, laundry machines, and a small restaurant corner.

The second is a larger store with a supermarket layout, featuring a large SPAR merchandise section. EUROSPAR stores, currently company-owned, will progressively be spun off to independents. As for its company-owned, INTERSPAR hypermarkets, they will continue to operate them as valuable assets, holding them as bargaining chips for a potential asset trade or possibly a merger in the future. In addition, SPAR is continuing to develop the very successful chain of NETTO discount stores, intending to expand from the current 250 stores to about 1000 of them in the near future.

Helmut Dotterweich is a busy man, and he has launched many other initiatives within SPAR. For example, the firm is busily developing new businesses that utilize its unique logistical ability to serve small retailers. The MIS capability is being totally revamped.

After the somewhat painful centralization of purchasing, Dotterweich now is concentrating on the second wave of organizational redesign. His focus this time is on governance issues, more specifically on empowering his leadership team and his regions, with the hope of getting SPAR to behave more and more like a networked organization. In particular, Dotterweich's aim is to delegate some of the powers traditionally held by the Vorstand (the very powerful management board under German law).

In the future, SPAR will be governed by three major committees. The first one, comprised of two members of the Vorstand (including Dotterweich as chairman) and the regional heads, will worry about the strategy and the overall steering of the firm. A second committee (also chaired by Dotterweich), comprised of representatives from all the major chains, the regional heads, and representation from the independent retailers, will deal with all store chain and related merchandising issues. The third committee will handle logistics, distribution, MIS, accounting, and other support, and will be chaired by Andreas Toth, member of the Vorstand.

Perhaps the most interesting aspect of the SPAR story is Dotterweich's view that the organization needed to be simultaneously more centralized and more empowered: more centralized, to reduce purchasing cost and increase its leverage with suppliers; more empowered, because the Vorstand couldn't pretend to know all the answers, particularly at the regional level, and because the firm needed to foster the development of leadership at the regional level.

USING TEAMS AS THE BASIC CONNECTING NODE AND THE DRIVER OF ORGANIZATIONAL ADAPTATION

As a model for developing the organization, we look to the human brain.

For years, it was thought that various human attributes could be isolated in specific areas of the brain. In particular, scientists long searched for "the rational area" and "the emotional area," only to discover that they were hopelessly intertwined. Furthermore, the brain appears to be capable of "moving things around," such that entire areas of the brain may be destroyed but other parts take over, resuming functioning that was thought to have become impossible. The essence of learning and intelligence appears to be in the movement across brain cells and through synapses of the electrochemical composites that somehow constitute thoughts and ideas. Creativity is therefore the process of connecting previously disjoined elements in new and useful ways.

Traditional leaders view their organizations in much the same way as scientists used to view the brain. Many corporations still view themselves as discrete blocks of functional capabilities, and they organize accordingly. Increasingly, however, companies are learning that it isn't so much how they're organized on the macro level, but what happens on the micro level that really counts. For example, the problem with functionally organized companies isn't their functional nature, per se, but rather the rigid organizational barriers that have grown between functions. Knowledge and learning doesn't flow across functions as it should, and people can't easily move within the organization to inject energy, talent, and creativity where it is most needed.

In approaching organizational renewal, many leaders tend to emphasize the formal, high-level reorganization component as the first major step. Where complete bureaucratic inertia has arrested forward progress, the shock of major reorganization is sometimes the best treatment. In many cases, however, this is like sticking a cattle prod into the center of the brain, sending the corporate body into misdirected convulsions due to over-stimulation. In such cases, predicting where the psychological dust will settle is anyone's guess.

A more prudent approach is to create small teams of multitalented people with the authority to take action. The idea is to fill the corporation's knowledge reservoir by tapping underground springs of entrepreneurial creativity. It is not necessary to pile up resources to ensure the success of entrepreneurial teams, for they rely on innovation more than resources to reach project goals. Each team can rely on knowledge as its greatest asset, and build its own business case as it progresses. If the team is to survive and be successful, it ultimately must pay its own way. Having a healthy sense of independence, self-reliance, and self-responsibility is the mark of a good team.

While independence is a virtue for these teams, *connectedness* is the goal. The role of leadership is to forge points of connectivity by redefining roles and responsibilities, driving communications, rewarding achievements, and allowing penalty-free failures. Many teams, especially those exploring new business opportunities, may indeed not succeed. But as more and more teams start succeeding, and as leaders continue building connectors across the teams, networks start to emerge.

Those networks then become the very core of the renewed organization, and the basis of the future organizational structure. For the CEO, these teams provide the ability to test both the future design and the leadership ability of the people who comprise them. If the project fails, either the design or the people have proven to be deficient. Either way, the CEO has avoided a potentially costly mistake. If the team succeeds, both the design and the leadership already have proven their ability to survive and thrive, and the CEO has reduced the risks involved.

More and more, transformational leaders are encouraging the formation of ad hoc structures of this type, deliberately sacrificing the call for clarity from the established organization to reap the benefits of experimentation. Much to the chagrin of the incumbents, a natural law of selection ensues, with some of the ad hoc teams challenging various dimensions of the established structure. While contrary to the traditional precepts of organizational teaching, this cohabitation of sometimes ambiguous mandates is an effective way to allow an organization to change spontaneously, rather than wait for the next discrete, top-driven reorganization.

The Small Outdoes the Establishment at Sony

We often think of small as good, big as bad. Part of the reason may be that it's intrinsically more rewarding to be surprised when the underdog wins. But when dealing with organizations, it's usually because big fosters rigidity and inflexibility. According to a manager at Sony, one way to overcome this problem is to be "intentionally disorganized."

He takes pleasure in describing the way the dual TV-VCR set was developed at Sony. An "organized" company would have worried about allocating resources, and wouldn't have dreamed of duplicating effort. Sony did. The goal seemed relatively simple: to produce a television with a built-in VCR. The project was given to two different groups within the Sony structure.

The first group actually was made up of two subgroups, the two large engineering departments at Sony's organizationally separate TV and VCR divisions. They were given the project under the assumption that by combining competences, they could produce the new hybrid device. The second group was a development team at Aiwa, a separate company 51-percent owned by Sony. It was a small group, operating out of Singapore. The team was formed just for the project, and operated in complete independence of Sony's engineering staff.

Intuitively, one would guess that the project should have been a cinch for the Sony engineers. As the months passed, however, they floundered, unable to get on the same wavelength. While they meandered around on unproductive pursuits, the small Aiwa team sailed ahead, producing the attractive integrated product now sold on the market.

This shows the value of turning projects over to people with free spirits, working within structures that are open, flexible, and easily changed. Score one for the small teams.

The Smile that Says, "I Work at Swedish Post"

It's 1987, and you're visiting Sweden. To sample some local color, you enter a neighborhood pub, where you strike up a conversation with a pleasant if somewhat morose fellow sitting at the bar. He seems to have been drinking fairly heavily, given that it's just 6:00 P.M., but that's okay, you've had your bad days too. After exchanging pleasantries, the conversation takes a slightly more personal turn, and you ask, "Do you work in the area?"

A shadow seems to cross the man's face as he offers reluctantly, "Yes, here in Stockholm."

You sense something wrong. Perhaps you've said something insulting without meaning to. But your curiosity is piqued, so you venture on. "Oh? Where exactly?"

Again the shadow, this time accompanied by furtive, sidelong glances, as if someone might hear. "Not far from here. I'm a civil servant."

There's something decidedly strange about this individual, you think, and you're determined to find out what it is. "Oh, really? And what do you *do*?" The emphasis is very slight, just to see if it gets a reaction.

It does. He slides into his shirt like a turtle, saying, "Well, actually...I work at Swedish Post."

Until Ulf Dahlsten, the president and CEO of Swedish Post, took over in 1987, this anecdote faithfully reflects the way employees felt about working at Swedish Post. The reputation of the agency was horrible, clouded by scandal and obscurity, not to mention terrible levels of service (which most of us can relate to with our own postal services).

Even the headquarters building seemed to reflect the organization's lack of human spirit. Dahlsten remembers approaching the massive gray facility just three days after being offered his leadership position. He couldn't even find the door! Finally he located it at the corner of the building. He opened it to find a dingy old staircase and lift, which led to his office on the first floor. He was greeted by a long-suffering civil servant, who offered words to the effect that he'd seen many before him, and few had lasted long. Dahlsten soon discovered that Swedish Post's future looked as gloomy as the building. It was a centuries-old, bloated bureaucracy, strangled by government control and threatened by technological change. The 358-year-old organization had lost its sense of purpose.

By 1994, however, Dahlsten could look back and point to some spectacular accomplishments. Swedish Post is now a network of some 1500 small enterprises, each a profit center working within the larger framework of five business areas. With the goal of breaking the entire organization into small profit centers now 60 percent complete, forty-six thousand people do more work than 58,000 did just four years ago. Productivity has gone up 10 percent between 1992 and 1994, while postal prices have dropped 10 percent in real terms. Once merely a civil service post, a job at Swedish Post is now a coveted position, with hundreds of applicants queuing up for the opportunity to work there. Perhaps the best measure of the organization's total transformation is that it was voted the most appreciated of all Swedish companies, public or private, in an independent survey in 1994.

When Dahlsten took the helm of Swedish Post, it was organized into postal districts, with each district run as an activity and cost center. Ostensibly, a postmaster was in charge of district operations. In reality, the postmasters had almost no accountability for performance. Now, local business managers run their businesses with "complete responsibility," in Dahlsten's terms. There are no more postmasters.

The entrepreneurial spirit has overtaken the organization. The ownership structure is now semi-private, and is likely to be completely privatized in the future. Forty of the top fifty executives are from the private sector. Each enterprise builds and implements its own plans, negotiating its interdependence through formal business plans within the five areas, as well as informal arrangements with its related business colleagues. The various enterprises share personnel policies and the IT platform, but beyond that each business is on its own, responsible for achieving financial success, customer satisfaction, and employee participation and involvement.

Swedish Post is no longer just a letter carrier. It still delivers letters and parcels, but it also offers extensive counter services, such as copying and faxing, and it manages messages and fund transfers (for payments) electronically through its Giro system. Swedish Post has become an integrated network of message, parcel, and payment-transfer specialists, operating primarily in Sweden and the European Community (EC), but also outside Europe.

Recently selected over heavy competition as the Swedish government's electronic carrier, Swedish Post has become a market leader in the area of electronic mail (E-mail). It offers an "E" post service in which messages are sent electronically to a distribution center and are then delivered physically to the final destination. The organization runs a 20,000 company "E-direct" network that connects the companies through its electronic network. Recently it has also created an electronic payment system that ties other European countries to its Giro system, becoming the first electronic payment system to meet EC requirements. Unlike the postal systems in most other European countries, Swedish Post has always been run independently of the country's phone system, meaning that it has accomplished this remarkable communications achievement without an installed base.

No territory is off-limits as far as Dahlsten is concerned. "Take on mail delivery within businesses or office complexes," he urges. "Distribute food as well as parcels, if you can make money at it." With this kind of entrepreneurial spirit, it's no wonder that world leaders such as FedEx and UPS have been unable to encroach on Swedish Post's package business, while they have beaten national postal companies on their own turf just about everywhere else.

So don't be surprised if the next time you meet a jolly group at a pub in Sweden, they raise their mug to your health and when asked what they do, sing out proudly: "We work at Swedish Post!"

CREATING GLOBAL LEARNING

Size still matters a lot to businesses, but not like it used to. Economies of scale are disappearing, being replaced by *the economies of global learning*.

Learning is a fairly new word in our corporate vocabulary. Our command-oriented mindset has long included words such as *plan, train, control, review,* and *decide*—but not *learn*. Skills and competences have stayed in the background, under the implicit assumption that they are the employees' responsibility—like lunch, to be brought with them to work. By and large, skills and competences have been externalized by the corporation, assumed to be provided by an unspecified third party called a school, a university, or "experience."

Everything that a company does, however, has both operational and learning aspects. Unfortunately, the learning aspect is usually ignored or regarded as incidental. At the core of the philosophy of renewal is recognizing that learning as vital.

We already have seen in Chap. 6 (Redesigning the Work Architecture) how a new, more fruitful approach to the reengineering of processes involves mapping the flow of knowledge rather than the chronology of operational steps to generate improvements. We also detailed how creative companies build wider and wider learning loops, in essence transporting knowledge across the entire corporation, bringing to bear the full firepower of the firm at all times rather than just the limited shelling ability of its farthest outposts.

When managed in an integrated way, learning loops form an integrated network, making the corporation a *learning organization*. A learning organization usually consists of at least three major elements:

1. *A knowledge architecture.* The knowledge architecture is the conceptual framework for generating an ever growing body of systematic knowledge, as well as the structure for matching knowledge to skill requirements. (See Chap. 11 for a further discussion of skills mapping.) The knowledge architecture should act as the road map for knowledge acquisition, career planning, and training.

2. *A knowledge management process.* The knowledge management process provides the formal methodology for collecting, integrating, and disseminating knowledge. Formal debriefing sessions, organized learning programs attended and supported by senior managers and executives, and recognition and reward systems are the key ingredients of an effective knowledge management process.

3. *A technical architecture.* The technical architecture, destined to become computer-based in virtually every organization, allows every individual to gain access to knowledge wherever and whenever it is needed. It ensures rapid dissemination of knowledge to the people who need it, increasingly through groupware and other network-based software.

A desire to keep pace with technology is driving many companies to invest massively in the creation of global electronic networks that connect their entire global employee population. As was the case with the frenzy of activity at the beginning of the IT wave, much of this activity is destined to fail, which will lead to disappointment and a poor return on some very large investments. *Content,* not technology, should drive the process. Many companies already are discovering that the most sophisticated learning system is of little help if users won't log on. They will log on only if the information available will help them in their individual jobs. Building the electronic superhighway may be aesthetically pleasing, but ultimately it is the quality of the cars riding on it that will make the journey worthwhile.

Making the Elephant Dance at John Brown

If independence is a *virtue,* then connectivity is a *necessity* when creating small, entrepreneurial teams. Technology plays a major role in making that connectivity possible. John Brown Engineers and Constructors (John Brown), a major company in the engineering division of Trafalgar House, is an excellent case in point. The company was founded at the dawn of the industrial revolution, making the steel for the first steam engine. It grew organically for a long time, and in the early 1980s it expanded even more through acquisitions. Today it has 100 autonomous local offices, operating in 30 countries around the world.

In the late 1980s, however, recession hit the construction industry hard, with a particularly strong drop in the process and petroleum industries that John Brown focuses on. This, combined with real estate problems plaguing the parent company, threatened the survival of the firm.

There were more structural problems as well. As in other industries, the customers of engineering and construction firms were becoming global. Owner/operators such as DuPont and Merck wanted their American, European, and Asian plants to be built by the same people, using the same specifications. It was growing increasingly difficult to defend the old, localized way of doing business, wherein individual offices managed their own profit-and-loss statements. Clients wanted the best possible talent brought to bear on their projects, wherever the construction site was. John Brown had the talent, but it was spread throughout the world. Like an elephant, the corporate body was so big and sprawling that it was hard to move. Generating new business meant flying engineers and contractors around the world, disrupting their family life, generating higher costs, and spreading resources too thin.

Or did it? John Brown decided to make the elephant *dance*, by using information technology. Jim Noble, IT director of Trafalgar House and of the engineering division, launched an effort to link the worldwide offices through a wide-band, open system network, creating what Noble now calls a "global office with electronic corridors."

Today, the 25,000 employees of the $4 billion design and construction business are linked together by a global, wide area network called John Brown International Network (JOIN). To date, the network links about 8000 PCs and nearly 1000 CAD (computer-aided design) workstations through more than 150 servers. It also supports video and engineering conferencing, which enables the construction site to illustrate real images of engineering and fabrication problems for the designer. In short, it enables workers throughout the world to contribute to a single task from any office, at any hour of the day. Noble refers to the people who work through the system on projects as "virtual teams." Virtual teams give John Brown global strength in terms of expertise, but a local presence.

Said Noble to *CIO* magazine in May 1994: "Now, with open systems, our offices are seamlessly integrated with the rest of the business. [The network] has transformed India [along with many of the company's other remote outposts] from operating autonomously to being an integral part of our worldwide office."

As one might imagine, installing the network wasn't simple. The organization had inherited proprietary systems from the many companies it had acquired, and linking them often turned into a nightmare. The cost, however, at $7.5 million per year for the four years it was under development, now appears almost modest, considering that the network is one of the largest of its type. For aficionados of the business case in information technology, Noble has a word of advice: "If we'd had a very rigorous financial analysis of our development plan, we probably never would have started."

Although Trafalgar House, the mother company, is still struggling financially, the network has had a tremendously positive impact on the engineering business. In 1993, Engineering and Construction contributed more than 75 percent of the parent firm's operating profits. From being a laggard in the late 1980s, the division emerged in 1994 as the number one international contractor and the number two international design firm, according to prestigious surveys conducted by

Engineering News Record. The 100 offices, once isolated throughout the world, have become the dancing elephant, pirouetting with ease and grace through electronic corridors.

Of Decathletes and Loose Particles at M&G Reinsurance

Reinsurance can be a tough business. Basically it's the business of providing insurance for insurance companies, wherein a reinsurance company takes on a portion of the primary insurer's risk in return for a percentage of the premiums. Since all of its clients are in the risk-management game, it's a lot like making book with only bookies as clients, or setting up a casino for casinos. The name of the game is to manage the interrelationships of risk, and to be exceptionally good at it in highly specialized areas. It requires constant innovation.

In 1992, Great Britain's largest reinsurance firm, The Mercantile & General Reinsurance Company (M&G), hit rock-bottom, losing a record $70.2 million (in December 1994 dollars). Many market watchers thought it was the beginning of the end for the company. But at the bottom, John Engestrom was appointed chief executive to turn the company around. Just one year later, M&G posted record pretax profits of $218.4 million, virtually all attributable to the performance of the general business account, the source of its previous malaise.

Engestrom worked out a two-pronged assault, staggered over time. The first assault was launched immediately, aimed outwardly at the marketplace. The second assault was focused inwardly, and would gather momentum to become a full-scale transformation effort starting in 1994.

In the short term, he tackled the market head-on, challenging not only M&G's market practices but those of the entire industry. As he said to *Post* magazine in September 1994, "You have to have the guts to go against some of the market forces if they are the core of the problem. And they were, because we were talking about overcapacity, underpricing, lax standards *as a market*. And we were part of that market, so we had to break out of that mould and say 'we now have to set things right'."

Engestrom understood that relationships with its customers were at the very heart of its business. According to Engestrom, developing a healthy, long-term business relationship is a lot like developing a relationship between husband and wife: "If there is a difference of opinion ... you must get it out on the table, talk about it, don't just shove it under the carpet—that won't work. Unless the relationship is sound, with open and transparent dialogue between adults, then you can't have a long-term relationship because of friction and misunderstandings and disputes."

Engestrom's view of the importance of long-term business relationships has been translated into the company's mission: "Forging successful partnerships through innovation and outstanding service." He views excellence in relationship-building as the nexus that links unique customer needs and M&G's organizational capabilities.

In 1994, Engestrom launched a major transformational effort, codenamed Rainbow. Now in its second phase, a major component of the program has been the reorganization of the company into a team-based, customer-focused organization. What has emerged is a whirring blend of interconnected teams representing an innovative—and somewhat daunting—organizational design (Fig. 12.1).

Figure 12.1. *The whirring blend of Interconnected Teams at M&G Reinsurance.* (*SOURCE:* M&G Reinsurance.)

In keeping with M&G's commitment to partnership relationships, customers form the heart of the organization. Teams are massed around specific customers, built on specialized expertise. The teams are multiskilled and multidisciplined, representing a cross-section of M&G's combined competences. Specialists move across teams, which are connected by the integration of roles and responsibilities. The teams around the client share a collective responsibility for meeting customer requirements.

Individual team members are described as "decathletes," referring to the way their responsibilities span 10 business areas. They serve on many different teams and have multiple bosses. Roles, responsibilities, and expectations aren't always clearly delineated, because as many as 30 different people may be circulating through a team. "Gradually, people are realizing that being a part of a network of teams is more fun and exciting than being in a specialized part of a hierarchical, functionally specialized machine," notes Engestrom.

Slightly further from customers are client team managers, who are singularly accountable for specific clients and jointly accountable for groups of clients, irrespective of the class of business. They are responsible for managing relationships across up to 10 business sectors. This gives clients a single point of contact if they need one, and a near direct channel into the many teams supporting them. Client team managers are responsible for profits at the customer level. They act as coaches for both the customer and the customer-focused teams (of which they are a member). They market, sell, and network to generate new business. And above all, they build trusting partnerships with customer executives.

Business managers support the client team managers, acting as the prime operational managers for a portfolio of businesses run by client team managers. They operate within a geographical domain across all business sectors, requiring them also to be risk-management "decathletes." They coach the client team managers and the client-focused teams, while also wearing the corporate hat. One of their major goals is to drive the organization toward achieving its mission.

Acting in a support capacity is the executive group, which shares collective responsibility for global results. They coach the business managers, representing both geographical and product perspectives. They also are responsible for coordinating global support in the finance, IT, human resource, and communications functions across all business sectors and teams. Even more than business managers, their responsibility is to drive the organization toward its strategic intent.

You may have noticed that the CEO doesn't appear in the picture. This isn't an error of omission, or even of commission. Engestrom describes himself as a "loose particle," floating through the whirring organization to the point of greatest need. "There are no higher or lower levels in this organization," he emphasizes. "There is only closer or further from the client."

Engestrom's ultimate ambition is to make himself obsolete, to evolve the organization to the point that he makes no decisions. His hope is that at least 80 percent of all decisions will be made by the inner circle of teams serving clients, perhaps 18 percent by the various outer rings, and 2 percent, preferably less, by himself.

A Vision of the CIGNA P&C to Come

Gerry Isom knows that the significant accomplishments made in the last year-and-a-half at CIGNA P&C have been necessary just to catch up.

"We've done the easy part," he grants, somewhat reluctantly. "Now comes the true challenge."

Isom is not yet sure whether CIGNA P&C will eventually succeed. "It's way too early to know," he concedes. But he knows they have traveled a long road already.

The main challenge now is about renewal. In Isom's view, renewal will come in two steps. First, the company has to realize that the key to its future growth lies in sharing knowledge across what have historically been three islands: underwriting, claims, and the producer. Instinctively, all employees know that if they can get the information to circulate quickly and freely between all parties, the customer will constantly be in good hands. Conceptually, everybody now understands that there is a nexus in the P&C business at the intersection of all three elements. If P&C can operationally link the three islands, it will become a top performer.

When the nexus is generated, it will be the corporate equivalent of accelerating the body's metabolism. All of a sudden the whole corporation will become more fit and more aware of its environment. Information will start flowing more quickly, decisions will be made faster and with greater precision. Individual processes will keep regenerating, constantly adapting to the impulses they receive both from outside and from the other processes. The customer will get the feeling that the firm is more responsive.

The road is still long, however. The obstacles are both behavioral and technical. On the behavioral front, there has never been such an integrated process. After much team building, underwriters, claims agents, and marketing people now have a positive relationship, but they still don't know each other well enough. Furthermore, the underwriting, claims, and producer management processes have just been redesigned, and everybody is a little reluctant to let the three, still-fragile processes start to reach out for each other.

On the technical front, Isom knows that CIGNA P&C will have to build an integrated learning system across underwriting, claims, and the producer. In the last year-and-a-half, the firm has created the necessary building blocks in the form of three computer-based performance support systems, which, assuming they get rolled out successfully, will have to be connected. It's an exciting prospect. For the first time, Isom can envision a desktop-based dialogue in which the claims agent calls the underwriter for advice, or the underwriter asks the agent for counseling on the payment of a claim. Isom dreams of functional silos crumbling left and right, of an integrated team moving quickly up and down the value chain.

But there is more to Isom's dream, a second act to his renewal opera. The newly found nexus across underwriting, claims, and the producers, which heretofore has focused on the *operational* connection, could also be used for *strategic* purposes.

Insurance, as Isom likes to repeat, is a game of constant innovation. What matters is to invent new segments all the time, ahead of competitors. The way to do that is to accumulate information faster than CIGNA's competitors, distill it into knowledge, and "invent" the segment before anybody else. Given the preemptor's advantage, if CIGNA sees an opportunity for segmentation before its competitor, it will own that segment and make money in it.

This, to Isom, is the ultimate form of specialization. One day, he dreams, CIGNA P&C will become a perpetual innovator, constantly scanning its experience base of claims and producer experience, and using it to invent new businesses ahead of everybody else. If it can do that, the learning and innovation section of the Balanced Scorecard will come alive, driving up the percentage of new segment premiums in the total of premiums collected. This in turn will cause the loss ratio to drop, and increase producer and end-user satisfaction.

Only then, when CIGNA P&C becomes a true specialist, will Gerry Isom be at peace.

EMBRACING THE CORPORATION'S SOUL AND ITS SHADOW

In this, the Communications Age, we believe that corporations have an opportunity to evolve from *dominance* to *preeminence,* to become loved and respected institutions. Like many others before us, we see them taking on a broader and broader social role: still in operation to generate profits, to be sure, but also becoming fundamentally important socioeconomic nodes in the individual's ever expanding connectivity networks. We see in corporations and in networks of corporations the resources and the know-how to help reclaim the inner cities, to become one of society's primary educational forces, to provide extensive family and community services, to be the environmental stewards of the products they create, and to play a key role in preserving mother earth. We see the corporation of the future as an environment in which high self esteem individuals can thrive, and in which struggling individuals can develop and improve themselves. We see corporations as the vehicle for putting more humanity, more soul, into economic life. And we see them doing all of this not because government mandates it, but because the people who *are* the corporation *want it*.

By contrast, we do *not* see corporations replacing governments, recognizing that the essential function of government should always be to preserve and protect individual freedom and rights, and by extension to protect individual nations from forceful foreign aggression. By its nature, however, government is an institution distinct from corporations and businesses. Its primary function is to *prevent* violence, not to *generate* wealth. Throughout history, governments have proven themselves time and again to be a less than effective in their attempt to promote the economic and spiritual welfare of the people who comprise societies. Only individuals can do that, and they do it best through voluntary cooperation. The corporation could be the primary vehicle for their cooperation, both economic and social, in the future.

One can envision, for example, a system of schools linked to corporations, each vying to fill its rooms with children and educate them to drive the performance of tomorrow. Instead of putting children through a standardized, compulsory system as we do today in most countries, parents and students could choose among competing schools that would provide both general education and specialized training. In all likelihood, companies could economically justify making the schools tuition-free, for education is the highest payout investment in the Communications Age.

Networks of insurance companies could provide fire protection and firefighting services to communities, in effect financing the protection of the assets they are paid to cover, thus reducing their own exposure. They also might help to finance police forces, again for the same reasons, relieving the community of a tax burden and augmenting the police force's investigative and enforcement capabilities with their knowledge networks.

The current trend toward networked health services could explode into universal family health education and services, as companies learn that their greatest assets, and their most significant contributors to the bottom line, are healthy, thinking people, not the machines they operate or the buildings they work in.

More people could work at home, closer to friends and family, as the electronically linked virtual corporation becomes more and more of a reality. As more people work at home, and as electronic wizardry reduces transaction costs, the personal touch of home-delivery services could once again be rekindled, becoming a booming cottage industry linked to corporate networks.

Chemical companies could extend themselves, leveraging their competences to learn how to make money by taking stewardship of the toxic products they produce. The petrochemical industry could put its collective head together, exploring new approaches to reclaiming polluted rivers, lakes, and streams.

All of this and more may occur, if what could happen, does.

If it is a worthwhile dream, it won't be an easy one to realize. For corporations that may choose to pursue such a future, the prerequisite will be to build trusting relationships with their people, the communities around them, and society as a whole. And if present-day cinema and television programming is any sort of cultural barometer, that will be no easy task.

A relatively brief channel surfing trip will reveal a predominantly negative view, not entirely unearned, of the modern corporation. Corporations and their leaders are among the most popular of present-day villains. Television portrays greedy companies trying to gratuitously dump unspecified toxic waste into Johnny Fishy's lake on early morning cartoons. Businessmen who enslave their workers are featured on daytime talk shows. Eager capitalists build unsafe nuclear power plants in movies and docudramas. Villainous executives smuggle drugs in doll heads, or sell children through adoption agencies. Think of any imaginable act of corporate wrongdoing, and the chances are good that someone has already produced a film or TV show about it.

Faced with this onslaught of corporation bashing, it's easy to forget that, like people, every company is unique. Corporations are just like us. In fact, they *are* us in the form of shareholders or employees. As such, they are neither saints nor devils, but a mixture of the good and the bad, of strengths and weaknesses. Like people, corporations are a composite of the hero within and the villain within. And as is true of most people, the hero triumphs more often than not.

So, where does the bad rap come from? Why do people seem to fundamentally distrust corporations?

Some of it is misconception. Some of it is philosophical animosity: A minority of people believe in their hearts that free enterprise and the profit motive are morally wrong. But the single largest component is *heritage*. Under the industrial model, the foundation of trust between corporations and society simply was never laid. The Marxist viewpoint of the exploitation of man by man is still at work, long after the death of Marx and even the collapse of the Berlin wall.

So what is a company to do? As the ancient Greek philosopher Epicurus wrote, "It is never too early or too late to care for the well being of the soul." Most psychologists agree that healthy change begins with self-acceptance, acceptance of one's entire identity in all its aspects, taking the positive with the negative. At the individual level this might be summarized by the following recognition: "So this is what I am, this is what I'm good at, this is what I'm afraid of or can't do. Okay, I'm enough. But I deserve to be more, so it's time to start moving!"

For a corporation, the same basic principle applies. For leaders, this means accepting and openly acknowledging the corporate heritage, both good and bad. It means recognizing that the economic universe consists of more than competition; that it also consists of community, social, and environmental problems. It involves a recognition by corporate leadership that turning a blind eye to society's ills won't generate any cures for them. At the leadership level, it means embracing both the hero and the villain within, both the corporation's soul and its shadow.

As psychologist Dr. Nathaniel Branden puts it, "Everyone who has any familiarity with psychology knows about the danger of disowning the murderer within. Far fewer people understand the tragedy of disowning the hero within." The tragedy in the heritage of most corporations is that they have never truly recognized their inner hero.

That hero is the individual human being, embodying the sanctity of human life. For those companies that feel reverence awakening in them as they recognize that fact, there is hope for a brighter tomorrow.

The Transformation of Woodbridge and Karl: Epilogue

It's celebration time in New Hampshire. Karl hasn't worn a tuxedo since his wedding day, and his waistline feels a lot tighter. But it's a wonderful day, marking the second anniversary of the transformation effort. He's so moved he could cry, but change agents don't do that.

The CEO is up there on the podium liberally praising a thousand folks, but discreetly taking credit. Outsiders listening to him will believe he led the charge all the way. Well, that's not exactly how Karl remembers the story. He remembers the CEO as being quite shy about supporting the change team when it went after the plant-based baronies, or when it pushed for the creation of an integrated materials management function. But on a day like today, Karl feels magnanimous. It's everybody's victory, even the CEO's. Karl goes from table to table shaking hands, hugging the women. Deep inside, he knows this story is about *him*, and many others like him.

The results have been staggering. After four years of failing to hit its Return on Net Assets (RONA) target, Woodbridge has now reached its target for the second year in a row, and at a time when the paper cycle is at its most depressed. The first major factor in this achievement has been a savings of close to 30 percent in all indirect production costs (scheduling, inventory control, cost of nonconformance, materials handling, and logistics) and close to 10 percent in direct purchasing and manufacturing costs. Karl has read company literature to that effect, but he never would have believed it if he hadn't seen the results firsthand.

The cost-savings stories pale in comparison to the results obtained on the revenue front, however. The CEO is claiming full strategic victory over the competition, and he may just be right. This product-proliferation strategy they have concocted, coupled with the concept of a manufacturing network of focused plants, has made a killing. Literally! Mountain View Papers, the lead competitor that got this whole mess started, has just announced that it's getting out of the packaging paper business because they can't keep up with Woodbridge. They used to have one advantage: lead time and service. This advantage has now been neutralized, and on top of that, the enemy is surrounded by the breadth of Woodbridge's product line. Their machinery is now for sale. What a tremendous satisfaction for the strategist Karl has become, this destruction of the opposing army. Karl feels like something between Julius Caesar and Alexander the Great.

After five years of watching its market share melt in the sun, Woodbridge now has regained five points in the last two years, largely by putting Mountain View out of business. The order fulfillment lead time is now at 10 days, and still dropping.

"I would hate to have to compete against us now," he says with a smile.

Many Woodbridge employees come up to him and invite him to come to dinner with them to celebrate their achievement, but Karl politely declines and makes a discreet exit.

"I have another commitment," he explains.

A half-hour later he is greeted at the door of a dark building on the campus of the University of New Hampshire by a young man who looks strikingly like him: his son, Karl Jr., 22 years old and a senior at the university. Both look awkwardly at each other, not sure what they should do next. Karl Jr. waves him through the door.

Inside the large conference room, the noise is deafening. On the back wall, a large banner announces the purpose of the gathering: UNH ENVIRONMENTAL CONFERENCE. A group of three students on the podium are facilitating a discussion of ecological disasters in New England. With the impetuosity of youth, students and other attendees in the audience are berating the behavior of large corporations, pouring chemicals into lakes and destroying Canadian and New England forests through acid rain. There are color slides showing dying fish in New Hampshire lakes, vibrant testimonials of greed by local corporations.

Karl Sr. is quite apprehensive. Less than an hour ago he was the focus of his firm's celebrations, and now here he is, ready to take the stage in Dante's inferno. He looks for possible support from the audience. There is none to be found. The audience seems to be made up of young men and women violently agreeing with each other that corporations are devilish creatures designed to destroy the earth. He knows there is some truth to the accusations, but at the same time he would like to introduce them to some of his colleagues, help them to see that they are made of the same flesh and blood, and as scared of life and death, as they are. But it's time for him to take the podium.

The tone is set early, when he is introduced as "one of the managers at Woodbridge Papers, the large paper conglomerate, rated by the Environmental Protection Agency as the third largest polluter of the state." A giant "boo" rolls like a wave from the back of the room, punctuated by a few catcalls.

Karl has a prepared speech in his hand, one that talks about the quality of effluent waters and atmospheric releases, how they are computed, how Woodbridge Papers has managed to reduce its environmental emissions by a factor of three in the last few years. He starts with that, but every statistic he offers is challenged and berated as a corporate lie. He sees that he can't win, so he decides to change his angle of attack. He talks about himself when he was a young student like them, and how he decided to join a paper company at a time when the word *ecology* didn't even exist. The hostile shouts don't stop but they are less frequent now, and a little less loud. By the time he's done, he sees that at least some of them have begun to understand what he's about. There's even some polite applause as he comes down from the podium.

In the parking lot, Karl Jr. escorts him back to his car. It's pitch-dark, and quite cold. Karl Sr. knows there won't be any hug, not even a thank-you, for young radical students at UNH are not into hugs and thank-yous. But by the light of the car, Karl Sr. can see a little humidity in the corner of his son's eyes.

It has been the nicest day of his life.

INDEX